Twenty Ways to Personnel

Different Techniques and Their Respective Advantages

ADRIAN FURNHAM

Norwegian Business School

CAMBRIDGE
UNIVERSITY PRESS

CAMBRIDGE
UNIVERSITY PRESS

University Printing House, Cambridge CB2 8BS, United Kingdom

One Liberty Plaza, 20th Floor, New York, NY 10006, USA

477 Williamstown Road, Port Melbourne, VIC 3207, Australia

314–321, 3rd Floor, Plot 3, Splendor Forum, Jasola District Centre,
New Delhi – 110025, India

103 Penang Road, #05-06/07, Visioncrest Commercial, Singapore 238467

Cambridge University Press is part of the University of Cambridge.

It furthers the University's mission by disseminating knowledge in the pursuit of
education, learning, and research at the highest international levels of excellence.

www.cambridge.org
Information on this title: www.cambridge.org/9781108844680
DOI: 10.1017/9781108953276

First published 2021

Printed in the United Kingdom by TJ Books Ltd, Padstow Cornwall

A catalogue record for this publication is available from the British Library.

Library of Congress Cataloging-in-Publication Data
Names: Furnham, Adrian, author.
Title: Twenty ways to assess personnel : different techniques and their respective
    advantages / Adrian Furnham.
Description: Cambridge ; New York, NY : Cambridge University Press, 2021. |
    Includes bibliographical references and index.
Identifiers: LCCN 2020051639 (print) | LCCN 2020051640 (ebook) |
    ISBN 9781108844680 (hardback) | ISBN 9781108948722 (paperback) |
    ISBN 9781108953276 (epub)
Subjects: LCSH: Employees–Rating of.
Classification: LCC HF5549.5.R3 F86 2021 (print) | LCC HF5549.5.R3 (ebook) |
    DDC 658.3/125–dc23
LC record available at https://lccn.loc.gov/2020051639
LC ebook record available at https://lccn.loc.gov/2020051640

ISBN 978-1-108-84468-0 Hardback
ISBN 978-1-108-94872-2 Paperback

For Alison and Benedict: Only five more books to go!

Contents

Tables

Preface

Three influences led me to be interested in this topic:

1. *A brilliant undergraduate teacher*: I grew up in South Africa and went to the University of Natal. I was extremely fortunate to have a brilliant teacher, Dr Bruce Faulds, who dedicated his life to teaching. Every Wednesday for 30 weeks, we completed a psychometric test and analysed the class and individual results. We did the standard tests of the day (MMPI, CPI, EPQ), but also some strange Freudian-inspired tests, projective techniques, even physiological tests. The major teaching aim was to be familiar with the background and theory of such tests, but most importantly to examine their psychometric qualities (evidence of reliability and validity). Because of Dr Faulds's interest in musical ability, he became interested in the measurement of art ability, but much else besides. To this day I am grateful for this exposure which has commanded my interest for 40 years. I discovered that I knew about and became fascinated with a huge range of tests, many forgotten and often overlooked.

2. *Psychological consultancy*: Soon after I got my first academic job (1981), a number of friends who graduated with me went into management consultancy and employed me as an associate of their organisations. Most worked for small(ish) psychology consultancies of 10–20 people who specialised in such things as assessment, organisational design and training. Their clients were usually HR specialists running assessment and development centres. Through my consultant and training work, I was taken into a new world where the Myers Briggs Type Inventory (MBTI) was king and there were enthusiasts for all sorts of tests I had hardly heard of, such as the Fundamental Interpersonal Relations Orientation – Behaviour (FIRO-B) and the Belbin Team Role Inventory.

One side effect of this experience was that I learned about these tests and have published various articles on them. Many of these tests (like the FIRO-B) had almost completely disappeared from the academic literature, while others (like the Belbin Team Role

Inventory) have struggled to find academics interested in evaluating them.

I have had numerous benefits from this academic–business association. Foremost is my close relationship with those few academics who have crossed the applied–academic (scientists-practitioners) divide, who devise and sell personality tests informed by theoretical considerations and rigorous research. My hero in this regard is Robert (and the late Joyce) Hogan from Hogan Assessments, whose major tools (Hogan Personality Inventory [HPI], Hogan Developmental Survey [HDS], Motives, Values and Preferences Inventory [MVPI]) are informed by theory and psychometric assessment. I was intrigued by the HDS, a unique instrument, and have published around 20 papers on it. Furthermore, I have developed my own commercial measures in conjunction with PhD students, including a very successful measure of Trait Emotional Intelligence and a talent measure called the High Potential Trait Inventory.

However, the experience of shifting between these two worlds is the difference between scientists (academic personality psychologists) and practitioners (HR/business specialists) in the way they evaluate and then choose personality tests. I also became aware of the costs of tests. Whilst I had purchased a few tests, many were available from the university test library, paid for by the department. Moreover, I knew many tests were available directly from journals or online. However, some had to be purchased at what seemed to be a high cost for a junior academic.

For academics, the choice of one test over another is usually based on the available data on test reliability and validity: thought to be essential by psychometricians and necessary for publication in a peer-reviewed journal. More than anything else, I was struck by how important the 'feedback' report was, which, the cynic in me noted, was aimed more towards making the tester look insightful and the client happy. The fact that practitioners need to take into account practical issues such as cost, time, the availability of multiple languages and the acceptability of a testing process by experiencing the assessment for themselves illustrates the complexity of the context in which they are working. Thus, their need to consider a wider range of 'evidence' than a more academic perspective is reasonable.

More importantly the test publisher soon becomes aware of the 'political issues'. Consider the problems with measuring one of the most important, fundamental and predictive of all personality traits, namely Neuroticism. Practitioners are terrified of offending their (internal) clients and consultants (their external clients) by suggesting they are neurotic, namely prone to anxiety, depression and psychosomatic illnesses. There are various solutions to this issue, such as renaming it the Adjustment dimension to Resilience and reverse scoring it.

Allied to this issue is the practitioner's sensitivity to words and concepts. While certain psychological concepts seem mysterious (e.g. schizotypal, histrionic), others (psychoticism) seem quite unacceptable. These either have to be relabelled or dropped. Thus, those with sub-clinical borderline personality disorder are defined by the Hogan Developmental Survey as excitable, mercurial, volatile or ambivalent. The language of the reports is all-important.

There is also the strange issue of dimensionality and parsimony. For many practitioners, the idea of 'reducing' the complexity of personality to three, even five, dimensions is preposterous. They expect somewhere between 10 and 20 factors. Hence the development of the EPP (Eysenck Personality Profiler), which has around seven facets for each of the three super-factors. I continue to 'walk the divide', to switch hats and to be 'bi-lingual'. I think I am enriched by the experience. However, I am consistently surprised by the 'ivory tower' academic psychometrician who has little or no knowledge of 'real-world concerns'.

3. *Talented collaborators*: Over my academic career I supervised 25 PhD students (as well as countless master's students). Because I was at an elite institution, we attracted highly talented students. Of these, Tomas Chamorro-Premuzic was one of the best. Energetic, inquisitive and

ambitious, he completed his PhD with nine empirical studies in record time. And it was him who persuaded me to write a book on this topic. Indeed, this book is a 'sort-of' second edition. Tomas is now engaged with other things but retains a great interest in this area.

But I have had other collaborators, many now professors, with sparkling CVs and worldwide reputations. They include Dino Petrides, who was one of the psychometric pioneers in Emotional Intelligence. Viren Swami has been a friend and co-author (of around 200 papers) for 20 years. We have explored, and indeed pioneered, the measurement of all sorts of things (like leg-to-torso ratio) as well as attitudes towards Brexit. Ian Macrae and I developed, commercialised and sold a very successful measure on the high-flying personality. Luke Treglown is now a very serious data scientist at a psychological test consultancy, and Simmy Grover, who inherited my job, is a rising star with her interest and ability in multivariate statistics.

This book is more than an update of *Psychology of Personnel Selection* published 10 years ago, although I rely heavily on that text for referencing older studies in the field. So much has changed in this field over the decade and will continue to do so.

Of course, I never forget the love and support of my wife Alison. For 30 years she has witnessed my workaholism and publishing fetish with equanimity and stoicism. She has never quite understood my rather strange desire to write 100 books, most (like this one) dedicated to her. It is also dedicated to my (only) son, who is equally puzzled by my obsessions but does not share them.

Acknowledgements

I have shown various chapters to associates, friends and colleagues all knowledgeable about, indeed often experts in, and working in the assessment business. I have incorporated many of their ideas and suggestions for which I have been very grateful. They include Phil Ackerman, Jan Ketil Arnulf, Tomas Chamorro-Premuzic, Philip Corr, Jason Devereux, Ian Florence, Marcus Gee, Simmy Grover, Alexandre Gruca, Mike Haffenden, Robert Hogan, John Hughes, Oyvind Martinsen, Mikael Nederstrom, David Pendleton, John Rauthmann, Ryne Sherman, John Taylor, Luke Treglown, Dice Van Daalen and Chris Woodman. I owe special thanks to George Home, my extraordinary research assistant, proofreader and cocktail mixer.

I also happily admit that I have drawn, often quite heavily, on other publications (papers, chapters and books) that I have written over the years, as I have always been interested in people assessment from a psychological perspective.

Of course, I remain responsible for errors of both omission and commission in the text.

I Introduction to Selection and Assessment

1.1 INTRODUCTION

Imagine, for all sorts of reasons, you really want to understand an individual: what 'makes them tick', what drives them; will they 'make something of their lives'? You want to be as accurate and efficient (in terms of time and money spent) as possible, leading to a perspicacious and valid assessment. What are your options: give them a standard questionnaire (pen and paper/online); interview them; ask others who know this individual; get a copy of their CV or work history; look them up on social media; contact previous employers with specific questions; determine their star sign; get a blood or saliva sample. This book is about the options people have in assessing others.

We spend much of our day assessing and evaluating people. We make judgements on how we are treated in restaurants and shops, how online people deal with our requests and on the competence and trustworthiness of people at work. Our data is in what they say and do. We also collect data, if not terribly systematically, on those we choose as long-term mates and spouses. Furthermore, we are regularly asked to provide information about ourselves.

This book is not about everyday assessment but rather the systematic collection of data designed to inform decisions. It involves measurement and evaluation. It does, or should, aim to provide accurate, insightful, precise and objective data that may be used to make better decisions. Because of the limitation of each data gathering method, it is usually recommended that one use multiple measures, sources, domains, settings, occasions and informants.

There is a great deal of interest in, and research into, assessing people at work. It is done for various reasons: selection, development, promotion, redundancy and appraisal. Assessment can be formal and informal, based on test data or personal intuitive judgements, with more or less serious consequences. The field is alive and well and thriving (Piotrowski, 2019). There are all sorts of developments, such as the development of video resumes, the screening of a person's social network profile and gamification of tests.

Essentially, most assessments and selection revolve around the concept of 'fit': helping people find the right environment, job, lifestyle and occupation for them and those who employ them.

In the ideal world, a selection process has various stages: do a comprehensive, up-to-date job analysis; identify the ability, attitudes and skills (competencies) required to complete the critical tasks in that job; develop or select the particular assessment devices; and apply them. There are, of course, all sorts of reasons why the ideal situation rarely occurs (Gatewood et al., 2015). Inevitably, some jobs have an easy-to-find measurement criterion such as sales: number of calls/orders; revenue/profit generated; number of customer complaints/returns; peer ratings. For other jobs it is much more difficult finding a set of accurate criteria for job success. One could assess a professor by the quality and quantity of publications (measured by the publicly available h-index), the amount of grant/fee money generated or students' satisfaction scores.

1.2   VOCATIONAL GUIDANCE AND PERSONNEL SELECTION

Vocational psychology concerns the reasons *why* people choose various vocations, the wisdom of those choices and the possibilities of giving them the best possible kind of advice, as to what to do and when and why to choose vocations. Many factors constrain job choices: ability, age, education and social, economic and political factors. Many jobs are not available to individuals, or competition for them is very strong. Quite simply, you cannot always get the job you want or are best suited to.

As there are striking individual differences in ability, aptitude, needs, personality and interests, different people will need different jobs with demands that better match their wants, expectations and skills. Vocational psychologists help people explore their long-range personal and professional goals, look at personal strengths and weaknesses and assess environmental threats and opportunities to examine salient and suitable career alternatives.

Many organisations are becoming aware of the career development of employees. Over time it is quite common for people to be promoted in rank or level (concomitant changes in responsibilities and skills) or move horizontally or laterally (with functional or technical changes). These lead to significant changes, which the individual might or might not be able to cope with.

It is usually assumed that vocational choice is based on a mix of things, such as a person's ability, personality and values, as well as their social background (Furnham et al., 2012). Furthermore, through experience and socialisation, people in different jobs become more homogenous in background within certain industries/sectors, and therefore different from those in other jobs.

The *Attraction-Selection-Attrition* (ASA) framework, proposed by Schneider (1987), suggests that people are attracted to specific jobs because of their interests and personalities, organisations then select people they believe are compatible for and ideally suited to different jobs and later people leave a job when they feel they do not fit in. Chatman et al. (2008) have noted how this ASA process leads organisations and groups within them to become increasingly *homogenous*, hence jokes and stereotypes about people in certain jobs (i.e. accountants) often sharing certain very noticeable characteristics.

In this sense it is possible to talk of person–job 'fit' or 'misfit', or of congruity between a person and their workgroup (Schneider et al., 1998). Schaunbroeck et al. (1998) found support for the application of ASA theory in the examination of differences between public and private sector employees.

One implication of ASA theory is within-group specialty homogeneity: that is because people with a particular profile are attracted to different jobs, they tend to end up being very like each other and, therefore, often very different from other specialists. Therefore, when specialists come together in a team, they are often very different from each other, not only in terms of their specialist knowledge and skills but in how they like to work.

1.3 PERSONNEL SELECTION

Assessment is *Big Business* but it difficult to get accurate results on who spends what with whom. A quick Google search will uncover a large number of businesses that have both their own bespoke, as well as traditional, tests on their platforms. Most now boast that they are AI powered, automated, comprehensive and very accurate.

Some concentrate on 'soft skills' others on more analytical skills.

Yet, as Ihsan and Furnham (2018) have noted:

> It is also important to note that job selection is essentially an
> arms race. For every improvement on the employer side (e.g., on-
> line personality assessments), there can/may/will be a reactive
> step-up on the applicant side. Thus, savvy applicants clean' their
> Facebook profiles and photos, in anticipation of an upcoming
> interview. Therefore, the question is whether it is widely known
> that your social media will be scraped for employability data.
> Many people will either create a dark social media presence or go
> off-the-grid for information that might be coded in a negative
> fashion
>
> *(p 165).*

There is a great deal of interest in the testing and assessment industry, and some work psychology academic journals dedicated to the whole issue (Greiff & Illiescu, 2017). There are many websites and test publishers that are happy to advise and sell their instruments (Gatewood, 2016).

It remains a 'hot topic', particularly in countries where it may have been abused in the past (Sehlapelo & Blanche, 1996). There are also a number of reviews on what companies currently do in assessing people, most of which have been done for long periods of time (multisource feedback, personality tests, interviews, etc.; Church & Rotolo, 2015).

There is also development in traditional approaches, such as trying to understand the dynamics of individual functioning: how people change over time and in different situations (Sosnowska et al., 2018). Indeed, Ferguson and Lievens (2017) argue that traits are no longer thought of as stable, deterministic predictors of future behaviour but rather as dynamic and flexible across generations, lifespan and contexts. In this sense, traits can be modified or trained.

This relates to the question of whether to invest most in selection (because people do not change a great deal) or training (because you can teach them all the skills they need).

1.3.1   Reasons for Selection

Assessing people at work is important for many reasons. The most important is the cost benefit analysis: *the benefits of the right decision* over *the costs of getting it wrong*. In other words, there are great financial benefits in hiring a positive and productive person, and many costs, especially financial, in hiring an unhappy, unproductive and difficult person.

Using good assessment tools has other benefits: it can 'up-skill' managers who use various tools and techniques and *increase their psychological mindedness*. It also has a major benefit for the interviewee as feedback can considerably *increase their self-awareness*. Furthermore, if a test is used widely in an organisation, people can often have a *useful shared language* to discuss issues in terms of psychological profiles and preferences.

With very few exceptions (handedness) all characteristics are normally distributed: intelligence, height, shoe size, ability to throw a ball, creativity. The same is true of work output measured qualitatively or quantitatively. We have data going back 100 years on this when it was possible to accurately measure an individual's contribution. It means, in effect, that the top 10–20% of what the top workers produce may be three to five times what the poorest workers produce. Hence the importance of selecting superior workers: it makes clear economic sense.

1.3.1.1 Costing Assessment and Value for Money

Often, HR specialists (and others) are required to justify the amount of money spent on selection and assessment exercises. Indeed, it may cost an organisation many thousands of pounds from recruitment to the final selection of a good candidate. We provide here one method to address this issue.

Start by asking 'what is the ratio of the *best to worst* performers in any job'? That is, assuming we could get a sensitive and accurate measure of various people's performance, how much more productive (measured by quality or quantity) is the best worker (in the top 10%) in comparison to the worst/least effective worker (bottom 10%)?

While the answer depends on the job, the simple rule appears to be that the best produce about *twice* as much as the worst and that this ratio increases for more difficult and complex jobs. It is therefore possible to calculate the difference between good and bad workers in any job. Another rule of thumb for researchers appears to be 40%–70%. That is, the difference between good and bad workers is between 40% and 70% of their salary whereas the difference between the best and worst may be much higher. So, the rule of thumb (Cook, 2004) is:

> The value of a good employee minus the value of a poor employee is roughly equal to the salary paid for the job.

At £60 000 one may assume one is getting around £81 000 worth from the good, and £39 000 from the bad, but £102 000 from the best and £18 000 from the worst. Whilst these exact calculations are in dispute, they do point to the importance of selecting the right people. There are also ways of calculating the return on selection. The calculation is based on five factors that are put into a formula, they are: the validity of the test, the calibre of the recruits, the distinction in value between good and bad employees, the cost of selection, and the proportion of applicants selected. Using this formula, it is quite possible to show that on a set salary of, say, £30 000, the savings for the organisation (per annum) by selecting good, over poor, candidates may be £5000 per annum. This number can be multiplied by the number of candidates.

So, can we determine when it is a good idea to invest more in selection procedures? The answer is clear. Spending more money on selection assessment is a good idea when firstly the calibre of the recruitment is high, rather than uniformly average. Secondly, employees differ quite widely in their worth to the organisation.

Cook (2016, pp. 170–172)

It is fairly easy to calculate the cost of selection, although many employers only think of doing so when asked to introduce new methods; they rarely work out how much existing methods, such as day-long panel interviews, cost. It is much more difficult to calculate the return on selection. The formula was first stated by Brogden in 1946, but for many years it had only academic interest because a crucial term in it could not be measured – SDy, the standard deviation of the value of employee productivity. Until the rational estimate technique was devised, there was no way of measuring how much more good employees were worth. Brogden's equation states:

SAVING per EMPLOYEE per YEAR = $(r \times SDy \times Z)-(C/P)$

Where:

r   is the validity of the selection procedure (expressed as a correlation coefficient)

SDy   is the standard deviation of the value of employee productivity, in pounds, dollars or euros

Z is the calibre of recruits (expressed as their standard score on the selection test used)

C is the cost of selection per applicant

P is the proportion of applicants selected

Here is a worked example:

- The employer is recruiting in the salary range £40,000 p.a., so SDy can be estimated – by the 40% rule of thumb – at £16,000.
- The employer is using a test of mental ability whose validity is 0.45, so r is 0.45.
- The people recruited score on average 1 SD above the mean (for present employees), so Z is 1. This assumes the employer succeeds in recruiting high-calibre people.
- The employer uses a consultancy, who charge £750 per candidate.
- Of ten applicants, four are appointed, so P is 0.40.

The SAVINGS per employee per year is:

$$(0.45 \times £16,000 \times 1) - (£750/0.40)$$

$$= £7,200 - £1,875$$

$$= £5,325$$

Each employee selected is worth some £5,000 a year more to the employer than one recruited at random. The four employees recruited will be worth in all £21,300 more to the employer each year. The larger the organisation, the greater the total sum that can be saved by effective selection, hence the estimate of $18 million for the Philadelphia police force. Note also that SDy increases as test validity increases: using the latest (and highest) estimate of MA test validity, incorporating correction for indirect range restriction, means SDy increases to £9.325 and the savings for four recruits increases to £37,300.

Selection pays off better when:

- The calibre or recruits is high.
- Employees differ a lot in worth to the organisation, i.e. SDy is high.
- The selection procedure has high validity.

Selection pays off less well when:

- Recruits are uniformly mediocre.
- SDy is low, i.e. workers do not vary much in value.
- The selection procedure has low validity.

Employers should have little difficulty attracting good recruits in periods of high employment (unless pay or conditions are poor). Rational estimate and other research shows SDy is rarely low. The third condition – zero validity – may apply quite often, when employers use poor selection methods. But if any of the three terms is zero, their product – the value of selection – is necessarily zero too. Only the right-hand side of the equation – cost – is never zero.

1.3.2   What to Assess

The question for assessors is essentially *what to assess, who is best suited to do it, when and how.* To some extent the 'what' can neatly be divided into three areas

Assessors need to know all three things about the person they are assessing.

What a person *can* do? This refers to their ability. It is about their capacity to do various tasks efficiently given that they have the desire to do so. It also refers to their ability to learn new tasks. Assessing what a person can do is more often measured by cognitive ability (intelligence) and skills tests, though it may also be useful to assess creativity as well as the ability to lead others

What a person *will* do? This refers to a person's motivation or what they want to do. Motivation refers to a person's values and drives. Everyone can be persuaded to do things as a function of rewards and punishments, but this refers to what a person will do on an everyday basis without strong rewards or punishments trying to shape behaviour.

What a person *wants to* do? This refers to preferences for certain activities over others. It is about want a person likes to do and will do so freely without any form of coercion. It is about their values and personality and motivation, which push them in one direction or another.

1.3.2.1   The Essential Methods

There are, in essence, five different methods to collect data on people. Of these, the first three are most commonly used.

A: **Self-Report**

This is essentially what people say about themselves in:

Interviews: both structured and unstructured.

Personality and other preference tests as well as projective techniques

Biodata data questionnaires and autobiographical data

The CV, personal statement or application form

The data may be given face-to-face or online. These are very common ways of assessing people, and candidates (not they) nearly always want and expect an interview where they can answer questions and talk about themselves.

There are however two major problems with self-report.

The first is called by various names: dissimulation, faking or lying. It concerns people giving false information, or embellished information about themselves.

This behaviour has been broken down by psychologist into two further types of behaviours.

Impression Management: This is where the person attempts to create a good impression by leaving out information, adding untrue information (errors of omission and commission) and giving answers that are not strictly correct but, they hope, create a good impression in the interviewer's mind. This is done consciously and is very common. Indeed, it is expected in the answer to some questions but it can be very serious when, for instance, people claim to have qualifications or experiences they have not had, or leave out important information (about their health, criminal past, etc.).

Self-Deception: This occurs when a person, in their own view, answers honestly but what they say is untrue because they lack self-awareness. Thus, they might honestly believe that they are a 'good listener' *whereas* all the evidence from reliable sources says this is not true. This can occur for both good qualities (cognitive and emotional intelligence) as well as weaknesses (impulsivity, depression). People with low self-awareness often self-deceive.

The way personality and other preference tests attempt to deal with this issue is by using Lie Scales. These are known by various names and many exist. They are generally known as measures of response bias. These will be considered in depth in the sections about questionnaires and interviews

The second is about self-insight. This is primarily concerned with what people can't say about themselves even if they want to. This is best seen with issues around motivation where people cannot, rather than will not, give honest answers about the extent to which they are motivated by power or security. Indeed, motivation is one of the most difficult topics to assess accurately, and yet, for business people it is amongst the most important.

One way psychologists have tried to deal with this issue is through projective techniques, such as the Thematic Apperception Test, or various sentence completion tasks. For instance, a person may be asked to complete the following sentence: 'My greatest regret is….'; 'At work I often appear to be….'; 'My parents would be most proud of my….' The idea is to content analyse these responses to detect themes. These methods are expensive in terms of time and unreliability, meaning too many minor factors (like a person's mood and where the interview takes place) affects their response.

B: **Observation Data**

This is what other people say about an individual in:

References and testimonials
360-degree ratings (multi-source feedback)
Appraisal and other performance management data

Most organisations attempt to get reliable reports from other people who know the candidate that they are attempting to assess. Many application processes ask candidates to list people who know them well in some salient setting and may be called upon. There are also problems with this type of data

---

The 'data bank'" of the observer. This essentially means what information the observer has about the candidate. For example, a boss has a different data set than a colleague or a subordinate. A schoolteacher or university lecturer will have a different data set than an employer. The question is *what they know*: the quality and quantity of data on a person's ability, motivation, workstyle, etc. Usually, but not always, the amount of time a person has known another and the quality and quantity of their feedback are the best predictors of the knowledge they have. Years ago, it was found that of all the background data that the military had of very senior officers, it was their peers' reports from bootcamp that were most useful. This means that the people who had lived and worked with them under extreme circumstances were best informed about their ability, personality and motivation.

The extent to which they are prepared to tell the truth about an individual. Some organisations refuse staff to do references because of litigation. They can be taken to court for what they say or do not say. They are told all they can say is that 'X worked here from date A to date B.' Next, people choose their own referees in the hope that they will be very positive. There seems to be an etiquette with respect to what people write or rate on references. Many know the power of negative information and therefore try strongly to resist providing any negative information. It is therefore rare to get very useful data on a person's weaknesses or challenges from references.

C: **Test Performance**

This refers to how well people do on tests:

*Power, Timed, Ability tests: These are of maximum
    performance*
*Preference, Untimed, Personality tests. These are of typical
    performance*
Behavioural tests often in groups
Games and gamified tests

There are thousands of different tests to choose from. Most professionals only know about a few of these. They also are often not clear about why one test may be better than the other. The issue is the choice of test, and this is discussed later. This is almost always a question of evidence of the psychometric properties of a test.

Tests differ enormously. Here are some examples:

Group vs individually administered tests. Some require a one-to-one administration, others can be easily and effectively administered in large groups.
Objective vs open-ended tests. The former requires the choice of several responses; the latter means one has to generate the response.
Pen-and-paper vs performance tests. The latter may involve the manual manipulation of apparatus, equipment and tools.

Test Reliability: does the test yield the same result at different times. There are different types of reliability (see questionnaires) but the essential question is, are test scores effected by all sorts of factors: time-of-day, mood of the test-taker; place where the test was taken. Some measures like blood pressure are highly unreliable while others like blood group are very reliable.

Test Validity: this is, quite rightly, thought of as the most important criteria for any test. There are again many different types of validity but perhaps the most important is construct and predictive validity: does the test actually measure what it is claiming to measure (i.e. do intelligence tests really measure intelligence) as well as predictive validity (do the test scores predict some specified behaviour at a later point).

D: **Physiological Evidence**

This is probably the newest and most disputed of all measures. Thus, for some jobs, employees have to go through a 'medical check-up', which they may have to do on a regular (i.e. annual) basis simply to keep their job. This would be true of such jobs as being an airplane pilot. In other jobs, for instance, working in the alcohol industry, it may be a requirement that people go through a liver function test.

Simple blood tests and saliva samples can be used for various diagnoses, including drug taking and stress levels. Every day, it seems new, simple physical measures are being devised that are claimed to be able to detect such things as whether a person is more likely to get a debilitating mental or physical disease.

There are many other physical measures such as voice evaluation and others (skin conductance, heart rate measurement from lie detectors). Some people 'trust' the 'reality' and supposed 'unfakeability' of physical as opposed to 'psychological' responses.

E. **Personal History/Biography**

This refers to a person's personal history, for instance where they were born and educated, the family from which they come and their present family and address. Some information is thought to be very important, such as the social class of the parents; does the person come from a minority race or religious group; how many brothers and sisters do they have and what is their place in the birth order; what was their schooling like and how successful were they at it.

This information is called biodata. It aims to determine, through empirical methods, the biographical markers of success in very particular jobs. It has limitations, which will be discussed later.

1.3.2.2   A Simple Selection Model

Here is the simplest selection model. The aim is to select the good and reject the bad.

There are ideal and non-ideal people, and we have the option to select or reject. So we can have

A: Select the ideal; B: Select the non-ideal; C: Reject the ideal; D: Reject the non-ideal.

Through job analysis, selectors usually have a list of competencies that they are looking for. However, there are two problems with this model: B and C are errors.

Most selectors are concerned with getting A but nobody with D.

The more important the job and the more the consequences of failure or derailment count, the more important it is to assess potential derailers (discussed below).

There are two major reasons why selection could go wrong:

1. The assumption of linearity: this is the idea that more is better. The more you have of a quality (intelligence, creativity, integrity) the better. The idea is linearity: a straight line. For most jobs you need an optimal amount rather than a maximal amount, or an inverse U. Neither too little, nor too much.
2. The failure to select out: this is to actively look for things that you do not want in the person being assessed. That is, not preparing a list of qualities that you should look for but that you don't want: that are essentially derailers.

1.3.2.3 Psychometric Details

All psychometricians are quite rightly obsessed with two factors with regard to many tests: do they give the same answer on two occasions (are they reliable) and do they measure what they say they are measuring. For each of the 20 methods we will ask these questions.

Figure 1.1 and Table 1.1 summarise these issues. Four fundamental points need to be made. First, a test cannot be valid if it is not reliable. Second, it takes a great deal of time and effort to establish test validity. The process is a little bit like trying to establish evidence for an alternative medicine or practice. Third, the most important types

	GOOD	BAD
SELECT	A I Good Decision	B I Bad Decision
REJECT	C I Bad Decision	D I Good Decision

FIGURE 1.1 A Simple Selection Model.

of validity are *predictive* validity (do test scores predict relevant behaviour?) and *construct* validity (does the test measure what it purports to measure, and is that important?). Fourth, has the validation process been carried out by independent assessors, rather than the people who are selling the test?

Where possible, it is a good idea to refer to the test manual, which should give you all the information you need on these topics.

1.3.2.4 Assessment Methods Compared

Both for the scientist and the practitioner a crucial question is what method(s) to choose. But different groups have different criteria:

Academic experts base their views primarily on studies of validity – and we will go on to provide some examples of these. One clear point emerging is how popularity and objectivity can be in conflict – i.e. that there are fads and fashions that influence usage and choice of methods.

Consultants are often more interested in what clients like and want rather than the data from validity studies. The structured interview, followed by structured peer reports, followed by a few psychometric tests seems to be the preferred approach.

Table 1.1 *Core and secondary types of validity in selection research*

Core types of validity in selection	
Criterion	Test predicts actual work performance
Content	Test looks plausible to experts (and test takers)
Construct	Test measures something meaningful/important to all concerned
Convergent/ divergent	Tests that 'should' correlate do correlate, while tests that 'should not' correlate with each other actually do not do so
Cross- validation	Test predicts work performance in two separate, unrelated samples
Incremental	Test measures something not already measured, or above (added to) what other tests measure
Differential	Test predicts better for one group/classification of people than another
Synthetic	Tests measure component traits and abilities that themselves predict work performance
Secondary types of validity in selection	
Face	Test look plausible, realistic, practical
Factorial	Test measures separate/distinct features or things
Mythical	People think/believe research has shown the test is valid

Adapted from Cook (2016, Table 2.1 p. 28)

HR specialists differ mainly depending on their background. Those with psychology training often like tests. Sometimes, they are zealous about the use of particular tests. However, most rate structured interviews and references as crucial.

Line managers most often like and use interviews (but frequently unstructured) and work samples.

Practitioners (i.e. consultants, HR specialists, line managers) are concerned about practicality and alienating candidates more than validity and even cost. In some organisations, the view is that any sort of testing, particularly on 'senior people', is seen as quite inappropriate.

While not all *academic experts* are in full agreement, there are clear areas of common view.

For example, there is the work of Schmitt (1989) (see Table 1.2), who argued for both the validity of, but also fairness in, employment selection and examined areas of bias based on gender, age, race, etc. His main conclusions were that assessment centres and peer ratings are perhaps the best selection methods to use. The former is very expensive and the latter very cheap. Secondly, many well-known methods are of very limited validity (i.e. interviews, references). Also, surprisingly little is known about the potential bias of these tests.

Table 1.2 *Level of validity and subgroup mean difference for various predictors*

Predictor	Validity	Subgroup mean difference
Cognitive ability and special aptitude	Moderate	Moderate
Personality	Low	Small
Interest	Low	?[a]
Physical ability	Moderate-high	Large[b]
Biographical information	Moderate	?
Interviews	Low	Small (?)
Work samples	High	Small
Seniority	Low	Large (?)
Peer evaluations	High	?
Reference checks	Low	?
Academic performance	Low	?
Self-assessments	Moderate	Small
Assessment centres	High	Small

[a] Indicates either a lack of data or inconsistent data.
[b] Mean differences largely between male and female subgroups.

Over the years, there have been many attempts at a *compare and contrast of methods*. The various reviews show a reasonable amount of concordance but also some important differences. The differences occur primarily because they use different data bases over different periods of time and use different criteria.

Because this is central to the very essence of this book, a number of works in order of date of publication will be reviewed. Thirty years ago, Schmitt (1989) argued for both the validity of, but also fairness in, employment selection. Subgroup mean refers to the fact that these tests show results for different groups of people (i.e. male vs female, black vs white, old vs young). This is obviously an important area of bias. Hence the Table 1.2. The bigger the subgroup mean, the more the potential bias in these tests which differentiate between various groups based on gender, age, race, etc.

At the turn of the millennium, Anderson and Cunningham-Snell (2000) made an interesting and important distinction between validity (i.e. predictive accuracy) and popularity, as given in Table 1.3.

Another recent summary by Arnold et al (2005) is presented in Table 1.4.

Pulakos (2005) provides a similar, but slightly different data (Table 1.5).

Cook (2004, 2016) give six useful criteria for judging selection tests (Table 1.6):

1. *Validity* is the most important criterion. Unless a test can predict productivity, there is little point in using it.
2. *Cost* tends to be accorded far too much weight by selectors. Cost is not an important consideration, so long as the test has validity. A valid test, even the most elaborate and expensive, is almost always worth using.
3. *Practicality* is a negative criterion – i.e. a reason for not using a test.
4. *Generality* simply means how many types of employees the test can be used for.
5. *Acceptability* to candidates is important, especially in times of full employment.

Table 1.3 *Accuracy and popularity of different methods*

Predictive accuracy	
Perfect prediction	1.00
Assessment centres promotion	0.68
Work samples	0.54
Ability tests	0.54
Structured interviews	0.44
Integrity tests	0.41
Assessment centres performance	0.41
Biodata	0.37
Personality tests	0.38
Unstructured interviews	0.33
Self-assessment	0.15
Reference	0.13
Astrology	0.00
Graphology	0.00
Popularity	
Interviews	(97%)
References	(96%)
Application forms	(93%)
Ability tests	(91%)
Personality tests	(80%)
Assessment centres	(59%)
Biodata	19%)
Graphology	(3%)
Astrology	(0%)

6. *Legality* can be another negative criterion – a reason for not using something. It is often hard to evaluate, as the legal position on many tests is obscure or confusing.

Cook then provides an evaluation of different assessment methods, using these six important and different criteria.

Schmidt et al. (2016) summarised the practical and theoretical implications of 100 years of research in personnel selection. On the

Table 1.4 *Summary of studies on the validity of selection procedures*

Selection method	Evidence for criterion-related validity	Applicant reactions	Extent of use
Structured interviews	High	Moderate to positive	High
Cognitive ability	High	Negative to moderate	Moderate
Personality tests	Moderate	Negative to moderate	Moderate
Biodata	Can be high	Moderate	Moderate
Work sample tests	High	Positive	Low
Assessment centres	Can be high	Positive	Moderate
Handwriting	Low	Negative to moderate	Low
References	Low	Positive	High

basis of meta-analytic findings, his research presents the validity of 31 procedures for predicting job performance and the validity of paired combinations of general mental ability (GMA) and 29 other selection procedures.

Overall, the two combinations with the highest multivariate validity and utility for predicting job performance were GMA plus an integrity test (mean validity of .78) and GMA plus a structured interview (mean validity of .76).

Similar results were obtained for these two combinations in the prediction of performance in job training programs (Table 1.7). A further advantage of these two combinations is that they can be used for both entry-level hiring and selection of experienced candidates.

Inspecting the Tables 1.2–1.7, one could be either struck either by their surprising *congruity and similarity* based on the fact they are different reviews looking at different studies with different measures

Table 1.5 *Evaluation of assessment methods based on four key criteria*

Assessment method	Validity	Adverse impact	Costs (develop/ administer)	Applicant reactions
Cognitive ability tests	High	High (against minorities)	Low/low	Somewhat favourable
Job knowledge tests	High	High (against minorities)	Low/low	More favourable
Personality tests	Low to moderate	Low	Low/low	Less favourable
Biographical data inventories	Moderate	Low to high for different types	High/low	Less favourable
Integrity tests	Moderate to high	Low	Low/low	Less favourable
Structured interviews	High	Low	High/high	More favourable
Physical fitness test	Moderate to high	High (against female and older workers)	High/high	More favourable
Situational judgement tests	Moderate	Moderate (against minorities)	High/low	More favourable
Work samples	High	Low	High/high	More favourable
Assessment centres	Moderate to high	Low to moderate, depending on exercise	High/high	More favourable
Physical ability tests	Moderate to high	High (against female and older workers)	High/high	More favourable

Note: there was limited research evidence available on applicant reactions to situational judgement tests and physical ability tests. However, because these tests tend to appear very relevant to the job, it is likely that applicant reactions to them would be favourable.

Table 1.6 *Summary of 12 selection tests by six criteria*

Selection test	Validity	Cost	Practicality	Generality	Acceptability	Legality
Interview	Low	Medium/low	High	High	High	Uncertain
Structured interview	High	High	?Limited	High	Untested	No problems
References	Moderate	Very low	High	High	Medium	Some doubts
Peer rating	High	Very low	Very limited	Very limited	Low	Untested
Biodata	High	High/low	High	High	Low	Some doubts
Ability	High	Low	High	High	Low	Major problems
Psychomotor test	High	Low	Moderate	Limited	Untested	Untested
Job Knowledge	High	Low	High	Limited	Untested	Some doubts
Personality	Variable	Low	High	High	Low	Some doubts
Assessment	High	Very high	Fair	Fair	High	No problems
Work sample	High	High	Limited	Limited	High	No problems
Education	Moderate	Nil	High	High	Untested	Major doubts

Table 1.7 *Operational validity for overall job performance of general mental ability (GMA) combined with a second supplementary predictor using multiple regression*

Selection Procedures/predictors	Operational validity (r)	Multiple R	Gain in validity (ΔR)	% Gain in validity	Standardised regression weights GMA	Supplement
1. GMA tests	.65					
2. Integrity tests	.46	.78	.130	20%	.63	.43
3. Employment interviews (structured)	.58	.76	.117	18%	.52	.43
4. Employment interviews (unstructured)	.58	.73	.087	13%	.49	.38
5. Interests	.31	.71	.062	10%	.64	.29
6. Phone-based interviews	.46	.70	.057	9%	.56	.29
7. Conscientiousness trait	.22	.70	.053	8%	.67	.27
8. Reference checks	.26	.70	.050	8%	.65	.26
9. Openness to experience trait	.04	.69	.039	6%	.74	−.25
10. Biographical data	.35	.68	.036	6%	.90	−.34
11. Job experience (years)	.16	.68	.032	5%	.66	.321
12. Personality-based EI	.32	.68	.029	5%	.61	.20
13. Person-organisation fit	.13	.67	.024	4%	.66	.18

14. SJT (knowledge)	.26	.66	.015	2%	.75	-.17
15. Person-job fit	.18	.66	.014	2%	.64	.13
16. Assessment centres	.36	.66	.013	2%	.78	-.18
17. T & E point method	.11	.66	.009	1%	.65	.11
18. Grade point average	.34	.66	.009	1%	.74	-.14
19. Years of education	.10	.65	.008	1%	.65	.10
20. Extraversion trait	.09	.65	.006	1%	.65	.09
21. Peer ratings	.49	.65	.006	1%	.57	.12
22. Ability-based EI	.23	.65	.004	0%	.68	-.08
23. Agreeableness trait	.08	.65	.002	0%	.64	.05
24. Work sample tests	.33	.65	.002	0%	.68	-.06
25. SJT (behavioural tendency)	.26	.65	.001	0%	.64	.03
26. Emotional stability trait	.12	.65	.00	0%	.64	.02
27. Graphology	.02	.65	.00	0%	.65	.02
28. Job tryout procedure	.44	.65	.00	0%	.63	.02
29. Behavioural consistency	.45	.65	.00	0%	.64	.02
30. Job knowledge tests	.48	.65	.00	0%	.65	.01
31. Age	.00	.65	.00	0%	.65	.01

Note. EI = emotional intelligence; SJT = situational judgement tests, T & E = training and experience.

over different time periods or by the fact that they seem surprisingly
different/incongruous/dissimilar from another. Whichever the reaction, various conclusions may be drawn.

Ability tests are possibly the most valid tests to predict work performance,
particularly in highly skilled jobs.

Interviews are only valid if thoughtfully structured and carried out.

Assessment centres, given that they are number of different methods, are
amongst the most valid.

Letters of reference have poor validity.

Where possible, work knowledge and job try-out data is highly valid.

Biodata has modest, but acceptable validity.

Depending on the test, and the traits measured, personality tests can be
very valid.

Individual personality traits have very different rates of predictiveness (i.e.
Conscientiousness vs Extraversion).

1.4   THE PERSPECTIVE OF PROFESSIONALS

Traditionally it has been HR professionals who have been tasked with
the main "burden" of selection, though in smaller organisations this
task could be done by anyone. A number of studies have looked at the
beliefs and approach of selectors.

Some years ago, Furnham (2008) looked at HR professionals'
beliefs about, and knowledge of, assessment techniques and psychometric tests. He asked 255 European HR professionals to rate various
tests in terms of validity, cost, reliability and perceived legality.
Table 1.8 shows that three techniques were thought to have high
validity: assessment centres, cognitive ability tests and work sample.
Least valid were judged to be personal hunch, references and biodata.
The techniques could be categorised into high, middle and low cost:
High – assessment centres, personality tests; *Medium* – 360-degree
appraisal data, cognitive ability tests, work sample, interview, biodata; *Low* – personal hunch, educational qualifications, references, job
knowledge, peer rating.

Table 1.8 *Rating of 12 techniques by four criteria: 1 = poor/cheap;*
5 = good/expensive

	Criteria			
Technique	A Validity	B Cost	C Practicality	D Legality
Interview	3.11	2.99	3.83	3.61
Reference	2.23	1.71	3.37	2.95
Peer ratings	3.08	2.39	2.74	2.56
Biodata	2.80	2.58	2.94	2.76
Cognitive ability tests	3.90	3.41	3.20	3.37
Personality tests	3.55	3.56	3.25	3.23
Assessment centres	4.03	4.42	2.71	3.70
Work sample	3.90	3.07	3.00	3.51
Job knowledge	3.65	2.27	3.49	3.47
Educational qualifications	3.13	1.64	3.69	3.43
360-degree appraisal data	3.56	3.46	2.73	3.03
Personal hunch	1.83	1.39	3.03	1.53

There was little range in ratings of practicality.

Interview was judged the most practical and 360-degree multi-source data the least.

There was relatively little variability in legality ratings with assessment centres and interviews getting the highest legality rating and peer ratings, biodata and, of course, personal hunch the lowest. Participants tended to be positive about the tests themselves, how they were used and about test publishers. They rated assessment centres, cognitive ability tests and work samples as the most valid, while interviews were rated as the most practical.

In another study, Furnham and Jackson (2011) looked at human resource practitioners' attitudes and beliefs about work-related psychological tests. In all, 255 practitioners from human resources and

related disciplines completed a 64-item questionnaire on their attitudes to, and beliefs about, work-related psychological tests. These
were measured on an 8-point scale where 8 = Strongly agree and 1 =
Strongly disagree. The 10 statements that were scored most high
(agree) and low (disagree) are shown in Table 1.9.

The general themes underlying the items that respondents
tended to agree with are the following: Tests are useful because interviews are unreliable. Many organisations are ignorant about test validity and which tests to use. Organisations have insufficient trained test
administrators. Tests predict job performance very well. Tests improve
on other techniques. Tests are scientifically biased, comprehensive and
explicit. Tests are objective, unbiased, practical and easy to administer.
Tests give a good impression to recruits. Tests provide useful, pre-
interview information. Tests explore/reveal individual motivation. It
is mainly resource constraints that stop tests from being used. Tests
can filter out unsuitable candidates. Tests can be intimidating to
potential employees. Online tests are efficient. Candidates may challenge their scores under freedom of information legislation. Tests help
understand under-performance and mis-deployment.

On the other hand, there were a number of items that generated
a fair amount of disagreement in the sense that they had lower mean
scores. They were all supportive of tests. That is, the respondents
strongly disagreed with the item that suggested psychological tests
did not add value (12), led to litigation (13), presented the wrong image
(16), were unfashionable (21), were no better than traditional
recruitment methods (1), were prejudiced against women (27), were
not specifically useful for individual development (7) or were a
pseudo-science (26). The general themes which respondents disagreed
with are as follows: 1. tests are no better than other methods; 2.
organisations use tests only because their competitions do; 3. online
tests reduce faking; 4. tests are more useful in deciding who to let go
rather than keep; 5. intelligence tests are too biased (race, age) to use
in selection; 6. psychological tests are only used for higher-level jobs;
7. organisations do not use tests for legal reasons; 8. tests are out of

Table 1.9 *The 64 items showing the mean score and standard deviation (ordered by mean) for the group (8 = Strongly Agree; 1 = Strongly Disagree)*

		Mean	SD
57.	It is very difficult for untrained people to differentiate between good and bad psychometric tests.	6.56	1.56
11.	Psychometric tests allow recruiters to find out about a person, not just their qualifications and background.	6.52	1.18
28.	Psychometric tests provide useful information before doing interviews.	6.34	1.65
36.	Psychometric tests can help filter out unsuitable candidates.	6.24	1.52
39.	Online tests offer both easier administration and faster turnaround.	6.18	1.56
10.	Psychometric tests definitely improve on our current recruitment techniques.	6.08	1.45
63.	We began to use psychometric tests because they improve on our recruitment techniques.	6.06	1.47
52.	Psychometric tests are useful because they help to counter the perception of corruption, favouritism and 'old-boy' networks being self-perpetuating.	5.91	1.44
38.	Psychometric tests provide numeric information, which means individuals can more easily be compared on the same criteria.	5.89	1.58
19.	Psychometric testing shows organisations are serious about recruitment practices.	5.85	1.51
55.	Psychometric test results are too complicated to implement.	3.12	1.62
49.	Most psychometric tests are invalid because they do not measure what they say they measure.	3.00	1.45
21.	Psychometric tests are now unfashionable.	2.86	1.57
1.	Even if properly used, psychometric tests are no better than traditional recruitment methods (e.g. interview, references, application forms)	2.68	1.59

Table 1.9 (cont.)

	Mean	SD
16. Psychometric tests present the wrong image to our employees in interviews.	2.55	1.55
27. Psychometric tests are biased against women.	2.41	1.55
13. We have stopped using psychometric tests for selection because we were worried about being sued.	2.34	1.68
7. Personality tests are more useful for individual development than selection.	2.27	1.48
12. Psychometric tests do not add value to existing recruitment techniques (e.g. interviews, references, application forms).	2.13	1.28
26. Psychometric tests are pseudoscience and are no better than graphology.	1.93	1.25

fashion; 9. tests necessitate too much feedback/monitoring after testing; 10. tests are poor predictors of work group compatibility; they do not measure the most essential organisationally prescribed dimensions of behaviour.

Later, Furnham (2018) tested 145 professionals who had a very wide variety of job titles with reference to assessment change, development, HR, learning, and talent being most common. They were asked, 'With regards to personality tests are you: an enthusiast (69.4%), a sceptic (10.4%), neither (20.2%)?'. Participants were asked how many personality tests they could name. They ranged from 0 to 30 with a mean of 8.85 (SD = 5.36). They were asked 'Are you currently licenced to use any personality tests?' In all, 84% said yes and they were asked to list them out. Most people were licenced to use around 3–5 tests of which the most common was the MBTI and the OPQ. They were then asked to rank order the various criteria given in Table 1.10.

The results indicate that the five highest criteria were validity, reliability, candidate feedback, assessor feedback and acceptability to employees. The least important were translations available, cost of

Table 1.10 *Rank order of the 19 criteria: low scores are associated with higher rank*

Criteria: label 0 item	1 = Crucially important, 10 = Not important	M	SD
Validity	Evidence of the validity of the test	3.51	3.29
Reliability	Evidence of the reliability of the test	3.70	2.83
Candidate feedback	The quality of the feedback report for the candidate	6.04	3.77
Assessor feedback	The quality of the report for the assessor	6.43	3.53
Acceptability employees	The acceptability of the test to employees	7.89	4.19
Number of traits	The number of dimensions/traits/types measured	8.23	4.25
Norms	Evidence of good local norms	8.47	4.42
Total cost	The total cost of each test	8.96	4.81
Minority groups	Evidence the test is fair to minority groups	9.78	4.57
Time	How long it takes to administer/ complete the test	9.87	3.78
Acceptability users	The acceptability of the test to the users	10.01	5.57
Modern	How modern/up to date the test is	10.54	4.40
Specific	How specific the test is (different versions for different levels)	12.02	5.24
Technical support	Technological support (online, website support, videos)	12.12	3.86
Languages	Whether the test is available in other languages	12.91	4.27
Cost training	The cost of certification training	13.99	4.70
Popularity	The popularity of the test	14.02	3.78
Previously licenced	Whether the organisation has subscribed or licenced the test in the past	15.58	3.59
Authorised HR	The test has been authorised by the HR department	15.94	4.02

training, test popularity, organisational licencing and HR authorisation. Thus, test purchasers were using the most important psychometric criteria in choosing tests: reliability and validity. These two psychometric fundamentals are ranked considerably above all other criteria. Furthermore, they both have low standard deviations, which indicates higher agreement among the respondents. They also noted the three criteria rated as least important were popularity, previously licenced and authorisation. The first, popularity, suggests that test users believe they are not prone to following the crowd, or simply choosing a test because others have. The fact they are 'licenced' to use the test, or that it was authorised in the organisation, seemed far less important. They concluded, 'Indeed, the increase of tests on the market and their availability on the web may have had, and will have, a big impact on current and future test selection by professionals in that they will not be as tied to one or other test publisher.'

Lundgren et al. (2019), in a more conceptual paper, identified six different strategies in test selection:

1. **Ethical-protective**: which is characterised by high ethical standards, being psychologically trained and motivated to protect the profession
2. **Scientific-selective**: which essentially meant the use of more complex/costly tools, an attempt to integrate negative aspects while offering a portfolio of assessments. The essential motivation was to select the best-fitting tool.
3. **Cautious-avoiding:** which was manifest by a sceptical attitude toward testing practice, negative personal experiences and being motivated to avoid pigeonholing.
4. **Cautious-embracing**: This also reflected a sceptical attitude toward testing practice but personal experience being mostly positive and motivated by 'light use'.
5. **User-friendly-pragmatic:** This was characterised by use of a simpler tool that is easy for the test taker to understand; working within organisational constraints and being motivated by high test-taker acceptance.
6. **Knowledgeable-accommodating**: This was seen by extensive knowledge on the personality-testing industry and tools, following ethics guidelines generally, breaking rules when demanded by client/employer and being motivated to accommodate clients' needs.

1.5 WHAT EMPLOYERS TYPICALLY USE

Most organisations, in practice, make distinctions by level of seniority (as illustrated in Table 1.11) typically in the broad categories of graduate trainees, junior management and senior management.

Historically, assessment for selection purposes would mainly be used for external appointments, rather than for promotion from within. Organisations tended to believe that they knew about individuals already working in the organisation, e.g. from performance records, so there is less need for any sort of formal assessment.

However, that has changed as organisations have started to be more scientific about understanding the depth of talent they possess and identifying gaps. The need for more comprehensive records has been underlined by the need to manage organisational change – including re-structuring, mergers and acquisitions – where the need to demonstrate fairness is an essential part of re-stabilising the organisation.

There are other factors as well which impact on the choice of assessment method:

1. *Select in or select out:* What are the organisation's operating circumstances? Is the organisation growing or shrinking? Is it actively recruiting or evaluating whether people should keep their job?
2. *Psychometric vs 'evaluative' (judgemental):* The choice between applying a range of standard tests of different sorts or relying on the expert evaluation of individuals using 'softer', non-numeric, self-report data, or a combination of the two.
3. *Mass vs individual:* What is the size of the group that is being assessed? Some organisations that either have high turnover or massive growth expect to have to assess many hundreds of individuals per annum. This inevitably affects how they go about cost-effective, and valid, testing.
4. *General vs specialist:* Whether they are attempting to select highly specialist individuals with specific experience and educational qualifications or selecting for more generic supervisory or managerial roles.
5. *Organisational sector and type:* A bank may have very different procedures for call centres, branch managers, and senior manager staff. Equally, public

sector administrative organisations assess very differently from, say, entrepreneurial or technology or retail companies.

6. *History*: Most organisations build habits and beliefs, particularly big public companies. Organisations tend to stick with particular assessment methods even though they have not fully assessed them. They are neither content nor confident in what to change to. In small companies, it can be the opinion of strong-minded bosses that effect choice of, and rejection of, particular methods.

7. *In-house vs outsourced*: Some organisations buy in specialist consultants to do their assessment, and thus buy the suppliers' preferred techniques; others prefer to do the whole thing in-house. Consultants have preferred assessment methods. Clinically oriented and headhunter consultants rely very heavily on long structured interviews and observer reports. Test publisher consultants often push particular tests. Organisations have a love-hate relationship with consultants, who they periodically change. These changes lead to different, possibly contradictory advice with the effect that assessment methods may equally suddenly be introduced or dropped.

8. *Training/background of senior HR managers*: Inevitably, the background of the senior person in selection/recruitment/ appraisal makes a difference. Just as the use of consultants can make a big difference in what assessment methods are chosen, so is the background and training of those who take managerial decisions equally important. A senior HR manager may come from a public relations or industrial relations background; they may or may not have Chartered Institute of Personnel and Development (CIPD) qualifications; they may be a psychology graduate or postgraduate. Furthermore, they may have had many HR jobs in different companies and been fully exposed to a range of assessment techniques. Their education and experience are often driving forces for further decision-making.

9. *Staff/applicant reactions*: Organisations are more than ever PR- and litigation-conscious. They are increasingly sensitive to assessor satisfaction with the process. If people think it is unfair or inaccurate, they increasingly complain. This can cause organisations to drop certain processes quite dramatically. There can be a difficult tension and trade-off between assessment methods, validity and acceptability. That is, the assessor may find that whilst the evidence points to both cost-effectiveness and validity for a particular method (e.g. intelligence testing), assessors seem very

Table 1.11 *Pre-hire assessments used*

Assessment types	2014	2014 rank
Skills/knowledge tests	73%	1
Personality tests	62%	2
Cognitive ability/general problem-solving tests	59%	3
Job-fit tests	47%	4
Specific ability tests	47%	4
Situational judgement	43%	6
Assessment centres	41%	7
Job-specific solutions	39%	8
Biodata (life history information)	37%	9
Culture-fit tests	33%	10
Job simulations	32%	11
Interest assessments	32%	12

unhappy about its use. Equally, they may favour methods such as the unstructured interview that provides remarkably little validity. Organisational cultures generally differ in their sensitivity to assessment feedback.

I.6   RECENT DEVELOPMENTS AND CURRENT TRENDS

There are a number of new definable products, trends and developments in the area. These are driven by the following factors:

- *Changes in the law*: Legal changes and litigation risks have driven some issues (e.g. integrity testing, diversity training).
- *Changes in business*: As many organisations attempt to become more flexible and competitive, they become concerned with specific assessment-related issues, e.g. in spotting and managing talent; in strengthening leadership; in managing re-structuring, acquisitions and mergers.
- *Ideas of gurus*: Popular books highlight various concepts, issues and methods, some of which are enthusiastically embraced by businesspeople (e.g. emotional intelligence).
- *Recommendations of consultants/academics*: They often have their own agenda, which might or might not be related to the above trends.

Thus, it is possible to see the emergence of various concepts, products and measures used to assess people for jobs and to develop them. Furthermore, just as some of these products begin to emerge, others tend to wane. Thus, 360-degree evaluation/feedback is probably at its zenith, but now it is much less popular than it was. Equally, outward-bound/outdoor training to strengthen teamwork seems on the wane.

Other factors have also played a part in the development of this area:

1. *Labour market shortages*: Shortages across Europe have led many companies to rethink their strategy and process to ensure it is fair to all concerned and that they can attract and correctly identify talented individuals.
2. *Technological developments*: Two issues are relevant; the administration of tests via computers as well as recruitment and testing online via the internet.
3. *Applicant perceptions*: This refers to the perceptions of applicants as to the fairness and validity of the assessment process. This is, in part, not only an impression management task for all organisations, but also refers to the effect of assessment methods on job acceptance and subsequent performance.
4. *Construct-driven approaches*: This refers to being clear about what one is trying to assess and why. That is, having a theory and evidence for the factors/constructs that one is trying to assess and show their predictive validity.

There have been very specific developments, and various trends are noticeable:

- There have been many advances in new data tools. For instance, there are now new *interactive tests* where people respond to carefully prepared video/ acted scenes on a computer. These can even be delivered using mobile devices. They can be adapted for very specific company uses.
- One of the newest, but as yet untested ideas is the use of avatars in assessment situations.
- There is now more and more interest in samples of real-life behaviour sometimes called 'thin slides', whereby people make accurate judgements of real-life behaviour, perhaps recorded by video.

- There is an increased interest in test-takers' experience and reactions.
- Most organisations are aware of the limitations of the traditional interview and are making efforts to introduce well-structured, panel interviews.
- Poor validity response rates and litigation issues have meant the traditional reference is being replaced by structured telephone calls asking specific questions of targeted interviewees (often peers).
- There is now great emphasis on the power and usefulness of peer and subordinate ratings for assessment purposes. This has been a major consequence of the interest in 360-degree multi-rater feedback work.
- Organisations are being very sensitive to the possibility of bias (sex, race, language) in ability tests. They are also particularly concerned that they have no face validity for candidates.
- There is always the development of tests to measure new (faddish) constructs, e.g. spiritual intelligence, practical intelligence. Psychometric tests continue to be developed in large numbers and put on the market. Some clearly chime with the spirit of time, like tests of *emotional intelligence*.
- Biodata, psychomotor tests and tests of job knowledge are *not* frequently used. They have, however, never disappeared and remain the favourite of particular clients in very particular settings.
- The concept of using work samples and probation periods appears to be gaining more attention. Probation periods, if strictly enforced, give both parties (employer and employee) a chance to revisit their decisions.
- Assessment centres remain the basis of many organisations' preferred methods. They are very expensive and time consuming but recognised as the best. Most are designed based on a company's specific requirements.
- There is great interest in assessing 'people with potential' or 'high-flyers', but people are not sure how to do it.
- Organisations differ widely in whether they should have assessment expertise in-house or outsource all or some of it.
- Much less interest and expertise is devoted to assessment for development purposes. This is done through mentoring and coaching which may or may not involve some formal assessment procedures.
- Organisations are beginning to realise that they can cost the effectiveness of successful assessment/selection in monetary terms, which can have important implications.

> ## Key Assessment Questions for Organisations
>
> ### Research Questions
> - What are the most frequently used methods and what are they used for?
> - What are the strengths and weaknesses of each method?
> - What is new in the area?
> - What guiding principles do employers use in choosing different assessment methods?
> - How effective are the methods perceived to be in identifying the right people?
> - What changes have been made and why?
> - What do suppliers and consultancies have to comment on current trends?

There are some important lessons for those working in these areas (Furnham, 2008):

1. Amateurism will not do: Assessment is a technical profession business requiring skill, education and training.
2. Learning from the past: Organisations need to validate their methods in-house and learn from successes and failures.
3. Spend assessment money in proportion to the job's value to the organisation, not according to the way it may have been done in the past.
4. Assess for failure as well as success: that is select out as well as in.
5. Study the job market and beware of all demographic and other changes in job applicants at all levels. This has important implications for the assessment methods used.
6. Be aware assessment is an HR, IR and PR business: Whatever method is used there are lots of consequences, both positive and negative, on employee relationships.
7. Differentiate between selection and development, which are different processes.
8. Update job analysis and competency profiles regularly as jobs evolve.
9. Know the costs and benefits of good and bad selection.
10. Keep up to date on both research and legal issues.

I.7 CURRENT TRENDS IN SELECTION AND ASSESSMENT

There are a number of new definable products, trends and developments in the area. Changes are typically driven by:

- *Changes in technology and tools*: Rapid developments in the way we can assess people and the commercialisation of these activities since 2000 has revolutionised the industry beyond all recognition. Assessment is done online; test-publishers are by-passed; big data is available.
- *Changes in the law*: Legal changes and litigation risks have driven some issues (e.g. discrimination, integrity testing, diversity training).
- *Changes in business*: As many organisations attempt to become more flexible and competitive, they become concerned with specific assessment-related issues (e.g. in spotting and managing talent); in strengthening leadership; in managing re-structuring, acquisitions and mergers.
- *Ideas of gurus and consultants*: Popular books highlight various concepts, issues and methods, some of which are enthusiastically embraced by businesspeople (e.g. emotional intelligence).
- *Applicant perceptions*: This refers to the perceptions of applicants as to the fairness and validity of the assessment process. This is, in part, not only an impression management task for organisations, but also refers to the effect of assessment methods on job acceptance and subsequent performance.

Based on a global survey called Trends in Testing, Ryan et al. (2015) concluded 'we see a number of directions for organizational psychology research and practice:

---

1) Reasons for using or not using testing were tied to the value of testing, suggesting that continued work to document and especially to communicate the value of testing should be a focus of research and practice efforts. In particular, enhanced communication regarding the incremental validity of testing may be important to adoption decisions.

2) Companies have taken advantage of the availability of technology to move away from using a paper-and-pencil format for most types of tests. However, most do not seem to be using the capabilities provided by recent technological advancements to the extent possible, in that less than half of respondents indicated using various elements made feasible by computerized

tests (e.g., video/multimedia, avatars, adaptive testing). Researchers and practitioners can focus efforts on enhancing these technological advances and promoting greater use.

3) Test security practices do not seem to be widely or fully employed for paper-and-pencil or supervised computerized testing let alone for unproctored computerized tests. The value of a selection system can be completely degraded by poor security so attention by practitioners to communicating the importance of security and data protection, as well as attention to means of making security measures easy to implement may help. Development of alternate forms in cases where adaptive pools are not in use should also be a focus given retesting policies. Note that this lack of attention to security may be due to beliefs that not many individuals cheat, willingness to tolerate a certain rate of cheating, and the rarity of detecting cheaters.

4) Global testing programs are likely to increase given the globalization of business, suggesting a need for greater attention to international testing standards. Many of the advocated practices for using testing worldwide did not appear to be followed.

5) Organizations increasingly track metrics that may be used to evaluate selection systems; further work to establish high-quality evaluation programs may even further support the value of test use in selection. Thus, it is possible to see the emergence of various concepts, products and measures used to assess people for jobs and to develop them. Further, just as some of these products begin to emerge others tend to wane; what was "all the rage" a decade ago now seems passed.' (pp. 150–151)

There have been very specific developments and various trends are noticeable:

- There have been many advances in new data tools. For instance, there are now new *interactive tests* where people respond to carefully prepared video/acted scenes on a computer. These can be delivered using mobile devices.
- Some of the newest are the exploration of Big Data (Chapter 10) as well as Gamification (Chapter 6), using physiological markers (wearables) (Chapter 7), the use of avatars in assessment situations.
- There is now more and more interest in samples of real-life behaviour sometimes called 'thin slices' whereby people make accurate judgements of real-life behaviour, perhaps recorded by video.

- Most organisations are aware of the limitations of the traditional interview and are making efforts to introduce well-structured, panel interviews.
- Poor validity response rates and litigation issues have meant the traditional reference is being replaced by structured telephone calls, asking specific questions of targeted interviewees (often peers).
- There is now great emphasis on the power and usefulness of peer and subordinate ratings for assessment purposes. This has been a major consequence of the interest in 360-degree multi-rater feedback work.
- Organisations are being very sensitive to the possibility of bias (sex, race, language) in ability tests. They are also particularly concerned that they have no face validity for candidates.
- There is always the development of tests to measure new (faddish) constructs, e.g. spiritual intelligence, practical intelligence agility. Psychometric tests continue to be developed in large numbers and put on the market. Some clearly chime with the spirit of time, like tests of *emotional intelligence.*
- Biodata, psychomotor tests and tests of job knowledge are *not* frequently used. They have, however, never disappeared and remain the favourite of particular clients in very particular settings.
- The concept of using work samples and probation periods appears to be gaining more attention. Probation periods, if strictly enforced, give both parties (employer and employee) a chance to revisit their decisions. However, this is not possible in many jobs.
- Assessment centres remain the basis of some organisations' preferred methods if they have the time and money. They are very expensive and time consuming but recognised as the best. Most are designed very specifically for each company and their particular requirements.
- There is great interest in assessing 'people with potential' or 'high-flyers', but people are not sure how to do it or how to define them.
- Organisations differ widely in whether they should have assessment expertise in-house or outsource all or some of it.
- Much less interest and expertise is devoted to assessment for development purposes. This is done through mentoring and coaching, which may or may not involve some formal assessment procedures.
- Organisations are beginning to realise that they can cost the effectiveness of successful assessment/selection in monetary terms, which can have important implications.

Serious Selection

Some jobs are more important than others: imagine trying to select an astronaut who has to spend months in a space station; or a commander for a nuclear submarine; or a spy. The consequences of failure would be extremely important. Hence the need to be very careful in the selection process, which inevitably will take considerable time and money.

Consider the following steps in how an anonymous organisation recruits its staff:

1. Head-hunters, talent scouts and trusted insiders are asked to keep a lookout for possible applicants who may be approached. These may be supplemented by very discreet advertisements.
2. Candidates complete a relatively short but very specific application form, and various checks are made with public data (social media Facebook, LinkedIn, police, health, migration). This is the first sift as many are rejected at this stage.
3. Potential candidates are first interviewed by a trained HR person from the organisation using a structured interview but on relevant attributes, skills and values, and the required to write a lengthy report.
4. If judged worth pursuing, the candidate goes through a due diligence process and asked to complete some online personality and IQ questionnaires and then interviewed by a second trained HR insider using the first interviewer's report.
5. If judged successful, the candidate is asked to take part in a two-day open, intensive assessment centre designed for high-flying managers and leaders across a range of organisations.
6. If successful, the candidate is asked to supply the names, email and phone details of between 10 and 20 people they have worked with and for, and/or who knows them well. They are asked also for permission to contact these people. A structured telephone interview of around 10 people is then done. Results are collected and written up. There are up to five referees and their comments are available at the later assessment centre.
7. If successful, a large document containing *all* the above details is sent to four people: three very senior people in the organisation and an outside expert (psychologist/psychiatrist) to read. They assemble two hours before the final interview with the candidate to structure a final interview based on their impressions from the documentation.
8. The candidate is interviewed by the 'final selection board' for around 1.5 hours. Their decision is communicated to the candidate later in the day.

REFERENCES

Anderson, N., & Cunningham-Snell, N. (2000) Personnel selection. In Chmiel, N. (Ed.), *Introduction to work and organizational psychology* (p. 69–99). Blackwell.

Arnold, J., Silvester, J., Cooper, C. L., Robertson, I. T., & Patterson, F. M. (2005). *Work psychology: Understanding human behaviour in the workplace.* Pearson Education.

Chatman, J. A., Wong, E., & Joyce, C. (2008). When do people make the place? In *The people make the place* (p. 63–86). New York: LEA.

Cook, M. (2004). *Personnel selection.* John Wiley & Sons.

Cook, M. (2016). *Personnel selection: Adding value through people-A changing picture.* John Wiley & Sons.

Ferguson, E., & Lievens, F. (2017). Future directions in personality, occupational and medical selection: myths, misunderstandings, measurement, and suggestions. *Advances in Health Sciences Education, 22*(2), 387–399.

Furnham, A. (2008). HR professionals' beliefs about, and knowledge of, assessment techniques and psychometric tests. *International Journal of Selection and Assessment, 16*(3), 300–305.

Furnham, A. (2018). The great divide: Academic versus practitioner criteria for psychometric test choice. *Journal of Personality Assessment, 100*(5), 498–506.

Furnham, A., & Jackson, C. J. (2011). Practitioner reactions to work-related psychological tests. *Journal of Managerial Psychology, 26*, 549–565.

Furnham, A., Trickey, G., & Hyde, G. (2012). Bright aspects to dark side traits: Dark side traits associated with work success. *Personality and Individual Differences, 52*(8), 908–913.

Gatewood, R., Feild, H. S., & Barrick, M. (2015). *Human resource selection.* Nelson Education.

Greiff, S., & Iliescu, D. (2017). A test is much more than just the test itself. *European Journal of Psychological Assessment, 33*(3), 145–148.

Ihsan, Z., & Furnham, A. (2018). The new technologies in personality assessment: A review. *Consulting Psychology Journal: Practice and Research, 70*(2), 147–167

Lundgren, H., Poell, R. F., & Kroon, B. (2019). "This is not a test": How do human resource development professionals use personality tests as tools of their professional practice? *Human Resource Development Quarterly, 30*(2), 175–196.

Piotrowski, C. (2019). Current research emphasis in the field of psychological assessment: A panorama of investigatory domain. *North American Journal of Psychology, 21*(3), 583–599.

Pulakos, E. D. (2005). *Selection assessment methods.* Society for Human Resource Management (SHRM) Foundation.

Rotolo, C. T., & Church, A. H. (2015). Big data recommendations for industrial–organizational psychology: Are we in whoville?. *Industrial and Organizational Psychology, 8*(4), 515–520.

Ryan, A. M., Inceoglu, I., Bartram, D., Golubovich, J., Grand, J., Reeder, M., Derous, E., Nikolaou, l., & Yao, X. (2015). Trends in testing: Highlights of a global survey. In I. Nikolaou & J. K. Oostrom (Eds.), *Current issues in work and organizational psychology. Employee recruitment, selection, and assessment: Contemporary issues for theory and practice* (p. 136–153). Routledge/Taylor & Francis Group

Schaubroeck, J., Ganster, D., & Jones, J. (1998). Organization and occupation influences in the Attraction-Selection-Attrition process. *Journal of Applied Psychology, 83,* 869–891.

Schmitt, N. (1989). Fairness in employment selection. *Advances in Selection and Assessment, 10,* 134–153.

Schmidt, F. L., Oh, I. S., & Shaffer, J. A. (2016). The validity and utility of selection methods in personnel psychology: Practical and theoretical implications of 100 years... *Fox School of Business Research Paper.*

Schneider, B. (1987). The people make the place. *Personnel Psychology, 40*(3), 437–453.

Schneider, B., Smith, D. B., Taylor, S., & Fleenor, J. (1998). Personality and organizations: A test of the homogeneity of personality hypothesis. *Journal of Applied Psychology, 83*(3), 462.

Sehlapelo, M., & Terre Blanche, M. (1996). Psychometric testing in South Africa: Views from above and below. *Psychology in Society, 21*(49), 45.

Sosnowska, J., Hofmans, J., & Lievens, F. (2018). Assessing personality dynamics in personnel selection. In J. F. Rauthmann (Ed.), *The handbook of personality dynamics and processes* (p. 61–87). Elsevier.

2 Complex and Sticky Issues in Assessment and Selection

INTRODUCTION

The business of assessment, recruitment and selection has come under a great deal of scrutiny over the past 50 years. There used to be a time when it was possible to use any form of assessment and choose any individual with impunity. Now there are great concerns about discrimination and laws against discriminating in favour of, or against, people in terms of disability, race, religion, sex, etc. That is, if people use an assessment method which helps them justify the preference for one category of candidate over another, irrespective of other evidence that they are equally qualified for the job, this is seen as a breach of the law.

In this chapter, we consider some of the issues that assessors need to be aware of. Studies have shown that supposedly the most trivial of factors have a direct effect on selection decisions. These include whether and what perfume a female candidate is wearing, the physical stature (i.e. firmness of hand grip) of the candidate, and the voice of the candidate. It is worrying, but of great psychological significance, that these factors influence judgement.

Some examples of research findings on applicant attributes that affect rating bias are given in Table 2.1.

2.1.1 The Role of Attractiveness in Selection

Are physically attractive people advantaged at work? Are they more likely to be selected for jobs, promoted in those jobs or given higher salaries? Does being physically attractive count more than being competent at work? Does physical attractiveness advantage females more than males, or does it depend on the job, the gender of the selector and the culture of the organisation?

Table 2.1 *Examples of research findings*

Attributes	Research findings
Gender bias	Influenced by type of job (role-congruent jobs) and competence. Female interviewers often give higher ratings than male interviewers.
First-impression effect	Early impressions are often more important than factual information for ratings and judgements. Decision to hire is related to the interviewer's causal interpretation (attribution) of an applicant's past outcomes.
Contrast effect	Interviewer's evaluations of a candidate are influenced by the quality and characteristics of previous candidates.
Nonverbal communication	Applicants who looked straight ahead, as opposed to downward, were rated as being more alert, assertive and dependable; they were also more likely to be hired. Applicants who demonstrated a greater amount of eye contact, head movement and smiling received higher evaluations.
Physical attractiveness	Those who are generally rated as physically attractive have a much higher chance of getting higher ratings after the interview and being accepted for the position.

The experimental and case study literature substantiates the oft-made claim that physical attractiveness has a powerful influence on people's decision-making in the workplace (Furnham & Swami, 2012; Judge & Cable, 2011; Langlois et al., 2000; Swami et al., 2008). Results show that attractive adults and children are *judged* to be more intellectually competent, emotionally adjusted and socially appealing. Physical attractiveness has manifold benefits in everyday life.

The 'what is beautiful is good' finding is so widely accepted that some organisations attempt to put in place processes and procedures which try to eliminate or reduce the possible influence of attractiveness. Some forbid the attachment of photographs to application forms; others try to ensure selection boards are made up equally of males and females; still others attempt through very strict competency-based, structured interviewing to focus on getting evaluations based only on work competency evidence. They all try to reduce impressionable ratings prone to the halo effect.

Here are the results of some studies in this area (Furnham & Swami, 2012):

- Concerning the attractiveness of politicians, for every 1 standard deviation in their measure of beauty, non-incumbent parliamentary candidates received a 20% increase in the number of votes!
- Overweight people are seen as disagreeable, emotionally unstable, incompetent, sloppy, lazy and lacking Conscientiousness.
- As people got heavier, men tended to get paid better (until they began to get obese, or 15–20 kg above the norm), while the opposite was true of women, where there was a decline in salary as a function of getting heavier. They showed that women were punished for weight gain, but that very thin women received the most punishment.
- Over time, more attractive men had higher starting salaries and continued to earn more over time.
- Highly qualified people were accepted irrespective of attractiveness or job whilst less qualified but attractive applicants were only judged more favourably than less qualified and unattractive ones in jobs involving relational skills.
- Taller people are judged as more attractive, persuasive and 'leader-like'.

Most selectors attempt to find people with the appropriate skills, aptitudes, attitudes and motivation to do the job well. It is rare to see physical attractiveness as a criterion of selection or competency. However, there are certain jobs, particularly in sales, customer service, theatre, fashion or the media, where physical attractiveness is seen to be a very distinct advantage and related to job performance. Hence, it can be argued that it is quite reasonable, indeed desirable, to take this into consideration in the selection process.

Can something be done to prevent discrimination sometimes called 'lookism' or 'face-ism' or 'weightism'? There are laws against discrimination in the workplace based on sex, age, race and religion. These are often more driven by morality and ideology than scientific evidence. Some believe that physically unattractive people already carry a burden, compared to their attractive peers, that penalises them further in the workplace, which is simply unjust. Hence the call for legislation that outlaws decisions made on the basis of attractiveness.

One problem with this issue is whilst things like age and gender are objectively verifiable, judgements about attractiveness are more subjective. There is usually considerable agreement at extremes but less so in the middle of the scale. There are, however, both cultural and idiosyncratic correlates of physical attractiveness judgements. It is possible to separate face from body ratings of attractiveness or look at very specific features like height or hair colour, but to sum those features holistically is far more difficult. In this sense, it may be difficult to defend a discrimination case where it is alleged that attractiveness discrimination has occurred.

There are three distinguishable theoretical/ideological positions in this area:

A. *Unfair, stereotypic and warranting intervention*: Some argue that the 'beautiful is good' belief is unfair, often denied and is an empirically unverified supposition and stereotype. As there is no evidence that physical attractiveness at any level (face vs. body) and/or associated with any feature (i.e. height, hair colour) is related to job performance, steps need to be taken to reduce this bias at work. Any evidence of an association between attractiveness and work performance is attributed to social processes rather than biological realities and ends up unfairly discriminating against those less physically attractive.

B. *An evolutionary fact and reality*: Others argue that there are both good theoretical reasons and empirical evidence to suggest that various physical features are associated with psychological factors and processes which directly relate to performance at work. In this sense the 'beautiful is good' idea is more an empirical fact than a stereotype. Hence, it is wise to take physical attractiveness into account in the workplace; trying to legislate against it would be extremely counterproductive.

C. *An association that develops*: Physical attractiveness has developmental advantages which influence an individual's personality and social behaviour. Attractive people are treated differently from unattractive people from an early age, by parents, peers and teachers, and later by employers. They are thus more likely to become more self-confident, assertive and socially skilled, which in turn means they become more able at work, particularly in interpersonal relations. While attractiveness is not a biological marker of work-related potentialities, it is a social marker. Furthermore, because of the 'beautiful is good' association, attractive people are liked, trusted and helped more by peers, subordinates and clients/customers.

This is a fraught and complicated area for anyone trying to make fair and accurate assessments of others.

2.2   UNCONSCIOUS BIAS

There is a comparatively new area of research of potentially great relevance to those in the assessment and selection field. It is nicely illustrated in this well-known riddle:

A father and his son are in a car accident. The father dies instantly, and the son is taken to the nearest hospital. The doctor comes in and exclaims, 'I can't operate on this boy.' 'Why not?' the nurse asks. 'Because he's my son', the doctor responds. How is this possible? Answer: because the doctor is his mother.

The thesis of unconscious bias is as given in the riddle. Psychologists have long accepted a dual process theory of thinking:

Conscious, propositional thinking, which is based on logic and acquiring information

Unconscious, associative thinking, which is based on relationships between stimuli that we learn from experience and observation

Throughout our lives, we develop a complex network of relationships between concepts. Thus, many people associate *business leader* as being a male and *carer* as being a female.

In order to be efficient thinkers, we delegate large proportions of thinking to our unconscious minds. However, issues emerge when the connections we make are not congruent with external realities. Unconscious bias occurs when we make dysfunctional decisions based on such inaccurate connections.

There are a number of tests to assess unconscious bias, including the well-known Implicit-Association Test. Pictures and words are shown to participants. They select button A or B in order to categorise the word in relation to predefined concepts: press button A for male words, and button B for female words. Stereotype attitudes and unconscious bias are seen through discrepancies in reaction times to associate certain words with specific concepts.

The idea is that although we believe we are not, and indeed try not to be, biased or (illegally) discriminatory in our (selection and assessment) decision-making, we often are and quite unaware of this.

Precisely how to deal with this phenomenon is not always clear, except in training courses which have proliferated. However, many evaluations have been negative. Consider the conclusion of Noon (2018):

> The latest fashion of 'unconscious bias training' is a diversity intervention based on unproven suppositions and is unlikely to help eliminate racism in the workplace. Knowing about bias does not automatically result in changes in behaviour by managers and employees. Even if 'unconscious bias training' has the theoretical potential to change behaviour, it will depend on the type of racism: symbolic/modern/colour-blind, aversive or blatant. In addition, even if those deemed racist are motivated to change behaviour, structural constraints can militate against pro-diversity actions. Agency is overstated by psychology-inspired 'unconscious bias training' proponents, leading them to assume the desirability and effectiveness of this type of diversity training intervention, but from a critical diversity perspective (sociologically influenced) the training looks pointless.

> *(p. 198)*

2.3 ACCEPTABILITY OF METHOD FROM THE CANDIDATE'S PERSPECTIVE

Every selection procedure is a PR opportunity for an individual or organisation. 'Word gets around' that a particular organisation is using a particular method, i.e. gamification or biodata, to select employees. Some methods are thought of as more or less accurate, fair and discriminating than others.

What would happen if as part of a bank's selection criteria they asked for a mouth swab or a blood sample? What if they simply took the candidate to lunch or asked them to write a 1,000-word biography?

For the selector, there are a series of trade-offs in choosing a selection instrument. Perhaps the three major ones are cost (time and money), known validity and acceptability to the candidate (perceived as accurate and fair). Ideally, the selector would want a method that was cheap and valid and rated well by the candidates. Certainly, the opposite would be highly undesirable. But what of the trade-off:

Cheap and Valid but Unacceptable: a very efficient method, but candidates are unlikely to accept it, which may cause adverse publicity.

Cheap and Acceptable but Not Valid: possibly a waste of time except from a PR perspective.

Expensive but Valid and Acceptable: surely the best option if one takes selection seriously, but still much depends on finding methods that have the latter two characteristics.

Over the years, there have been a number of academic papers on this topic.

A good lunch as a selection opportunity

What about taking people to lunch as a selection device? This is actually done in some organisations.

A one- to two-hour lunch offers the opportunity to visit many issues that may seem inappropriate in a traditional stilted office atmosphere. A chat about previous jobs; bosses they admired; policies they thought innovative; what factors had most influence over their career; and, indeed, their out-of-work activities. Also, people drop their guard in such events, unable to keep up various pretences for all that time.

It may also show their understanding of etiquette and politeness. Most would (usually) refuse alcohol, but what if the host said, 'I fancy a glass of wine, will you join me?' The skilled executive knows the power of mirroring when it comes to negotiation and general 'friend-raising'.

Dealing with staff – it is possible over the course of lunch the candidate might interact with a range of serving staff. Does the candidate treat them like 'plebs' or are they intimidated by them? Are they annoyed by over- or under-attentiveness? What do they think of how the restaurant is run? How do they react to tipping?

Peculiarities will out at luncheons. It is difficult to believe that food fetishes are not related to social difficulties. Strong dislikes, intolerances and restrictions may reveal rigidities of one sort or another.

It is quite possible to bring up issues of health over food, as well as other habits – these are important details especially if the job involves a lot of travel to foreign countries, entertainment and selling.

Is the cost of time and money worth it? And what about the retributive, litigious interviewee who, having been rejected, is convinced it was pure prejudice against teetotal vegans who insist on bringing their own cutlery to meals?

And do not forget that an interview, be it over lunch or not, gives the candidate a much better understanding of the interviewer, who may turn out to be their boss. Many interviewers themselves appear to be too guarded and socially insecure to pull off luncheon interviews. Both parties may disclose more, which must help good decision-making.

So, does the old-fashioned lunch allow a recruiter to get a much better idea of the social and negotiation skills of a (reasonably) senior manager? Or is this also fraught with all sorts of assumptions and biases?

McCarthy et al. (2017) reviewed 145 papers on applicant reactions to selection procedures since 2000. Their first question was 'is applicant reaction research much ado about nothing?' They concluded that the literature on assessment consequences like fairness and justice, levels of anxiety and motivation all point to the fact that 'applicant reactions have significant and meaningful effects on attitudes, intentions and behaviours' (p. 1695). Experiences of the selection process are clearly related to applicants' perceptions of how attractive the organisation appears and their intentions to accept the job and recommend it to others. The development of the internet and other electronically based technology has presented new issues for organisations who saw them as simply both cheaper and less discriminative. They have recognised that website aesthetics have an influence on whether candidates apply, and that not all candidates like video-conferencing and online testing. Issues like the degree of formality, user-friendliness and applicant control are important.

Candidates are well aware of the use of new screening technologies and the ever-increasing use of content and structure-based analytics, as well as third-party providers (screening CVs, matching CVs to jobs). The promise of testing anybody, anywhere and anytime in an unproctored way can easily invite all sorts of problems, like cheating, and a range of response distortions. This quickly translates into perceptions of fairness, invading privacy and justice.

The surprisingly rich literature in this field has shown that candidates' reactions are, in part, a function of the selection ratio (accept/ reject), job type, job desirability and social context. They also vary as to when reactions are measured (before or after feedback) as well as whether the candidates are internal or external to the organisation.

It has also been established that there are cultural, personality, ethnicity and gender factors involved as these relate to values, expectations and perceptions of justice. In essence, people have cognitive (attitudinal; belief) and affective (emotional) reactions to the way they are assessed, which have various consequences like their evaluation of the organisation and themselves, their intentions to accept/reject and recommend others (as well as pursue litigation) and even their future job performance.

2.4   REACTIONS OF THOSE BEING ASSESSED

As noted above, organisations are becoming more concerned with candidates' reactions to assessment and selection methods, particularly in times of labour shortage. Some have been known to whistle-blow to the press and even advocate a boycott on purchasing the products of organisations whose assessment methods are thought of as biased, unfair or inappropriate. Some HR personnel are also nervous about senior managers rejecting a particular method.

Some organisations see their assessment technique as an 'employer brand' opportunity. They see it as helping them in the 'war for talent'. Candidates like interviews, work samples and assessment centres. Candidates dislike biodata, peer assessment and personality tests. The more job-related the method (simulations, interviews, concrete ability tests), the more they are as seen to be fair. Candidates do not like being assessed on aspects of themselves (i.e. ability, personality) that they believe they cannot (easily) change.

Lievens et al. (2003) came to some similar conclusions. They found that interviewers' beliefs about the validity and fairness of tests had little impact. But the more people taking the tests thought tests were valid, the fairer they thought personality and cognitive ability tests were.

In a useful review study, Truxillo et al. (2004) looked at both 'soft' and 'hard' outcomes of applicants' perceptions of fairness of assessment procedures. They point out that many factors influence perception of fairness. These include applicants' expectations of assessment, familiarity with the selection process, personality and socio-economic and national culture.

Meanwhile Hausknecht et al. (2004) found that four sets of factors predicted applicants' perceptions. These were the *personal characteristics* of the applicant (their work and test experience, age, sex and personality), the *nature of the job* they were applying for (e.g. how attractive it is), the *organisation* (history, resources), but most importantly the *process outcome,* (intrusion of privacy). All these factors determined the candidates' test anxiety and motivation and, most importantly, their belief in the justice of the whole experience. The techniques they thought most valid and fair were interviews and work samples followed by cognitive ability tests and then followed by personality tests, honesty tests, biodata and graphology.

Privacy is an issue in assessment. Organisations do themselves a favour by explaining assessment procedures when training assessors and considering the possibility of selection fairness very seriously. Some organisations are now beginning to base their assessment strategies on the feedback they get, specifically around appropriation, ability, fairness and validity.

Furnham and Chamorro-Premuzic (2010) investigated students' perception of the accuracy and fairness of 17 different assessment methods to measure different traits/characteristics (see Table 2.2). The results of accuracy and fairness judgements were similar, with drug, general knowledge and intelligence tests being thought of as *least* accurate and fair and panel interviews and references thought of as among the fairest selection methods. Factor analyses of the accuracy data showed that two underlying components existed, labelled test and face-to-face methods.

The problem with these results is obvious: there seems to be a negative relationship between accuracy/validity and acceptability. Usually, as we shall see, references are quite useless and intelligence tests very accurate.

Issues around acceptability to the interview change over time as new techniques are introduced. Also, as information expands, potential candidates become more aware of the use and abuse of certain techniques

2.4.1 Reactions to Integrity tests

How do people react when asked to do an integrity test? Are they offended, insulted or accepting? One study looked at student reactions

Table 2.2 *Ratings on the perceived accuracy and fairness of 17 different assessment methods*

Accuracy: selection method	M	SD
Face-to-face interview	25.69	8.65
Outward-bound leadership	26.59	9.34
References	27.43	9.34
Panel interview	27.64	8.91
Discussion	28.62	8.56
Oral presentation	30.78	9.11
Personality test	32.93	8.21
Telephone interview	33.77	10.94
Video	34.54	10.43
Essay	35.17	10.39
Situation exam	35.54	10.78
Assessment centre	36.45	10.97
Unseen course-related exam	36.45	10.31
Application form	38.46	12.89
General knowledge test	42.60	11.81
Intelligence test	44.08	11.11
Drug test	52.17	15.84
Fairness: selection method	**M**	**SD**
Face-to-face interview	33.28	12.97
Outward-bound leadership	30.66	10.38
References	27.49	12.34
Panel interview	30.18	10.78
Discussion	30.65	9.84
Oral presentation	32.26	11.09
Personality test	35.30	12.03
Telephone interview	34.93	11.88
Video	35.37	11.09
Essay	35.89	11.76
Situation exam	38.86	12.63
Assessment centre	38.74	12.82
Unseen course-related exam	42.04	12.53
Application form	37.42	14.17
General knowledge test	42.94	13.99
Intelligence test	43.28	12.97
Drug test	54.08	15.89

Note: a low score implies high accuracy and fairness.

to honesty testing as an abstract concept (Ryan & Sackett, 1987). They found:

68% felt it was appropriate for an employer to administer such a test.

10% would refuse to take such a test.

25% would enjoy being asked to take such a test.

42% felt this type of test was an invasion of privacy.

46% said if they had two comparable job offers, they would reject the company using such a test.

26% would resent being asked to take such a test.

59% felt that a test such as this is sometimes an appropriate selection procedure.

33% believe that administering a test such as this reflects negatively on the organisation.

42% indicated that being asked to take such a test would not affect their view of the organisation.

56% indicated that tests such as this are routinely used in industry.

In another study with job applicants, Jones (1991) found the following:

90% felt it was appropriate for an employer to administer such a test.

4% would refuse to take such a test.

63% would enjoy being asked to take such a test.

11% felt this type of test was an invasion of privacy.

2% said if they had two comparable job offers, they would reject the company using such a test.

3% would resent being asked to take such a test.

82% felt that a test such as this is sometimes an appropriate selection procedure.

5% believe that administering a test such as this reflects negatively on the organisation.

80% indicated that being asked to take such a test would not affect their view of the organisation.

80% indicated that tests such as this are routinely used in industry.

The issue is that there is a thin line between what may be seen as benign and intrusive/invasive monitoring technologies. Zweig and Webster (2003) found that employees' acceptance of monitoring systems was a function of their perceived usefulness, fairness and privacy invasion, which in turn were dependent on the precise characteristics of the monitoring system involved and the justification for its use. They argue:

> There is a delicate balance in the line between benign and invasive. People form expectations about the degree of personal information they will communicate with others in their daily lives. Often, there are shared expectations that are respected by all and serve to guide social interactions among them. When these expectations are violated, people can experience feelings of discomfort, embarrassment and even anger. From these studies, it was suggested that when awareness systems are put in place, employees might be unsure about the expectations guiding their own and others' behaviours. That is, awareness systems appear to cross this line and are considered invasive. Thus, we believe that the notion of boundary violations represents a key construct in explaining employees' reactions to technologies such as awareness systems. Awareness systems violate boundaries for sharing personal information with others, constrain employees' ability to control how they present themselves to others, and are construed as unfair. Even if attempts are made to respect individuals through manipulations of the system's characteristics, overall violations of psychological boundaries can lead to rejection.
>
> (p. 627–628).

What would be particularly interesting is to compare these results with those from other tests. Would people be happier to complete ability or personality tests than honesty tests? Are people simply wary of tests in general? It seems many people tend to accept tests are job relevant and many even find them enjoyable.

Much, no doubt, depends on the type of test used, the way it is presented, the candidate's previous experience of testing and their personality and values. Certainly, results appear to indicate that neither extreme view is correct: people neither happily embrace the idea of being tested nor do they find the whole idea irrelevant, immoral or offensive.

Anyone in the business of assessment and selection understands this. Unless in a totalitarian state or where such things as military conscription occurs, a candidate's beliefs about and reaction to assessment methods can affect both their behaviour with respect to that method as well as the impression it leaves on them

2.5 HOW WOULD YOU LIKE TO BE ASSESSED?

What insights do we get when we ask people how they would like to be assessed? There is now an extensive and growing literature on student's perceptions about assessment and evaluation in higher education.

Some have looked at the possibility of using peer assessment. Struyven, Dochy and Janssens (2005) reviewed 35 salient papers on the topic. They concluded that a student's approach to learning is a clear and logical correlate of assessment preferences and that the assessment method has an impact on the student's learning approach and vice versa. There appear to have been various studies in the area of student preference for assessment method (Chamorro-Premuzic et al., 2005; Furnham & Chamorro-Premuzic, 2005; Furnham et al., 2008, 2011).

They show consistent findings: students prefer Multiple Choice Questionnaire (MCQ) and continuous assessments the most, and oral exams, group work and final-year dissertations the least. Given the advantages and disadvantages of both assessment method, it is not surprising that there has been a growing interest to evaluate the consequences of shifting from exams to coursework assessment method, particularly as there is evidence for the fact that students' performance varies across different assessment method. However, little previous research has investigated whether and how such variability in assessment method preference and performance may be explained by any individual difference constructs, notably personality traits.

In a number of studies, Furnham and colleagues gave students the questionnaire shown in Table 2.3.

Table 2.3 *Rating preferences for how you would like to be assessed*

Please rate the extent (1 = Not at all, 5 = Very much) to which you prefer each of the seven academic assessment methods listed below (you may wish to consider how fair you perceived each method to be)

Assessment method	Rating				
Multiple choice exams	1	2	3	4	5
Essay-type exams (e.g., answer two questions in 2 hours)	1	2	3	4	5
Final year dissertation (e.g., supervised thesis, 4 month research project)	1	2	3	4	5
Oral examination (viva voce)	1	2	3	4	5
Continuous assessment (e.g., participation in class, attendance, course work)	1	2	3	4	5
Group work (team assignment, one mark for everybody in the group)	1	2	3	4	5

2.6   ACCEPTING FEEDBACK

For 70 years, psychologists have been investigating a problem called the Barnum effect. It was Phineas T Barnum who said, 'there's a sucker born every minute', and his formula for success 'a little something for everybody'.

The Barnum effect refers to the phenomenon whereby people accept personality feedback about themselves, whether it is universally valid or trivial, because it is supposedly derived from valid and possibly mysterious personality assessment procedures. People fall victim to the *fallacy of personal validation*, which means they accept the generalisations, the trite bogus descriptions that are true of nearly everybody, to be specifically true of themselves.

Consider a psychological study to illustrate this point. Over 70 years ago Stagner (1948) gave a group of personnel managers a well-established personality test. Instead of giving them the actual results, he gave each of them bogus feedback in the form of

13 statements derived from horoscopes, graphological analyses, fortune cookies and the like.

Each manager was then asked to read over the feedback (supposedly derived for him/herself from the 'scientific' test) and decide
how accurate the assessment was by marking each sentence on the
scale (a) amazingly accurate; (b) rather good; (c) about half and half; (d)
more wrong than right; (e) almost entirely wrong. Over half felt their
profile was an amazingly accurate description of them, whereas 40%
thought it was rather good. Almost none believed it to be very wrong.

These are the classic Barnum statements:

---

1. You have a great need for other people to like and admire you.
2. You have a tendency to be critical of yourself.
3. You have a great deal of unused capacity which you have not turned to
   your advantage.
4. While you have some personality weaknesses, you are generally able to
   compensate for them.
5. Your sexual adjustment has presented problems for you.
6. Disciplined and self-controlled outside, you tend to be worrisome and
   insecure inside.
7. At times you have serious doubts as to whether you have made the right
   decision or done the right thing.
8. You prefer a certain amount of change and variety and become dissatisfied
   when hemmed in by restrictions and limitations.
9. You pride yourself as an independent thinker and do not accept others'
   statements without satisfactory proof.
10. You have found it unwise to be too frank in revealing yourself to others.
11. At times you are extroverted, affable, sociable, while at other times you are
    introverted, wary, reserved.
12. Some of your aspirations tend to be pretty unrealistic.
13. Security is one of your major goals in life.

People have a strong penchant for the positive. As Furnham (1990)
noted, many researchers have replicated this result. A French psychologist advertised his services as an astrologer in various newspapers and

received hundreds of requests for his services. He replied to each letter by sending out mimeographed identical copies of a single ambiguous 'horoscope'. More than 200, clearly gullible, clients actually wrote back praising his accuracy and perceptiveness.

An Australian professor regularly asks his first-year students to write down in frank detail their dreams, or he might ask them to describe in detail what they see in an inkblot – the more mystical the task the better. A week later he gives them the 13 statements shown in the table for rating as before. Only after they have publicly declared their belief in the test, are they encouraged to swap feedback. The humiliation of being so easily fooled is a powerful learning experience.

Research on the Barnum effect has, however, shown that belief in bogus feedback is influenced by a number of important factors: some to do with the client/applicant and the consultant/selector (their personality, naïveté, etc.) and some to do with the nature of the test and the feedback situation itself. Women are not more susceptible than men, although of course generally naïve or gullible people are (tautologically!) more susceptible to this effect. However, the status or prestige of the consultant is only marginally important, which is of course good news for the more bogus people in this field.

However, some variables are crucial. One of the most important is perceived specificity of the information required. *The more detailed the questions the better* – so you have to specify the exact time, date and place of birth to astrologers. In one study an American researcher gave all his subjects the same horoscope and found that those who were told that the interpretation was based on the year, month and day of birth judged it to be more accurate than those who were led to believe that it was based only on the year and month. Again and again studies show that after people receive general statements they think pertain just to them, their faith in the procedure and in the diagnostician increases. A client's satisfaction is no measure of how well the diagnostician has differentiated him or her from others, but it is utterly dependent on the extent to which they believe it is specific to them.

The second factor belies the truth that *we are all hungry for compliments but sceptical of criticism.* That is, the feedback must be favourable. It need not be entirely, utterly positive but if it is by-and-large positive with the occasional mildly negative comment (that itself may be a compliment) people will believe it.

People do not readily accept the negative version even if it is seemingly specifically tailored to them. This confirms another principle in personality measurement – the 'Pollyanna principle', which suggests that there is a universal human tendency to use or accept positive words or feedback more frequently, diversely and facilely than negative words and feedback. It has been shown that, according to the evaluation of two judges, there were five times as many favourable as unfavourable statements in highly acceptable interpretations and twice as many unfavourable statements in rarely accepted interpretations.

Hence the popularity of astrology and graphology: feedback is based on specific information (time and place of birth for astrology; slant and size of writing, correctness of letters, dotting of 'i's and crossing of 't's, use of loops and so forth in graphology). It is nearly always favourable. It is often the anxious (worried, depressed, insecure) who visit astrologers, graphologists or fortune tellers who are particularly sensitive to objective positive information about themselves and the future. Therefore, the very type of feedback and the predisposition of clients make acceptance highly probable.

If the general description seems true (and it probably is), people frequently conclude that it must be even more true when even more other information is given. Furthermore, this process is enhanced over time for two reasons: People selectively remember more positive events about themselves than negative and are thus likely to remember the feedback; people have to pay for the consultation and rationalise their decision.

There are other attractions: they not only give useful, 'fascinating' information about oneself, but they are also claimed to predict the future, thus reducing anxieties and uncertainties about what will happen. Moreover, unlike other forms of therapy, which require psychological work and/or behaviour change to obtain any benefit, they require little effort to change

There is also the role of the self-fulfilling prophecy. It is quite possible that if one is told 'as a Virgo, you are particularly honest', this may lead one to notice and subsequently selectively recall all or any instances, albeit trivial ones, of behavioural confirmation (pointing out that a person had dropped a bus ticket; giving back excess change). The self-fulfilling prophecy may work on both a conceptual and a behavioural basis. Thus, Virgos come to include the trait of honesty in their self-concept, but they may also actually become more honest. In this way graphology and astrology predictions may come true because accepting the predictions partly dictates that our behaviour will change appropriately!

2.7   DISCRIMINATION AND FAIRNESS

More than anything else, the idea (indeed threat of) illegal, immoral or unwise discrimination in selection methods and procedures frightens anyone in the business world. The idea of costly court cases and very bad publicity is enough for some HR managers to not use very valid assessment methods that they know will cause a massive negative response.

The problem is that selection is about discrimination in the old sense of the word. You used to see advertisements which suggested that people who bought a particular product were people of 'taste and discrimination': they could tell the difference between superior and inferior products and act on that judgement.

Now, however, the term has acquired an almost universal negative connotation. This is what you read in Wikipedia:

> **Discrimination** is the act of making an unfavourable distinction for a being based on the group, class, or category to which they are perceived to belong. Discrimination can be justified or prejudicial. Serious criminals may be discriminated against by sending them to jail while other groups may be unjustly discriminated against through bias and prejudice. People may discriminate on age, caste,

criminal record, height, disability, family status, gender identity, gender expression, generation, genetic characteristics, marital status, nationality, color, race and ethnicity, religion, sex and sex characteristics, sexual orientation, social class, species, as well as other categories. Discrimination consists of treatment of an individual or group, based on their actual or perceived membership in a certain group or social category, 'in a way that is worse than the way people are usually treated'. It involves the group's initial reaction or interaction going on to influence the individual's actual behavior towards the group leader or the group, restricting members of one group from opportunities or privileges that are available to another group, leading to the exclusion of the individual or entities based on illogical or irrational decision making.

This may, in part, explain the antipathy to the use of intelligence tests which have been shown to discriminate in terms of sex, ethnicity and social class. This is an active and changing area where some societies that have been well known for their discriminatory practices are attempting to change them. There are studies which have insisted that job advertisements can be discriminatory.

Gendered Wording in Job Ads

Consider the following alternative words in job ads:
  The job responsibilities are to (a) provide general support to project teams in a manner complementary to the company and help clients with relevant activities, (b) direct project groups to manage project progress and ensure accurate task control and determine compliance with clients' objectives. Or
  (a) develop interpersonal skills and understanding of the business, (b) develop leadership skills and business processes. Or (a) consider patient symptoms in order to select appropriate treatment and support, (b) analyse patient symptoms to determine appropriate intervention.

What about qualifications? Is there anything different between (a) a pleasant attitude, dependable judgement and attention to detail, (b) a self-confident attitude, decisive judgement and detail oriented. Or (a) cheerful with excellent communication skills and being capable of working with minimal supervision, (b) strong communication skills and the ability to work independently.

Is there much of a difference between the requirements in (a) and (b) for these jobs? Do you prefer the clarity and directness of (b) over (a)? Are you more attracted to the jobs using the (a) description?

Gaucher et al. (2011) argued that 'gendered wording may emerge within job advertisements as a subtle mechanism of maintaining gender inequality by keeping women out of male-dominated jobs' (p. 111).

The idea is that you can choose to use masculine or feminine words in job ads. Male words are *aggressive, ambitions, analytic, assertive* and *autonomous.* So is *challenge, compete, confident* and *courage; dominant, determination* and *decisive* as well as the 's' words: *superior, self-confident, self-sufficient* and *self-reliant.*

By contrast consider some feminine words: *committed, communal, compassionate, connect, considerate* and *co-operative.* Or their 's' words: *sensitive, submissive, supportive, sympathetic.* So the male 'l' words are *lead* and *logic,* and the female word is *loyal.* Equally the male 'i' words are *independent, individual* and *intellect,* and the female 'i' words are *interpersonal* and *interdependent.* Get the idea?

What these researchers did was systematically vary the job descriptions for prototypically male-dominated, female-dominated and neutral jobs and asked students to rate them for how appealing they were to them personally, the perceived male-to-female ratio in the job, their chances of getting the job and how well they believed they would fit in.

They found, regardless of the job, their appeal was higher if the words matched the student's gender, but the effect for women was stronger than that for men. The conclusion was 'gendered wording signals who belongs and who does not, and thus, in part, affects the appeal of the job, independent of whether one perceives one has the personal skills to perform that job' (p. 119).

Various organisations and societies have rules about these issues. Consider the recommendations of the British Psychological Society (BPS, 2017):

> Equality Act 2010: This Act protects people against unfair treatment, promotes equality and prevents discrimination against any of nine protected characteristics: age, disability, gender reassignment, marriage and civil partnership, pregnancy and maternity, race, religion and belief, sex, and sexual orientation. Respect is a core ethical value for psychologists and a commitment to equality of opportunity is embedded in all aspects of psychological practice. Psychologists, where they operate in an organisational context, must also seek to encourage and influence others in ensuring that equality of opportunity is embedded in all thinking and all practice relating to access to services for client groups and recruitment and employment practices.
>
> Providers of service to the public must also make reasonable adjustments for people who have a disability under the Act. This requirement is anticipatory so requires consideration, and adjustment where reasonable, of any barriers which may prevent a person with a disability from using a service.

At a later point they note:

Reflective practice One of the key processes that should be encouraged for psychologists is having a complex understanding of self in the context of others. The HCPC requires reflection in the record of continued professional development in order to retain continued registration. Psychologists will need to make decisions about clients which may have a profound impact on their lives. Decision-making is often subject to various competing biases. Psychologists should be aware of the possibility that they may be influenced by considerations which are not driven by professional knowledge, skills or experience. Maintaining awareness of these biases is important when trying to think through dilemmas.

Sources of influence and bias may include:

- Cognitive Biases – More than 150 have been described, including salience (how readily something comes to mind), confirmation bias (the human tendency to look for evidence that confirms their belief and to ignore other evidence), loss aversion (risky behaviour to avoid loss), beliefs about disclosure (tendency to be more honest when they believe their actions will be known by others) and dissonance reduction (justifying actions if consequences are considered worth it).
- Personal Experience – The experience of the psychologist may affect how they view or treat a client or situation. This may include current or historical trauma, or the kind of organisation and culture with which they are most familiar. Interventions which may be appropriate in one context may be ineffective and cause distress in another.
- Motivation – The original reasons for undertaking the profession may change or be challenged due to fatigue or experience within the profession, which may affect the psychologist's viewpoint.
- Health – Psychologists should be mindful of the potential effect of health conditions or medications which they may be taking, on their practice.
- Control over the psychologist's own practice – This refers to clarity and openness in the management of the psychologist's business and maintaining the professional's autonomy in their interactions with clients.
- Pro bono public work – Psychologists are encouraged, and personally motivated, to engage in such work, while being mindful of impact on the value that is placed on the profession as a whole.
- An unethical environment – Maintaining self-recognition of what the appropriate ethical standard should be, irrespective of the prevailing situation.
- Environment – Political realities may lead the psychologist to make compromises; while there is nothing wrong with compromises, their constant use may mean a decline in overall standards.

The literature is generally pessimistic about the ability of practitioners to overcome some of these biases, considering them to be inherent in human thinking patterns. By being aware of and acknowledging them, it can be possible to manage their influence. For example, biases can be levelled out by presenting information in different ways, by engaging the perspectives of people with different experiences and expectations, or by priming thinking with different examples.

> A key factor in developing and maintaining these skills is the use of consultation or supervision and having a space where it is possible to empathise with others to develop oneself.
>
> It is important that psychologists from all disciplines look after their own wellbeing. This is not only important for them as individuals, but also for the quality of the care they give their clients. In their practice and, for example, within their CPD plans and supervision, psychologists should consider self-care and how they can maintain their own wellbeing.

It is also important for psychologists to evaluate effectiveness of practice, by welcoming feedback from clients. This can be difficult due to fear of criticism, but reflective practitioners are eager to improve and welcome any feedback that will support this process.

There are many examples of organisations attempting to confront these issues. The question is about legality, but also general fairness.

The Society for Industrial and Organisational Psychology of South Africa (2005) produced a document titled *Guidelines for the Validation and Use of Assessment Procedures for the Workplace.* They note four different meanings of fairness:

1. Firstly, there is the view that fairness means equal outcomes for all groups (equal pass rates for the various groups being assessed). This definition is rejected by all professionals involved in assessment.
2. The second meaning involves the *equitable treatment* of all groups in terms of access to materials, conditions during the assessment process, time limits, etc. This includes the notion of *reasonable accommodation* which means adjusting conditions to meet the needs of physically handicapped people.
3. The third meaning of fairness is that participants have equal opportunity to experience and learn from situations that may have an impact on later assessment. This is most obvious in the educational setting, where people who have not been taught certain content cannot be expected to do as well on an assessment as those who have been taught the material. Schmidt (1988) refers to this as *pre-market discrimination.*

4. The fourth meaning of fairness discussed in the *Guidelines* is the absence of predictive bias – an assessment has the same meaning (in terms of future behaviours) irrespective of group membership. The regression models and other approaches to ensuring fairness discussed below are all based on this definition of fairness.

Moerdyk (2016) noted the following fairness models (Table 2.4).

Moerdyk (2016) goes on to looking at different approaches to ensure fairness in assessment:

1. **Do nothing**: Differences seen as natural and inevitable. Accept that people, and groups of people, differ in terms of their personality, motivation and abilities, as a result of different backgrounds and experiences. There is little we can do, except to accept this as a fact of life. Some cultures seem happier with this solution than others who will not accept this basic premise.
2. **Remove all test items that discriminate between groups**: We need to find which of the elements of the assessment process account for these differences and eliminate them. Thus, for example, because we know that men do better at visuo-spatial tests compared to women, we take these out of IQ test batteries.
3. **Use separate tests**: Separate tests are devised and standardised for different groups and people get compared to one another exclusively within their own group. Thus, a 'talented' person is one who compares favourably only to their own group.
4. **Use same tests, but different norms**: The approach is to administer a single test (or battery of assessments) to different individuals, but then to use different norms for interpreting the results. This is illegal in some countries.
5. **Single tests, same norms**: This approach in effect tries to develop 'fair' tests that do not discriminate legally or morally against any group but still provides useful information in work settings.

Moerdyk also notes six ways of ensuring fairness in practice:

1. **Do not assess**: This, one could argue, is defeatist and unwise. People are assessed and evaluated every day on all sorts of criteria. The idea is to find the method that is both fair and accurate.
2. **Interviews only**: This is a common solution but with drawbacks: they are tedious, costly and time-consuming processes and also often with very poor

Table 2.4 *Summary of fairness models*

Model	Method	Rationale	Effect on minorities	Effect On Organisation
No assessment	All comers selected on a first come first served basis	Because assessment methods are unfair, applicants are allowed to demonstrate their ability over time	Number of minorities maximised – high failure rates	Poor investments as large numbers fail at a great cost to the organisation
Unqualified individualism	Top down selection using single norm used	Assessment methods are equally valid for all groups and scores, therefore, represent merit	Relatively few minority members are selected	Good performance achieved, not good for EE targets
Qualified individualism	Group membership (race, gender, language, etc.) taken into account	Separate norms and/or correction factors used to generate separate top-down selections	Minority groups well represented	Poorer achievement of objectives, EE targets more easily met
Cleary Regression model	Regression lines used to show fairness and to calculate highest criterion scores: people selected accordingly	This is fair because those with the highest predicted criterion score are selected	Minority groups well represented	Poorer achievement of objectives
Quota system	Appointment of minority groups should be proportional to their availability in the population (or within 4/5ths thereof)	Because potential is equally distributed across all groups (psychic unity), all groups must be proportionally represented.	Best representation of minority groups	Poorer achievement of objectives

validity data. Indeed, it has been shown that unstructured interviews introduce many other very subtle forms of bias.

3. *Observation at, or outside, work*: Place people in a situation (either a sample of the real situation or some kind of simulation) and then observe how they perform in this situation. This may be a form of 'job try-out' but could be biased to groups who have for various reasons been more exposed to these tasks.

4. *Separate (different) assessment processes*: This is to develop separate assessment processes (such as tests) for different groups, that are actually comparable. These may or may not look similar to each other, but a great deal of work needs to be done to show the tests scores are actually comparable in terms of reliability and validity.

5. *Same measure, different norms*: Another approach that was widely used in the past (and is used widely in many multicultural societies) is to use a single set of assessment measures and to then develop separate norms for different cultural groups.

The concepts of ethics, fairness and legality in assessment are indeed very testing. American books give extensive reports on court cases of people claiming discrimination and how to avoid it (Gatewood, 2016). It is something psychometricians are not always experienced in, though over the years they are often found in court cases explaining how, when and why particular assessment methods are biased in favour of or against certain groups.

2.8 CONCLUSION

For the academic, the choice of a selection instrument is usually based on psychometric criteria (see Chapter 1). However, they are also aware of, and indeed research, some of the systematic biases known to affect human judgement.

For the HR practitioner or the business person tasked with selection, it is inevitably much more complicated. They have to be aware of the effect of the exercise method on their organisation's reputation as well as the many changes in employment law.

REFERENCES

Chamorro-Premuzic, T., & Furnham, A. (2014). *Personality and intellectual competence.* Psychology Press.

Chamorro-Premuzic, T., Furnham, A., Dissou, G., & Heaven, P. (2005). Personality and preference for academic assessment: A study with Australian University students. *Learning and Individual Differences, 15*(4), 247–256.

Furnham, A. (1990). Can people accurately estimate their own personality test scores? *European Journal of Personality, 4*(4), 319–327.

Furnham, A. (2018). Estimating one's own and other's psychological test scores. *Psychology, 9*(8), 2231–2249.

Furnham, A., Batey, M., & Martin, N. (2011). How would you like to be evaluated? The correlates of students' preferences for assessment methods. *Personality and Individual Differences, 50*(2), 259–263.

Furnham, A., & Chamorro-Premuzic, T. (2005). Individual differences and beliefs concerning preference for university assessment methods. *Journal of Applied Social Psychology, 35*(9), 1968–1994.

Furnham, A., & Chamorro-Premuzic, T. (2010). Consensual beliefs about the fairness and accuracy of selection methods at university. *International Journal of Selection and Assessment, 18*(4), 417–424.

Furnham, A., Christopher, A., Garwood, J., & Martin, N. G. (2008). Ability, demography, learning style, and personality trait correlates of student preference for assessment method. *Educational Psychology, 28*(1), 15–27.

Furnham, A., & Swami, V. (2012). Occupational and economic consequences of physical attractiveness. In T. F. Cash (Ed.), *Encyclopedia of body image and human appearance* (pp. 581–587). Oxford: Elsevier.

Gatewood, R. D., Feild, H. and Barrick, M. (2016). *Human resource selection.* Thomson South-Western.

Hausknecht, J. P., Day, D. V., & Thomas, S. C. (2004). Applicant reactions to selection procedures: An updated model and meta-analysis. *Personnel Psychology, 57*(3), 639–683.

Hovorka-Mead, A. D., Ross Jr, W. H., Whipple, T., & Renchin, M. B. (2002). Watching the detectives: Seasonal student employee reactions to electronic monitoring with and without advance notification. *Personnel Psychology, 55*(2), 329–362.

Jones, J. W. (1991). Assessing privacy invasiveness of psychological test items: Job relevant versus clinical measures of integrity. *Journal of Business and Psychology, 5*(4), 531–535.

Judge, T. A., & Cable, D. M. (2011). When it comes to pay, do the thin win? The effect of weight on pay for men and women. *Journal of Applied Psychology, 96*(1), 95–112.

Langlois, J. H., Kalakanis, L., Rubenstein, A. J., Larson, A., Hallam, M., & Smoot, M. (2000). Maxims or myths of beauty? A meta-analytic and theoretical review. *Psychological Bulletin, 126*(3), 390.

Lievens, F., Harris, M. M., Van Keer, E., & Bisqueret, C. (2003). Predicting cross-cultural training performance: The validity of personality, cognitive ability, and dimensions measured by an assessment center and a behavior description interview. *Journal of Applied Psychology, 88*(3), 476–489.

McCarthy, J. M., Bauer, T. N., Truxillo, D. M., Anderson, N. R., Costa, A. C., & Ahmed, S. M. (2017). Applicant perspectives during selection: A review addressing "So what?," "What's new?," and "Where to next?". *Journal of Management, 43*(6), 1693–1725.

Moerdyk, A. (2016). *The principles and practice of psychological assessment*, 2nd edn. Van Schaik.

Noon, M. (2018). Pointless diversity training: Unconscious bias, new racism and agency work. *Employment and Society, 32*(1), 198–209.

Ryan, A. M., & Sackett, P. R. (1987). Pre-employment honesty testing: Fakability, reactions of test takers, and company image. *Journal of Business and Psychology, 1*(3), 248–256.

Society for Industrial and Organisational Psychology of South Africa. (2005). *Guidelines for the validation and use of assessment procedures for the workplace.* SIOP(SA), Pretoria.

Stagner, R. (1948). *Psychology of personality.* McGraw-Hill.

Struyven, K., Dochy, F., & Janssens, S. (2005). Students' perceptions about evaluation and assessment in higher education: A review. *Assessment & Evaluation in Higher Education, 30*(4), 325–341.

Swami, V., Furnham, A., & Joshi, K. (2008). The influence of skin tone, hair length, and hair colour on ratings of women's physical attractiveness, health and fertility. *Scandinavian Journal of Psychology, 49*(5), 429–437.

Truxillo, D. M., Steiner, D. D., & Gilliland, S. W. (2004) The importance of organizational justice in personnel selection: Defining when selection fairness really matters. *International Journal of Selection and Assessment, 12*, 39–52.

Zweig, D., & Webster, J. (2003). Personality as a moderator of monitoring acceptance. *Computers in Human Behavior, 19*(4), 479–493.

Traditional and Mainly Discredited Assessment Methods

INTRODUCTION

People have always been interested in selection and assessment for obvious reasons: the costs of getting it wrong and the benefits of getting it right. It has been suggested that the ancient Chinese had selection tests for their civil servants. An early example can be found in the Bible where Gideon was selecting soldiers. He asked them to drink at the river: some cupped their hands and drank a number of scoops; others put their mouths in the water and sucked up the water. Supposedly he chose the former because they could look around for potential danger while drinking.

Many different cultures have developed strange and superstitious ways of determining whether people are innocent or guilty of some crime. For instance, one popular pseudoscience is chiromancy (or palmistry), the art of characterisation and foretelling the future through the study of the palm. There are twenty-nine features that may be read. Various lines ('life-line', 'heart line' and so on) and mounts (bumps) purportedly suggest interpretations by their relative sizes and intersections. Some palmistry claims that you can tell what a person is like by the shape of their hands: creative people are said to have fan-shaped hands and sensitive people have narrow, pointy fingers and fleshy palms. However, there is no scientific evidence for any of these claims. Palm readers are more likely to be found at the 'end of the pier' than in a selection interview.

Also, many have noticed that we have *idiosyncratic systematic preferences* for all sorts of things: our food choices; the colours we wear; the art we like; the music we listen to; the way we decorate our offices; the friends we make and the people we marry. As a result, it is very common to see popular articles titled something like 'What (you choose, like, use) says about you!'. The claim is these preferences provide good (accurate), insightful and very revealing insights or facts about an individual's abilities, personality or motives. Furthermore, because people are unaware of what they are revealing/signalling, they do not manipulate or disguise things. We therefore get 'amazing' data about 'the real person'.

There are indeed innumerable studies that look at the correlates of various choices with personality. For instance, there is rich literature on personality and choice of art (paintings, music, architecture), which shows replicable and explicable relationships (Cleridou & Furnham, 2014). There are studies on everything from the choice of spicy vs bland food to sports and recreation preferences and their relation to individual differences. Indeed, it is not uncommon for people to enquire into sporting preference, skill and activity in interview questions. Hence, it is assumed that people who play team, as opposed to solo-sports are more team oriented. Similarly, inferences are made about team position (attack vs defence) or whether it is an endurance sport or not.

It is nearly always the case that these observations inform interview questions rather than selection procedures, though they may be used for biodata and biographical methods (see Chapter 8).

In this chapter we will review some of the older methods to evaluate and assess people. Some of them have shown something of a revival as new technology and theories have been proposed.

Interest in these 'ologies' wax and wane. Thus, Genovese (2015) showed that while an interest in astrology has been pretty stable over the last two centuries, the interest in phrenology rose rapidly in the 1800s but then declined. One reason for the decline in phrenology was that it was more 'materialistic' and less romantic (celestial events shaping human affairs), but also because it lent itself to be more easily tested scientifically.

3.2   ASTROLOGY

What is it?
It is belief that the precise time and place of birth, as determined by the position of the planets, determines many aspects of our lives, particularly our personality.

How does it work?
This is unclear and disputed in the sense that no mechanism or process has been proposed to explain how planetary positions impact on individual functioning.

What of the evidence?
There is sufficient overwhelming evidence that there is no evidence that this data predicts any worthwhile outcomes.

Practical problems: cost, ethics, politics
There are no practical problems as people are usually happy to disclose the relevant data, though date (and place) of birth are now less acceptable questions in application forms.

Recommendations for use
Avoid completely as there is no evidence star sign is related to any issue of interest to those involved in job selection.

Astrology claims the apparent positions of celestial bodies is useful in understanding, interpreting and organising knowledge about reality and human existence on earth.

Astrologers suggest it is a useful intuitive tool by which people may come to better understand themselves and others, and the relationships between them. It is a topic of considerable interest to many with more than 6000 books with the word 'astrology' in the American Library of Congress.

There are a number of technical terms used like ascendant, aspects, birth chart, elements, houses, planets and zodiac signs. Furthermore, there is not always agreement about how to present the astrological data. That is, the reliability of analysis is poor, inevitably threatening any possible validity.

Over the years, surveys done in many different countries have shown than around 20–40% of the population believes that indeed the position of the stars and planets do impact on people's lives. This is in contrast to the scientific evidence that condemns it roundly in many ways. Most academics have been scathing. In 1975, 186 leading scientists (including 18 Nobel Prize winners) published a paper in *The Humanist* which showed the evidence roundly condemned the claims of astrology. However, they did not support their argument with data which provoked Eysenck to investigate it further (Nias, 2016).

In some celebrated research, Eysenck examined relationships between astrological and personality factors (Gauquelin et al., 1979; Mayo et al., 1978). Astrologers claim that Mars occupies certain positions in the sky slightly more often at the birth of sports champions than at the birth of 'ordinary' people (the so-called Mars effect, based on Gauquelin, 1969). Gauquelin et al. (1979) reported an association between established traits and astrological factors: extraverts were significantly more frequently born just after the rise or upper culmination of Mars and Jupiter, whereas introverts where more frequently born when Saturn had just risen or passed their upper culmination. Psychoticism, on the other hand, has been found to relate to the position of Mars and Jupiter.

There have, over the years, been many serious attempts to investigate the claims of astrology. Sachs (1999) explored associations between the zodiac and human behaviour (in particular, criminal behaviour). Many other results failed to support the role of astrology in personality (van Rooij, 1994). Carlson (1985) found that astrologers had no special ability to interpret personality from astrological readings and performed much worse in tests than they predicted they would. Similarly, Clarke et al. (1996) explored the effect of the positions of the sun, moon and planets in the zodiac at the moment of birth and found no evidence that tendencies towards extraversion and emotionality are explained by such signs. Astrologers also fail comprehensive tests when they themselves provide the required information (Nanninga, 1996).

Using the Eysenck Personality Inventory, Dean (1987) selected 60 people with a very high Introversion score and 60 people with a very high Extraversion score. He then supplied 45 astrologers with the birth charts of these 120 subjects. By analysing the charts, the astrologers tried to identify the Extraverts from the Introverts. The results were disappointing for astrologers: their average success rate was only about 50 per cent (i.e. no better than random guesswork).

Indeed, Dean, in a series of papers 20 years ago, became the most well researched critic of astrology which in many ways ended psychological studies attempting to validate it. However, research continues in the area with nearly always the same results. For instance, Burke (2012), a practicing astrologer, did a PhD on the relationship between 'the moon variable' and personality and found no significant results.

In a comprehensive review, Kelly (1997) concluded that: 'first, the majority of empirical studies undertaken to test astrological tenets did not confirm astrological claims; and second that the few studies that are positive need additional clarification' (p. 1231). Similarly von Eye et al. (2003) concluded that if there is a scientific basis to astrology, this basis remains to be shown, and if there exists a link between the signs of the zodiac and human behaviour, this yet to be seen.

Despite the lack of association between astrological predictions and personality, many people still believe in astrology (Hamilton, 1995) and accept the personality descriptions. However, it seems few academics bother to work in the area because the *jury is in.* As pointed out by Nias (2016): '. . .astrology has nothing to do with "as above, so below" but is simply a time honoured cover for artifacts that better explain the outcomes' (p. 145).

3.3   GRAPHOLOGY

What is it?
It is the assumption that a number of specific features associated with an individual's handwriting are markers of their personality.

How does it work?

By scoring a specific group of handwriting factors (slant, crossing of 't's, dotting of 'i's), it is possible to infer specific personality (and possibly other) traits.

What of the evidence?

There is enough evidence to conclude that the claims of graphology are false.

Practical problems: cost, ethics, politics

This can be very cheap depending on the costs of the graphologist; there can be ethical issues depending on how handwriting samples are secured.

Recommendations for use

Do not use for lack of empirical evidence.

Graphology is the study and analysis of handwriting and has been used for centuries as a way of understanding personality. There has long been a claim that 'hand writing is brain writing'. Graphology is still used, where estimates for the percentage of organisations using the technique range from 38% (Shackleton & Newell, 1994) to 93% (Bruchon-Schweitzer & Ferrieux, 1991). In the USA, graphology gained some acceptance in many corporate workplaces during the late 1980s and early 1990s (Davey, 1989; Edwards & Armitage, 1992). In Europe, the French led the way in the use of graphology (Furnham, 2004); this is in line with a strong psychodynamic tradition in France, particularly compared to the UK. It is difficult to find reliable statistics on its current use.

Some organisations are happy to boast of their usage of graphology, while others often keep it quiet for fear perhaps of ridicule or perhaps because they believe they have an efficient but hidden means to evaluate candidates' suitability.

There is still an interest in the topic even among clinicians who have recently investigated whether graphology can be usefully employed to assess major depression. It has been thought to be useful in criminal cases for analysing ransom notes, blackmailing and poisoned pen letters (Mishra, 2017).

3.3.1 The Method

Part of the appeal of graphology is that people cannot supposedly fake their 'real' personality because they are unaware of how they show it in their writing.

The problem is that since interpretation is subjective, differentiators' (even when they are clinical experts) end up making different interpretations, making graphology untestable at best, and unreliable at worst.

There also appear to be different schools of psychology which interpret specific aspects of handwriting differently. Also, as a necessary condition for valid inference, the reliability of predictions based on graphology must first be established (Goldberg, 1986). However, reliability of graphological prediction has its own precondition: handwriting features must first be reliably encoded. This precondition appears to be met; the mean agreement between different judges measuring objective handwriting features (such as slant or slope) is high, and the mean agreement about subjective handwriting features (like rhythm) is still respectable (Dean, 1992).

There has been considerable unreliability between the scoring of different graphologists, hence the recent invention of computerised graphology, which is the application of AI technology to score handwriting on many different scales (Garoot et al., 2017; Sen & Shas, 2017)

There seems no strong agreement as to what aspects of writing mean what. Thus, Mishra (2017, p. 3) suggests the following:

Large size handwriting: It indicates towards the extravert as well as confident behavior of the person.

Small size handwriting: It indicates towards the introvert as well as academic behavior of the person. If the handwriting is small and delicate then the person may be comfortable only to those who are known (or are similar in one way or the other) to him/her.

Position and Shape of i-dots

a. If an 'I' is written without any dot then it indicates toward the absentmindedness of the writer.
b. If the dot on the letter 'I' is placed high above then it indicates that the writer is imaginative.
c. If the dot on the letter 'I' is formed like a circle then it indicates towards the artistic personality of the writer.
d. However an open dot may also indicates towards the affection and a visionary.

Position and Shape of T-bars

i. There are various ways in which the stem as well as the cross bar can be written and hence the letter 't' is very revealing in terms of graphology.
ii. If the letter 't' looks like a star then it is a sign that the person has the strong sense of responsibility.
iii. If the cross bar is slanted in the upwards direction then it is a sign that the writer is ambitious.
iv. If the cross bar is high and rises away from stem in the right side direction then it indicates leadership qualities and intelligence.

Furnham et al. (2003) used two coders to analyse exam script writing using the following features of handwriting and testing various hypotheses they found in the literature:

Handwriting analysis

1. *Colour*: Candidates choose either blue or black ink. Whilst there is evidence on colour choice being linked with personality no hypotheses were tested.
2. *Connectedness*: This represents the link between handwritten letters. The major types of connections are arcades, angles, garlands and threads. Arcades (negatively) and garlands (positively) can be theoretically associated with Extraversion, whereas angles can be associated with high Conscientiousness. Threads do not seem to have a clear relationship with any of the Big Five traits.

3. *Crossed t's*: This refers to the extent to which t's were crossed or not. It does not refer to where they were crossed but whether they were crossed. It maybe thought as an index of Neuroticism and Conscientiousness.

4. *Dotted i's*: This refers to the nature of the dot itself – where it is placed, its shape and size. It is suggested that these can be good indices of originality and creativity (Openness to Experience).

5. *Loops above*: This refers to the width and roundness of letters with a loop above the line like 'l' or 'f'. It has been suggested that very small loops (if they exist at all) are a sign of both Introversion and Neuroticism.

6. *Loops below*: This is same as above but refers exclusively to loops below, in particular in the letter 'g'.

7. *Percentage used*: This refers to the percentage of the lined page used. Some candidates use every line; others skip one line ensuring double spacing writing. Others use a margin on both sides of the paper. It was anticipated that extraverts use less space than introverts, and neurotics more than stable individuals.

8. *Dotted i's/i-dots*: Same as above, this refers to whether i's are dotted or not.

9. *Pressure*: This is a measure of stamina. Light pressure indicates lethargy and powerlessness; heavy pressure indicates forcefulness and confidence. Pressure may therefore be associated with Extraversion and (negatively) with Neuroticism.

10. *Size*: This is a measure of Extraversion (large writing is associated with Extraversion).

11. *Slant*: Vertical slant is related to independence and secrecy, whereas reduced slant is associated with change resistance and low emotional intelligence. Like pressure, slant may also be related to Extraversion and (negatively) Neuroticism.

12. *Spacing*: Normal spacing is associated with characteristics of Conscientiousness, whereas wide spacing (between letters) has been said to represent independent personalities. Jumbled spacing is related to low intelligence, whereas wide spacing (between lines) is associated with high intelligence and high Conscientiousness.

13. *T crosses*: graphological analysis of the placement of the t-crosses has also been theoretically related with characteristics of the Big Five traits. Left and right placements have both been negatively associated with Conscientiousness, while placement above the stem seems to relate (positively) with Openness to Experience.

14. *Width*: Same as in size.

It was not until the late nineteenth century that the foundations of modern graphology were laid by Jean-Hippolyte Michon (1872), who claimed he was able to discern the particular features of handwriting that writers with similar personalities had in common. He developed an inventory of about 100 graphological features or 'fixed signs', such as a particular way of crossing the t or dotting the i, which were associated with certain types of personalities.

Jean Crepieux-Jamin (1909) further developed this research and claimed to have found further associations between particular features of handwriting and personality traits. However, this process of matching particular features of handwriting with particular types of personality traits began to produce conflicting results: the associations found by one graphologist would often contradict those found by others (Hartford, 1973). This remains the case today with different schools of thought emphasising the 'meaning' of particular letters. Inter-interpreter reliability is nearly always unacceptably low. Furthermore, validity is preconditioned on the reliability of diagnoses. It is hard for unreliable measures to be valid.

Ludwig Klages (1917, 1930) took a different approach to the subject. This approach favoured a more intuitive, theoretical psychology of expressive behaviour. It is probably this approach to handwriting that has had the greatest influence, and Klages is held in high esteem by most contemporary graphologists (Lewinson, 1986).

Contemporary graphologists still use these 'insights' to determine personality characteristics of individuals through the analysis of their handwriting. Furnham et al. (2003) factor-analysed fourteen graphological criteria and found they were reduced to two fundamental areas: dimension of writing (size, width, slant) and details (connections, loops, etc.). However, these variables were unrelated to established (and validated) personality inventories.

Eysenck and Gudjonsson (1986) suggested that there appear to be two different basic approaches to the assessment of both handwriting and personality, namely holistic vs analytic. This gives four basic types of analyses.

Holistic analysis of handwriting: This is basically impressionistic, because the graphologist, using his or her experience and insight, offers a general description of the kind of personality he or she believes the handwriting discloses.

Analytic analysis of handwriting: This uses measurements of the constituents of the hand writing, such as slant, pressure, etc., which are then converted into personality assessment on the basis of a formula of code.

Holistic analysis of personality: This is also impressionistic, and may be done after an interview, when a trained psychologist offers a personality description on the basis of his or her questions, observations and intuitions.

Analytical analysis of personality: This involves the application of psychometrically assessed, reliable and valid personality tests (questionnaires, physiological responses to a person and the various grade scores obtained).

This classification suggests quite different approaches to the evaluation of the validity of graphological analysis in the prediction of personality. Holistic matching is the impressionistic interpretation of writing matched with an impressionistic account of personality, and holistic correlation is the impressionistic interpretation of writing correlated with a quantitative assessment of personality. Analytic matching involves the measurement of the constituents of the handwriting matched with an impressionistic account of personality, and analytic correlation is the measurement of the constituents of handwriting correlated with a quantitative assessment of personality.

Study after study with different personality tests, different graphological measures and different population groups seem to come to the same conclusion: e.g. there is no relationship between handwriting and practically any individual difference factor of note.

Some organisations are happy to boast of their usage of graphology, while others often keep it quiet for fear perhaps of ridicule or perhaps because they believe they have an efficient but hidden means to evaluate candidates' suitability.

3.3.2 *Scientific Evidence for Graphology*

Early studies appeared to provide some support for this form of personality assessment (Allport & Vernon, 1933; Hull & Montgomery, 1919). Some more recent studies have also claimed to have found evidence that graphologists can recognise certain personality traits from handwriting samples (Linton et al., 1962; Nevo, 1988; Oosthuizen, 1990). There are also many articles in professional journals and serious newspapers advocating graphology through evidence involving personal experience (Watson, 1993).

However, when studies are carefully selected in terms of their methodological veracity, then the evidence is overwhelmingly negative (Eysenck & Gudjonsson, 1986; Neter & Ben-Shakhar, 1989; Tett & Palmer, 1997).

Furnham (1988) listed the conclusions drawn from six studies conducted in the 1970s and 1980s, which have been updated.

---

(1) 'It was concluded that the analyst could not accurately predict personality from handwriting.' This was based on a study by Vestewig et al. (1976) from Wright State University, who asked six handwriting experts to rate 48 specimens of handwriting on fifteen personal variables.

(2) 'No evidence was found for the validity of graphological signs.' (Lester et al., 1977)

(3) 'Thus, the results did not support the claim that the three handwriting measures were valid indicators of Extraversion.' (Rosenthal & Lines, 1978)

(4) 'There is thus little support here for the validity of graphological analysis.' (Eysenck & Gudjonsson, 1986)

(5) 'The graphologist did not perform significantly better than a chance model.' (Ben-Shakhar et al.,1986)

(6) 'Although the literature on the topic suffers from significant methodological negligence, the general trend of findings is to suggest that graphology is not a viable assessment method.' (Klimoski & Rafaeli, 1983)

(7) No evidence was found to validate the graphological method as a measure of personality (Dazzi & Pedrabissi, 2009)

(8) 'No writing characteristics were specific to personality traits. There is no evidence for assessment of personality on the base of handwriting.' (Gwada, 2014)

Furthermore, Furnham and Gunter (1987) investigated the 'trait' method of graphology, which attempts to predict specific personality traits from individual features of handwriting. Participants completed the Eysenck Personality Questionnaire (EPQ) and copied a passage of test in their own handwriting. The writing samples were coded on thirteen handwriting-feature dimensions (size, slant and so on) that graphologists report to be diagnostic of personality traits. Only chance-level correlations were observed between writing features and EPQ scores.

Furnham et al. (2003) reported two studies with a similar methodology. Students completed well-established personality and intelligence tests after arriving at university. These scores were then related to a reliable graphological analysis of their handwriting in exam scripts a few months later (Study 1) and 20 months in another (Study 2). Correlation and regression analyses in both studies showed fewer associations with the Big Five personality variables than maybe expected by chance. Graphological variables did correlate with both participants' gender and intelligence, but the pattern was different in the two studies, reinforcing the idea that chance factors were influential. They noted:

> Yet this paper must conclude with many others using different tests and measures of handwriting that the two are essentially unrelated. Whatever graphological analysis measures it is not stable personality or ability traits. Hence , it would be particularly unwise to use graphological analysis in selection to attempt to understand an applicant's personality. However there remain two interesting and important questions in this research area. The first is whether there are indeed any consistent correlates of handwriting. They may well be demographic correlates like age, education and nationality, but it is unclear whether there are any psychological correlates of handwriting. It may be suggested that handwriting is associated with indices of impression management like self-monitoring, self-concept or social awareness. However, most of

these variables are logically and significantly correlated with personality traits, which as has been demonstrated are unrelated to graphological variables. The second question concerns why despite published and unequivocal evidence dating back fifty years so many people still believe that handwriting reflects personality.

3.3.3   Meta-Analyses

In a meta-analysis (a review of many studies in an area that provides a quantitative estimate of the average statistical relationship among the examined variables) of over 200 studies assessing the validity of graphological inferences, Dean (1992) found only a small effect size for inferring personality from handwriting and noted that the inclusion of studies with methodological shortcomings may have inflated the effect-size estimate. The liberal estimated effect size of 0.12 for personality from neutral-content scripts (scripts with fixed content not under the control of the writer) is not nearly large enough to be of any practical value and would be too small to be perceptible. Thus, even a small, real effect cannot account for the magnitude of hand-writing–personality relationships reported by graphologists.

Furthermore, gender, socio-economic status and degree of literacy, possibly predictable from handwriting, may predict some personality traits. Thus, any weak ability of graphology to predict personality may be merely based on gender or socio-economic status information assessed from handwriting. Graphological accuracy attributable to these variables is of dubious value because simpler, more reliable methods for assessing them are available.

In a meta-analytic review of seventeen studies, Neter and Ben-Shakhar (1989) found that graphologists performed no better than non-graphologists in predicting job performance. When handwriting samples were autobiographical, the two groups achieved modest accuracy in prediction. When the content of the scripts was neutral (i.e. identical for all writers), neither group was able to draw valid inferences about job performance. Thus, belief in the validity of graphology, as it is currently used to predict job performance, lacks empirical support.

3.3.4 Graphology and Job Performance

Given its apparent lack of validity for predicting personality, it would be surprising if graphology proved to be a valid predictor of job performance. Indeed, the results of research investigating the validity of graphology for predicting job performance has generally been negative (Kravitz et al., 1996; Rafaeli & Klimoski, 1983).

Ben-Shakhar et al. (1986) used two empirical studies to test the validity of graphological predictions. In one study, bank employees were rated by graphologists on several job-relevant traits. A linear model developed for the study outperformed the graphologists. In the second study, the professions of 40 successful professionals were judged. The graphologists did not perform significantly better than a chance model. The results of both studies led to the conclusion that, when analysing spontaneously produced text, graphologists and non-graphologists achieve similar validities.

As a necessary condition for valid inference, the reliability of predictions based on graphology must first be established (Goldberg, 1986). However, reliability of graphological prediction has its own precondition: handwriting features must first be reliably encoded. This precondition appears to be met; the mean agreement between different judges measuring objective handwriting features (such as slant or slope) is high, and the mean agreement about subjective handwriting features (like rhythm) is still respectable (Dean, 1992).

3.3.5 Why, Then, Does Graphology Persist?

Many of the purported relationships between handwriting and personality appear almost intuitive. For example, small handwriting is believed to imply modesty and large handwriting implies egotism. In many examples like this, the empirical relationships between handwriting features and personality traits identified by graphologists closely parallel semantic associations between words used to describe handwriting features (e.g. regular rhythm) and personality traits (e.g. reliable).

This has been confirmed by a careful study by King and Koehler (2000), who showed that illusory correlations in graphological evidence was rife. They also concluded that this may partially account for continued use of graphology despite overwhelming evidence against its predictive validities (p. 336).

This is an example of what is known as the 'confirmation bias' (Nickerson, 1998). When a person is inspecting some evidence in a search for systematic relationships, semantic association is likely to guide the formulation of hypotheses about what goes with what, producing a kind of expectation. Other potential relationships may not be considered and hence not detected even if they are consistent with the observed evidence.

Graphology persists because when we examine evidence in the light of semantically determined hypotheses, ambiguous aspects of the evidence are interpreted in a manner consistent with the hypothesised relationship. Driver, Buckley and Frink (1996) asked 'should we write off graphology' as a selection technique? Their answer was 'yes'. They note ' the overwhelming results of well-controlled empirical studies have been that the technique has not demonstrated acceptable validity ... (and that) while the procedure may have an intuitive appeal, graphology should not be used in a selection context' (p. 76).

Recent reviews of the literature have by and large supported previous reviews on the low validity of graphological analyses and their potential harm for personnel selection.

3.4 PHRENOLOGY (THE SCIENCE OF BUMP READING AND ITS MODERN RELEVANCE)

What is it?
It is the science of skull reading, namely the shape of the skull in particular places which indicates abilities, personality and morality

How does it work?
Phrenology suggests that different parts of the brain are responsible for different features of human behaviour and that these can be measured in head and skull shape.

What of the evidence?
There is considerable evidence that many of the early claims of phrenology were completely false.

Practical problems: cost, ethics, politics
Many indeed, given the evidence on invalidity. It would be unacceptable and possibly illegal to do a classic phrenological analysis.

Recommendations for use
Do not use!

Phrenology is based on a simple idea that is current today. The brain is the 'organ of the mind': it is structured in a way that different parts are responsible for different functions. So different parts of the brain, which are reflected in the shape of the head, control different facilities. However, there are crucial disagreements between the traditional phrenological and the modern neuropsychological view. First, phrenologists believe the size of the brain area 'dedicated' to a particular function is proportioned in size to the 'importance' of that mental facility. Second, craniometry, which is the measurement of things like skull size and shape, represents the form of the brain and therefore all human functions. Third, that both moral and intellectual facilities are innate.

Franz-Josef Gall, at the end of the eighteenth century, is usually attributed as the developer of phrenology which became very popular in the nineteenth century. It can be credited as a protoscience for the idea that the brain is the organ of the mind and that certain brain areas have localised, specific functions. In this sense he could be seen as a forefather of neuroscience.

Gall observed that his fellow students who had good memories all had prominent eyes, and so he assumed that the part of the brain concerned with memory was located behind the eyes (Davies, 1955). Gall believed that the mind and brain were one and the same thing. His ideas developed the notion of *cerebral localisation:* various parts of the brain have relatively distinct functions. Thus, understanding the brain would come through identifying which pieces were responsible for which functions.

Later Johann Spurzheim argued that parts of the brain which correspond to functions that an individual used a great deal would *hypertrophy*, while those functions which were neglected would *atrophy*. This has been validated on studies with taxi drivers and violinists. The vision of the brain was that it had a lumpy and bulbous surface, with a landscape unique to each individual based upon their particular set of intellectual and neurological strengths and weaknesses. It was believed that the skull overlying the lumpy parts of the brain would bulge out to accommodate the hypertrophied brain tissue underneath. Therefore, by measuring those bumps, one can infer which parts of the brain are enlarged and therefore which characteristics are dominant.

This idea later acquired some fame with the 'phrenology head', a china head on which the phrenological faculties were indicated. These heads are widely available today and often found on the shelves of psychologists! A typical phrenological chart outlines 37 brain functions, each with a corresponding bearing upon the shape of one's head (see Davies, 1955, p. 6).

During the nineteenth century, phrenology gained a rapidly growing interest. By the 1820s, every major British city had its own phrenological society, and many people consulted phrenologists to get advice in matters like hiring personnel or finding a marriage partner (see Cooter, 1984; Davies, 1955). Although the theory of phrenology was eventually rejected by official academia, phrenological parlours remained popular for some time, but they were considered closer to astrology, chiromancy and the like.

The Victorians took phrenology very seriously. Their busts, casts, journals, callipers and machines survive through the fine white china busts produced by the London Phrenology Company. The Victorians had phrenological surgeries, schools, foods and doctors. The average man had apparently a head size of 22″ and a woman ½ to ¾ inch less. Head size was linearly related to brain capacity and intellect.

However, they believed that shape was more important than size. A good cranioscopy could, they believed, show special talents. Phrenologists made diagnoses and predictions about motives, abilities and temperament.

Phrenologists examined skeletons like the skull and bones of Thomas à Beckett. Queen Victoria had her children 'read' because phrenologists professed both self-knowledge and the keys to developmental, moral and occupational success.

In 1896 Sizer and Drayton published a phrenology manual titled *Heads and Faces and How to Study Them*. It illustrated how to recognise idiots and poets, as well as those with a criminal vs moral character.

3.4.1   Measuring the Head

The traditional analysis began by first considering the overall shape of the head:

A *rounded head* supposedly indicates a strong, confident, courageous, sometimes restless nature.

A *square head* reveals a solid, reliable nature, deeply thoughtful and purposeful. A wider the head suggests an energetic, outgoing character, while a narrower head suggests a more withdrawn, inward-looking nature.

An *ovoid shape* belongs to an intellectual.

It is important to gently, but firmly, run your fingers over the skull to feel the contours of the skull. One has to measure the individual size of each faculty and its prominence in comparison to other parts of the head. As the brain consists of two hemispheres, each faculty can be duplicated: check both sides of the skull.

A faculty that is underdeveloped in comparison to the others indicates a lack of that particular quality in the personality while one that is well developed indicates that the quality is present to a considerable degree. So a small organ of 'alimentiveness' indicates a light and finicky eater, possibly a teetotaller; if this faculty is well developed, it indicates a person who enjoys food and wine; and if over-developed, a glutton, who may also drink to excess.

The phrenological head has over 40 regions, but it depends on which list or system you read. Some have rather old-fashioned concepts, like #20 'veneration', which is respect for society, its rules and institutions; #26 'mirthfulness', which is cheerfulness and sense of humour; and #24 'sublimity', which is the love of grand concepts. There are also head regions for #1 'amativeness' (sex appeal), #3 'philoprogenitiveness' (parental, filial love); #10 'alimentiveness' (appetite, love of food), #31 'eventuality' (memory) and #5 'inhabitiveness' (love of home). These areas have been further described or classified into eight sentiments or propensities.

---

1. *The 'domestic' propensities*, which are characteristics common to humans and animals and are basically responsible for one's emotions and instinctive reactions to objects and events.
2. *The 'selfish' propensities* provide for man's wants and assist him in self-protection and self-preservation.
3. *The 'self-regarding' sentiments* are concerned with self-interest and expression of personality.
4. *The 'perceptive' faculties* are responsible for awareness of surroundings.
5. *The 'artistic' propensities* give rise to sensitivity and aptitude in art and artistic creation.
6. *The 'semi-perceptive' faculties* occur in such fields as literature, music and language, and are responsible for the appreciation of cultural surroundings.
7. *The 'reflective', 'reasoning' and 'intuitive' faculties* are concerned with styles of thinking.
8. *The 'moral' sentiments*, including religious faculties, humanise and elevate the character.

In the early twentieth century, phrenology benefited from a new interest with physiognomy. But like physiognomy, much of this resurgence had to do with questions of racial difference and degeneration (Cooter, 1984). Frequent pictorial representations of racialised groups (notably black Africans and Australian Aborigines) are found within the phrenological journals at this time. For their effectiveness, they depended on the view of the external body as a site that could be used to divide assumed racial superiority from inferiority. Phrenology was used by "science" to naturalise racism, class, inequality and patriarchy (Gould, 1981). Needless to say, it to appealed to the Nazis.

3.4.2 Appraising Phrenology

We accept that the phrenologists were correct when it came to the central debate of neurology of the time (Miller, 1996): the brain is somewhat compartmentalised, with each section serving a specific function.

Yet the modern 'map' of the brain does not correlate at all with the classic map used by phrenologists. Theirs was more personality (even morality) based, while the modern map is based on fundamental functions, such as the ability to perform mathematical functions (Butterworth, 1999). Furthermore, all the other assumptions of phrenology are false:

- The brain is not a muscle, but may hypertrophy or atrophy depending on use.
- The brain is very jelly-like in consistency: the soft brain conforms to the shape of the skull and the skull does not conform itself to the brain.

Modern phrenology is not based on head shape but on brain structure and function. In fact, the speed of developments in PET scanning and other related technologies suggests that this may become, in time, the new selection methodology. Understanding individual differences in brain structure and function is the new science of the twenty-first century (see Chapter 7). Furthermore, it is possible that future candidates may be brain-scanned as part of their selection process. That raises interesting ethical issues, though it will be a long time before the science is going to be sufficiently specific to be used to inform selection decisions.

Despite its popularity mainstream science has always dismissed phrenology as quackery and pseudoscience. The idea that 'bumps' on the head were related to personality structure and moral development was dismissed as nonsense. The evidence has been evaluated and is wanting.

The rise of neuroscience has shown how many of the claims of phrenology are fraudulent. However, there remain other popular brain myths like the idea that we only use 10% of our brain in day-to-day processing. There are also myths about brain energy, brain tuners and brain tonics, which seem as plausible as phrenology.

Yet there have been attempts to do modern scientific research. For instance, Jones et al. (2018) noted that whereas nineteenth-century phrenologists had access to coarse measurement tools, they could re-examine phrenology using a twenty-first-century method. In a study using thousands of subjects MRI was used to quantify local scalp curvature. The curvature statistics were compared against life-style measures matching a subset of lifestyle measures to phreno-logical ideas of brain organisation.

They concluded:

> The present study sought to test in the most exhaustive way currently possible the fundamental claim of phrenology: that measuring the contour of the head provides a reliable method for inferring mental capacities. We found no evidence for this claim... In summary, we hope to have argued convincingly against the idea that local scalp curvature can be used to infer brain function in the healthy population. Given the thoroughness of this study, it is unlikely that more scalp data would yield significant effects. But we would advocate that future studies focus on the brain
>
> *(p. 31–33)*

However, there remain some aspects of phrenology that seem relevant and very controversial today. We know, for instance, that brain size is positively correlated with mental ability test scores and within and between species: head size is correlated with brain size. There is a modest relationship (r = .10 to .20) between head size (length and breadth) and IQ. However, when corrected for body size, this relationship drops and possibly disappears.

> Certainly, new technology has increased our knowledge of, and interest in, cognitive neuropsychology and psychiatry. We are now able to map the brain electronically and metabolically. Through studies both of accident victims as well as 'normal' people we are building up a new detailed map of the brain and what 'parts' are primarily responsible for what functions. But this 'electrophrenology' is empirically based and bares no relationship to old, prescientific moralistic ideas of the founders of phrenology
> *(Furnham, 2010).*

3.5 PHYSIOGNOMY AND BODY BUILD

What is it?
It is the idea that aspects of body size and shape are good indicators of ability, personality and motivation.

How does it work?
Body shape is determined by our lifestyle as well as our genetic inheritance. Shape is a good marker of both nature and nurture.

What of the evidence?
Much depends on the nature of claim (i.e. what body feature is involved) and whilst overall the evidence is weak in some instances it is reasonably good.

Practical problems: cost, ethics, politics
There are problems in how to get ethical access to body shape statistics and the possibility these differ by gender, ethnicity, etc.

Recommendations for use
Choose metrics with caution and have the data supplemented by other factors.

Physiognomy is the study of inferring psychological attributes from physical traits. It is the idea that a person's outer appearance reflects their psychological functioning: morphology reflects psychology. Thus, wider faces and levels of aggression are both positively affected by testosterone levels during puberty and would therefore covary. The same is true of finger length. It seems to be a belief held by both the ancient Greeks and Chinese.

For many it seems common-sensical that body shape must be an indicator of psychological functioning. We inherit many physical characteristics: height, facial characteristics, psychological characteristics like intelligence and various medical conditions; even our lifestyle is related to personality which inevitably effects our body shape. Similarly, our appearance effects how other people treat us: height, physical attractiveness, body weight have been shown to be important. Thus, a combination of nature and nurture could mean that body shape is a powerful, and relatively undisguisable, indicator of personality.

It is clear that *many people make inferences about others based on appearance.* There is an extensive literature on lookism, which will be considered shortly. Hassin and Trope (2000) argue that there are four reasons to assume that physiognomy plays an important role in social cognition:

1. The face is almost always seen whenever an interaction takes place. Thus, the face always represents information that is available and is hard to neglect in any judgements.
2. Until quite recently in human evolution, facial features (unlike facial or behavioural expressions) could not be wilfully altered.
3. The structure of the face is relatively stable (except in extreme conditions, such as accidents or surgery).
4. There are areas in the human brain specialised for face perception and processing.

Considerable experimental evidence suggests that people can and do infer personality traits from faces. This research shows that the process of inferring traits from faces is highly reliable. That is, different judges tend to infer similar traits from given faces. Some studies have shown that this inter-judge agreement is cross-cultural, thus suggesting that the cognitive work of reading traits from faces has some universal characteristics (Zebrowitz-McArthur & Berry, 1987).

3.5.1 History

European scientific interest can be traced to Johann Caspar Lavater who published his *Essays on Physiognomy* (1775–1778). In turn, his ideas were based on the writings of the Italian Giambattista Della Porta, the French physiognomist Barthelemy Cocles and the English philosopher and physician Sir Thomas Browne. For example, the method for divining the character of a person during this period was metoposcopy, or the interpretation of facial wrinkles (especially those on the forehead).

At the beginning of the twentieth century, physiognomy enjoyed renewed popularity. Various vocational institutes used physiognomy as one of their main tools in assessing candidates, while others put it to more dubious use. Cesare Lombroso's criminal anthropology (1895), for example, claimed that murderers have prominent jaws and pickpockets have long hands and scanty beards. This work is very often put forward as preposterous and deeply prejudicial.

However, the picture that emerges regarding the validity of physiognomic judgements is more ambiguous. Early studies that attempted to answer this question concluded that there was no significant correlation between facial features or physiognomic inference and the traits individuals actually possess (Cohen, 1973). In a later review of the literature on physiognomic inferences, Alley (1988) reached a similar conclusion.

More recent research suggests that face-based impressions may sometimes be valid. Berry (1990) asked students to report their impressions of their classmates (after one, five and nine weeks of the semester elapsing), and used these impressions as the criteria with which she compared independent evaluations of the classmates' photographs. She found significant correlations between peer impressions and photographs on three dimensions: power, warmth and honesty.

Recent studies of what has been called *lookism* have noted that features associated with an individual's physical attractiveness (face, body shape) can have a great influence on their employment opportunities (Swami & Furnham, 2008). One of the most widely researched settings of weight-based discrimination is in the workplace, where overweight individuals are vulnerable to stigmatising attitudes and anti-fat bias (Phul & Brownell, 2003). The literature points to prejudice and inequity for overweight and obese individuals, often even before the interview process begins.

3.5.2 *Body Build*

There is a large literature on body build dating from Hippocrates but made most famous by Kretschmer (1925) and later by Sheldon et al. (1940). Kretschmer argued that people could be divided into four distinct categories according to body type:

---

(1) Asthenic (slight, long-boned, slender persons with a predisposition towards a schizophrenic personality type);

(2) Pyknic (round, stocky, heavy individuals with a predisposition towards manic-depressive reactions);

(3) Athletic (strong, muscular, broad-shouldered people with a tendency more towards schizophrenic than manic-depressive responses); and

(4) Dysplastic (individuals exhibiting disproportionate physical development or features of several body types with personality predispositions similar to the athletic type).
    The argument was that body shape was systematically related to personality, specifically mental illness.

Sheldon argued for the existence of three distinct body types: endomorph, mesomorph and ectomorph. It represented a long-standing interest in anthropometrics. First a great deal of the research concentrated on the delineation of clear physiological types based on a variety of skeletal measures. This remains far less in contention than the second claim, namely that these types are related to personality and ability. Research in the area, however, produced weak and equivocal correlations between anthropomorphic measures and personality.

These ideas have been examined extensively, particularly in the period 1950–2000 but found wanting. Eysenck (1967) did a great deal of work in the area but abandoned the idea after finding very little evidence.

3.5.3 Body Mass Index and Shape

Over the last 20 years evolutionary psychologists have made a contribution to this area. They have worked on facial and bodily correlates of attractiveness, which are related to youth and health (and fecundity). It is possible to describe characteristics of the body and face that are consistently rated attractive by others.

- **BMI**: body mass index or shape which is Weight/(Height × Height); an attractive shape is 21–23 BMI points
- **WHR**: waist-to-hip ratio in females. A desirable score is .7 to .8
- **CTH**: chest-to-hip ratio in men (less than 0.95)
- **LTR**: leg-to-torso ratio (higher ratio or longer legs is preferred in women, smaller ratio or shorter legs in men)

As well as the 'crude' body indexes, there are factors like symmetry, height and skin texture. There are a whole range of characteristics that signal health and attractiveness. Consider hair: this indicates age (bald, grey) and race as well as fitness. Many cultures require body hair to be removed, especially by women.

People attempt to improve their attractiveness by various methods. These include possibly dangerous and certainly expensive plastic surgery but also cosmetics and nearly always clothes. Clothes are used to enhance and disguise, to flatter and to distract: to change the state of both wearer and observer.

3.5.4   The Waist-to-Hip Ratio

The ultimate success or failure of evolutionary psychology must of course be judged on its products. Does it provide us with plausible and illuminating insights into human nature or human behaviour? One example of evolutionary psychological research which highlights both its predictive power and its limitations are studies that highlight the waist-to-hip ratio (WHR) as an indicator of a woman's attractiveness.

One of the key determinants of attractiveness that prefigured in early attractiveness research was an individual's overall *body weight*, measured as the body mass index (BMI). Various studies found that women were considered more attractive, better mate choices and more positive in general if they were thin. However, Singh (1993) presented evidence that it was *body fat distribution*, rather than overall weight, which was related to judgements of both a woman's attractiveness and potential reproductive success. Singh's reasons for investigating this particular morphological feature are primarily due to its uniqueness. The features concerned with the measurement of the WHR, the waist and the buttocks, are unique to humans and it is therefore possible that it serves some unique functional significance.

Before and after puberty, body shape differences between men and women are negligible and only during early reproductive life is there maximal differentiation. This is brought about by the active sex hormones during and after puberty, which influence the anatomical distribution of adipose tissue. In women, oestrogen stimulates fat cells to accumulate in the buttocks and thighs and inhibits accumulation in the abdominal region. By contrast, testosterone in men maximally stimulates accumulation of fat cells in the abdominal region and inhibits fat deposits in the thighs and buttocks. These differences produce *gynoid* and *android* fat distribution, respectively, which in turn can be measured by the WHR (the ratio between the circumference of the waist and the circumference of the hips).

An important part of Singh's evolutionary predictions is the finding that the WHR is related to a variety of life outcomes.

Susceptibility to various major physical diseases and psychological disorders is conveyed by the WHR. In addition, Singh pointed out that the WHR signals all conditions that affect women's reproductive status. For example, in his summary of this research, Singh (1993) argues that the probability of successful pregnancy induction is affected by the WHR and that married women with higher WHRs have more difficulty becoming pregnant.

For Singh, the main problem facing our hunter-gatherer ancestors in evolutionary history was the identification of mate value. Over evolutionary time, therefore, *perceptual mechanisms* were selected in men to detect and use information conveyed by the WHR in determining a women's potential as a mate. To investigate, Singh developed a set of two-dimensional line drawings of the female figure, which were systematically varied with respect to overall body weight and the WHR. In a series of experiments, Singh reported that low WHRs (indicative of curvaceousness) were judged as the most attractive.

Singh argued the WHR acts as a *wide first-pass filter*, which serves to exclude women who are unhealthy or who have low reproductive capacity. It is only after this *culturally invariant filter* is passed that other features, such as the face, skin or weight, become utilised in mate selection. The filter is 'culturally invariant' or universal to all men because it was an adaptive assessment of female mate value for all males in the environment of evolutionary adaptation. Singh's studies have been replicated in a whole host of (industrialised) countries, with the similarity of results being taken as evidence for the universal nature of the WHR as a signal for mate selection.

Yet others have questioned the universal nature of preferences for low WHRs. Several studies among hunter-gatherer tribes have found that they generally prefer high over low WHRs, and in any case body weight is a better predictor of attractiveness ratings (Wetsman & Marlowe, 1999). Among the Matsigenka of Peru, for example, Yu and Shepard (1998) found that an isolated group ranked line-drawings first by weight (high preferred to low) and only then high WHR over low WHR, diametrically opposed to findings in industrial societies.

Swami and Tovée (2005) compared the relative contributions of BMI and WHR to ratings of female attractiveness in different cultures. Their results have corroborated the previous finding that BMI is the greater predictor of attractiveness than WHR, regardless of the cultural setting. Indeed, this study showed that what is an attractive body weight varies with *resource availability*, with observers of higher socio-economic status (SES) in general finding thinner women more attractive than observers of low SES. Evolutionary psychological explanations of this finding based on 'adaptive' body weights for different ethnicities have been partially ruled out, and possible psychological mechanisms that emphasise core cultural attributes and individual learning have been proposed instead.

What, then, should we make of the WHR and attractiveness? One possibility is that the WHR affects attractiveness ratings only indirectly. Recent research has highlighted the possibility that the WHR is used to make social judgements about gender. In other words, the WHR seems to be involved in differentiating men from women, or pregnant from non-pregnant women. Moreover, the WHR is strongly linked to perceived femininity, and to the extent that femininity is associated with female attractiveness, women with sex-typical WHRs should be considered highly attractive.

Within this paradigm, there is room for both evolutionary and socialisation explanations. The underlying biology may direct a preference for WHRs that are sex-typical, but culture and learning may influence proximate preferences more strongly. Indeed, there is now a greater recognition that evolutionary psychological models of attraction are altogether too one-sided.

Accepted uncritically, most evolutionary psychological theories degenerate into absurd, misogynistic claims that serve to perpetuate prejudices and discrimination (e.g. the idea that men occupy positions of power in society because it is 'natural' or the idea that men have mental modules that direct them to rape under appropriate circumstances). At a more basic level, most contemporary researchers are keen to emphasise learned and experiential components of attraction alongside possible evolutionary preferences. That is, culture and biology should be seen as working together and not in isolation.

3.5.5   New Body Metrics

New technologies – three-dimensional (3D) body scanners and image processing – have transformed our ability to accurately measure, visualise and interpret an individual's 'body metrics' (Treleaven et al., 2006). The capacity to automatically collect digital data on body size, shape and surface area represents a significant innovation, because more detailed information on body size and shape is transforming the way we look at human physical attractiveness, health and well-being.

The new technologies include video silhouette images, white light phase measurement, laser-based scanning and radio wave linear analysis. The most common form of body scanners are based on an array of depth sensors, which fire a laser beam at an object and measure the direction of the reflected ray in order to calculate the distance between the sensor lens and the incident surface.

Hundreds of measurements can be extracted using a scan lasting for seconds and produces a so-called point cloud from which a computer extracts surface details, such as measurements associated with surface features (body landmarks). If a group of people are scanned, the database can be searched efficiently for comparison, analysis and viewing of averaged scans within a range of body shapes using software tools developed for this purpose. Three-dimensional body scanning is also useful for the monitoring of longitudinal changes in body morphology, whether due to exercise, nutrition or diet programmes, or as part of clinical treatment.

There are, of course a number of ethics, privacy and data protection issues to be considered. In Britain, for example, the Data Protection Act of 1998 stipulates that participants be given fair notice of how, why and by whom their personal data may be used (it is also necessary for participants to consent to data being used in such a way).

3.5.6   Other Markers

Whilst there is now considerable interest in the psychology of body shapes (BMI, WHR), this is concerned with evolutionary psychological explanations of attractiveness. There remains very little evidence that body shape is a robust marker of temperament or ability and should therefore be used for personnel selection. That said, it is to be expected that people's (e.g. interviewers') perceptions of others' (e.g. interviewees' or job applicants') psychological traits will be influenced by physical traits, but this will inevitably represent a distorted and erroneous source of information and should therefore be avoided.

There is currently a good deal of interest in related topics like *fluctuating asymmetry* and digit ratio. Fluctuating asymmetry consists of within-individual differences in left- vs right-side body features (length of ears, fingers, volume of wrists, etc.). Asymmetry is associated with both ill health and lower IQ. In a recent study, Luxen and Buunk (2006) found 20% of the variance in intelligence was explained by a combined measure of fluctuating asymmetry. However, unless these factors are very noticeable in an individual, they are unlikely to affect hiring decisions.

The *2D:4D ratio* has been known for some 100 years and has recently attracted a great deal of attention. The idea is that a person's hand shape – the length of the 2nd to 4th finger – is determined by physiological processes in the womb which influence the sex-linked factors (Brosnan, 2006).

In line with this view, a seminal study by Lippa (2003) showed that 2D:4D determined sexual orientation (though only for men). Subsequent studies in this area have attempted to link 2D:4D to individual differences in established personality traits, notably those related to aggression or masculine behaviours. Although evidence has been somewhat inconsistent, a number of meaningful connections have indeed been found. In a large-scale study, Lippa (2006) found positive, albeit weak, associations between 2D:4D and extraversion, as well as a negative, albeit weak, link between 2D:4D and openness to experience. Overall, however, associations between finger-length measures and personality were modest and variable.

In a similar, smaller-scale study, 2D:4D was a significant predictor of different aggression subscales (e.g. sensation-seeking, verbal aggression) (Hampson et al., 2008). The authors concluded that 'the 2D:4D digit ratio may be a valid, though weak, predictor of selective sex-dependent traits that are sensitive to testosterone' (p. 133). More recently, Lindova et al. (2008) reported that more feminine women – those with higher right-hand 2D:4D ratio – were more neurotic and less socially bold than their less feminine (those with a lower right-hand 2D:4D ratio) counterparts.

Although 2D:4D measures are still unlikely to be used as a personnel selection device, there is growing research in this area and the findings reviewed here show some promising potential to provide an alternative approach for assessing individual differences (see Chapter 7).

3.5.7   Body Build and Selection

Experimental studies have typically investigated hiring decisions by manipulating perceptions of employee weight, either through written descriptions or photographs. One early study of job applicants for sales and business positions reported that written descriptions of target applicants resulted in significantly more negative judgements for obese women than for non-obese women (Rothblum et al., 1988).

One study used videotaped mock interviews with the same professional actors acting as job applicants for computer and sales positions, in which weight was manipulated with theatrical prostheses (Pingitore et al., 1994). Participants indicated that employment bias was much greater for obese candidates than for average-weight applicants, and that the bias was more apparent for women than for men. An earlier study using videotapes of job applicants in simulated hiring settings showed that overweight applicants were significantly less likely to be recommended for hiring than average-weight applicants, and were also judged as significantly less neat, productive, ambitious, disciplined and determined (Larkin & Pines, 1979).

Where overweight individuals have been hired, negative perceptions of them persist throughout their career (Paul & Townsend, 1995). Roehling (1999) summarised numerous work-related stereotypes reported over a dozen laboratory studies. Overweight employees were assumed to lack self-discipline and be lazy, less conscientious, less competent, sloppy, disagreeable and emotionally unstable. Furthermore, these attitudes have a negative impact on wages, promotions and decisions about employment status (Register & Williams, 1990; Rothblum et al., 1990).

There is a mass of literature on how assessors are influenced by observable characteristics in an interview. In a recent study, Hu et al. (2018) created 140 realistic male and female body models using data from laser scans of actual human bodies. Participants in their study saw each body from two angles and indicated whether 30 trait words shown on screen applied to that body. The trait words reflected dimensions of the Big Five personality traits typically seen as positive (e.g. enthusiastic, extraverted, dominant) or negative (e.g. quiet, reserved, shy).

The researchers analysed whether participants consistently associated specific traits with certain types of bodies. They found people judged heavier bodies as being associated with more negative traits, such as being lazy and careless; they judged lighter bodies as having more positive traits, such as being self-confident and enthusiastic. Also, they classified classically feminine (e.g. pear-shaped) and classically masculine (e.g. broad-shouldered) bodies as being associated with 'active' traits, such as being quarrelsome, extraverted and irritable. Male and female bodies that were more rectangular were associated with relatively passive traits, such as being trustworthy, shy, dependable and warm. In short, they found, as many have before, that they could reliably predict personality trait judgements from specific combinations of different body shape features.

Thus, whether or not there is any evidence that physiognomy and body build do indicate personality, people believe it to be true.

3.5.8 Conclusions

Each age has its own belief system and technology which claims there are ways of assessing and understanding individuals by different metrics: their body build, head shape, handwriting and birth place/time. Many people take the claims seriously and livelihoods are dependent on the use of these technologies.

It takes the scientist a long time to do the validation of these claims, Inevitably the early results are equivocal and often remain so. However, it is probably safe to conclude that the evidence available on the various techniques reviewed in this chapter suggests it would be very unwise to use them in any formal assessment of an individual.

REFERENCES

Alley, T. R. (1988). Physiognomy and social perception. In T. R. Alley (Ed.), *Resources for ecological psychology. Social and applied aspects of perceiving faces* (p. 167–186). Lawrence Erlbaum Associates, Inc.

Allport, G. W., & Vernon, P. E. (1933). The present status of experimental graphology. In G. W. Allport & P. E. Vernon, *Studies in expressive movement* (p. 185–211). MacMillan Co

Ben-Shakhar, G., Bar-Hillel, M., Bilu, Y., Ben-Abba, E., & Flug, A. (1986). Can graphology predict occupational success? Two empirical studies and some methodological ruminations. *Journal of Applied Psychology, 71*(4), 645.

Berry, D. S. (1990). Taking people at face value: Evidence for the kernel of truth hypothesis. *Social Cognition, 8*(4), 343–361.

Brosnan, M. J. (2006). Digit ratio and faculty membership between prenatal testosterone and academia. *British Journal of Psychology, 97,* 455–466.

Bruchon-Schweitzer, M., & Ferrieux, D. (1991). Les méthodes d'évaluation du personnel utilisées pour le recrutement en France. *Orientation Scolaire et Professionnelle.*

Burke, K. (2012). Big Five personality traits an astrology. Unpublished PhD thesis. Pacific Graduate University, Ann Arbor.

Butterworth, B. (1999). *The mathematical brain.* Macmillan.

Carlson, S. (1985). A double-blind test of astrology. *Nature, 318*(6045), 419–425.

Clarke, D., Gabriels, T., & Barnes, J. (1996). Astrological signs as determinants of extroversion and emotionality: An empirical study. *Journal of Psychology, 130*(2), 131–140.

Cleridou, K., & Furnham, A. (2014). Personality correlates of aesthetic preferences for art, architecture, and music. *Empirical Studies of the Arts, 32*(2), 231–255.

Cohen Jr, M. M. (1973). A new syndrome with hypotonia, obesity, mental deficiency, and facial, oral, ocular, and limb anomalies. *Journal of Pediatrics, 83*(2), 280–284.

Cooter, R. (1984). *The cultural meaning of popular science: Phrenology and the organization of consent in nineteenth-century Britain.* Cambridge University Press.

Crepieux-Jamin, J. (1909). *L'ecriture et le caractere.* Alcan.

Davey, D. M. (1989). *How to be a good judge of character: Methods of assessing ability and personality.* Kogan Page

Davies, J. D. (1955). *Phrenology, fad and science: A 19th century American crusade.* Yale University Press.

Dazzi, C., & Pedrabissi, L. (2009). Graphology and personality: an empirical study on validity of handwriting analysis. *Psychological Reports, 105*(3), 1255–1268.

Dean, G. (1987). Does astrology need to be true? Part 2: The answer is no. *The Skeptical Inquirer, 11*(3), 257–273.

Dean, G. (1992). Does astrology need to be true? In K. Frazier (Ed.), *The hundredth monkey and other paradigms of paranormal* (pp. 279–319). Prometheus.

Driver, R. W., Buckley, M. R., & Frink, D. D. (1996). Should we write off graphology? *International Journal of Selection and Assessment, 4*(2), 78–86.

Edwards, A. G., & Armitage, P. (1992). An experiment to test the discriminating ability of graphologists. *Personality and Individual Differences, 13*(1), 69–74.

Eysenck, H. J., & Gudjonsson, G. (1986). An empirical study of the validity of handwriting analysis. *Personality and Individual Differences, 7*(2), 263–264.

Eysenck, H. (1967). *The biological basis of personality.* Thomas.

Furnham, A. (1988). Write and wrong: The validity of graphological analysis. *Skeptical Enquirer, 12*: 64–69.

Furnham, A. (2004). The future (and past) of work psychology and organisational behaviour: A personal view. *Management Review, 15*: 420–436.

Furnham, A. (2008). *Personality and Intelligence at Work.* Routledge.

Furnham, A. (2010). Phrenology. In *50 Schlüsselideen Psychologie* (pp. 184–187). Spektrum Akademischer Verlag.

Furnham, A., & Gunter, B. (1987). Effects of time of day and medium of presentation on immediate recall of violent and non-violent news. *Applied Cognitive Psychology, 1*(4), 255–262.

Furnham, A., Chamorro-Premuzic, T., & Callahn, I. (2003). Does graphology predict personality and intelligence? *Individual Differences Research, 1*(2), 78–94.

Furnham, A., McClelland, A., & Mansi, A. (2012). Selecting your boss: Sex, age, IQ and EQ factors. *Personality and Individual Differences, 53,* 552–556.

Garoot, A. H., Safar, M., & Suen, C. Y. (2017, November). A Comprehensive Survey on Handwriting and Computerized Graphology. In *2017 14th IAPR International Conference on Document Analysis and Recognition (ICDAR)* (Vol. 1, p. 621–626). IEEE.

Gauquelin, M., Gauquelin, F., & Eysenck, S. B. (1979). Personality and position of the planets at birth: An empirical study. *British Journal of Social and Clinical Psychology, 18*(1), 71–75.

Gauquelin, M. (1969). *The scientific basis of astrology.* Stein and Day.

Gauquelin, M., Gauquelin, F., & Eysenck, S. B. (1979). Personality and position of the planets at birth: An empirical study. *British Journal of Social and Clinical Psychology, 18*(1), 71–75.

Genovese, J. E. (2015). Interest in astrology and phrenology over two centuries: A Google Ngram study. *Psychological Reports, 117*(3), 940–943.

Goldberg, L. R. (1986). Some informal explorations and ruminations about graphology. In B. Nevo (Ed.), *Handbook of scientific aspects of graphology* (p. 281–293). Charles C. Thomas.

Gwada, B. (2014). Lack of evidence for the assessment of personality traits using handwriting analysis. *Polish Psychological Bulletin, 45*(1), 73–79.

Hamilton, M. M. (1995). Incorporation of astrology-based personality information into long-term self-concept. *Journal of Social Behavior and Personality, 10*(3), 707.

Hampson, E., Ellis, C. L., & Tenk, C. M. (2008). On the relation between 2D: 4D and sex-dimorphic personality traits. *Archives of Sexual Behavior, 37*(1), 133.

Hartford, H. (1973). *You are what you write.* Macmillan Publishing Company.

Hassin, R., & Trope, Y. (2000). Facing faces: studies on the cognitive aspects of physiognomy. *Journal of Personality and Social Psychology, 78*(5), 837.

Hu, Y., Parde, C. J., Hill, M. Q., Mahmood, N., & O'Toole, A. J. (2018). First impressions of personality traits from body shapes. *Psychological Science, 29* (12), 1969–1983.

Hull, C. L., & Montgomery, R. B. (1919). An experimental investigation of certain alleged relations between character and hand writing. *Psychological Review, 26*(1), 63.

Kravitz, D. A., Stinson, V., & Chavez, T. L. (1996). Evaluations of tests used for making selection and promotion decisions. *International Journal of Selection and Assessment, 4*(1), 24–34.

Jones, O. P., Alfaro-Almagro, F., & Jbabdi, S. (2018). An empirical, 21st century evaluation of phrenology. *Cortex, 106*, 26–35.

Kelly, I. W. (1997). Modern astrology: a critique. *Psychological Reports, 81*(3), 1035–1066.

King, R. N., & Koehler, D. J. (2000). Illusory correlations in graphological inference. *Journal of Experimental Psychology: Applied, 6*(4), 336.

Klages, L (1917) *Handschrift und charakter*. Bovier Verlag Herbert Grundman.

Klages, L. (1930). *Graphologisches Lesebuch [A graphology reader]*. Johann Ambrosius Barth.

Klimoski, R. J., & Rafaeli, A. (1983) Inferring personal qualities through handwriting analysis. *Journal of Occupational Psychology, 56*, 191–202.

Kretschmer, E. (1925). *Physique and character* (trans. WJH Sprott). Kegan Paul, 266.

Larkin, J. C., & Pines, H. A. (1979). No fat persons need apply: experimental studies of the overweight stereotype and hiring preference. *Sociology of Work and Occupations, 6*(3), 312–327.

Lester, D., McLaughlin, S., & Nosal, G. (1977). Graphological signs for extraversion. *Perceptual and Motor Skills, 44*(1), 137–138.

Lewinson, T. S. (1986). Handwriting analysis in diagnosis and treatment of alcoholism. *Perceptual and Motor Skills, 62*(1), 265–266.

Lindová, J., Hrušková, M., Pivoňková, V., Kuběna, A., & Flegr, J. (2008). Digit ratio (2D: 4D) and Cattell's personality traits. *European Journal of Personality: Published for the European Association of Personality Psychology, 22*(4), 347–356.

Linton, H. B., Epstein, L., & Hartford, H. (1962). Personality and perceptual correlates of primary beginning strokes in handwriting. *Perceptual and Motor Skills, 15*(1), 159–170.

Lippa, R. A. (2003). Are 2D: 4D finger-length ratios related to sexual orientation? Yes for men, no for women. *Journal of Personality and Social Psychology, 85*(1), 179.

Lippa, R. A. (2006). Finger lengths, 2D: 4D ratios, and their relation to gender-related personality traits and the Big Five. *Biological Psychology, 71*(1), 116–121.

Lombroso, C. (1895). *Criminal Anthropology: Its Origin and Application*. Forum Publishing Company.

Luxen, M. F., & Buunk, B. P. (2006). Human intelligence, fluctuating asymmetry and the peacock's tail: general intelligence (g) as an honest signal of fitness. *Personality and Individual Differences, 41*(5), 897–902.

Mayo, J., White, O., & Eysenck, H. J. (1978). An empirical study of the relation between astrological factors and personality. *The Journal of Social Psychology, 105*(2), 229–236.

McArthur, L. Z., & Berry, D. S. (1987). Cross-cultural agreement in perceptions of babyfaced adults. *Journal of Cross-Cultural Psychology, 18*(2), 165–192.

Michon, J. H., & Desbarrolles, A. (1872). *Les Mystères de l'écriture,... art de juger les hommes sur leurs autographes, par A. Desbarrolles et Jean-Hippolyte [Michon]*. Garnier frères.

Miller, E. (1996). Phrenology, neuropsychology and rehabilitation. *Neuropsychological Rehabilitation, 6*(4), 245–256.

Mishra, A. (2017). Forensic graphology: Assessment of personality. *Forensic Research & Criminology International Journal, 4*(1), 00097.

Nanninga, R. (1996). The astrotest. *Correlation, 15*, 14–20.

Neter, E., & Ben-Shakhar, G. (1989). The predictive validity of graphological inferences: A meta-analytic approach. *Personality and Individual Differences, 10*(7), 737–745.

Nevo, B. (1988). Yes, graphology can predict occupational success: Rejoinder to Ben-Shakhar, et al. *Perceptual and Motor Skills, 66*(1), 92–94.

Nias, D. K. (2016). Hans Eysenck: Sex and violence on television, the paranormal, graphology, and astrology. *Personality and Individual Differences, 103*, 140–147.

Nickerson, R. S. (1998). Confirmation bias: A ubiquitous phenomenon in many guises. *Review of General Psychology, 2*(2), 175–220.

Oosthuizen, S. (1990). Graphology as predictor of academic achievement. *Perceptual and Motor Skills, 71*(3), 715–721.

Paul, R. J., & Townsend, J. B. (1995). Shape up or ship out? Employment discrimination against the overweight. *Employee Responsibilities and Rights Journal, 8*(2), 133–145.

Puhl, R. M., & Brownell, K. D. (2003). Psychosocial origins of obesity stigma: toward changing a powerful and pervasive bias. *Obesity Reviews, 4*(4), 213–227.

Pingitore, R., Dugoni, B. L., Tindale, R. S., & Spring, B. (1994). Bias against overweight job applicants in a simulated employment interview. *Journal of Applied Psychology, 79*(6), 909.

Rafaeli, A., & Klimoski, R. J. (1983). Predicting sales success through handwriting analysis: An evaluation of the effects of training and handwriting sample content. *Journal of Applied Psychology, 68*(2), 212.

Register, C. A., & Williams, D. R. (1990). Wage effects of obesity among young workers. *Social Science Quarterly, 71*(1), 130.

Roehling, M. V. (1999). Weight-based discrimination in employment: Psychological and legal aspects. *Personnel Psychology, 52*(4), 969–1016.

Rosenthal, D. A., & Lines, R. (1978). Handwriting as a correlate of extraversion. *Journal of Personality Assessment, 42*(1), 45–48.

Rothblum, E. D., Brand, P. A., Miller, C. T., & Oetjen, H. A. (1990). The relationship between obesity, employment discrimination, and employment-related victimization. *Journal of Vocational Behavior, 37*(3), 251–266.

Rothblum, E. D., Miller, C. T., & Garbutt, B. (1988). Stereotypes of obese female job applicants. *International Journal of Eating Disorders, 7*(2), 277–283.

Sachs, G. (1999). *The astrology file.* Orion.

Sen, A., & Shah, H. (2017). *Automated handwriting analysis system using principles of graphology and image processing.* ICIIECs Conference.

Shackleton, V., & Newell, S. (1994). European management selection methods: A comparison of five countries. *International Journal of Selection and Assessment, 2*(2), 91–102.

Sheldon, W. H., Stevens, S. S., & Tucker, W. B. (1940). *The varieties of human physique.* Harper and Bros.

Singh, D. (1993). Body shape and women's attractiveness. *Human Nature, 4*(3), 297–321.

Swami, V., & Tovée, M. J. (2005). Female physical attractiveness in Britain and Malaysia: A cross-cultural study. *Body Image, 2*, 115–128.

Tett, R. P., & Palmer, C. A. (1997). The validity of handwriting elements in relation to self-report personality trait measures. *Personality and individual differences, 22*(1), 11–18.

Van Rooij, J. J. (1994). Introversion-extraversion: astrology versus psychology. *Personality and Individual Differences, 16*(6), 985–988.

Vestewig, R. E., Santee, A. R., & Moss, M. K. (1976). Validity and student acceptance of a graphoanalytic approach to personality. *Journal of Personality Assessment, 40*(6), 592–598.

von Eye, A., Losel, F., & Mayzer, R. (2003). Is it all written in the stars? A methodological commentary on Sachs' astrology monograph and re-analyses of his data on crime statistics. *Psychological Test and Assessment Modeling, 45*(1), 78.

Watson, P. R. (1993). Benefits of graphology. *Professional Manager*, May 4.

Wetsman, A., & Marlowe, F. (1999). How universal are preferences for female waist-to-hip ratios? Evidence from the Hadza of Tanzania. *Evolution and Human Behavior, 20*(4), 219–228.

Yu, D. W., & Shepard, G. H. (1998). Is beauty in the eye of the beholder? *Nature, 396*, 321–322.

4 Self-Report Tests

4.1 THE INTERVIEW

What are interviews?
Traditionally, they are live face-to-face conversations between an assessor and an assessee where both get the opportunity to interrogate each other for information. They can be done online or over the telephone remotely. They differ in many features (i.e. structured vs unstructured; individual vs panel).

How do they work?
The idea is that they provide rich, subtle and invaluable information about all aspects of the individual, not only what they say but how they say it. Furthermore, candidates can get information about the job itself and the organisation.

What of the evidence?
There is a great deal of data which shows the following: unstructured interviews have very low validity but well-structured interviews have very high validity. Most people doing selection arrange an interview and most of those being selected expect one. Interviewers need careful training to be accurate and consistent. There are subtle differences in online interviews.

Practical problems: cost, ethics, politics
The cost in terms of working time and assessee travel costs for face-to-face is high, but much less so for online interviewing. The ethics and politics are getting more complicated given legal restrictions on what can and cannot be asked.

Recommendations for use
Only use well-trained interviewers to deliver carefully structured interviews after a thoughtful job analysis.

4.1.1   Introduction

Most people expect to be interviewed for any job. While some organisations 'gave up' interviewing potential staff because they believed it was too expensive and not valid, many had to return to the process because of the bad publicity they got from such a decision. Candidates nearly always want to be interviewed.

There are many variations in job interviews: how long they last, how many interviewers they have, whether there are more than one interview/er, whether they are panel/board interviews and most importantly whether they are structured or not. Certainly, applicants expect to be interviewed at some stage of the selection process.

Interview is a two-way process of observation and rating. By and large, candidates approve of interviews and are surprised if they are not asked to them. Thus, they have two types of validity: that from the organisational perspective (which has been the focus of academic validity studies on personnel selection techniques) and that from the candidate perspective. Because it is an interview where both parties assess and evaluate each other, candidates can get some idea of the nature of the job, the organisation and possibly senior management. This makes it rather different from many other methods of assessment.

Schuler (1993) described the latter as the *social validity* of the interview. He argued that people tend to base the social validity of interviews on four factors: how informative they are to the candidate in terms of the total information they get about the job; the quality, quantity and control they have over participation in the process (and its outcome); how transparent the whole approach is; and the amount and type of feedback provided.

What sort of things do interviewers look for? These can include intelligence, job knowledge, personality, social skills, physical attributes, interests and preferences. Some interviewers prepare exhaustively, others very little. Some develop their questions using highly salient typical situations, which is a bit like the Situational Judgement Test (Chapter 13) either with forced choice or free response.

Why are interviews so poor at predicting performance? There is a long and growing list of factors that collectively explain this.

- Interviewers differ in insight, skills and preferences.
- Interviewers are not as logical and rational and able to deal with complexity as they suppose.
- Interviewers' motives, attention and need for justification of their decisions differ.
- Interviewees try hard to manage a positive (not totally realistic) impression by self-promotion and self-enhancement.
- Interviewers look for novel information which they weigh too heavily
- Interviewees are increasingly being coached on how to behave in interviews.
- Interviewees (and interviewers and referees) lie.
- Variations occur in how interviewers use the rating scale used during or after the interview.
- The interviewer is trying to predict the unpredictable, namely totally good work on all aspects of the job at a much later period in time.
- There is range restriction in ratings meaning that raters never use the full scale particularly the two ends. They do not discriminate/differentiate clearly enough between different candidates.
- Interviewers make up their mind before the interview.
- Interviewers simplify the task and cannot cope with the complexity of integrating the information.
- Interviewers are susceptible to forming a first impression and ignoring later data.
- Reasons to reject (i.e. select out) factors have disproportionate weight compared to select-in factors.
- Interviewers have their own (wrong, unproved, bizarre) implicit personality theories (i.e. red heads are intelligent, rugby players are good team workers).

It seems almost inconceivable that any form of selection task is not informed by one or many job interviews. These have been used in selection for over two centuries (e.g. the Royal Navy used job interviews as early as 1800). Many use the words 'chemistry', 'fit' and 'feel', all of which speak primarily to the intuitive nature of the process.

An interview candidate may have to sit before large panels of people eager to have a 'good look' at him or her or else go through a large number of sequential 'one-to-ones' from the, often many, stake-holders in the job. Interviews differ on many dimensions: how long they last, how many interviewers there are, how much they are pre-planned and what the real purpose of the interview is.

The very popularity and ubiquity of interviews has spawned a huge industry in interview training. There are a number of books for both interviewers and interviewees. Interviewers are 'taught' how to ask 'killer questions' that get 'to the heart of the interviewee'. Equally, interviewees are taught how to give diplomatic (somewhat evasive) answers to those really 'tough' questions. Interviews are therefore presented as a minefield of dishonesty; a game of intellectual cha-rades, where both parties are essentially out to 'trick' and 'out man-oeuvre' one another. This is, of course, far from the truth but has no doubt served to influence how both parties see selection interviews.

As a result, some organisations have argued that the data show-ing the extremely poor reliability and validity of (mostly unstruc-tured) interviews effectively means that they often hinder rather than help effective decision-making. Interview data and ratings have been accused of being *invalid, unreliable and biased*. Furthermore, considerable time and travel costs are often involved for both parties.

Hence, in the UK, it is still common for universities not to inter-view prospective undergraduate students, believing that the school exam results, letters of recommendation and other application form data pro-vide sufficient information for them to make the 'optimal' decision. Some universities do interview for highly selective courses because they are interested in weeding out unsuitable candidates (judged by personal-ity, motivation or values) rather than electing desirable candidates.

Yet interviews are part of nearly all selection-decision, data-gathering method because they are rated as the most acceptable (fair, reasonable, important) method. They are used to collect information, make inferences about suitability and determine an individual's com-munication skills.

The literature on this topic is scattered between various aca-demic and applied disciplines from Human Resource Management to

Differential Psychology. Some researchers appear to be less disinterested than others in their attempt to demonstrate the validity of particular types of interview techniques or styles. However, there remains considerable consensus on the validity of structured and non-structured interview data.

4.1.2 Description, Types and Functions of Interviews

Research on interviews addresses a number of quite specific issues.

First, it is important to distinguish between different types of interviews, given both their purpose and methodology.

Second, there is a literature on the cognitive psychology of interviews that looks at how people obtain, evaluate and combine information to arrive at a final judgement.

Third, by far the greatest research effort has gone into looking at the psychometrics (reliability and validity) of interviews, as well as how to improve it.

Fourth, there is a growing literature on candidate evaluation in interviews.

Fifth, there is a small literature on legal aspects of interviews.

It is difficult to characterise the *typical* selection interview. Most are unstructured, or semi-structured at best; few interviewers are properly trained. The easiest aspect to score highly on (i.e. self-confidence and presentation) are frequently relatively unimportant job criteria; the interview is usually done by the person (alone or with others) who will 'manage'; the only preparation the interviewer has done is a perfunctory reading of the completed application form and the candidate's CV. Despite the wide range of interviews, most tend to ask a relatively invariant number of questions, such as 'What persuaded you to work for us?' 'What are your greatest strengths and weaknesses?' and the cliched finale of 'Do you have any questions for us?'

There are many different types of interviews: *appraisal, disciplinary, motivational* and *selection* interviews, though most research is probably on selection interviews. Candidates have a clear expectation of interviews. They usually expect an interview to be thorough, lasting anywhere between 30 and 120 minutes. They expect the interview to be a one-to-one; that they must be smartly dressed, that they will answer question honestly and that they will be allowed themselves to ask various questions at some point.

There are usually four phases to the interview: welcome, information gathering, information supplying and conclusion. The welcome phase usually lasts a few minutes and is designed to put the candidate at ease. The gathering data phase may constitute as much as 80–90% of the total interview. The third, relatively short phase near the end occurs when the interviewer invites the candidate to pose any question they might have. Some of the questions are genuine and others often impression-management questions designed to impress the interviewer. The fourth phase usually involves the interviewer explaining the decision-making process to the candidate, and how and when they will be informed about the outcome.

There are many courses that attempt to teach managers interview skills, especially how to plan an appraisal interview, as well as how to ask very perceptive, high-yield questions. These can, or should, have highly defined job outcome criteria measurable usually by one of five factors: time, money, quality, quantity and customer feedback.

All interviews should have an agenda that demonstrates that at least the interviewer has planned the process. Also, it should end with a clear summary statement from both parties regarding what they got from the interview, ideally with the interviewee summarising his/her understanding first.

Potential qualities or areas typically assessed by a structured job interview include the following (see Table 4.1), although individuals and organisations have favourite questions and topics which they believe yield very high-quality data.

Appraisal interviews have very specific functions: to improve utilisation of staff resources by promoting work performance, assigning work more efficiently, meeting employee's need for growth, etc.

Table 4.1 *Six areas of assessment*

Upbringing	• Base point against which person makes decisions • Info needed – where born, siblings (ages, academic and work achievements), childhood events *Evaluate: economic and social stability, degree of supportiveness*
Education	• Focus is on intellect • Info needed – schools, university, exam results, other interests and achievements (cultural, social, technical) *Evaluate: choice of subjects, performance, causes and results of failures*
Work History	• Look at the most recent experience first • Info needed – job titles, main tasks, relationships, objectives/results, part of job liked/done well and vice versa, reasons for changing *Evaluate: significance of job within the organisation, standing of the firm in the industry, competence of candidate against demands of job*
Aspirations	• Reality check • Info needed – what candidate wants to do in the short/long term, what plans for achieving ambitions *Evaluate: how realistic aspirations are when set against academic and work achievements to date plus personal attributes*
Circumstances	• Establish pressures on career • Info needed – willingness to move, marital status, social family constraints, financial liabilities, driving licence *Evaluate: any constraints which may affect work effectiveness by exploring marital and financial stability*
Interests	• Ask what they enjoy about their interests to find out motivations • Info needed – main interests, with what intensity and for how long *Evaluate: to what extent the proposed job gives an outlet for these interests, and to what extent it is a barrier*

Often, training programmes concerning interviews spend a great deal of effort on looking at formulating, asking and interpreting the answers to questions.

Appraisal interviews, often considered much more problematic, look at how best to give (both positive and negative) feedback. Thus, clear recommendations are made such as:

- Begin with a clear brief about the context and purpose of the feedback.
- Start with the positive feedback. Ask the candidate for their positive, then negative feedback first followed by that of the assessor.
- Be specific in both positive and negative comments.
- Refer always to behaviour that can be changed.
- Offer alternative suggestions for how things can be done differently.
- Always be descriptive rather than evaluative in feedback.
- Attempt to get the person to acknowledge the feedback.
- Check on whether there are any hidden agenda in how, when and why you are giving the feedback.
- Give the person the choice in how they accept and respond to the feedback.
- Consider what the feedback says about you.

Equally, it may be advisable to train people in how to receive feedback in interviews. Thus, they are usually advised to listen to, and to consider carefully, precisely what is being said before rejecting it or arguing with the giver. It is important to understand and be clear about what is being said. Receivers of feedback should be encouraged to ask for feedback that they wanted but did not get. They may also be encouraged to check it out with other senior people who know them rather than rely on only one source. Furthermore, they will need to decide on precisely what they intend to do with the feedback.

4.1.3   Impression Management: Dissimulation and Lying

Although people dismiss questionnaires as pointless because people lie, they often seem quite happy with the interview, despite similar possibility for deceit.

Many have considered the problem of faking and impression management in interviews.

Max Eggert, an expert on selection, has argued that there are many different types of lies. They make a good checklist for the potential interviewer.

1. *White lies*: These are found in the 'puff' statement gormless people are encouraged to write on their CV. 'I am a totally committed team player'. 'I have excellent social skills and the ability to read people'. 'I am utterly trustworthy and loyal'. The question of course is 'who says?' Where is the evidence? The best solution is to ignore all this flim-flam and say: 'I will be the judge of that, thank you'.

2. *Altruistic lies*: These are lies that attempt a cover-up but look as if they are helping others. So rather than say they left their last job because their manager was a bully, or the company was patently dodgy, they say they resigned to look for new challenges.

3. *Lies of omission*: For many these are the most frequent and easiest of lies. People might omit details of school or university grades because of they had poor marks. Whole periods of their life are obfuscated. The most common lie concerns dates, often to disguise the fact that the candidate seemed to spend a surprisingly short amount of time in a succession of jobs. It is no more or less than concealment.

4. *Defensive lies*: The defensive lie is one that conceals by generalisations or vagaries. Ask a person about their previous boss's management style, their reason for leaving or their health record and you are often faced with a string of vague expressions such as 'like others in the company', 'much the same as my co-workers', 'at that time'. Ask vague questions, you get defensive lies.

5. *Impersonation lies*: This is also called the transfer lie and occurs mostly where people take credit for others' work. Statements such as 'I doubled sales over the year' or 'I was responsible for a budget of over three million'. All others in the hierarchy are forgotten in these lies. And it is often difficult to establish the facts as to who exactly was responsible for particular successes (and disasters which are, of course, omitted).

6. *Embedded lies*: This is a clever subterfuge to confuse the interviewer. The idea is to suggest than an experience, qualification or achievement was very different from the actuality. 'It was good fun being with the BBC' could mean practically anything from 'I once went to a show there' to 'They filmed at my school'.

7. *Errors of commission or fact*: This is lying 101. They are explicit, verifiably, false claims. It is about claiming qualifications you don't have; starting up or working for companies that never existed; skills that don't exist. It is the most blatant form of lie.

8. *Definition lies*: This is the sport of lawyers and of presidents. What precisely does it mean 'to have sex with' someone; what is a company turnaround; what does it mean to be in the latest group? This approach involves working with a very specific and obscure definition so that for all intents and purposes you are telling the truth.

9. *Proxy lies:* This is where the candidates get others to lie for them. It is usually referees but could be former teachers. They may skilfully work on their previous employers' poor memory, vanity or other bribes to persuade them to obfuscation.

Liars leak deceit. Most try hard to cover up their deceit, but it is difficult trying to control your words, voice, face, feet and hands all at the same time. The voice and the face carry important cues.

Vrij (2000, p. 33) has identified 17 non-verbal behaviours that may be directly related to lying.

Overview and descriptions of non-verbal behaviours that indicate lying:

Vocal Characteristics

1. *Speech hesitations*: use of the words 'ah', 'um', 'er' and so on.
2. *Speech errors*: word and/or sentence repetition, sentence change, sentence incompletions, slips of the tongue and so on.
3. *Pitch of voice*: changes in pitch of voice, such as a rise or fall in pitch.
4. *Speech rate*: number of words spoken in a certain period of time.
5. *Latency period:* period of silence between question and answer.
6. *Frequency of pauses:* frequency of silent periods during speech.
7. *Pause durations:* length of silent periods during speech.

Facial Characteristics

8. *Gaze*: looking at the face of the conversation partner.
9. *Smile*: smiling and laughing.
10. *Blinking*: blinking of the eyes.

Movements

11. *Self-manipulations*: scratching the head, wrists and so on.
12. *Illustrators*: functional hand and arm movements designed to modify and/or supplement what is being said verbally.
13. *Hand and finger movements*: non-functional movements of hands or fingers without moving the arms.
14. *Leg and foot movements*: movements of the feet and legs.
15. *Head movements*: head nods and head shakes.
16. *Trunk movements*: movements of the trunk (usually accompanied by head movements).
17. *Shifting position*: movements made to change the sitting position (usually accompanied by trunk and foot/leg movements).

One of the major aims of interviewer training is how to catch those involved in some sort of deception (see Table 4.2)

Table 4.2 *Seven specifically verbal indicators that relate to lying*

Verbal characteristic	Description
1. Negative statements	Statements indicated aversion towards an object, person or opinion, such as denials and disparaging statements, and statements indicating a negative mood
2. Plausible answers	Statements which make sense and which sound credible and reasonable
3. Irrelevant information	Information which is irrelevant to the context, and which has not been asked for
4. Overgeneralised statements	The use of words such as 'always', 'never', 'nobody', 'everybody' and so on.
5. Self-references	The use of words referring to the speaker himself or herself, such as 'I', 'me' or 'mine'
6. Direct answers	To-the-point and straightforward statements (e.g. 'I like John' is more direct than 'I like John's company')
7. Response length	Length of the answer or number of spoken words

4.1.4 *Structured vs Unstructured Interviews*

It has long been common practice to differentiate between what have been called structured and unstructured interviews, though strictly speaking, they are really on a continuum from completely unstructured (and possibly unplanned) to rigidly and inflexibly structured.

An ultimately unstructured interview is a like an informal discussion where interviewers ask whatever questions come to mind and follow up answers in an intuitive and whimsical way. Crucially, questions are open-ended and attempt to avoid 'leading' the interviewee's answers in any specific direction. Conversely, and rather self-explanatorily, in a structured interview the questions are thoughtfully planned. Indeed, there are so many attempts at standardisation that it has been suggested that the interview questions be recorded, as indeed are the answers (Cook, 2016).

The structured interview is pre-planned to ensure every candidate receives exactly the same questions in the same order at the same pace. Structured interviews employ rating scales and checklists for judgement, allow for few or no follow-up questions (to limit interviewees' response time and standardise it), take into account previous job analyses and leave little autonomy for the interviewer. In that sense, totally structured interviews resemble standardised psychometric tests (see Chapter 6). The question is how much structure vs flexibility should be built in to maximise the point of the whole exercise.

A structured interview is essentially a planned interview. It often requires interviewers to make pre- and post-interview decisions. The idea is that a job analysis leads one to decide on a limited number of abilities and skills that one is looking for.

A structured interview then follows a rigorously planned sequence of question areas in an attempt to get all the salient information upon which to make an accurate rating.

The importance of structured interviews to ensure validity cannot be overrated, as we shall see. However, they are not always popular with interviewers who feel they should have discretion in conducting the interview, they lose 'the personal touch' and rapport and dislike the amount of time spent in developing the questions (Cook, 2016).

4.1.5   Accepted Guidelines for a Good Selection Interview

The central problem for those interested in the selection interviews are psychometric issues of reliability and validity (see Chapter 1). They refer to the question of whether interviewers' ratings of the candidates agree (sufficiently) with one another. Do candidates leave the same impression about their skills, aptitudes, dispositions and attitudes with all those that interview them? Second, and always more salient, do the interview ratings predict future job performance? The answer to this simple question is far from simple. The reliability and validity of the interview is dependent on all sorts of things from the skill and training of the interviewers to the types of ratings made and the length of the interview, and rather than asking 'whether' interviews predict performance, the question is 'to what extent' they do.

As a consequence of a great deal of research and excellent recent meta-analyses, it is possible to list some rules of thumb that have been shown to increase the reliability and validity of interviews: train interviewers, ask standardised questions, do a good job analysis, ignore salient prior information; do the ratings before and after the interviews, make specific ratings.

Interviews can be improved to increase their reliability and validity by various relatively simple steps. These are very important to make the ever-popular interview a useful assessment method:

1. Select good, insightful, natural interviewers.
2. Use more than one interviewer in panel or board interviews.
3. Use the same interviewers throughout the process.
4. Train interviewers in the fundamental skills of interviewing.
5. Take notes to help memory and settle arguments.
6. Make ratings rather than use descriptors.

Structured Interviews: this means pro- and pre-scribing *what* is questioned, by *whom*, for what *purpose*. Some become almost spoken questionnaires and deprive the interviewers of their traditional autonomy and flexibility. But we know that a good interview is one that is planned and structured.

Arnold et al. (2005, p. 182) provide 10 tips for best practice structured interview design:

1. Base questions on a thorough job analysis.
2. Ask exactly the same questions of each candidate, limit prompting, use follow-up questions, but limit elaboration.
3. Use relevant questions and design them as either situational, competency-based, biographical or knowledge questions.
4. Use longer interviews or larger number of questions; control the input of ancillary information (e.g. CV (resume), references).
5. Do not allow questions from the candidate until after the interview (when the data have been collected).
6. Rate each answer using multiple rating scales.
7. Use detailed anchored rating scales and take detailed notes.
8. Use multiple interviewers where possible.
9. Use the same interviewer(s) across all candidates and provide extensive training to enhance reliability.
10. Use statistical rather than clinical prediction.

Gatewood et al. (2016) have a slightly different list (p. 471):

1. Restrict the range of the interview to selection (not recruiting) and focus on the most job-relevant WRCs (Work Related Criteria), preferably just two or three WRCs
2. Limit the use of pre-interview data about applicants
3. Adopt a structured format by predetermining major questions to be asked
4. Use job-related questions
5. Use multiple questions for each WRC
6. Rely on multiple independent reviewers
7. Apply formal scoring that allows for the evaluation of each WRC separately
8. Train interviewers in the process of the selection interview

Interviewers need training in how they present themselves: how to pose questions and how to interpret often subtle non-verbal cues as well as certain answers. This is mainly about social skills and emotional intelligence. More importantly, they need to know what salient questions to ask that relate to the very specific nature of the job that they are selecting for.

A thorough job analysis should reveal the full range of skills, aptitudes and dispositions required. This should drive the interview structure. Interviewers should not only know what questions to ask and why but also how to interpret the answers. In addition, interviewers need to make judgements on only the salient features of the candidates and to ignore various impression-management techniques.

Next, interviewers need training on how to accurately distinguish between the different criteria assessed. Just as wine and tea tasters have to be taught to make reliable and accurate ratings, so should interviewers be taught – through both practice and special training – how they and other raters see the same candidate and to ensure that they provide consistent or at least compatible evaluations. Finally, it is important that the rating scales used by interviewers are clear and comprehensive, allowing a wide range of ratings, including an index of uncertainty

4.1.6 The Psychometrics of Interviews

The two strong pillars of psychometrics are reliability and validity, both of which come in many forms. Furthermore, they are interdependent: interviews cannot be valid if they are not reliable.

For interviews, it is crucial to have interviewer (judge, observer, rater) reliability. This means that two people conducting or watching an interview with the same person must have the same (or very similar) ratings. Low reliability, particularly in unstructured interviews, is no doubt mainly due to interviewer variability. Interviewers ask different questions, record and weight answers differently and may have radically different understandings of the whole purpose of the interview.

Most reviewers have seen that the simplest way to improve reliability is to introduce a consistency and structure to the interview. It is almost tautological to suggest that consistency leads to reliability, as they are in essence the same thing. Studies also show that it is possible to increase interviewer reliability by different but important steps, including doing a job analysis, training interviewers, having structured interviews, having behaviourally based and anchored rating scales.

How much do different interviewers agree? The answer is about $r = .50$, and better and more so in *structured* interviews. Validity is much lower. For structured interviews it is about the same for one-to-one vs board interviews $(r = .35)$ but for unstructured interviews the one-to-one $(r = .11)$ is about half as good as board interviews $(r = .21)$. This means that interviewers of the same person do not agree very much on their assessments *and* that these assessments are not very useful in predicting success (or failure) on the job. Only planned, structured interviews offer good data to really be useful in assessment.

At best it seems an interview's poor predictive validity means that it can only account for the 10% of the variance in the candidate's later job performance – or, in other words, 90% of the employees' later, on-the-job effectiveness is *not* accounted for by the data acquired in the interview.

Many studies have examined the issue of reliability with a useful meta-analysis by Conway, Jako and Goodman (1995), who reviewed 160 empirical studies. They found reliabilities of 0.77 when observers watched the same interview, but that this dropped to 0.53 if they watched different interviews of the same candidate. Given that candidates react to different questions by different interviewees often quite differently, some would argue that 0.53 is surprisingly good.

Research in this area has gone on for 50 years at least. Over the years small, relatively unsophisticated studies have been replaced by ever more useful and important meta-analyses. There are now a sufficient number of meta-analyses that some have done helpful summaries of them. Cook (2004) reviewed Hunter and Hunter (1984; 30 studies), Wiesner and Cronshaw (1988; 160 studies), Huffcutt and Arthur (1994; 114 studies) and McDaniel, Whetzel, Schmidt and Maurer (1994; 245 studies). These meta-analyses covered many different studies done in different countries over different jobs and different time periods, but the results were surprisingly consistent. Results were clear: the validity coefficient for unstructured interviews as predictors of job performance is around $r = .15$ (range .11–.18), while that for structured interviews is around $r = .28$ (range .24–.34). Cook (2004) calculated the overall validity of all interviews over three recent meta-analyses – taking job performance as the common denominator of all criteria examined – to be around $r = .23$.

There may be rather different reactions to this validity coefficient. An optimist might point out that given the many differences in interview technique – some are psychological, some situational, some job related – and the fact that they were attempting to assess very different issues from creativity to Conscientiousness, the validity is impressively high. Indeed, compared to various other job selection methods, this result is rather impressive.

The pessimist, however, may point out that a value of $r = .25$ means in effect an interview is accounting for a paltry 5% in explaining the variance in later work behaviour. However, given the unreliability of the criterion, the unaccounted variance may be as low as 70%, and even seemingly small percentages of variance explained may have very important utility. If, for instance, 5% of the variance in an outcome is explained, the categorical (yes or no) prediction of that outcome would improve from 50% (the chance rate) to 55%, and probably more (as the 5% figure is 5/70 rather than 5/100). That said, given that interviews are used to infer information about candidates' abilities or personality traits, they provide very little unique information about a candidate and show little incremental validity over established psychometric tests (of ability and personality) in the prediction of future job performance (Schmidt & Hunter, 1998).

It is not difficult to list reasons for the relatively low reliability. Essentially, these have to do with three issues: *factors associated with the interviewer, factors associated with the interviewee, and factors associated with the process.*

Another question addressed is how well interviews can predict the results of intelligence, personality, etc. The results in this area suggest they are better at predicting ability than personality, but more interestingly they have incremental validity over and above intelligence and personality tests.

From an interviewer's perspective, low validity may be attributable to individual difference in values, intelligence, perceptiveness, etc. of the various interviewers; the motives of interviewers in the selection process; the training they received; and their understanding of the job itself. Whatever their training, interviewers differ in terms of their natural ability, perceptiveness and courage to make 'thorough but accurate' ratings. From an interviewee's perspective there are two major problems which come under the heading of dissimulation: notably impression management and self-deception. This means in effect not presenting themselves honestly either because of their desire to get the job or not having sufficient self-insight to tell the truth. Thus, the person who is presented at the interviews is not the same as the person at work on the job.

The third factor lies not in the two parties involved, but in the information provided. What criterion/criteria is the interviewer trying to predict? Is there clear, reliable and valid evidence on the criteria? Does the question being rated lead to ceiling effects, or restriction of range? In short, how easy is it for the interviewer to do a good job even if both parties are well briefed and honest?

Cook (2004) offers evidence-based recommendations for improving interview reliability and validity:

1. Select interviewers with talent. As in every aspect of life, some people appear to have the optimal mix of abilities, temperaments and traits to do good interviews. Many studies have demonstrated considerable

interviewer variability. Though it can cause organisational problems, it is recommended that interviewers be elected for this task, which inevitably leads to some being rejected. This inevitably leads to the interesting question of how interviewers are selected. Is the best interviewer selected by interview?

2. Train interviewers in the relevant skills like asking open-ended questions, doing sufficient preparation, etc. It is possible to improve all skills though training, but only within the limits of the ability of the trainee.

3. Be consistent in using the same interviewers for all interviews. This simply avoids unwanted variance. Although, for practical and political reasons it may not always be possible to have the same (well-chosen and well-trained) interviewer for all interviews.

4. Use dyad, board or panel interviewers because they are more reliable. This point does not contradict the previous point. Rather it suggests that a well-chosen, well-trained, perceptive group of interviewers will be more accurate and reliable.

5. Have planned, structured interviews with clarity about precisely what questions to ask. And when and why. It means taking notes, making systematic ratings and later checking interview reliability and validity.

4.1.7 The Cognitive Basis of Interviews

The result of an interview is usually an accept/reject decision. Ideally this process involves collecting, evaluating and integrating specific salient information into a logical algorithm that has shown to be predictive.

However, there is an academic literature on impression formation that has examined experimentally how precisely people select and weight particular pieces of information. Studies looking at the process in selection interviews have shown all too often how interviewers may make up their minds *before* the interview even occurs (based on the application form or CV of the candidate) or too quickly based on first impression (superficial data) or their own personal implicit theories of personality. Equally, they overweigh or over-emphasise negative information or bias information not in line with the algorithm they use.

Early research examined whether information was added or weighted, that is, how people combined positive and negative 'pieces of information' about an individual to come up with some overall rating. Thus, researchers in the area of interpersonal perception examined the way interviews looked for 'favourite cues' or facts they believed particularly diagnostic. Some wondered whether people did 'linear regressions' in their head in the sense that they assigned different importance to certain predictors of a given outcome. The question is how interviewers make configural judgements: what causes them to have multiple cut-off points (e.g. are candidates qualified enough, young enough, friendly enough) or, instead, single disqualifying factors, such as evidence of going to a mental hospital or having taken drugs? Clearly, more research is needed to answer this question.

Social psychologists have also been interested in implicit personality theories, which are concerned with how individual, idiosyncratic, lay theories of personality influence a person's judgement in the interview (Cook, 2016). They have also worked for years on attribution theories, which are concerned with how people attribute social causation, notably whether they explain success and failure in terms of personal or situational factors. In the interview it is common to ask candidates why certain events occurred, i.e. to try to assess their attribution style, but the interviewer also infers causation. Thus, a candidate may be asked why their school results were so different from their university results, or why they seem to change jobs so regularly.

Certainly, understanding how people collect and integrate information in the interview must be central to the whole enterprise.

4.1.7.1   Cognitive Interviewing

Perhaps the most important development in interviewing over the last 25 years is in *cognitive interviewing techniques*. The police and others in the forensic world have really embraced these ideas because of their proven efficacy.

Interviewing is mainly about information exchange. Both parties give and receive information, usually about the past: an event or series of very specific events. – an example of bullying, shoplifting, a fight, how an irate and rude customer was dealt with or about not following some serious work procedures.

Indeed, it can become more like a police, legal or inquisitional interview, which is why the cognitive interview takes place where the actual event to be recalled took place. First, get them into a *similar frame of mind or mood state*. Contextual fit can have a big impact on memory.

Second, *depth and time*. Ask the recaller to report everything that comes to mind, however supposedly trivial or irrelevant: the colour of the customers suit, temperature, lighting and smells, their accent, background noises. Give them time: do not ask leading or closed questions.

Third, *ask for a retell of the story* backwards. From the perspective of the other person, and then an onlooker. Ask the interviewee to imagine what it looked like on camera. Each retelling brings out different information. The picture gets richer, but is it consistent?

Fourth, after the many retellings you may ask some *specific questions*. About, for instance, the person's appearance or mood, perhaps the exact words they used or perhaps the colour or the material some disputed object was made of.

The idea is to get the full story of the event in the words of the interviewee. An uninterrupted narration of the incident. The idea is to get it with few distractions. The interviewer's role is almost that of an appreciative enquirer. Listen attentively. Help the interviewee concentrate. Assist the interviewee in 'going back' to the event and 'reliving' it as much as possible.

Cognitive interviewing certainly takes (a lot) more time, effort and concentration on the part of the interviewer. There are no guarantees. But the data are clear. When interviewed this way, often more is recalled *and* the relationship between interviewer and interviewee is much better. A no brainer then?

4.1.8   Automated Digital Interviews

Traditional interviews are very expensive in terms of time and money. Usually the interviewee has to travel, sometimes long distances to be interviewed by one or more individuals who have to make time for the process. The outcome may be a set of notes, a relatively simple score sheet or simply a yes/no recommendation. Unless audio-recorded, there is no reliable data about what went on during the interview, which could be challenged in a court of law.

Even with structured interviews where people are asked the same questions, it is possible that the verbal tone and non-verbal behaviour of the interviewer could be importantly or subtly different eliciting different reactions in interviewees.

The advent of automated interviews offers many advantages over more traditional interviews. Usually this involves an interviewee responding on camera to a set of standardised, pre-recorded (text, audio or video) questions. These interviews are recorded and analysed by a whole range of techniques, ranging from state-of-the-art AI technology or more modest techniques. Indeed, this methodology has become so widespread that various HR technology providers offer their services to do this.

From the recorded interviews it is possible to measure a very wide range of particularly interesting variables such as facial expressions, vocabulary and word speed and latency of response. They might even be used to measure body temperature changes, and, in time, other physiological factors. These interviews are recorded and thus may be used at any time to link data from them to any subsequent behaviours.

Everything depends on a number of things. *First*, typical problems with interviews: the honesty of the interviewees, impression management, acquiescence all of which make the interview unreliable in the sense that the data are inaccurate and unreliable. *Second*, that the questions asked are perceptive and high yield. *Third*, that of the many variables measured, the most relevant (to the selection task) are chosen.

One paradoxical finding at the moment is, however, reactions to digital interviews (Wood et al., 2020). A number of studies have shown that candidates do not like them and that they lead to a negative perception of the organisation (Langer et al., 2019, 2020). Participants report feeling less in control and that they have an impression of lower social presence and fairness. Interviewees express concerns with privacy and seem less attracted to organisations that use these techniques. Langer et al. (2020), in a study where students responded online to voice recordings, showed that these participants engaged in less deceptive impression management, provided shorter answers and felt that they had fewer opportunities to perform at their best.

Early studies in this area showed that the more positive the interviewee was about the usefulness and ease of use with the technology the happier they were with it (Brenner et al., 2016).

Thus, it seems that as this technology becomes more sophisticated, user-friendly and widespread, the more it will be accepted by the candidate.

4.1.9   Fairness, Bias and the Law

The fact that one is interacting with another person has led researchers, clients and lawyers to suggest that all sorts of biases occur in the interview, particularly gender, race and generation, as well as accent, appearance, body shape and sexual preference, all of which have been researched (see Chapter 2).

Factors possibly irrelevant to the job influence interviewers. These factors play a less relevant role in other methods – i.e. completing psychometric tests and biodata. Thus, the interview may seem particularly susceptible to bias. Studies show clearly the more interviews are planned and structured, the more likely these biases are reduced. However, they are never completely eliminated. Hence the legal issues of interviews.

Most developed countries have legislated against forms of discrimination in terms individuals and organisations try not to let appearance and social background influence their decision-making.

There is plenty of evidence to suggest that interviews in the past have been, and no doubt will continue in the future to be, systematically biased against ethnic minority groups, older people and women (Cook, 2016). This tends to occur where raters are not trained or interviews are not structured. All sorts of extraneous factors like the perfume a person wears at the interview have been shown to influence ratings.

The literature is essentially driven by two main areas of research: one well established, namely the social-psychological literature on discrimination, favouritism and prejudice; the other, more recent research on socio-legal features of selection. Studies on the legal and illegal aspects of selection have nearly all come out of the USA, whose reputation for litigation is well known. Inevitably, one has to acknowledge many national differences in legal procedures and the law itself, suggesting that studies are less likely to discriminate in terms of age, gender, race and religion. Whilst there are no laws about lookism (discriminating by physical appearance), weightism (discriminating by body mass index) or classism (discriminating by dress or accent), there are reasons why selectors should pay attention to this as a potential problem.

4.1.10   The Personality of Interviewers

There are countless books for interviewing professionals on what traits to look for, what questions to ask and how to interpret the answers to those tricky, perspicacious questions. But there is no explicit recognition that the personality of the interviewer may play a very significant role in the whole interview process. Do different types/personalities make different decisions on the same people given the same criteria? Presumably, they know what they are looking for and have agreed specific criteria in terms of a candidate's abilities, attitudes, experiences, personality and values. So why is there ever any disagreement? Were the criteria not clear? Did the questions not elicit data to satisfy the criteria? Often both of these are true. But there remains one other factor – differences in the personalities of the interviewers have to be factored into this equation.

Extraverts usually enjoy interviewing. They are 'people people', sociable and eager to be amused and entertained and to entertain. Extraverts probably talk too much and listen too little. They may not do their preparation as thoroughly as they should. They may be impatient and inattentive in long interviews. Also, they are attracted to vivacious (if vacuous) candidates.

Introverts make very different, and often diffident, interviewers. They pause more, seeming hesitant, when they are processing information. They can find the whole process tiring and intimidating and feel more for those candidates who are similar to themselves. They usually take the data gathering more seriously and see the whole interview less as a social occasion than a semi-scientific exercise. Certainly, the introverted candidate probably gets a 'better deal' (more favourable hearing) from the introverted interviewer. The trouble is that introverts eschew, while extraverts volunteer for, interviewing assignments.

What of the 'sensitive' (**neurotic**) interviewer? They are stress prone and do not like people in general, whom they see as threatening. They can be moody and critical, wary and judgemental. Neurotic interviewers can easily feel threatened by the potential 'mover and shaker'. They worry about things: the future, the present; their reputation, their security; their ability, their worthiness, etc. They listen carefully to the candidates' answers to questions about work-life balance, diversity, counselling and other issues. If they do not like what they hear in response to salient as well as less relevant questions, their instinct is to push the rejection button.

Emotionally stable interviewers, like stable employees, are better news. They are less irritable and moody and better able to weigh the information. They worry less about what might go wrong and cope with all the little dramas at interviews well. They tend to be calm, focused and rational.

Agreeable interviewers are warm, empathic and trusting. They are for the most part likeable. They understand that interviews can be stressful. They are concerned about making the candidate comfortable, relaxed and able to be their real selves. They are slow to chide and swift to bless and believe they get the best out of others by giving them a chance.

Disagreeable interviewers believe you understand people best by 'putting them on the spot'. They treat the interview as a political interview. They cross-examine individuals, often pushing them to give details of success and failure which their CV overlooks. They are hard to please: cynical, tough, world-weary and they care little for interviewee comfort.

Conscientious interviewers are not only conscientious about how they approach the task of interviewing, but also what they are looking for. Hard work is a virtue. Some are even prepared to 'trade off' ability for the work ethic: preferring the loyal plodder to the capricious wunderkind. Conscientious interviewers are concerned that the applicant follows orders, obeys rules and has a sense of duty.

Less conscientious interviewers want to have fun. They tend to be less achievement orientated, less careful and with a much weaker work ethic. All that 'postponement of gratification' stuff never works with them. They prefer what the Freudians call 'the pleasure principle'. They seek out playmates more than solid and reliable colleagues.

The ambition and achievement needs of interviewers are also relevant. Paradoxically, both the low and high ambitious interviewer may be intimidated by the obviously ambitious candidate. Those with low ambitions can feel intimidated by newly minted MBAs who want to be on the board at 30 and retired at 40 years old. The highly ambitious see a potential threat.

What of the **abilities** of the interviewer? How are bright, educated interviewers different from their less-talented peers? Another paradox: the clever prefer discriminating questions, the dim prefer 'clever' questions. Brighter people tend to have a bigger vocabulary and think fast. They ask good questions which sort the wheat from the chaff. The less bright and less-educated interviewers might rehearse 'killer' questions that make them appear intelligent, even if they cannot process the answers. They can be intimidated in group interviews and behave badly. They often have 'crackpot' theories, refreshingly evidence free about desirable characteristics in candidates.

The interview is a social process. It can be a sophisticated intellectual theatrical show, a hall of mirrors, a game of bluff and counter-bluff. There is no doubt that there is a lot of 'gut feeling' going on in both parties, despite all their training.

> **First**, acknowledge that the interviewers' make-up (ability and personality) does inevitably play a part.
>
> **Second**, try to work out how specific interviewers react to particular candidates.
>
> **Third**, use multiple interviewers but particularly those with the ability and personality profiles found among those actually doing the job in question.
>
> **Fourth,** where possible, encourage these insights in interviewers.
>
> **Fifth,** choose (test and train) interviewers who are bright, stable and conscientious.

4.1.11 Conclusion

It is almost unthinkable for a person to be selected for any type of job without an interview. Some interviewees 'pull out of an application' after the interview as they did not like what they saw. They did not feel the job was for them: they did not feel they were a good fit for the organisation or the people in it. Some prepare obsessively for interviews; others wing it. Some are very nervous; others enjoy the whole experience. The same is true of the interviewers.

It is argued that a good interview can have a validity of $r = .4$, which according to Cook (2016), make it 'a moderately good, disguised mental ability test'. As noted earlier there are certain factors that are known to increase the validity of an interview, which are advisedly followed.

REFERENCES

Basch, J., & Melchers, K. (2019). Fair and flexible?! Explanations can improve applicant reactions toward asynchronous video interviews. *Personnel Assessment and Decisions*, 3, 1–11.

Horn, R., & Behrend, T. (2017). Video killed the interview star. Personnel Assessment and Decisions, *1*, 51–59.

Melchers, K., Ingold, P., Wilhelmy, A., Kleinmann, M. (2015). Beyond validity: Shedding light on the social situation in employment interviews. In Nikolaou

& J Osstrom (Eds.), *Employee Recruitment, Selection and Assessment* (pp. 154–171). London: Psychology Press.

Roulin, N., Bourdage, J., & Wingate, T. (2019). Who is conducting "better" employment interviews. *Personnel Assessment and Decisions, 1,* 37–48.

4.2   PERSONALITY TESTS

What are they?
They are a series of questions which have been chosen to measure a particular trait (i.e. Extraversion). They differ enormously in length, response format and psychometric properties.

How do they work?
They are based on the assumption that most people observe and understand themselves well and if asked questions, will accurately and honestly respond to them. This shows consistent behavioural tendencies which can be grouped into independent traits.

What of the evidence?
Personality tests have been extensively investigated and been shown to be reliable and valid under particular circumstances; however, they differ widely.

Practical problems: cost, ethics, politics
Most applicants are very used to doing personality tests. Some are very well known, others very obscure. Costs vary, though are coming down on all tests. There is evidence of small group (age, race, sex, culture) differences which can be dealt with in various ways.

Recommendations for use
It would be very unwise not to use some self-report data, though it is important to ensure it is valid. Decide on what traits relate to work success and then seek out the test that best measures those.

4.2.1   *Introduction*

There are well over 10,000 personality tests in print: some suggest more than 10 times that number. They differ enormously in terms of *what* they are trying to measure and *how* they measure it. Sometimes there may be 20–30 measures all attempting to measure the same personality traits. Others are quite unique, in both what they are trying to measure and how they do it.

The debate about the usefulness of using personality tests in selection waxes and wanes. Cynics and sceptics complain about consultant greed and test costs, and others about the fact that people tend to lie on the tests. Supporters and apologists point to the costs of making bad decisions and the validity evidence of tests.

Although the assessment of these characteristics is complex, a wide range of measurement instruments have been developed and tested, with relatively solid measurement properties and a range of applications. What is more, these instruments are more efficient than those designed to measure cognitive skills, with some of them being able to provide a broad assessment of basic personality dimensions in just one minute of testing time.

Kankaras (2017) noted personality characteristics shape human behaviour and influence a wide range of life events or outcomes. They do so not only through their immediate effects on life outcomes, but also through their indirect effects on other important personal factors and intermediate life events, such as the development of cognitive capacities, the attainment of educational qualifications or the formation of a family.

> 'However, it is important to be aware of the complexity of the relationships between personality characteristics and other personal and situational factors in their influence on important life outcomes. This dynamic interplay between complex task requirements, constantly changing contexts and often conflicting individual and social goals and preferences makes it less likely that any single personality characteristic will be appropriate or influential across different situations, cultures or eras. Thus, care is needed when evaluating the relative importance of personality characteristics, both in relation with one another or when compared to other personal or external factors' (p. 86).

A central feature of the argument is about how much personality counts in explaining business success and failure. Robert Hogan in his book *Personality and the Fate of Organisations* makes a very strong case for the personality of leaders being extremely influential factors in business success and failure. Judge and Zapata (2015) made some simple but important points about the role of personality at work. They suggested a dozen factors where personality makes all the difference:

(1) The impact of decisions on co-workers/results, or 'whether the decisions an employee makes impact the results of co-workers, clients, or the company'. Thus, in some jobs (e.g. aviation inspector) the way they do the job (as a function of their personality) can make all the difference

(2) The consequences of error, or 'how serious the results would be if the worker made a mistake that was not readily correctable'. Not so important for the librarian or language teacher, all important for the surgeon and ship's captain

(3) The responsibility for health/safety of others, or 'the degree to which the employee is responsible for the health and safety of others'. Of little relevance to a proofreader but all important for a dentist or ambulance driver

(4) The unstructured (vs. structured) work, or 'the extent to which the job allows the worker to determine tasks, priorities, and goals' (unstructured work) versus 'the degree to which the job is structured for the worker' (structured work)

(5) The freedom to make decisions, defined as 'the degree to which the job offers considerable decision-making freedom, without supervision'

(6) The variety, which refers to 'the extent to which the job requires the employee to do many different things at work, using a variety of skills and talents' (low scores reflect little variety, high scores reflect significant variety)

(7) The independence in completing work, where 'the job requires developing one's own ways of doing things, guiding oneself with little or no supervision, and depending on oneself to get things done', as opposed to working under a predetermined set of rules, under close supervision or in dependency on others for guidance

(8) The attention to detail requirement, or 'the extent to which the job requires being careful about detail and thoroughness in completing work tasks'

(9) The social skills requirement, defined as 'the degree to which an occupation frequently involves working with, communicating with, and teaching people'

(10) The level of competition requirement, referring to 'the extent to which the job requires the worker to compete or to be aware of competitive pressures'

(11) The innovation/creativity requirement, which is 'the extent to which the job requires creativity and alternative thinking to develop new ideas for and answers to work-related problems'

(12) When dealing with unpleasant or angry people, or 'how frequently employees have to deal with unpleasant, angry, or discourteous individuals'

The bottom line in this complex and very hotly debated area is this: the validity of personality tests in predicting future work performance depends on (a) the test, (b) the criteria, (c) the population sample. The tests are at their most useful/accurate when a good, well-validated test is used, and the criteria are clear, well measured, and theoretically related to the trait being measured.

As a result of some 100 years of research and disagreement, researchers have (for the most part) agreed on what is the underlying structure (i.e. personality, periodic table) of traits.

The question is what sort of questions have been asked. Consider three:

i. *Are people at different levels of an organisation different in their personality profile?*

A number of studies using different tests have compared people at different levels, from the supervisor level through management and senior management to chief executive. Despite this, there remains a major issue that is not easily solved – whether the person's personality profile in some way was responsible for their level. Thus, because Conscientious people are more reliable, responsible and productive, and less Neurotic people less stress prone, these traits lead to greater productivity, which is rewarded by promotion or appointment to senior levels. On the other hand, it is possible that personality may change as a person moves up levels in organisations learning to become better organised and less stressed. The studies in the area inevitably give equivocal results, though it seems that more senior people tend to be more Extraverted and Conscientious and less Agreeable and Neurotic.

ii. *Is there evidence that personality profile is related to both the speed and number of promotions at work?*

It is possible to do either a retrospective or a prospective study to determine how long it takes people to get promoted to middle or senior management within any organisation as well as between them. This is about leader emergence rather than effectiveness

iii. *Is personality linked to salary?*

Many factors dictate a person's salary. These include the type of job they do (bankers tend to get paid more than bar staff; doctors more than dock workers) as well as their seniority and age. However, it is possible to take many confounding factors into account and demonstrate that indeed personality is related to personal wealth as a function of salary.

The central question for the researcher is to describe and explain the mechanism or process whereby personality traits are related to various related aspects of work success. Most researchers believe that personality is related to various specific behaviours that directly impact on work productivity:

a. *Lifestyle*: these refer to diet and personal habits, including exercise. Thus, traits influence mental and physical health, which impacts on such things as efficiency and absenteeism, which impacts on productivity at work.
b. *Risk taking*: this includes things outside work, such as driving and hobbies, but also risk taking in the workplace.
c. *Stress*: this includes the extent to which people cause and experience personal stress, which can have many consequences.
d. *Social support*: this includes a person's ability to establish personal bonds, support networks and succeed in teams.

It is self-evident to any observer that people have unique characteristics and preferences which are consistent across situations and stable over time. This is called personality and it is therefore very useful to know about and assess in the workplace.

In this chapter we will focus on 'bright-side' normal personality, 'dark-side' personality disorders, personality and motivation and, finally, personality and integrity.

4.2.2 Bright-Side Normal Personality

Psychologists have fought each other for around 100 years over the basic dimensions of personality. Some argued there were three, others five and some even sixteen. For many years, the *Gigantic Three* of Hans Eysenck dominated the research but this was replaced by the now widely accepted *Big Five* of Costa and McCrae. There remains a lot of overlap between them.

The Eysenckian model still has three super-factors: Psychoticism, Extraversion, and Neuroticism (known as P-E-N). Eysenck was quite convinced that these three conceptual and descriptive categories are necessary and sufficient for a thorough understanding of individual differences in personality. On the other hand, the Big Five model, which is now very widely established, has been employed in most studies looking at personality at work.

However, the model that has dominated the area now for around 30 years is the Big Five model (see Table 4.3 and 4.4).

Table 4.3 *Labels used by various authors to refer to the so-called Big Five factors in personality*

1	2	3	4	5
Social Adaptability	Conformity	Will to achieve	Emotional control	Enquiring intellect
Surgency	Agreeableness	Conscientiousness	Emotionality	Culture
Assertiveness	Likeability	Responsibility	Emotionality	Intelligence
Extraversion	Friendly compliance	Will to achieve	Neuroticism	Intellect
Extraversion	Agreeableness	Conscientiousness	Neuroticism	Openness to experience
Power	Love	Work	Affect	Intellect

Table 4.4 *Examples of adjectives, Q-sort items and cost benefits defining the five factors of personality*

Factor	Factor Definers		Positive Benefits	Negative Costs
	Adjectives	Items		
Extraversion	Active	Talkative	Big social networks	Accidents and risk-taking
	Assertive	Skilled in play, humour	Relationship and mating	Impulsivity and poor decision-making
	Energetic	Rapid personal tempo	success	
	Enthusiastic	Facially, gesturally	Explorer of opportunities	Relationship instability
	Outgoing	expressive	Happiness	
	Talkative	Behave assertively		
		Gregarious		
Neuroticism	Anxious	Thin-skinned	Hyper vigilant	Poor mental health
	Self-pitying	Brittle ego defences	Achievement-striving	Stress sensitivity
	Tense	Self-defeating	Emotional sensitivity	Poor physical health
	Touchy	Basically anxious	Competitiveness	
	Unstable	Concerned with		
	Worrying	adequacy		
		Fluctuating moods		
Openness	Artistic	Wide range of interests	Social Attractiveness	Mental illness
	Curious	Introspective	Creativity	Social exclusion
	Imaginative	Unusual though	Flexibility	Bizarre belief system and
	Insightful	processes	Change orientated	lifestyle

	Adjectives	Description	Positive correlates	Negative correlates
	Original Wide interests	Values intellectual matters Judges in unconventional terms Aesthetically reactive		
Agreeableness	Appreciative Forgiving Generous Kind Sympathetic Trusting	Not critical, sceptical Behaves in a giving way Sympathetic, considerate Arouses liking Warm, compassionate Basically trustful	Psychological mindedness Social networks Strong relationships Valued group member	Vulnerable to exploitation Failure to maximise personal advantages Too conflict-avoidant Low assertiveness
Conscientiousness	Efficient Organised Planning ability Reliable Responsible Thorough	Dependable, responsible Productive Able to delay gratification Not self-indulgent Behaves ethically Has high aspirational level	Long-term planning Longer life expectancy Good citizenship Dependable and dutiful team member	Obsessionality and perfectionism Rigidity with poor flexibility Slow to respond

Labels in the rows are (in order) from Fisk (1949), Norman (1963), Borgatta (1964), Digman (1990) and Costa and McCrae (1985). The final row provides a characterisation by Peabody and Goldberg (1989) of the life domain to which the trait pertains.

There have been as many speculations in studies that have investigated the relationship between the Big Five dimensions and different work outcomes which could be classified as positive or negative. Table 4.5 presents some of these hypotheses. This is not a meta-analysis, though hopefully in time that might be done. Three points about the table are noteworthy. First, the strongest and most consistent personality correlate of work-related behaviour is Conscientiousness. The second most consistent predictor is Neuroticism (low Adjustment). Third, Extraversion seems to be related to both positive and negative work outcomes.

2.1 **Extraversion** is perhaps the best known and is at the very 'heart' of many theories of personality and well understood by laypeople. Introversion–Extraversion is a dimension from very high to very low. So, most of us are *ambiverts*: in the middle and not strongly the one or the other. Extraverts are seen as more likeable, interesting and popular; introverts more honest, stable and reliable. Extraverts are attracted to 'people jobs' such as sales and the service industry and do well.

Extraverts are less distracted than introverts. The open-plan office, the mobile phone, the relentless meetings all favour extraverts who like stimulation, whereas introverts are distracted by people, noise or stimulants of any kind. They are less comfortable, less efficient and less helpful in the noisy world of work.

Introverts take longer to retrieve information, longer to marshal their ideas and thoughts and longer to respond to the demands of the world around them. From a motivational point of view, we know extraverts respond better to carrots and care less about sticks, while introverts are less motivated by rewards and more sensitive to, and inhibited by, threats of punishments.

Table 4.5 *Possible relationships between personality traits and work outcomes*

| | Positive | | | | Negative | | |
	Creativity	Engagement	Productivity	Promotion	Absenteeism	Accidents	Derailment	Turnover
N	+	–	–	–	+++	+	+	+
E	+	+	+	++	+	+++	+	+
O	+++	+	+++	+++			+	+
A		+		–	–	–	–	–
C		+++	+++	+++	– – –		–	–

People like extraverts because they tend to be more socially confident and comfortable.

There have always been serious known *disadvantages* of being a (strong) extravert:

Accidents: Extraverts are risk takers. They drive fast and choose risky recreational activities. They trade off accuracy for speed.

Crime: Extraverts are sociable and impulsive. They are excitement seekers interested in novel experiences, which often leads them to be poorer learners than introverts at many tasks, including the acquisition of general social rules. They can be difficult to train and be rebellious.

Learning: Extraverts do well at primary school but less well at university. The idea of sitting in a quiet room for hours learning complicated abstract ideas just does not suit the extravert.

Sex: Extraverts tend to be less prudish and nervous than their introverted cousins and more excited and satisfied with sex. But extraverts are more likely to have premarital sex and more likely to experiment.

Most people are able to accurately rate themselves and others on Introversion and Extraversion.

2.2 **Neuroticism** is also called 'negative affectivity' or 'poor emotional adjustment'. Researchers believe it is based on activation thresholds in the sympathetic nervous system or visceral brain. This is the part of the brain that is responsible for the fight-or-flight response in the face of danger.

Neurotic persons have a low activation threshold: when confronted with even mild stressors or anxiety inducing situations, they quickly and easily experience negative emotions and moods and sometimes become seriously upset. These manifestations can range from physiological changes in heart rate and blood pressure, cold hands, sweating and muscular tension to feelings of apprehension and nervousness and to the full effects of fear and anxiety.

In contrast to Neurotics (or emotionally unstable and labile persons), their emotionally stable peers have a much higher activation threshold, and thus will experience negative affect only when confronted by major stressors. Such individuals tend to be calm even in situations that could be described as anxiety inducing or pressure laden. They are stable not moody, robust not vulnerable, hardy not overly sensitive.

Many higher-order theories of personality – like the Eysenckian Giant Three, the Big Five, the six-factor HEXACO model or the seven-factor Hogan Personality Inventory – describe and measure Neuroticism at the Domain, but also at the Facet level, though there remains very little agreement in the description of these facets. For instance, the *Eysenck Personality Profiler* (EPP) has six N facets labelled: Inferiority, Unhappiness, Anxiety, Dependence, Hypochondria and Obsessiveness; the *HEXACO* model has four facets labelled Fearfulness, Anxiety, Dependence and Sentimentality; and the *Multidimensional Personality Questionnaire* (MPQ) has three facets labelled Stress Reaction, Alienation and Aggression.

Even the name of the domain changes: for the EPP it is *Neuroticism*, for the HEXACO it is *Emotionality* and for the MPQ it is *Negative Emotional Temperament*. This indicates subtle but important differences in the conceptualisation of Neuroticism.

People who score high on Neuroticism are prone to anxiety, depression and psychosomatic illness and hence higher levels of stress at work. However, they are very vigilant and able to pick up the emotional tones around them better than stable individuals.

2.3 **Agreeableness.** Trait Agreeableness is associated with being altruistic, appreciative, compliant, trusting and tender minded. People high in Agreeableness have been shown to be generous, kind, sympathetic and warm. Agreeableness facets include easy to live with, sensitive, caring, likes people and no hostility. Others have suggested facets labelled forgiveness, gentleness, flexibility, patience, and altruism vs. antagonism.

To some extent Agreeableness has been the 'Cinderella' trait of the Big Five, as it seems less related to many education, health and work outcomes. Also, doubt has been expressed as to whether it is a trait (as opposed to a social desirability or social-relational concept).

Furthermore, it is often seen to be a disadvantage to be high in Agreeableness. Those low, rather than high, in Agreeableness have been associated with success as business leaders.

Studies on Agreeableness in children have demonstrated that it predicts academic performance and social competence. Agreeableness is often highly valued in the workplace. People like to work with others who are helpful, kind, and empathic. They tend to be liked and valued. However, the workplace is often a competitive and 'win-lose' philosophy environment where those who are more disagreeable, egocentric and tough minded do best.

2.4 **Openness to Experience.** Of all the Big Five personality traits, Openness to Experience is often shown as the strongest correlate of ability, particularly creativity and intelligence. Openness is associated with having a vivid imagination and an active fantasy life; a deep appreciation for art and beauty; a receptivity to one's own and other's emotions; a willingness to try new experiences; intellectual curiosity and a readiness to examine political, social and religious values.

People high in Openness have been shown to be unconventional, questioning and emotionally literate. Other personality theories and systems have described Openness as Intellect or Culture and had different ideas about the facets of the super-factor or domain. These include Aesthetic Appreciation, Inquisitiveness, Creativity and Unconventionality. Whilst there is confusion and disagreement about facets of Openness, there is agreement that it is a stable trait that reflects intellectual curiosity, imaginativeness and inquisitiveness.

Those interested in personality correlates of educational, health and occupational outcomes have tended to show that of the Big Five traits Neuroticism and Conscientiousness account for most of the variance, with Openness being related to very specific issues like aesthetic preferences or leisure pursuits. In most individual difference studies personality traits are the predictor variables and some salient beliefs or behaviours the criterion variables, but in this study the trait Openness is the criterion or outcome variable. One relevant theory is

Cattell's (1971) investment theory, which suggests personality and fluid intelligence contribute to the development of crystallised intelligence. Our research question is what are the early determinants, including intelligence, of Openness in adulthood? Few studies have done this because of the difficulty in obtaining longitudinal data, though there are some recent exceptions (Furnham & Cheng, 2015).

Studies have used different measures of both Openness and intelligence and have all tended to show a significant positive correlation (Chamorro-Premuzic et al., 2005; DeYoung et al., 2014).

2.5 **Conscientiousness.** This is associated with being efficient, organised, reliable and responsible. People high in Conscientiousness have been shown to be achievement oriented, competent, dependable and productive. It is not surprising therefore that parents, teachers and employers value the trait and attempt to shape and encourage it in their children, students and employees. Students who are more Conscientious earned higher university grades than their intelligence scores would predict.

There are consistent findings from correlational studies that show a very small, but significant positive, association between Conscientiousness and educational achievement and occupational prestige. There is also some evidence to suggest sex differences in Conscientiousness, which has been used to explain why females outperform males in school grades despite the evidence of very small differences in intelligence between the genders (Furnham, 2008).

The taxonomists of Conscientiousness argue that there are eight distinguishable but related parts:

Industriousness: This is about working hard, always putting in an effort and frequently exceeding expectations. In all work places people push themselves (and others) very hard to succeed.

Perfectionism: This is aiming for high quality, no mistakes, no rejection of work. It is about being detail orientated and striving always to be the best.

Tidiness: This is strong preference for order, regularity and the 'everything in its place' philosophy. Conscientious people have a strong aversion to disorder and mess. They like things correctly filed and tasks completed.

Procrastination refrainment: The really Conscientious are not easily distracted or have difficulty getting started. They don't put off unpleasant tasks to do the easy ones. They go to work at once: they prioritise and spend their time and effort wisely.

Control preference: This should not be confused with control freakery. It's about being planful, thoughtful and decisive. It is also about understanding the role of authority. The opposite is rushed, rash impulsive behaviour.

Caution: Because of the above the Conscientious person is careful to avoid mistakes, get their facts right and think ahead. They think before they speak; they choose their words carefully.

Task planning: The Conscientious person is planful. They carefully devise a plan, a schedule, a considered path. They stick to it and require others to do likewise. They like to work out an efficient routine and stick to it.

Perseverance: The Conscientious deal well with frustrations and set-backs. They don't give up easily, they don't avoid responsibility, they don't lose interest. They are calm under pressure.

There are many measures of the Big Five, including the NEO-PI-R (Costa & McCrae, 1985), which is a 240-item inventory, assessing the FFM Domains of Neuroticism (N), Extraversion (E), Openness to experience (O), Agreeableness (A) and Conscientiousness (C), with 6 Facets (8 items each) structured under 5 Domains. Its psychometric properties and validity have been well documented cross-culturally. There is also a very simple 10-item measure used by researchers called the TIPI (Gosling et al., 2003)

4.2.3   High-Flyer Personality

There have been many attempts over the years to develop models and measures of 'high-flyers' or talented people who succeed in organisations. The idea is to identify those abilities, motives and traits that are, in most organisations, clearly linked to occupational success.

MacRae and Furnham (2014) have developed the High Potential Traits Inventory (HPTI), a measure of personality traits directly relevant to workplace behaviours, thoughts and perceptions of the self and others at work. The HPTI can be used to investigate which personality traits in the workplace might predict career success and

thus predict high potential (MacRae & Furnham, 2014). Six scientifically validated personality traits:

1. Conscientiousness – planning, organisation, strong work ethic,
   achievement drive.
2. Openness/curiosity – openness to new information, adopting
   new approaches.
3. Approach to risk – willingness to confront difficult situations, thrive during
   adversity, solve difficult problems, have difficult conversations.
4. Stress reactivity – resilient to the impact of stressors, not overly worried
   about others' judgement.
5. Tolerance of ambiguity – approach to ambiguous situations and
   information, make use of mixed information, cope (and thrive)
   with ambivalence.
6. Competitiveness – need to achieve, drive to exceed one's own or another's
   performance, desire for control.

The test obviously has an overlap with the Big Five, but data
suggest it predicts work-related behaviour better than the Big Five.

4.2.4 The Personality Disorders

Psychologists are interested in personality traits, psychiatrists in personality disorders. Psychologists interested in personality have made
great strides in describing, taxonomising and explaining the mechanisms and processes in normal personality functioning. Psychiatrists
also talk about personality functioning. They talk about personality
disorders that are typified by early onset (recognisable in children and
adolescents), pervasive effects (on all aspects of life) and relatively
poor prognosis (that is difficult to cure).

Both argue that the personality factors relate to *cognitive,
affective and social aspects of functioning*. It is where a person's
behaviour 'deviates, markedly' from the expectations of the individual's culture where the disorder is manifested. The psychiatric
manual is very clear that 'odd behaviour' is not simply an expression
of habits, customs, religious or political values professed or shown by
a people of particular cultural origin.

Psychiatrists and psychologists share some simple assumptions with respect to personality. Both argue for the *stability* of personality. The DSM criteria talk of 'enduring pattern', 'inflexible and pervasive' and 'stable and of long duration'. The DSM manuals note that personality disorders all have a long history and have an onset no later than early adulthood. Moreover, there are some gender differences: thus, the anti-social disorder is more likely to be diagnosed in men while the borderline, histrionic and dependent personality is more likely to be found in women.

One of the most important ways to differentiate personal style from personality disorder is flexibility. There are lots of difficult people at work but relatively few whose rigid, maladaptive behaviours mean they continually have disruptive, troubled lives. It is their *inflexible, repetitive, poor stress-coping responses* that are marks of disorder.

Personality disorders influence the *sense of self* – the way people think and feel about themselves and how other people see them. The disorders often powerfully influence *interpersonal relations at work*. They reveal themselves in how people 'complete tasks, take and/or give orders, make decisions, plan, handle external and internal demands, take or give criticism, obey rules, take and delegate responsibility, and co-operate with people' (Oldham & Morris, 1991, p. 24). The anti-social, obsessive, compulsive, passive-aggressive and dependent types are particularly problematic in the workplace.

People with personality disorders have difficulty expressing and understanding emotions. It is the intensity with which they express them and their variability that makes them odd. More importantly they often have serious problems with self-control.

Many others have been influenced by the usefulness of the DSM classification of the personality disorders. In order to explain and describe these disorders other writers have changed the names to make them more interpretable to a wider audience. Table 4.7 describes each Personality Disorder from the DSM Manual as well as from the Hogan (HDS) test manual.

There is a higher-order, three-fold classification based both on theory and research. This makes things a little easier as one can concentrate on 3 rather than 10–13 disorders.

Table 4.6 *Different labels for personality disorders*

DSM-IV personality disorder	Hogan and Hogan (1997)	Oldham and Morris (1991)	Miller (2008)	Dotlich and Cairo (2003)	Moscosco and Salgado (2004)
Borderline	Excitable	Mercurial	Reactors	Volatility	Ambivalent
Paranoid	Sceptical	Vigilant	Vigilantes	Habitual	Suspicious
Avoidant	Cautious	Sensitive	Shrinkers	Excessive caution	Shy
Schizoid	Reserved	Solitary	Oddballs	Aloof	Lone
Passive-aggressive	Leisurely	Leisurely	Spoilers	Passive resistance	Pessimistic
Narcissistic	Bold	Self-Confident	Preeners	Arrogance	Egocentric
Antisocial	Mischievous	Adventurous	Predators	Mischievous	Risky
Histrionic	Colourful	Dramatic	Emoters	Melodramatic	Cheerful
Schizotypal	Imaginative	Idiosyncratic	Creativity and vision	Eccentric	Eccentric
Obsessive-compulsive	Diligent	Conscientious	Detailers	Perfectionistic	Reliable
Dependent	Dutiful	Devoted	Clingers	Eager to please	Submitted

Table 4.7 *The DSM-IV and the HDS*

DSM Labels	Theme	PROFILE		HDS	
		Issues	Theme	Scale	Theme
Borderline	Inappropriate anger; unstable and intense relationships alternating between idealisation and devaluation	Unstable Relationships	Flighty; inconsistent; forms intense albeit sudden enthusiasms and disenchantments for people or projects	Excitable	Moody and hard to please; intense, but short-lived enthusiasm for people, projects or things
Paranoid	Distrustful and suspicious of others; motives are interpreted as malevolent	Argumentative	Suspicious of others; sensitive to criticism; expects to be mistreated	Sceptical	Cynical, distrustful, and doubting other's true intentions
Avoidant	Social inhibition; feelings of inadequacy and hypersensitivity to criticism or rejection	Fear of Failure	Dread of being criticised or rejected; tends to be excessively cautious; unable to make decisions	Cautious	Reluctant to take risks for fear of being rejected or negatively evaluated
Schizoid	Emotional coldness and detachment from social relationships; indifferent to praise and criticism	Interpersonal Insensitivity	Aloof; cold; imperceptive; ignores social feedback	Reserved	Aloof, detached, and uncommunicative; lacking interest in or awareness of the feelings of others

Passive-aggressive	Passive resistance to adequate social and occupational performance; irritated when asked to do something he/she does not want to	Passive-aggressive	Sociable, but resists others through procrastination and stubbornness	Leisurely	Independent; ignoring people's requests and becoming irritated or argumentative if they persist
Narcissistic	Arrogant and haughty behaviours or attitudes; grandiose sense of self-importance and entitlement	Arrogance	Self-absorbed; typically loyal only to himself/herself and his/her own best interests	Bold	Unusually self-confident; feelings of grandiosity and entitlement; overvaluation of one's capabilities
Antisocial	Disregard for the truth; impulsivity and failure to plan ahead; failure to conform with social norms	Untrustworthiness	Impulsive; dishonest; selfish; motivated by pleasure; ignoring the rights of others	Mischievous	Enjoying risk taking and testing limits; needing excitement; manipulative, deceitful, cunning and exploitative
Histrionic	Excessive emotionality and attention seeking; self-dramatising, theatrical and exaggerated emotional expression	Attention seeking	Motivated by a need for attention and a desire to be in the spotlight	Colourful	Expressive, animated, and dramatic; wanting to be noticed and needing to be the centre of attention

Table 4.7 (*cont.*)

DSM Labels	Theme	PROFILE		HDS	
		Issues	Theme	Scale	Theme
Schizotypal	Odd beliefs or magical thinking; behaviour or speech that is odd, eccentric or peculiar	No common sense	Unusual or eccentric attitudes; exhibits poor judgement relative to education and intelligence	Imaginative	Acting and thinking in creative and sometimes odd or unusual ways
Obsessive-compulsive	Preoccupations with orderliness, rules, perfectionism, and control; over-conscientious and inflexible	Perfectionism	Methodical; meticulous; attends so closely to details that he/she may have trouble with priorities	Diligent	Meticulous, precise, and perfectionistic; inflexible about rules and procedures; critical of others' performance
Dependent	Difficulty making everyday decisions without excessive advise and reassurance; difficulty expressing disagreement out of fear of loss of support or approval	Dependency	Demand for constant reassurance, support and encouragement from others	Dutiful	Eager to please and reliant on others for support and guidance; reluctant to take independent action or go against popular opinion

In a critical and comprehensive review, Furnham et al. (2014) attempted a systematic review of current PD measures together with a decision tree to choose among them. They noted that over the years a large number of measures have been devised for research and practice. They also pointed out that the available PD measures differed on at least four major characteristics.

First, some instruments attempt to be comprehensive and measure *all* of the PDs currently (or previously) thought to exist. Some describe disorders that others discount, but the usual number is around 10–15 disorders. However, some instruments set out simply to measure *one* very specific disorder.

Second, there seem to be four common methods to assess the PDs: structured diagnostic interviews, rating instruments for clinicians, self-report questionnaires and other-report questionnaires (Friedman et al., 2007). Thus, two use observer data (clinician, family) and two use self-report data approaches towards measurement. By far the most common, however, are questionnaires and structured interviews.

Third, some measures are about subtypes of the PD in the sense that they are multidimensional measures that yield scores on different but related facets of the disorder. For example, some measures and theorists may distinguish between grandiose and vulnerable, or communal and agentic Narcissistic PD (NPD; Gebauer et al., 2012). Most measures, however, mimic DSM-5 categorical criteria and are not about the distinction among subtypes of a specific PD.

Fourth, PD measures have been developed for essentially five target groups. The first group of users are clinicians attempting a reliable and valid diagnosis of a PD. The second is a related group, namely academic researchers who may be testing theories of the aetiology or prognosis of a PD eventually after treatment. Industrial and organisational psychologists form a third professional group interested in evaluating aberrant personality and subclinical forms of personality pathology in the context of personnel selection or career coaching and development. Finally, there are two other groups, namely 'laypeople' who may be interested in self-diagnosis, but also relatives of those with a specific PD requiring information about personality disorder symptoms and its prognosis.

In the review they documented 22 measures (interview and questionnaire) of all the PDs as well as those designed to measure the specific disorders. Interestingly, these differed considerably for each disorder. For instance, there are seven for Borderline, none for Avoidant and nine for Narcissistic.

There continues to be an interest in, and development of, instruments in this area.

4.2.4.1   The Hogan Development Survey (HDS)

Perhaps the most widely used measure for the dark side is the HDS. The HDS contains 168 true/false items that assess dysfunctional interpersonal themes (see Table 4.7). These dysfunctional dispositions reflect one's distorted beliefs about others that emerge when people encounter stress or stop considering how their actions affect others. Over time, these dispositions may become associated with a person's reputation and can impede job performance and career success.

The HDS is not a medical or clinical assessment. It does not measure personality disorders, which are manifestations of mental disorder. Instead, the HDS assesses self-defeating expressions of normal personality. The DSM-5 (American Psychiatric Association, 2013, p. 647) makes this same distinction between behavioural traits and disorders – self-defeating behaviours, such as those predicted by the HDS, come and go depending on the context. In contrast, personality disorders are enduring and pervasive across contexts.

The HDS is now extensively used in organisational research and practice to measure dysfunctional personality in the 'normal population' (Furnham, 2006, 2008; Furnham & Crump, 2005; Hogan & Hogan, 1997a). Its aim is partly to help selectors, executive coaches and management development consultants, and individuals themselves diagnose how they typically react under work stress. It has the advantage of being psychometrically valid; of measuring all the personality disorder categories in DSM-IV and being appropriate for a 'normal' population.

The latest development in HDS are facets for each of the scales. This will inevitably lead to a finer grain analysis of the different concepts and a better understanding of how the process works.

4.2.4.2 *The Dark Triad*

There is a relatively new area of research into a concept called the 'Dark Triad' which is an individual differences construct proposed by Paulhus and Williams (2002). Since then, there has been an asymptotic rise in papers and most of a 2014 issue of the journal *Personality and Individual Differences* was dedicated to it.

Paulhus and Williams (2002) proposed a psychologically coherent triad construct of previously studied unique constructs – namely Narcissism, Machiavellianism and Psychopathy at their subclinical or 'normal' level of functioning. This is in essence the combination of well-known measures and is therefore not an example of the 'jingle-jangle' fallacy.

Of these three constructs, Machiavellianism is the only one that is not traditionally seen as a clinical syndrome (i.e. a personality disorder), but rather a normal personality belief dimension or personal philosophy characterised by cynical, manipulative behaviour, expedient and self-interested rather than principled behaviour and cold affect. A measure was derived from a selection of statements from Machiavelli's original books and experimental and correlational work by Christie and Geis (1970) called the Mach-IV inventory.

Narcissism and Psychopathy are constructs traditionally seen as clinical in nature, though there are measures of both at the subclinical level. Specifically, they are usually thought of in *DSM IV-TR* as personality disorders. 'Normal' (Grandiose) Narcissism was originally operationalised by Raskin and Hall (1979). It is characterised by an inflated sense of self-worth, entitlement, dominance and superiority. Frequently, the construct is measured using the Narcissistic Personality Inventory (NPI; Raskin & Hall, 1979), although sometimes it is measured using the NPI-40 (Raskin &

Terry, 1988), as well as the NPI-16 (Ames et al., 2006) in the Dark Triad literature.

Psychopathy has been noted as the most 'dangerous' of the three (Paulhus et al., 2001). Subclinical psychopathy manifests itself mainly in part by high levels of impulsivity and thrill-seeking behaviour along with low levels of empathy and anxiety. The Self-Report Psychopathy scale has, at its core, the same four-factor solution as the Psychopathy Check List (Hare, 1991), which is the 'gold standard' for the measurement of psychopathy. It has been validated by Forth, Brown, Hart and Hare (1996) as useful in the assessment of non-forensic samples. The SRP is not the only measurement of subclinical psychopathy used in the dark triad research.

One of the best used measures is the 'Dirty Dozen' devised by Jonason and Webster (2010). The items are

1. I tend to manipulate others to get my way.
2. I have used deceit or lied to get my way.
3. I have used flattery to get my way.
4. I tend to exploit others towards my own end.
5. I tend to lack remorse.
6. I tend to be unconcerned with the morality of my actions.
7. I tend to be callous or insensitive.
8. I tend to be cynical.
9. I tend to want others to admire me.
10. I tend to want others to pay attention to me.
11. I tend to seek prestige or status.
12. I tend to expect special favours from others.

The central questions for this new research area are both theoretical and psychometric. The first concerns the conceptual and empirical coherence of the triad as well as evidence for the psychological processes that underlie the Dark Triad. Related to this is the explanation for the aetiology and the dark triad. The second question concerns the measurement of the triad, namely the psychometric properties of any instruments used as well as the correlates of these measures. Inevitably, the most important psychometric questions are the construct, incremental and predictive validity of measures of the Dark Triad over other measures and their individual parts.

Research in this area had recently taken off exponentially (Andersen et al., 2020). It has electrified the individual difference and work psychology area as people have begun to value the importance of the select-out issue (see Chapter1).

4.2.5 Motives and Values

The question that so many assessors are asked is 'What motivates this person?' It is one of the more difficult areas to attempt to assess. It is often done through values at work, which are individual judgements about the importance or relevance of actions and outcomes. They are, according to Latham and Pinder (2005), rooted in needs, acquired through experience and the basis of transitional life goals. Ascertaining values is often thought of as the best way to measure motivation as values reduce problems of dissimulation found in more standard work motivational questionnaires (Furnham, 2008; Hogan & Hogan 1997).

Values are important because they can significantly influence goal setting and decision-making (Parks & Guay, 2009). Whilst there are many old and new work motivational scales, there are many fewer measures of work values (Gagne et al., 2010, 2015). However, both work motivation and values measures have similar themes or structures. There has been extensive work on attempting to map and measure general values (Schwartz, 1992) and further attempts to map these onto work values (Cable & Edwards, 2004).

The value theory (Schwartz, 1992, 2006, 2012) adopts a conception of values that specifies six main features that are implicit in the writings of many theorists: (1) Values are beliefs linked inextricably to affect. When values are activated, they become infused with feeling. (2) Values refer to desirable goals that people are motivated to pursue. (3) Values transcend specific actions and situations. Obedience and honesty values, for example, may be relevant in the workplace or school, in business or politics, with friends or strangers. (4) Values serve as standards or criteria. Values guide the selection or evaluation of actions, policies, people and events. People decide what is good or bad, justified or illegitimate, worth doing or avoiding, based on possible consequences for their cherished values. But the impact of values in everyday decisions is rarely conscious. (5) Values are ordered by importance relative to one another. People's values form an ordered system of priorities that characterise them as individuals. (6) The relative importance of multiple values guides action. Any attitude or behaviour typically has implications for more than one value.

Values influence actions when they are relevant in the context (hence likely to be activated) and important to the actor. Swartz (2012) argues that values are ordered by importance relative to one another. People's values form an ordered system of priorities that characterise them as individuals.

The Schwartz theory of basic values identifies 'ten basic personal values that are recognised across cultures and explains where they come from'. They are:

1. *Self-direction*: independent thought and action – choosing, creating, exploring.
2. *Stimulation*: excitement, novelty, and challenge in life.
3. *Hedonism*: pleasure or sensuous gratification for oneself.
4. *Achievement:* personal success through demonstrating competence according to social standards.
5. *Power*: social status and prestige, control or dominance over people and resources.
6. *Security:* safety, harmony and stability of society, of relationships and of self.
7. *Conformity:* restraint of actions, inclinations, and impulses likely to upset or harm others and violate social expectations or norms.
8. *Tradition:* respect, commitment and acceptance of the customs and ideas that one's culture or religion provides.
9. *Benevolence:* preserving and enhancing the welfare of those with whom one is in frequent personal contact (the 'in group').
10. *Universalism:* understanding, appreciation, tolerance and protection for the welfare of all people and for nature.

Hogan and Hogan (1997) argue that the best way to tap into motivation is though values, because people are motivated to achieve and obtain that which they value. Hence, the terms are used interchangeably.

The 10 Hogan values are given in Table 4.8. The idea is that people are motivated to achieve what they value most. Thus, it is

Table 4.8 *The 10 Hogan values*

Recognition	Desire to be known, seen, visible and famous, which leads to a lifestyle guided by a search for opportunities to be noticed and dreams of fame and high achievement, whether or not they are fulfilled.
Power	Desire to succeed, make things happen, make a difference and outperform the competition.
Hedonistic	Pursuit of fun, excitement, pleasure and a lifestyle organised around eating, drinking and entertainment.
Altruistic	Desire to help others, a concern for the welfare of the less fortunate in life, and a lifestyle organised around public service and the betterment of humanity.
Affiliation	Needing and enjoying frequent and varied social contact and a lifestyle organised around social interaction.
Tradition	A belief in, and dedication to, old-fashioned virtues such as family, church, thrift, hard work, appropriate social behaviour and a lifestyle that reflects these values.
Security	A need for predictability, structure and efforts to avoid risk and uncertainty – especially in the employment area – and a lifestyle organised around minimising errors and mistakes.
Commerce/ business	Interest in earning money, realising profits, finding new business opportunities and a lifestyle organised around investments and financial planning.
Aesthetics/ culture	Need for self-expression, a dedication to quality and excellence, an interest in how things look, feel and sound and close attention to the appearance of things.
Science/ rationality	Being interested in science, comfortable with technology, preferring data-based as opposed to intuitive decisions and spending time learning how things work.

possible to see the motivational profile of an entrepreneur (high on commerce, power and recognition) vs those interested in completely different jobs (HR, IT). This is based on the Holland model of fit (see Chapter 1) where it is important to get a good fit between a person's values and motives, and the job they do.

4.2.5.1   Two Factors of Motivation

One of the most well-known theories regarding motivation at work is Herzberg, Mausner and Snyderman's (1959) two motivational dimensions: *hygiene* and *motivator* variables. Hygiene is more often referred to as *extrinsic* motivation, which describes external pressures to obtain rewards or avoid punishment. Motivator variables, often referred to as *intrinsic* motivators, are an internal drive to complete a task for its own sake or for personal enjoyment. However, researchers have sought to investigate subfactors of both basic motives suggesting a hierarchical model (Deci & Ryan, 1985). It should also be noted that there are other measures of work values and motivation that have more than two factors.

The following is a simple but robust measure of job motivation developed by Furnham and MacRae (2020) (see Table 4.9): 'Below are listed various different work-related factors that may be important to you when *you look for* or *change* jobs. Please indicate **how much you personally value** each one of them by circling the appropriate number. Give *higher* ratings to factors that are *more important* to you and lower ratings to factors that are less important to you. There are no right or wrong answers – we are interested in your personal opinions.'

This questionnaire yields six scores across two categories. *Extrinsic Motivation* – 1. Security, 2. Compensation, 3. Conditions; and *Intrinsic Motivation* – 1. Autonomy, 2. Recognition, 3. Affiliation. The measure has been shown to have construct and predictive validity.

4.2.6   Integrity Tests

It is well recognised that integrity (honesty) is of fundamental importance in the workplace. It is one of the virtues/traits that people most

Table 4.9 *Measuring Motivation*

	Unimportant									Important
1. Balance – a job that allows me to lead a balanced life.	1	2	3	4	5	6	7	8	9	10
2. Benefits – a job that provides many features additional to pay (e.g. pension top-ups, extra holidays).	1	2	3	4	5	6	7	8	9	10
3. Bonuses – a job that provides many opportunities for topping up the basic salary.	1	2	3	4	5	6	7	8	9	10
4. Clarity – a job with clear and well-defined roles and responsibilities.	1	2	3	4	5	6	7	8	9	10
5. Comfort – a job that can be carried out in physically comfortable conditions.	1	2	3	4	5	6	7	8	9	10
6. Competition – a job that provides me with opportunities to compete with others.	1	2	3	4	5	6	7	8	9	10
7. Conditions – a job that can be carried out in conditions, that are safe, modern, and clean.	1	2	3	4	5	6	7	8	9	10
8. Contribution to society – a job that allows me to work for a good cause.	1	2	3	4	5	6	7	8	9	10
9. Creativity – A job that brings out your personal creative talents.	1	2	3	4	5	6	7	8	9	10
10. Effortlessness – a job that is relatively easy and does not require excessive effort.	1	2	3	4	5	6	7	8	9	10
11. Entrepreneurial – a job that is about new business opportunities, making extra money.	1	2	3	4	5	6	7	8	9	10
12. Equipment – a job that can be carried out with up-to-date equipment and technology.	1	2	3	4	5	6	7	8	9	10
13. Fame – a job that gives you a high profile	1	2	3	4	5	6	7	8	9	10
14. Flexibility – a job that allows me to work flexible hours to suit my personal needs.	1	2	3	4	5	6	7	8	9	10
15. Fun – a job that is about the pursuit of excitement, pleasure and play.	1	2	3	4	5	6	7	8	9	10
16. Independence – a job that allows me to work autonomously without much supervision.	1	2	3	4	5	6	7	8	9	10
17. Insurance – a job that provides health and life insurance.	1	2	3	4	5	6	7	8	9	10

Table 4.9 (*cont.*)

	Unimportant									Important
18. Intellectuality – a job that is challenging and involves a lot thinking and analysis.	1	2	3	4	5	6	7	8	9	10
19. Location – a job that is conveniently located and easily accessible.	1	2	3	4	5	6	7	8	9	10
20. Organizational image – a job within an organization that is widely recognized and respected.	1	2	3	4	5	6	7	8	9	10
21. Pay – a job that is very well paid.	1	2	3	4	5	6	7	8	9	10
22. Perks – a job that provides many extras (e.g. company car, discounts on goods, etc.)	1	2	3	4	5	6	7	8	9	10
23. Personal growth – a job that provides opportunities for self-improvement.	1	2	3	4	5	6	7	8	9	10
24. Personal relevance – a job that provides me with opportunities to use my personal talents, education, and training.	1	2	3	4	5	6	7	8	9	10
25. Power – a job that allows me to control my destiny and be influential.	1	2	3	4	5	6	7	8	9	10
26. Promotion – a job that provides opportunities for rapid advancement.	1	2	3	4	5	6	7	8	9	10
27. Rationality – A job that values science, technology, data.	1	2	3	4	5	6	7	8	9	10
28. Recognition – a job that leads to clear and wide recognition of my achievements.	1	2	3	4	5	6	7	8	9	10
29. Regularity – a job that can be performed in a standard, stable, and controlled manner.	1	2	3	4	5	6	7	8	9	10
30. Responsibility – a job with many appropriate responsibilities.	1	2	3	4	5	6	7	8	9	10
31. Safety – a job that can be carried out in safe and secure conditions.	1	2	3	4	5	6	7	8	9	10
32. Security – a job that is secure and permanent.	1	2	3	4	5	6	7	8	9	10
33. Self-Expression – a job that allows you to be the real you.	1	2	3	4	5	6	7	8	9	10
34. Simplicity – a job that is not overly complicated.	1	2	3	4	5	6	7	8	9	10
35. Social interaction – a job that provides many good opportunities for social contact with others.	1	2	3	4	5	6	7	8	9	10

Table 4.9 *(cont.)*

	Unimportant									Important
36. Status – a job that is generally recognized as 'high-status' in our society.	1	2	3	4	5	6	7	8	9	10
37. Stimulation – a job that I personally find very interesting.	1	2	3	4	5	6	7	8	9	10
38. Supervision – a boss who is fair and considerate.	1	2	3	4	5	6	7	8	9	10
39. Teaching – a job that allows me to train others and to pass on my expertise.	1	2	3	4	5	6	7	8	9	10
40. Teamwork – a job that provides me with opportunities to cooperate with others.	1	2	3	4	5	6	7	8	9	10
41. Tradition – a job that celebrates old fashioned values like history, thrift, hard-work.	1	2	3	4	5	6	7	8	9	10
42. Tranquillity – a job that is not particularly stressful.	1	2	3	4	5	6	7	8	9	10
43. Variety – a job that allows me to get involved in many different kinds of activities.	1	2	3	4	5	6	7	8	9	10
44. Visibility – a job that gives me a fair amount of publicity.	1	2	3	4	5	6	7	8	9	10

want in their boss. Furthermore, it is very important in numerous areas where people are trusted with money or confidential information.

There have been pencil-and-paper tests for over 50 years that have attempted to measure integrity. These tests are fairly varied but appear to concentrate on the following four areas: first, direct, explicit admissions of dishonest behaviour (lying, cheating, stealing, devious whistle-blowing); second, opinions/attitudes about the acceptability of dishonest behaviour (prevalence in society, justification of causes); third, traits, value systems and biographical factors thought to be associated with dishonesty; fourth, reactions to hypothetical situations that do or do not feature dishonest behaviour. Simple items from a test used in World War II asked how frequently respondents lied, whether they had ever been expelled from school and whether they thought people trusted them. Still others enquired about illegal or disapproved activities, such as drug-taking or forgery.

Another approach is to ask questions about honesty: how much respondents believe others are honest or dishonest, and how they themselves have behaved. Other questions are about personality attributes associated with dishonesty.

Often, these self-report measures can be distinguished in terms of whether they are overt, explicit, 'clear purpose' tests, or personality-based, 'veiled purpose' tests. The sort of issues that an overt test examines include: honesty attitudes/admission of previous dishonesty; substance abuse, drug avoidance; personal past achievements; service orientation, customer relations; work values; clerical, mathematical, verbal skills, technical abilities and aptitudes.

On the other hand, 'veiled purpose' tests are more likely to try to measure conscientiousness, dependability, prudence; hostility to rules and regulations; impulsivity, thrill-seeking, disinhibition; alienation and lack of commitment.

Bennett and Robinson (2000) developed a two-part questionnaire: one part measuring *organizational* deviance (behaviours directly harmful to the organization), the other measuring *interpersonal* deviance (behaviours directly harmful to individuals). They also provided validity data for their questionnaire. Again, what is striking is the variability in behaviours from nearly trivial to very serious, from every day to rare, from generally condoned to completely unacceptable. This is an important issue. The assumption is that honesty/integrity is a stable 'trait' that informs *all* behaviour at work. Some looking at these items may say those who are 'grumpy' or 'emotionally volatile' or those who have significant responsibilities outside the workplace are unfairly labelled as lacking in honesty.

Clearly, one obvious advantage of the so-called veiled purpose test is that they are less open to faking or not admitting wrongdoing. Faking threatens test reliability. However, it has been shown to be significantly reduced when people are aware that the investigators (potential employers) have (many) other sources of information about their honesty.

There are different themes tapped into by self-report integrity tests. Furthermore, there is an assumption that the honest, reliable person with integrity acts somewhat differently from the dishonest person on this dimension. Thus, the following behaviours can be expected:

1 *Report incidences of explicit dishonesty*: Honest people will honestly report that they have been less dishonest in the past.
2 *Leniency towards dishonesty*: Honest people are less likely to excuse, forgive or explain away dishonesty in others and themselves.
3 *Rationalisation for thieving*: Honest people are less likely to try to excuse or provide rationalisation for theft in organisations.
4 *Brooding and rumination about theft*: Honest people are less likely to even think (plan, plot, fantasise) about thieving from their organisation.
5 *Rejecting dishonest norms*: Honest people are likely to question or reject dishonest behaviour of all sorts perceived within the organisation as acceptable.
6 *Impulse control*: Honest people are less likely to act on their impulses, preferring to think through an issue before acting.
7 *Punitive attitude*: Honest people have less punitive attitudes towards themselves and others.

Karren and Zacharias (2007) list four concerns with all paper-and-pencil self-report integrity tests:

1 The nature of what is being measured – integrity or some related construct (like conscientiousness), because tests do show a relationship with a wide range of work performance measure.
2 Tests can and do lead to decision errors – *false positives* (where those with integrity are accused of not having it) and the opposite, *false negatives* (where dishonest respondents appear honest).
3 Recent studies show that faking, coaching or retaking integrity tests can affect scores.
4 Tests may be considered an invasion of privacy because they seek intrusive information about past undesirable behaviour.

4.2.6.1   Do Integrity Tests Work?

The most obvious and fundamental questions about honesty testing must be about *validity*. There have been various studious and excellent reviews. Those who are positive conclude that integrity tests are often good at detecting CounterWork Behaviours (CWBs), as well as supervisors' ratings of good/poor performance. Others believe that the 'jury is out' and that we need more high-quality disinterested and sceptical research before making a judgement.

While validity is always the single and simply most important criterion of any test, there are others, some of which have a direct effect on validity. These include reliability, dimensionality and so on, but perhaps the most important is *fake-ability*. Can clever (and dishonest) people 'beat the test' and come out looking virtuous when they are not. This problem applies to all tests, but particular honesty tests. Results suggest that one can catch dissimulators but that there is a general – and quite understandable – trend to overemphasise honesty.

The issue with testing is the problem of false positives and negatives – that is classifying the honest as dishonest and vice versa. Both are equally undesirable but have quite different consequences.

While it is not difficult to make a case for the use of integrity tests, it seems ironic that test publishers seem to make possibly fraudulent claims for the efficacy of their tests in detecting dishonest people, thence reducing theft and shrinkage problems. Honesty testing is a competitive business.

It is possible honesty testing in the future will attempt to measure very specific, rather than general, types of honesty. Furthermore, it is likely that the tests will be computer-administered.

Is there evidence that these relatively simple questionnaires mean that people are more or less likely to engage in dishonest CWBs? Can they predict who will be honest or dishonest? There are various ways of checking the variability of tests. They include:

1 *The 'known' or contrast groups method*: People who are known to be both honest and dishonest are given the test, and the quantity and quality of the difference in response is recorded.
2 *Background, biographical check*: A thorough background check (number of convictions) using police, school, organisations' records are related to test scores.

3 *Admissions and confessions*: Separate (perhaps confidential) admissions to a wide range of tests covering dishonest behaviours from the trivial to the very serious are correlated with test scores

4 *Predictive or future method*: People are tested at organisational entry and scores are related to documented (proven) dishonest behaviours over their career.

5 *Time series or historic method*: Before honesty tests are used in selection, all sorts of indices are collected (loss, shrinkage); the same data are collected after tests are used in selection to see whether there is a noticeable difference.

6 *Correlations with polygraph or anonymous admissions*: of theft or absenteeism.

Each method has its limitations and failings. For instance, background checks will not show working on company time. Predictive methods can take a decade to get results. A reduction in shrinkage (stealing) may have as much to do with the installation of a new security system as it does the use of tests. Studies have shown individual differences in faking integrity tests.

Certainly, tests have been validated against very different criteria – theft, faking credentials, CWBs – and they do tend to produce rather different results. Working on private issues on company time, taking lunch breaks are called 'time theft'. Stealing office stationery (pens, paper) is strictly theft. But both of these could be considered trivial, certainly quite different from the theft of company secrets, or of valuable materials used for production or the products themselves. But what is the latest thinking around these tests?

First, it is agreed that these tests are certainly useful. They are valid enough to help prevent various problems.

Second, testing alone will not stop theft, dishonesty or sabotage as many factors other than dishonest individuals cause them.

Third, integrity tests may be measuring aspects of human personality which are stable over time, though it is not certain which.

Fourth, there are problems in testing because some testing codes and standards insist that people being tested give informed consent on details about the test, such as what it measures. Hardly the best thing to give a dishonest person.

Fifth, there may be legal issues in how 'cut-off' scores are used and labelled. One could classify people as 'pass/fail' or 'very, highly, moderately dangerous'. How this information is used or recorded can cause expensive legal action. Sixth, integrity tests are used to 'select out', not 'select in'. They are designed to help people screen out high-risk applicants, not identify 'angels'.

The issue of the validity of integrity tests and interpreting the evidence is technical. Four issues are relevant:

1 What are the criteria against which test scores are measured? How specific or serious are these criteria? Global (like job performance) or specific (like absenteeism or stealing)?
2 What type of measure is made: subjective or objective? Is the measure recorded electronically (on camera), by others' disinterested observations or is this done by a person's own self-report?
3 What is the validation strategy? That is, is it concurrent – are things compared at the same time (test scores and cheating data), or is it predictive – when scores are seen to predict future behaviour?
4 Who comprise the validation sample of people on whom to do the study? Job applicants or job incumbents?

Whereas personality psychologists want to emphasise personality trait prediction and correlates of CWBs, social psychologists want to stress how group, organisational and situational factors influence situations. Inevitably, the two interact. Related to this is whether the trait of integrity – if it exists – is immutable. Can it change over time as a consequence of experience?

4.2.7   Other Measures

As noted, there are hundreds of other measures of personality. Consider the ones discussed here, which have become very popular over the past decade or so.

4.2.7.1   Strengths

Coming out of positive psychology there was a great emphasis on assessing character strengths, which were characterised as the 'psychological processes or mechanisms that define virtues'.

It was suggested that different strengths are employed to exhibit a particular virtue, although generally only one or two strengths would be exhibited from a particular virtue group. These virtues include: *Wisdom and knowledge* (including the strengths of creativity, curiosity, open-mindedness, love of learning and perspective), *Courage* (including bravery, persistence, honesty and zest), *Humanity* (including love, kindness and social intelligence), *Justice* (including teamwork, fairness and leadership), *Temperance* (including forgiveness, modesty, prudence and self-regulation) and *Transcendence* (including appreciation of beauty and excellence, gratitude, hope, humour and spirituality).

Together, it was argued the strengths and virtues are the foundation of psychological health, which in modern-day contexts is significantly reduced. People experience greater levels of stress and pressure that use up their resources to cope. Numerous studies have shown that the strengths of character are positively related to subjective and psychological well-being. Research on the development of strengths in individuals has also showcased a decrease in depressive symptoms.

Furthermore, strengths such as gratitude, hope, zest, curiosity and, most importantly, love have been demonstrated to be related to life satisfaction (Park et al., 2004). For example, Luthans and Jensen (2002) highlighted the importance of hope in maintaining worker's motivation in an environment increasingly threatened by mergers, bankruptcies, new technologies and an uncertain global economy. Hope is a strength that allows people to overcome uncertainty. These findings have important implications for people involved in the promotion of positive development among society.

In light of such evidence, a measurement of the strengths of character and core virtues was needed. So, Peterson and Seligman (2004) took up the task of assessing the positive traits than facilitate human flourishing and answering the fundamental question of how one can define the concept of a human 'strength'. Subsequently, the Values in Action Inventory of Strengths (Peterson & Seligman, 2004) was first established. Since then, various versions of this measurement have been developed, alongside other separate measurements. Furnham and Lester (2012) devised the following test (see Table 4.10).

WHAT ARE YOUR STRENGTHS?

We all have various specific strengths and weaknesses. This questionnaire focuses on your ratings of your strengths. We are going to ask you to rate 24 strengths on what is called a normal distribution which is how IQ is measured. IQ tests measure a person's intelligence. The average or the mean score on these tests is 100. Most of the population (68%) score between 85 and 115. Very bright people (around 2–3%) score around 130 and scores have been known to go over 145.

In this two-page questionnaire we want you to estimate various things about yourself like your intelligence but also your general **personal strengths**.

Look at the above scale and simply put a number between 55 and 145 based on what you think reflects your ability compared to the general population. For example, if you put 120 you think that you are fairly good but a score of 105 means you are only just above average. You can put any number between 55 and 145. Please try to be accurate and honest in your answers.

4.2.7.2 Locus of Control

Spector (1982) noted that locus of control is related to motivation, effort, performance, satisfaction, perception of the job, compliance with authority and supervisory style, as well as an important moderating factor between incentives and motivation, satisfaction and turnover. For instance, 'internals' tend to prefer piece-rate systems, whereas 'externals' tend to be more satisfied with direct supervision, to comply more with demands of coercive supervisors and to be more compliant with social demands than internals. Spector concludes that much more organisational theory may be applicable to internals. Similar studies on employment, unemployment and labour market discrimination have demonstrated different levels of internality and externality as a function of work experience.

Table 4.10 *Personal Strengths.*

Personal Strengths	ESTIMATE YOU
1. **Curiosity**: interest in, intrigued by many things	
2. **Love of learning**: knowing more, reading, understanding	
3. **Good judgement**: critical thinking, rationality, open-mindedness	
4. **Ingenuity**: originality , practical intelligence, street smart	
5. **Social intelligence**: emotional/personal intelligence, good with feelings	
6. **Wisdom**: seeing the big picture, having perspective	
7. **Bravery**: courage, valour, fearlessness	
8. **Persistence**: perseverance, diligence, industriousness	
9. **Integrity:** honesty, genuineness, truthfulness	
10. **Kindness**: generosity, empathic, helpful	
11. **Loving**: able to love and be loved; deep sustained feelings	
12. **Citizenship**: team worker, loyalty, duty to others	
13. **Fairness**: moral valuing, equality and equity	
14. **Leadership**: able to motivate groups, inclusive, focused	
15. **Self-control**: able to regulate emotions, non-impulsive	
16. **Prudence**: cautious, far-sighted, deliberative, discreet	
17. **Humility**: modesty, unpretentious, humble	
18. **Appreciative of beauty**: seeking excellence, experience of awe/wonder	
19. **Gratitude**: thankful, grateful	
20. **Optimism**: hopefulness, future-mindedness, positive	
21. **Spirituality**: faith, philosophy, sense of purpose/ calling	
22. **Forgiveness**: mercy, benevolent, kind	
23. **Playfulness**: humour, funny, childlike	
24. **Enthusiasm**: passion, zest, infectious, engaged	

Work locus of control:

1. A job is what you make of it.
2. In most jobs, people can pretty much accomplish whatever they set out to accomplish.
3. If you know what you want out of a job, you can find a job that gives it to you.
4. If employees are unhappy with a decision made by their boss, they should do something about it.
5. Getting the job you want is mostly a matter of luck.
6. Making money is primarily a matter of good fortune.
7. Most people are capable of doing their jobs well if they make the effort.
8. In order to get a really good job, you need to have family members or friends in high places.
9. Promotions are usually a matter of good fortune.
10. When it comes to landing a really good job, who you know is more important than what you know.
11. Promotions are given to employees who perform well on the job.
12. To make a lot of money you have to know the right people.
13. It takes a lot of luck to be an outstanding employee in most jobs.
14. People who perform their jobs well generally get rewarded for it.
15. Most employees have more influence on their supervisors than they think they do.
16. The main difference between people who make much money and people who make a little money is luck.

   Each item has a True (T) or False (F) score which is calculated 1–4 (T) 5–6 (F); 7 (T) 8–10 (F);11 (T);12–13 (F);14–15 (T);16 (F) Low scores indicate high on fatalism; high scores indicate high in instrumentalism (Spector,1988).

4.2.8 Conclusion

In his review of the use of personality tests in selection, Cook (2016) concluded that personality is a vaguer and more diffuse concept than ability, and there are many models of personality. He suggests that personality inventories have limited value in predicting how well a person can do a job, but may be more successful in predicting how hardworking a person is. They may also be more successful in predicting avoidance of deviant or problematic behaviour at work. The relationship between team personality and team performance may be complex, and low scorers may be able to hold back the entire group. Personality inventories have been criticised on the grounds that some of their questions are unduly intrusive.

There are however clear *advantages* of personality testing, which are:

- Tests provide *numeric information*, which means individuals can more easily be compared on the same exacting criteria.
- Tests give *explicit and specific results* on temperament and ability rather than the ambiguous coded statements that are often found in references.
- Tests are *fair* because they eliminate corruption, favouritism and networks from self-perpetuating.
- Tests are *comprehensive* in that they cover all the basic dimensions of personality and ability from which other behaviour patterns derive.
- Tests are *scientific* in that they are empirically based on theoretical foundations; that is, they are reliable, valid and able to discriminate the good from the mediocre and the average from the bad.

Equally it could be argued that they have various *disadvantages*

- Many of these tests can be *faked*.
- Some people do not have *sufficient self-insight* to report on their own feelings and behaviour; that is, it is not that people lie, but that they *cannot*, rather than *will not*, give accurate answers about themselves (some tests only look for simple behavioural data to overcome this).
- Tests are *unreliable* in that all sorts of temporary factors, such as test anxiety, boredom, weariness, a headache, and period pains all lead people to give different answers on different occasions (although this is partly true, it is only a minor factor).
- Most importantly, tests are *invalid*; they do not measure what they say they are measuring and those scores do not predict behaviour over time. For many tests, this is indeed the Achilles heel and they are often lamentably short of robust proof of their validity.
- They might be able to measure all sorts of dimensions of behaviour, but *not the crucial ones* to the organisation, such as trustworthiness and likelihood of absenteeism.

- People have to be *sufficiently literate* or articulate to do these tests, not to mention sufficiently familiar with modern jargon.
- There are no *good norms* (normative population data), at least for the population they want to test, and comparing them to White US students can be dangerously misleading.
- *The tests are unfair and biased* towards WASPs (White Anglo-Saxon Protestants).
- *Interpretation of the tests* takes skill, insight and experience, and this is either too expensive or not available.
- *Freedom of information legislation* may mean that candidates would be able to see, and hence challenge, either the scores themselves or their interpretation of the decisions made on them.
- As tests become known, people could buy copies and practise, so that they know the correct or *most desirable answers.*

All assessment methods have advantages and disadvantages. Personality tests can greatly facilitate assessment. But the user needs to have some knowledge of test construction and theory both to choose tests wisely and how and when to implement them in the process. We do know that two of the Big Five factors seem to be important for all jobs – *Neuroticism*, which is a select-out factor because it is correlated negatively with success at work, and *Conscientiousness*, which is a select-in factor because it predicts work success. Test users would do wisely then to select tests which measure *both* these important traits.

But if tests do not predict behaviour at work very well – why not? First, there may be problems with the theoretical formulation in the first place, in that the personality theory or system has been poorly or inaccurately conceived. That is, the theory upon which the test is based is wrong. Next, the measurement of the personality trait is poor for a variety of reasons; for example, it measures a single trait which is actually multidimensional. Also, the measure has poor reliabilities (e.g. Cronbach's alpha, which is a measure of the internal coherence of questionnaires) or is not a valid measure of what is being tested.

Also, various systematic errors involved with self-report, such as attribution errors or dissimulators, render scores meaningless. People do not or cannot report accurately.

Although the personality measures and theory are satisfactory, there is no reason to suppose that the trait(s) selected actually predict the occupational behaviour specified. That is, the outcome work variable (sales figures, appraisal reports) are quite simply, and for good theoretical reasons, not related to the trait variable (e.g. extraversion).

Next, the measurement of occupational behaviour (e.g. absenteeism, productivity) is poor for several reasons, for example only one measure or very few measures have been taken, threatening the reliability of the measure (i.e. no good aggregate measure is used). Also, the occupational behaviour measure is subject to systematic error, whether it is derived by observation, test data or self-report.

We know that occupational behaviour is shaped and constrained by *other factors* more powerful than personality traits. That is, although there is a coherent and consistent relationship between personality and occupational behaviour, other factors such as union agreements, unalterable working conditions or incentive schemes (usually the lack of) suppress or diminish the relationship that actually exists. It should be noted that personality is a moderator variable rather than a direct predictor of occupational behaviour, and thus its force depends on a wide range of other variables (such as social class, intelligence and organisational structure) being present.

Finally sampling problems may have 'washed' out or suppressed the relationship because of self-selection – or indeed, rigorous recruitment to many jobs – that is, the effect is that the people in them may be too homogeneous in terms of their personality to show strong findings. For all these reasons people may conclude, often erroneously, that tests never or even rarely predict behaviour at work.

REFERENCES

Al-Dajani, N., Gralnick, T., & Bagby, R. (2016). A psychometric review of the personality inventory for DSM-5 (PID-5). *Journal of Personality Assessment*, 98, 62–68.

American Psychiatric Association. (1980). *Diagnostic and statistical manual of mental disorders* (3rd ed. rev.). Washington, DC: APA.

American Psychological Association. (1994). *Diagnostic and statistical manual of mental disorders* (4th ed.). Washington, DC: American Psychological Association.

American Psychiatric Association. (2000). *Diagnostic and statistical manual of mental disorders*. (4th ed. rev.). Washington, DC: APA.

Ashton, M. C., & Lee, K. (2007). Empirical, theoretical, and practical advantages of the HEXACO model of personality structure. *Personality and Social Psychology Review*, 11, 150–166. https://doi.org/10.1177/1088868306294907

Babiak, P., & Hare, R. (2006). *Snakes in suits: When psychopaths go to work*. New York: Regan Books.

Bagby, R. M. (2013) Introduction to special issue on the Personality Inventory for DSM-5 (PID 5). *Assessment*, 20, 267–268.

Barkoukis, V., Lazuras, L., Tsorbatzoudis, H., & Rodafinos, A. (2011). Motivational and sportspersonship profiles of elite athletes in relation to doping behavior. *Psychology of Sport and Exercise*, 12(3), 205–212. https://doi.org/10.1016/j.psychsport.2010.10.003

Basch, J., & Melchers, K. (2019). Fair and flexible?! Explanations can improve applicant reactions toward asynchronous video interviews. *Personnel Assessment and Decisions*, 3, 1–11.

Bastiaansen, L., Rossi, G., & De Fruyt, F. (2012). Comparing five sets of Five-Factor model personality disorder counts in a heterogeneous sample of psychiatric patients. *European Journal of Personality*, 2, 377–388.

Bastiaansen, L., Rossi, G., Schotte, C., & De Fruyt, F. (2011). The structure of personality disorders. *Journal of Personality Disorders*, 25, 378–396.

Benson, M. J., & Campbell, J. P. (2007). To be, or not to be, linear: An expanded representation of personality and its relationship to leadership performance. *International Journal of Selection and Assessment*, 15(2), 232–249.

Blashfield, R., Keeley, J., Flanagan, E., & Miles, S. (2014). The cycle of classification: DSM-1 through DSM-5. *Annual Review of Clinical Psychology*, 10, 25–51.

Bryant, F. B., & Yarnold, P. R. (1995). Principal components analysis and exploratory and confirmatory factor analysis. In L. G. Grimm & R. R. Yarnold (Eds.), *Reading and understanding multivariable statistics* (pp. 99–136). Washington, DC: American Psychological Association.

Cable, D. M., & Edwards, J. R. (2004). Complementary and supplementary fit: A theoretical and empirical integration. *Journal of Applied Psychology, 89*(5), 822–834. https://doi.org/10.1037/0021-9010.89.5.822

Carroll, B. (1973). *Job satisfaction: A review of the literature.* Ithaca, NY: Cornell University.

Carver, C. S. & Schier, M. F. (1992) *Perspectives on Personality.* Boston, MA: Allyn & Bacon.

Cattell, R. B. (1978). *The Scientific Use of Factor Analysis.* New York: Plenum.

Cook, J., Hepworth, S., Wall, T., & Warr, P. (1981). *The experience of work.* London: Academic Press.

Coolidge, F. (2001). *Short Form of the Coolidge Axis-II inventory (SCATI).* Colorado Springs, CO: Manual.

Coolidge, F. L., Segal, D. L., Cahill, B. S., & Simenson, J. T. (2010). Psychometric properties of a brief inventory for the screening of personality disorders: The SCATI. *Psychology and Psychotherapy: Theory, Research and Practice, 83*(4), 395–405.

Costa, P.T., & McCrae, R. (1985). *The NEO personality inventory manual.* Odessa, FL: Psychological Assessment Resources.

Costa, P. T., & McCrae, R. R. (1992). Four ways five factors are basic. *Personality and Individual Differences, 13,* 653–665.

Cotton, L., Bynum, D., & Madhere, S. (1997). Socialization forces and the stability of work values from late adolescence to early adulthood. *Psychological Reports, 80*(1), 115–124. https://doi.org/10.2466/pr0.1997.80.1.115

Cronbach, L. J., & Shavelson, R. J. (2004). My current thoughts on coefficient alpha and successor procedures. *Educational and Psychological Measurement, 64*(3), 391–418.

Davison, M., & Furnham, A. (2018). The personality disorder profile of professional actors. *Psychology of Popular Media Culture, 7,* 33–46.

De Fruyt, F., De Clercq, B., Milley, J., Rolland, J. P., Jung, S. C., Taris, R., Furnham, A., & Hiel, A. (2009). Assessing personality at risk in personnel selection and development. *European Journal of Personality, 23,* 51–69.

Deci, E. L., Koestner, R., & Ryan, R. M. (1999). A meta-analytic review of experiments examining the effects of extrinsic rewards on intrinsic motivation. *Psychological Bulletin, 125*(6), 627–668. https://doi.org/10.1037/0033-2909.125.6.627

Deci, E. L., & Ryan, R. M. (1985). *Self-determination and intrinsic motivation in human behavior.* New York: Plenum Publishing Co.

Digman, J. M. (1997). Higher-order factors of the Big Five. *Journal of Personality and Social Psychology, 73,* 1246.

Eysenck, H. J. (1967). *The biological basis of personality.* Springfield: Thomas.

Eysenck, H. J. (1970). A dimensional system of psychodiagnostics. In A. R. Mahrer (Ed.), *New approaches to personality classification and psychodiagnosis* (pp. 169–208). New York: Columbia University Press.

Faul, F., Erdfelder, E., Lang, A.-G., & Buchner, A. (2007). G*Power 3: A flexible statistical power analysis program for the social, behavioral, and biomedical sciences. *Behavior Research Methods, 39*(2), 175–191. https://doi.org/10.3758/BF03193146

Floyd, F. J., & Whidaman, K. F. (1995). Factor analysis in the development and refinement of clinical assessment instruments. *Psychological Assessment*, i(3), 286–299.

Furnham, A. (2008). *Personality and intelligence at work*. London: Routledge.

Furnham, A. (2010). *The elephant in the boardroom: The psychology of leadership derailment*. Basingstoke: Palgrave Macmillan.

Furnham, A. (2015). Bringing order and reason to the personality disorders. *PsycCRITIQUES, 60*, 14.

Furnham, A. (2018). A Big Five facet analysis of sub-clinical Dependent Personality Disorder (Dutifulness). *Psychiatry Research, 270*, 622–626.

Furnham, A. (2019). The Personality Disorders and Money Beliefs and Behaviours. *Financial Planning Review, 2*, e1046.

Furnham, A., & Crump. J. (2005). Personality traits, types and disorders. *European Journal of Personality, 19*, 167–184.

Furnham, A., & Crump, J. (2013). A bright side, facet analysis of Schizotypal Personality Disorder. The relationship between the HDS Imaginative Factor, the NEO-PI-R personality trait facets in a large adult sample. *Thinking Skills and Creativity, 11*, 42–47.

Furnham, A., & Crump, J. (2014a). A bright side facet analysis of Histrionic Personality Disorder: The relationship between the HDS Colourful Factor and the NEO-PI-R facets in a large adult sample. *Journal of Social Psychology, 154*, 527–536.

Furnham, A., & Crump, J. (2014b). A bright side facet analysis of Borderline Personality Disorder: The relationship between the HDS Excitable Factor and the NEO-PI-R facets in a large adult sample. *Borderline Personality Disorder and Emotional Dysregulation, 1*, 1–7.

Furnham, A., & Crump, J. (2014c). A Big Five facet analysis of sub-clinical Narcissism: Understanding Boldness in terms of well-known personality traits. *Personality and Mental Health, 8*, 209–217.

Furnham, A., & Crump, J. (2015). A Big Five facet analysis of a Paranoid personality disorder: The Validity of the HDS Sceptical scale of sub-clinical Paranoia. *Journal of Individual Differences, 36*, 199–204.

Furnham, A., & Crump, J. (2015). Personality and management traits: traits that differentiate leadership levels. *Psychology*, *6*, 549–559.

Furnham, A., & Crump, J. (2016a). A Big Five facet analysis of a psychopath: The Validity of the HDS Mischievous scale of sub-clinical Psychopathy. *Scandinavian Journal of Psychology*, *57*, 117–121.

Furnham, A., & Crump, J. (2016b). Personality correlates of passive-aggressiveness: A NEO-PI-R domain and facet analysis of the HDS leisurely scale. *Journal of Mental Health*, *6*, 496–501.

Furnham, A., & Lester, D. (2012). The development of a short measure of character strength. *European Journal of Psychological Assessment*, *28*, 95–101.

Furnham, A., & Macrae, I. (2019). The dark side of work values. *Current Psychology*, 1–7. https://doi.org/10.1007/s12144-018-9873-z

Furnham, A., & Trickey, G. (2011). Sex differences and dark side traits. *Personality and Individual Differences*, *50*, 517–522.

Furnham, A., Crump, J., & Chamorro-Premuzic, T. (2007). Managerial level, personality, and intelligence. *Journal of Managerial Psychology*, *22*, 805–818.

Furnham, A., Eracleous, A., & Chamorro-Premuzic, T. (2009). Personality, motivation and job satisfaction: Herzberg meets the Big Five. *Journal of Managerial Psychology*, *24*(8), 765–779. https://doi.org/10.1108/02683940910996789

Furnham, A., Forde, L., & Ferrari, K. (1999). Personality and work motivation. *Personality and Individual Differences*, *26*(6), 1035–1040. https://doi.org/10.1016/S0191-8869(98)00202-5

Furnham, A., Guenole, N., Levine, S., & Chamorro-Premuzic, T. (2013). The NEO Personality Inventory-Revised. *Assessment*, *20*, 14–23.

Furnham, A., Humphries, C., & Zheng, E. (2016). Can successful sales people become successful managers? Differences in Derailers and Motives across two jobs. *Consulting Journal: Practice and Research*, *68*, 252–268.

Furnham, A., Hyde, G., & Trickey, G. (2014). Do your dark side traits fit? Dysfunctional personalities in different work sectors. *Applied Psychology*, *63* (4), 589–606.

Furnham, A., Milner, R., Akhtar, R., & De Fruyt, F. (2014). A review of the measures designed to assess DSMV personality disorders. *Psychology*, *5*, 1646–1686.

Furnham, A., Petrides, K.V., Jackson, C., & Cotter, T. (2002). Do personality factors predict job satisfaction? *Personality and Individual Differences*, *33*(8), 1325–1342. https://doi.org/10.1016/S0191-8869(02)00016-8

Furnham, A., Petrides, K. V., Tsaousis, I., Pappas, K., & Garrod, D. (2005). A cross cultural investigation into the relationships between personality traits and work values. *Journal of Psychology*, *139*(1), 5–32. https://doi.org/10.3200/JRLP .139.1.5-32

Furnham, A., Richards, S. C., & Paulhus, D. L. (2013). The dark triad of personality: A 10-year review. *Social and Personality Compass, 7*, 199–216.

Furnham, A., Richards, S., Rangle, L., & Jones, D. (2014). Measuring malevolence: Quantitative issues surrounding the dark triad of personality. *Personality and Individual Differences, 67*, 114–121.

Furnham, A., Trickey, G., & Hyde, G. (2012). Bright aspects to dark side traits: Dark side traits associated with work success. *Personality and Individual Differences, 52*(8), 908–913.

Furnham, A., Crump, J., & Ritchie W. (2013). What it takes: Ability, demographic, bright and dark side trait correlates of years to promotion. *Personality and Individual Differences, 55*, 952–956.

Gagné, M., & Vansteenkiste, M. (2013). Self determination theory's contribution to positive organizational psychology. In A. B. Bakker (Ed.), *Advances in positive organizational psychology* (pp. 61–82). Rotterdam: Erasmus University. https://doi.org/10.1108/S2046–410X(2013)0000001006

Gagné, M., Forest, J., Gilbert, M. H., Aubé, C., Morin, E., & Malorni, A. (2010). The Motivation at Work Scale: Validation evidence in two languages. *Educational and Psychological Measurement, 70*(4), 628–646. https://doi.org/10.1177/0013164409355698

Gagné, M., Forest, J., Vansteenkiste, M., Crevier-Braud, L., Van den Broeck, A., Aspeli, A., & Halvari, H. (2015). The multidimensional work motivation scale: Validation evidence in seven languages and nine countries. *European Journal of Work and Organizational Psychology, 24*(2), 178–196. https://doi.org/10.1080/1359432X.2013.877892

Georgel, J. M., & Jones, G. R. (1997). Experiencing work: Values, attitudes, and moods. *Human Relations, 50*(4), 393–416. https://doi.org/10.1177/001872679705000404

Gosling, S. D., Rentfrow, P. J., & Swann, W. B., Jr. (2003). A Very Brief Measure of the Big Five Personality Domains. *Journal of Research in Personality, 37*, 504–528.

Gøtzsche-Astrup, O., Jakobsen, J., & Furnham, A. (2016). The higher you climb: dark side personality and job level in a sample of executives, middle managers, and entry-level supervisors. *Scandinavian Journal of Psychology, 57*, 535–541.

Hare, R. D. (1999). *Without conscience: The disturbing word of the psychopaths among us.* New York, NY: Guilford.

Harms, P., Spain, S., & Hannah, S. (2011) Leader development and the dark side of personality. *Leadership Quarterly, 22*, 495–509.

Hauber, F. A., & Bruininks, R. H. (1986). Intrinsic and extrinsic job satisfaction among direct-care staff in residential facilities for mentally retarded people.

Educational and Psychological Measurement, 46(1), 95–105. https://doi.org/10.1177/0013164486461009

Hedman, E., Ljótsson, B., Rück, C., Furmark, T., Carlbring, P., Lindefors, N., & Andersson, G. (2010). Internet administration of self-report measures commonly used in research on social anxiety disorder: A psychometric evaluation. *Computers in Human Behavior, 26*(4), 736–740.

Herzberg, F. (1966). *Work and the nature of man.* Cleveland, OH: World Publishers.

Herzberg, F., Mausner, B., & Snyderman, B. (1959). *The motivation to work.* New York: Wiley.

Hogan, R. (1986). *Hogan Personality Inventory manual.* Minneapolis: National Computer Systems.

Hogan, R. (2007). *Personality and the fate of organizations.* Mahwah, NJ: Lawrence Erlbaum.

Hogan, J., & Hogan, R. (1997). *Motives, values, preferences inventory manual.* Tulsa, OK: Hogan Assessment Systems.

Hogan, R. & Hogan, J. (2001). Assessing leadership: A view from the dark side. *International Journal of Selection and Assessment, 9,* 40–51.

Hogan, R., & Hogan, J. (2009). *Hogan Development Survey manual* (3rd ed.). Tulsa, OK: Hogan Assessment Systems.

Hogan, R., & Hogan, J. (2009). *Hogan Development Survey Manual.* Tulsa, OK: HAS.

Hogan, R. & Hogan, J. (2009). *Hogan development survey manual.* Tulsa, OK: HAS.

Hogan, J., Hogan, R., & Kaiser, R.B. (2010). Management derailment. In S. Zedeck (Ed.), *APA handbook of industrial and organizational psychology* (Vol. 3, pp. 555–575). Washington, DC: American Psychological Association.

Hogan, R., Hogan, J., & Roberts, B. W. (1996). Personality measurement and employment decisions: Questions and answers. *American Psychologist, 51,* 469–477.

Hogan, R., & Kaiser, R.B. (2005). What we know about leadership. *Journal of General Psychology, 9,* 169–180.

Hooper, D., Coughlan, J., & Mullen, M. R. (2008). Structural equation modelling: Guidelines for determining model fit. *Electronic Journal of Business Research Methods, 6*(1), 53–60. Retrieved from https://maynoothuniversity.ie

Horn, R., & Behrend, T. (2017). Video killed the interview star. *Personnel Assessment and Decisions, 1,* 51–59.

Hu, L. T., & Bentler, P. M. (1999). Cutoff criteria for fit indexes in covariance structure analysis: Conventional criteria versus new alternatives. *Structural Equation Modeling: A Multidisciplinary Journal, 6*(1), 1–55. https://doi.org/10.1080/10705519909540118

Huprich, S. K. (Ed.). (2015). *Personality Disorders: Toward theoretical and empirical integration in diagnosis and assessment.* Washington, DC: American Psychological Association.

Igalens, J., & Roussel, P. (1999). A study of the relationships between compensation package, work motivation and job satisfaction. *Journal of Organizational Behavior, 20*(7), 1003–1025. https://doi.org/10.1002/(SICI)1099-1379(199912)20:7<1003::AID-JOB941>3.0.CO;2-K

Jopp, A., & South, S. (2014). Investing the personality inventory for DSM-5 using self and spouse reports. *Journal of Personality Disorders, 28*, 1–22.

Judge, T. A., Bono, J. E., Ilies, R., & Gerhardt, M. W. (2002). Personality and leadership: A qualitative and quantitative review. *Journal of Applied Psychology, 87*, 765–780.

Judge, T. A., Heller, D., & Mount, M. K. (2002). Five-factor model of personality and job satisfaction: A meta-analysis. *Journal of Applied Psychology, 87*(3), 530–541.

Judge, T., & LePine, J. (2007). The bright and dark sides of personality. In J. Langan-Fox, C. Cooper, & R. Klimoski (Eds.), *Research companion to the dysfunctional workplace* (pp. 332–355). Cheltham: Elgar.

Kaiser, R. B., LeBreton, J. M., & Hogan, J. (2015). The dark side of personality and extreme leader behavior. *Applied Psychology, 64*(1), 55–92.

Kerr, S., Harlan, A., & Stogdill, R. M. (1974). Preference for motivator and hygiene factors in a hypothetical interview situation. *Personnel Psychology, 27*(1), 109–124. https://doi.org/10.1111/j.1744-6570.1974.tb02067.x

Knoop, R. (1994a). Work values and job satisfaction. *Journal of Psychology, 128*(6), 683–690. https://doi.org/10.1080/00223980.1994.9921297

Knoop, R. (1994c). The relationship between importance and achievement of work values and job satisfaction. *Perceptual and Motor Skills, 79*(1), 595–605. https://doi.org/10.2466/pms.1994.79.1.595

Kohn, A. (1993) *Punished by Rewards.* Boston: Houghton Mifflin.

Krueger, R.F., & Markon. K. E. (2014). The role of the DSM-5 personality trait model in moving toward a quantitative and empirically based approach to classifying personality and psychopathology. *Annual Review of Clinical Psychology, 10*, 477–501.

Latham, G. P., & Pinder, C. C. (2005). Work motivation theory and research at the dawn of the twenty-first century. *Annual Review of Psychology, 56*, 485–516. https://doi.org/10.1146/annurev.psych.55.090902.142105

Lepper, M. R., & Greene, D. (1975). Turning play into work: Effects of adult surveillance and extrinsic rewards on children's intrinsic motivation. *Journal of Personality and Social Psychology, 31*(3), 479–486. https://doi.org/10.1037/h0076484

Locke, E. (1976). The nature and causes of job satisfaction. In M. Dunnette (Ed.), *Handbook of industrial and organizational psychology*. Chicago: Rand McNally.

Lönnqvist, J. E., Paunonen, S., Nissinen, V., Ortju, K., & Verkasalo, M. (2011). Selfenhancement in military leaders: Its relevance to officer selection and performance. *Applied Psychology*, 60(4), 670–695.

MacRae, I., & Furnham, A. (2014). *High Potential: How to spot manage and develop talented people at work*. Bloomsbury: London.

MacRae, I., & Furnham, A. (2017). *Motivation and performance: A guide to motivating a diverse workforce*. London: Kogan Page.

MacRae, I., & Furnham, A. (2020). Psychometric Analysis of the High Potential Trait Inventory (HPTI). *Psychology*, 11(8), 1125–1140.

McCall, M. W. (1997). *High-Flyers: Developing the next generation of leaders*. Boston, MA: Harvard Business School.

McCrae, R. R., & Costa, P. T. (1996). Toward a new generation of personality theories: Theoretical contexts for the five-factor model. In J. S. Wiggins (Ed.), *The five factor model of personality: Theoretical perspectives* (pp. 51–87). New York, NY: Guilford Press.

McCrae, R. R., & Terracciano, A. (2005). Universal features of personality traits from the observer's perspective: Data from 50 cultures. *Journal of Personality and Social Psychology*, 88, 547–561.

Melchers, K., Ingold,P., Wilhelmy, A., Kleinmann, M. (2015). Beyond validity: Shedding light on the social situation in employment interviews. In Nikolaou & J Osstrom (Eds.), *Employee Recruitment, Selection and Assessment* (pp. 154–171). London: Psychology Press.

Miller, L. (2008). *From Difficult to Disturbed*. New York: AMACOM.

Miller, J. D., Campbell, W. K., & Pilkonis, P. A. (2007). Narcissistic personality disorder: Relations with distress and functional impairment. *Comprehensive Psychiatry*, 48(2), 170–177.

Moscoso, S., & Salgado, J. F. (2004). 'Dark side' personality styles as predictors of task, contextual, and job performance. *International Journal of Selection and Assessment*, 12(4), 356–362.

Musek, J. (2007). A general factor of personality: Evidence for the Big One in the five-factor model. *Journal of Research in Personality*, 41, 1213–1233.

Netter, P. (1997). Digging forward into the past: Modern research on the neurochemical basis of individual differences rooted in Hans Eysenck's theory. ISSID Conference, Giessen, July.

Nord, W., Brief, A., Atieh, J., & Doherty, E. (1990). Studying meanings of work: The case of work values. In A. Brief and W. Nord (Eds.), *Meanings of occupational work* (pp. 21–64). Lexington, MA: Lexington Books.

O'Boyle, E. H., Forsyth, D. R., Banks, G. C., & McDaniel, M. A. (2012). A metaa-nalysis of the dark triad and work behavior: A social exchange perspective. *Journal of Applied Psychology*, 97(3), 557.

Oldham, J., & Morris, L. (1991). *Personality self-portrait*. New York: Bantam.

Overhuin, M., & Furnham, A. (2012). Assessing Obsessive-Compulsive Disorder (OCD): A review of self-report measures. *Journal of Obsessive-Compulsive and Related Disorders*, 1, 312–324.

Palaiou, K., & Furnham, A. (2014). Are bosses unique? Personality facet differences between CEOs and staff in five work sectors. *Consulting Psychology Journal: Practice and Research*, 66, 173–196.

Parks, L., & Guay, R. P. (2009). Personality, values, and motivation. *Personality and Individual Differences*, 47(7), 675–684. https://doi.org/10.1016/j.paid.2009.06.002

Paulhus, D. L. (1991). Measurement and control of response bias. In J. P. Robinson, P. R. Shaver, & L. S. Wrightsman (Eds.), *Measures of personality and social psychological attitudes* (pp. 17–59). San Diego, CA: Academic Press.

Paulhus, D. L. (2002). Socially desirable responding: The evolution of a construct. In H. I. Braun, D. N. Jackson, & D. E. Wiley (Eds.), *The role of constructs in psychological and educational measurement* (pp. 49–69). Mahwah, NJ: Erlbaum.

Paulhus, D. L., & Jones, D. N. (2014). Measures of dark personalities. In G. J. Boyle, D. H. Saklofske, & G. Mathews (Eds.), *Measures of personality and social psychological constructs* (pp. 562–594). San Diego: Academic Press.

Pink, D. H. (2009). *Drive: The Surprising Truth About What Motivates Us*. New York: Riverhead Books

Rauthmann, J. F. (2012). The Dark Triad and interpersonal perception: Similarities and differences in the social consequences of narcissism, Machiavellianism, and psychopathy. *Social Psychological and Personality Science*, 3(4), 487–496.

Resnick, C., Whitman, D., Weingarden, S., & Hiller, N. (2009). The bright-side and the dark-side of CEO personality. *Journal of Applied Psychology*, 94, 1365–1381. https://doi.org/10.1037/a0016238

Rice, R., Gentile, D., & McFarlin, D. (1991). Facet importance and job satisfaction. *Journal of Applied Psychology*, 76(1), 31–39. https://doi.org/10.1037/0021-9010.76.1.31

Roulin, N., Bourdage, J., & Wingate, T. (2019). Who is conducting "better" employment interviews. *Personnel Assessment and Decisions*, 1, 37–48.

Samuel, D.B., & Widiger, T.A. (2008). A meta-analytic review of the relationships between the Five-Factor Model and DSM-IV-TR personality disorders: A facet level analysis. *Clinical Psychology Review*, 28, 1326–1342.

Saulsman, L., & Page, A. (2004). The five factor model and personality disorder empirical literature: A meta-analytic review. *Clinical Psychology Review, 23,* 1055–1085.

Schwartz, S. H. (1992). Universals in the content and structure of values: Theory and empirical tests in 20 countries. In M. Zanna (Ed.), *Advances in experimental social psychology* (Vol. 25, pp. 1–65). New York.

Schwartz, S. H. (1994). Are there universal aspects in the content and structure of values? *Journal of Social Issues, 23,* 14–30.

Schwartz, S. H. (1996). Value priorities and behavior: Applying a theory of integrated value systems. In C. Seligman, J. M. Olson, & M. P. Zanna (Eds.), *The psychology of values: The Ontario Symposium* (Vol. 8, pp. 1–24). Hillsdale, NJ: Erlbaum.

Skodol, A., Bender, S., Morey, L., Clark, L., Oldham, J., Alarcon, R., Krueger, R., Verheul, R., Bell, C., & Siever, L. (2011). Personality disorder types proposed for DSM-5. *Journal of Personality Disorders, 25,* 136–169.

Skodol, A. E., Oldham, J. M., Bender, D. S., Dyck, I. R., Stout, R. L., Morey, L. C., Shea, M.T., Zanarini, M.C., Sanislow, C.A., Grilo, C.M., McGlashan, T.H., & Gunderson, J.G. (2005). Dimensional representations of DSM-IV personality disorders: relationships to functional impairment. *American Journal of Psychiatry, 162*(10), 1919–1925.

Smith, S. F., & Lilienfeld, S. O. (2013). Psychopathy in the workplace: The knowns and unknowns. *Aggression and Violent Behavior, 18*(2), 204–218.

Spain, S. M., Harms, P., & LeBreton, J. M. (2014). The dark side of personality at work. *Journal of Organizational Behavior, 35,* 41–60.

Steiger, J. H. (2000). Point estimation, hypothesis testing, and interval estimation using the RMSEA: Some comments and a reply to Hayduk and Glaser. *Structural Equation Modelling,* 7(2), 149–162. https://doi.org/10.1207/S15328007SEM0702_1

Super, D. E. (1970). *Work values inventory.* Boston, MA: Houghton Mifflin.

Teodorescu, A., Furnham, A., & MacRae, I. (2017). Trait correlates of success at work. *International Journal of Selection and Assessment, 25*(1), 36–42.

Swami, V., Weis, L., Lay, A., Barron, D., & Furnham, A. (2016). Associations between belief in conspiracy theories and the maladaptive personality traits of the personality inventory for DSM-5. *Psychiatry Research, 236,* 86–90.

Van Kampen, D., De Beurs, E., & Andrea, H. (2008). A short form of the dimensional assessment of personality pathology (DAPP-BQ): The DAPP-SF. *Psychiatry Research,* 160:115–128.

Van Leeuwen, K. G., Mervielde, I., De Clerco, B. J., & De Fruyt, F. (2007). Extending the spectrum idea: Child personality, parenting and psychopathology. *European Journal of Personality, 21*(1), 63–89.

Waters, L. L., & Waters, C. W. (1972). An empirical test of five versions of twofactor theory of job satisfaction. *Organizational Behaviour and Human Performance, 7*(1), 18–24.

Wernimont, R. (1966). Intrinsic and extrinsic factors in job satisfaction. *Journal of Applied Psychology, 50*(1), 41–50.

Widiger, T. (2011). Integrating normal and abnormal personality structure: A proposal for DSM-V. *Journal of Personality Disorders, 25*, 338–363.

Widiger, T. A, Gore, W. L., Crego, C., Rojas, S. L., & Oltmanns, J. R. (2017). Five factor model and personality disorder. In T. A. Widiger (Ed.), *The Oxford handbook of the five factor model* (pp. 449–478). New York: Oxford University Press.

Widiger, T. A., & Costa, P. T., Jr. (2002). Five-factor model personality disorder research. In P. T. Costa, Jr. & T. A. Widiger (Eds.), *Personality disorders and the five-factor model of personality* (pp. 59–87). American Psychological Association.

Widiger, T. A., Trull, T. J., Clarkin, J. F., Sanderson, C. & Costa, P. T. (2002). A description of the DSM-IV personality disorders with the five-factor model of personality. In P. T. Costa & T. A. Widiger (Eds.), *Personality disorders and the five factor model of personality* (2nd ed., pp. 89–99). Washington, DC: American Psychological Association.

Widiger, T., & Costa P. (1994). Personality and personality disorders. *Journal of Abnormal Psychology, 103*, 78–91.

Winsborough, D. L., & Sambath, V. (2013). Not like us: An investigation into the personalities of New Zealand CEOs. *Consulting Psychology Journal: Practice and Research, 65*, 87–107.

Wissing, B., & Reinhard, M.-A. (2017). The dark triad and the PID-5 maladaptive personality traits. *Frontiers in Psychology, 8*, article 1549.

Wright, A., & Simms, L. J. (2014). On the structure of personality disorder traits: Conjoint analysis of the CAT-PD, PID-5, and NEO PI-3 trait models. *Personality Disorders: Theory, Research, and Treatment, 5*, 43–54.

4.3 PROJECTIVE TECHNIQUES

What are they?

They can be a number of different techniques which require a person to say what they think or feel about something they hear, read or see: i.e. what they see in a picture, associate with a word, etc.

How do they work?

The idea is that people project onto the stimulus important and deep seated (unconscious) thoughts and feelings that reveal a great deal about them. They 'pour out' their 'inner soul' without realising it.

What of the evidence?

There is lots of evidence of absence of evidence: except for very few examples, these tests are unreliable and invalid. The danger is in over-interpreting responses that have little meaning and therefore being, quite simply, wrong.

Practical problems: cost, ethics, politics

It is relatively easy and cheap to obtain the materials but it is difficult to find, and expensive to hire, an 'expert' who is able to *validly* interpret the data.

Recommendations for use

It could be dangerous, unwise and unethical to rely on the results of any projective techniques. They are more of a party trick than a useful assessment device.

4.3.1 Introduction

Most of us have probably been exposed to a party-game projective technique. For instance, you are told that you are on a walk, and going through a forest. You come across a stream/river. Please describe it. Next to the river is a hut. Again, describe it. Ahead of you is a road through the forest. What is it like? The budding psychologist does the interpretation. Whatever you say (the river is deep, the river is shallow, the river has rocks) is deeply symbolic of our frustrated *unconscious* needs for sex, power or domination! The road is narrow, then forks, which of course indicates difficult decisions ahead. A simple game apparently says more about you than you know yourself. It not only reveals your cleverly hidden secrets, but things you don't know about deep desires and motives, and that appear to emerge from projective technique analysis. But is this merely an evidence-free party game with no proof that these 'interpretations' are true? Does it indeed have the effect of discrediting psychological assessment?

Projective tests have stayed alive in psychology for a long time partly because psychologists seem less good at uncovering people's motivations. One of the most consistent criticisms of those using interviews or questionnaires to get information about others is that they *cannot*, rather than *will not*, tell you the answer to certain questions. What really motivates you? How aggressive or altruistic are you? How much do you enjoy power? What effect did your childhood have on you? It is not that they won't tell you the answer to these questions but rather that they do not have the insight, or language to answer honestly, even if they wanted to.

It is possible that projective techniques have been sustained by psycho-analytic concepts which are essentially the following:

Behaviour is a result of *fights and compromises* among powerful, often unconscious motives, drives and needs.

Behaviour can reflect a motive in a subtle or disguised way.

The same behaviour can reflect different motives at different times or in different people.

People may be more or less aware of the forces guiding their behaviour and the conflicts driving them.

Behaviour is governed by an energy system, with a relatively fixed amount of energy available at any one time.

The goal of behaviour is *pleasure* (reduction of tension, release of energy, the pleasure principle).

People are driven primarily by *sexual* and *aggressive* instincts.

The expression of these drives can conflict with the demands of society – so the energy that would be released in the fulfilment of these drives must find other channels of release.

There is a *life* (*eros*) and *death* (*thanatos*) instinct.

Three distinctions are frequently made between *Conscious* (what we are aware of), *Preconscious* (what we can become aware of, if we attend to it) and *Unconscious* (what we cannot become aware of, except under special circumstances). The idea that seems to underlie a great deal of the projective tests is that they offer us a way to get at the pre- and unconscious which has powerful and long-lasting effect on our behaviour. Freud argued that dreams were the 'royal road' to the unconscious. It seems that some in assessment believe projective techniques have a similar useful function.

> There are essentially five categories of tests:
>
> *Inkblot* or abstract pictures: These can be constructed very simply by dropping a large 'blob' of wet ink on the middle of a page folding it in half and then looking at the resultant pattern.
>
> *Sentences completion*: Thus you complete the following 'I wished I had never....', 'I am....', 'My greatest fear is....', 'I am rather proud about....'
>
> *Free drawing*: People are asked to draw certain objects, a house, a car, a parent and are then asked questions about them.
>
> *Solid objects*: The person is given dolls, block, sand, etc. and is asked to play with, construct or manoeuvre the object while describing what they are doing.
>
> *Sounds*: People listen to sounds (familiar songs, baby crying, car crashing) or music and describe what they feel.

In some countries, people have been known to ask to what one sees in cloud formations. Others assume that many personal choices, like the colour of clothes have deep psychological foundations.

4.3.2   The Rorschach Inkblot Test

If people are unwilling or unable to discuss their innermost fears and hopes and aims, could we find these out by asking them what they see in pictures: the idea, common in 'popular' psychology that choices and descriptions 'tell you a lot about a person'? But it was a Swiss psychologist, Hermann Rorschach, who started a great movement nearly 80 years ago.

Since its creation, the famous Rorschach inkblot test has become an icon of clinical psychology and popular culture. Administered over a million times worldwide each year, the Rorschach is used to assess personality and educational placement decisions, employment and termination proceedings, parole determinations and even investigations of child abuse allegation. But is the Rorschach more than a modern variant of tea leaf reading?

There are versions of this famous test. An idea had been suggested in 1895 by Binet, the person later to be become famous for the first IQ test. The most well-known test consists of 10 half-coloured, half-monochrome cards with symmetrical inkblots. They were found to show the shapes that were most diagnostic. The tester gives the person a card at a time and asks them to say what they see. This is repeated with all the cards. Testers note what is said, how long they spend looking at each card, which way up they hold it, etc.

Scoring the test

The orthodox administration of the test goes through four phases:

The *performance phase* requires the testee to spontaneously say what he/she sees on each card. Everything said should be written down.

The second is the *inquiry phase*, which is more structured. The tester tries to enquire about two things and goes back over each card. He or she asks about location and detail. Location is what part of the inkblot was interpreted (whole, large detail, small detail, etc.). An enquiry is also made about what made the inkblot resemble the object the testee saw: form, movement, shading, colour.

The *third* stage is called the *analogy phase* where the tester probes into the choices made by the testee and wonders what they could mean or indicate.

In the final *testing-the-limits phase* the tester offers other 'popular' perceptions and wonders aloud if the test can see those as well.

This begins the 'interpretation'. This is surprisingly elaborate and has a number of letters that scorers use to indicate various phenomena. M refers to imagination and the extent to which the readings are 'peopled'. K refers to anxiety and is picked up by colour and movement. D lets the tester know much common sense the person has, and this is picked up by form. S refers to the testees oppositional tendencies and this is picked up by interpreting the white space or very small details. The scoring system can easily look like a strange mixture of a cookbook and a magic book.

The following are typical types of interpretations:

Frequent responses to small, clearly defined parts of the inkblot patterns	Obsessional personality with perfectionism and meticulousness
Frequently sees moving animals	Impulsive, demanding immediate gratification
Responses often purely determined by colour (alone)	Emotionally uncontrolled, explosive
Often sees small, passive animals	Passive, dependent personality and attitudes
Tendency to see maps	Guarded and evasive
Often sees facial masks	Reluctance to show the real self

There are different expert systems to score this test, but many look at many different aspects of the cards. The idea is to do a diagnosis or paint a profile of the real individual.

There are many serious and acrimonious debates in psychology concerning whether the test is valid (Garb et al., 2005). Careful examinations of the technique have shown that it 'does not work': for instance Wood et al, (2010) concluded 'The present findings contradict the view that the Rorschach is a clinically sensitive instrument for discriminating psychopaths from non-psychopaths' (p. 336).

The inkblot tests are not the only *projective techniques* in psychology. What they have in common is giving a person a stimulus (usually a picture; it could be a sound, or smell) and then encouraging them to *project into* or *onto* it their immediate, innermost and intense thought, feelings and desires. They say how they react to an ambiguous stimulus. The more unclear, ambiguous, vague the stimulus the more the person projects themselves onto it.

4.3.3   *The Thematic Apperception Test*

David McClelland, who worked extensively with the second most famous projective test psychology – Thematic Apperception Test – which is a series of drawings rather than inkblots, claimed that it uncovered three of the most important and fundamental of all drives or needs. They are need for Achievement, Power and Affiliation. The idea is that people tell stories about these pictures which give accurate insights into these drives which they cannot talk about.

This is perhaps the most well-known and widely used projective test. It is also known as the *picture interpretation technique* because it uses a series of around 20 provocative yet ambiguous pictures about which the person is asked to tell a story. The pictures look very dated now and some are famous.

The person is asked to tell as dramatic a story as they can for each picture presented, including the following: what has led up to the event shown; what is happening at the moment; what the characters are feeling and thinking; what the outcome of the story is.

Each story to each test is carefully scored looking for evidence of three themes. For instance:

Achievement: George is an engineer who (**need, +1**) wants to win a competition in which the man with (**achievement imagery: standard of excellence +1**) the most practical drawing will be awarded the contract to build a bridge. He is taking a moment to think (**goal anticipation, +1**) how happy he will be if he wins. He has been (**block, world, +1**) baffled by how to make such a long span strong, but remembers (**instrumental act, +1**) to specify a new steel alloy of great strength, submits his entry, but does not win and (**goal state, negative, +1**) is very unhappy. Total *n* achievement score = +7

Affiliation: George is an engineer who is working late. He is (**affiliation imagery, +1**) worried that his wife will be annoyed with him for neglecting her (**block, world, +1**). She has been objecting that he cares more about his work than his wife and family (**block, personal, +1**). He seems unable to satisfy both his boss and his wife (**need, +1**), but he loves her very much, and (**instrumental act, +1**) will do his best to finish up fast and get home to her. Total *n* affiliation score = +6

Power: This is Georgiadis, (**prestige of actor +1**) famous architect, who (**need, +1**) wants to win a competition which will establish who is

---

> (**power imagery, +1**) the best architect in the world. His chief rival,
> Bulokovsky (**block, world, +1**) has stolen his best idea, and he is
> dreadfully afraid of the (**goal anticipation, negative, +1**) disgrace of
> losing. But he comes up with a great new idea, which absolutely
> (**powerful effect, +1**) bowls the judges over, and he wins.
> Total n power score = 7

This is clearly a highly 'expensive' task. The stories have to be transcribed, then at least two raters (for evidence of reliability) have to go through each of the 20 stories to get three scores and these scores have to be aggregated to yield three scores for an individual. Compare this with completing a simple and short need for achievement test.

4.3.4 Sentence Completion

Sentence completion requires people filling the gaps in statements, and in doing so, revealing specific values/attitudes which would otherwise be unmentioned and/or unrealised:

> My biggest regret in life is...
> Compared to most others of my age and stage I am considerably
>   more...
> The thing I fear most is...
> Secretly I really admire...
> If I won a million dollars I would...
> What I would like to be remembered for is...
> Assuming that I know you well, and am being honest, what is the
>   nicest compliment I can give you?

Once the answers have been obtained, the issue is how they are scored (see earlier):

Another related technique is the 'I am...' or Twenty Statements test. A person has to complete the same sentence twenty times. So, you may say 'I am 27 years old'; 'I am a Muslim'; 'I am very fond of tennis'. One way in which this test has been used is to measure self-concept and whether this is done by social category (i.e. membership of a particular group) or whether it is strictly individual characteristics.

These are called sentence completion techniques. They are used to fill newspaper and magazine columns by journalists. They are interview techniques without the interviewer. They offer the responder a wonderful opportunity to show off, to disclose or to carefully manage others' impressions.

Why use sentence completion techniques in business? The rationale behind sentence completion is threefold.

Firstly, and perhaps most importantly, to get at motives and motivation. The problem with many motivations – motives for power and dominance; motives for inclusion and affiliation; motives for achievement and success – is not that people will not, but they cannot tell you.

Could famous politicians, entrepreneurs or scientists tell you what drives and motivates them? They could no doubt give you an answer. But it might be a politically correct or self-justifying story, not the actual truth.

Secondly, they are, it is argued, much less prone to faking, dissimilation or social desirability. People 'see through' questionnaires but much less so in sentence completion. The scorer looks for themes that they contain and is prepared to entertain contradiction and paradox.

Thirdly, why people like and use sentence completion tests is the mystery that surrounds them. Personality tests that reduce an individual to as few as five or six numbers may seem as unspecific, impersonal and even boring in comparison. It seems to many that you answer the test by saying how you typically behave, and then the testers, using slightly different language, tell you back how you behave.

4.3.5 Evaluation

There are four – arguably *devastating* – objections to the use of these tests on scientific grounds:

> First, they are unreliable because different experts or scorers come up with quite different interpretations. If the testers can't agree on the meanings, we can't get anywhere.

Second, they are invalid because the scores don't predict anything. In short, they don't measure what they say they are measuring.

Third, context makes all the difference. The mood of the person, the characteristics of the tester, the setting of the test all effect results, which suggests they are picking up on trivial rather than essential underlying factors.

Fourth, the testers can't agree on what the tests measures: attitudes, abilities, defences, motivation, deep desires. By measuring everything they may measure nothing.

So why are these tests still used despite their limitations?

1. They provide often unique and intriguing data relatively easily that cannot be obtained as cheaply, quickly and easily elsewhere.
2. Skilled and trained practitioners seem able to obtain impressive, reliable and insightful findings which they cannot get from other tests or interviews.
3. The richness of the data makes other test data often look crude, colourless and constipated.
4. They can complement and confirm other findings and ideas.

Although 20 years old, and indeed challenged by other academics, the review by Lilienfeld et al. (2000) called the *Scientific Status of Projective Techniques* requires careful reading. They noted:

'1. Projective techniques are highly controversial.
2. Projective techniques are susceptible to faking, as well as to subtle situational influences.
3. Projective techniques are routinely used for purposes for which they are invalid or poorly supported by research.
4. The scoring of many projective techniques can be unreliable or poor
5. Norms for projective techniques are often non-existent, poor, or misleading.
6. Projective techniques may be biased against North American minority groups and individuals who live outside North America.

First, given the relatively weak evidence for the zero-order and incremental validity of most projective indexes, the amount of time devoted to educating and training students in the administration and scoring of projective techniques should be reduced ... Second, if instructors intend to cover projective techniques in their courses, they should expose students to the research and meta-analytic literature regarding their psychometric properties. In particular, instructors should teach students to distinguish between projective indexes that do and do not have empirical support. ... Third, all graduate students in clinical and counselling psychology should be systematically exposed to the extensive body of research on clinical judgment and decision making. Drawing stimuli and psychopathological features increases as information processing load increases... Foremost and finally, graduate students should be taught the crucial and sometimes painful lesson that this research literature imparts – clinical experience and clinical intuition can sometimes be misleading.'

(pp. 56–58)

4.3.6 Conclusion

Projective techniques are, quite rightly, used very little in formal assessments, though they do go in and out of fashion. They are difficult to justify on cost, ethical or psychometric grounds.

They retain a mystery factor but have not completely disappeared because of their ability to tap into the subconscious.

REFERENCES

Binet, A. (1895). Measuring visual illusions in children. *Philosophical Review of France and Abroad*, 40, 11–25.

Garb, H. N., Wood, J. M., Lilienfeld, S. O., & Nezworski, M. T. (2005). Roots of the Rorschach controversy. *Clinical Psychology Review*, 25(1), 97–118.

Lilienfeld, S. O., Wood, J. M., & Garb, H. N. (2000). The scientific status of projective techniques. *Psychological Science in the Public Interest*, 1(2), 27–66.

McClelland, D. C. (1999). How the test lives on: Extensions of the thematic apperception test approach. In L. Gieser & M. I. Stein (Eds.), *Evocative images: The thematic apperception test and the art of projection* (pp. 163–175). Washington, DC: American Psychological Association.

Wood, J. M., Lilienfeld, S. O., Nezworski, M. T., Garb, H. N., Allen, K. H., & Wildermuth, J. L. (2010). Validity of Rorschach Inkblot scores for discriminating psychopaths from nonpsychopaths in forensic populations: A meta-analysis. *Psychological Assessment*, 22(2), 336.

5   Observer Reports

What are they?
Responses to requests to describe or evaluate the (often unspecified) characteristics of an individual, usually about their typical behaviour and abilities as well as the extent to which they would succeed in a particular educational course or job.

How do they work?
Selectors contact people who supposedly know the candidate well, asking them to comment on particular individuals because they have taught them or worked for or with them. It is the quantity and quality of information/data that they have on an individual that makes them suitable for the task.

What of the evidence?
They are useful only under very specific conditions: when referees know, and are asked about very specific *and* relevant characteristics of an individual *and* tell the truth as they know it.

Practical problems: cost, ethics, politics
It is very cheap and, for the most part, does not incur many ethical problems. However, there are now many potential legal and political problems which explains why many companies do not allow their staff to write them.

Recommendations for use
If contacts/recommenders/writers know an individual well, have insight, *and* are prepared to be completely honest it is a good idea to get information from them.

5.1.1 Introduction

For many decades, selection involved the standard trio of application forms, interviews and references. It was standard practice that a candidate's teachers, colleagues or bosses from the past were contacted and asked to write about the candidate's aptitudes, attitudes and potential to complete a course or succeed in a job. Many candidates still expect this to occur.

They attempt to gather all sorts of facts: dates of employment, salary, work habits and organisational citizenship. They are often highly idiosyncratic, revealing more about the writer than the candidate. There are many jokes about the meaning of certain phrases like 'He left us fired with enthusiasm'; 'She always achieved the standards she set'; 'He is a deeply sensitive person'. They are about referees subtly 'encoding' negative information.

The average length of a reference is around 500 words, though this can vary enormously.

Potential referees may be sent a letter saying that X is applying for a job (they many include details of roles and responsibilities) and that they have nominated them as one who can provide an informed reference. This may include some specific questions like details on their absenteeism/illnesses or not. Because, mainly in America, various people have sued their referees for negative references, many only give barest details like years of employment.

The question is what data these references provide. *Are some negative points cleverly encoded? What is the exact relationship between referee and candidate? Does it make a difference if these references are collected by phone, email or post?*

Gatewood et al. (2015) noted that people felt the really only useful information that people get from letters of reference were the *dates of previous employment.* Only occasionally did they get useful information like salary history, reason for leaving previous employment, work ethics, skills, history of malpractice or personality. Furthermore, they pointed out a number of problems, like the possible defamation of character in references.

Sometimes, the contacts are given very little details about the course/job and encouraged to write about any aspect of the individual. Other times they are asked broad or specific questions. It is often assumed that employment reference letters cover issues such as the employee's tasks and responsibilities while in the job; the duration of employment; the reporting relationship with the writer; the employee's abilities, knowledge, skills and personality; the employee's qualifications; the employee's attitude and beliefs (i.e. job satisfaction); the employee's social skills, emotional intelligence and power to build relationships.

References are almost as widely used in personnel selection as the interview. Yet there has been a surprising dearth of research on the reliability and validity of the reference letter, and an assessment of the existing evidence suggests that the reference is a poor indicator of candidates' potential. Indeed, Judge and Higgins (1998) concluded that 'despite widespread use, reference reports also appear to rank among the least valid selection measures' (p. 207). Furthermore, studies using experts show less consensus than controversy around letters of recommendation with (surprisingly perhaps) academics still placing more weight on the references than applied (non-academic) people (Nicklin & Roch, 2009).

Early research attempted to do a content analysis of letters to pick up certain traits and competencies like dependability (Peres & Garcia, 1962).

Given the potentially important consequences of the information in a letter of recommendation (LOR), they have not attracted a great deal of interest (Kuncel et al., 2014; Nicklin & Roch, 2009; Saudek et al., 2018). Referees have usually been used to check for prior discipline problems, confirm details on an application form or discover new and salient information about a possible employee (Aamodt et al., 1998). Thus, referees are expected to have sufficient knowledge of the applicant's previous work experience and his or her suitability for the job applied. That is, they ideally have a thorough record of the candidate's work performance and an understanding of how, why and when their abilities and skills impacted on the outcomes but also (most unusually) a full understanding of the position they are applying for.

However, it is widely known that these letters often contain many exaggerations (Nicklin & Roch, 2008). Though cheap and popular, they are thought of as unreliable and of poor validity.

There are three main reasons for their poor reliability.

1. Leniency: Most references are indiscriminately positive. This is for three reasons. Candidates themselves choose those they know are most likely to be very positive; respondents worry negative evaluations may result in a libel suit; respondents have no incentive to take the time or tell the truth.
2. Idiosyncrasy: People can and do use idiosyncratic language, examples and criteria to describe and evaluate others.
3. Free-form references: Reference writers are often offered no guidelines in what they are required to do. They can offer long/short, descriptive/evaluative and relevant/irrelevant data.

Some recent studies have shown interesting findings. In an experimental study, a group of medical researchers (Saudek et al., 2018) found the factors rated most important about the letter of reference were (in order):

1. Depth of interaction with the applicant
2. Specific traits of the applicant
3. Applicant's abilities
4. Summative statement or strength of recommendation
5. Personal stories about the applicant

The least important three factors were: Community service activities; applicant's advanced (post-graduate) degrees and an increased length of reference (4+ paragraphs). They also noted the three most positive rating phrases: 'I give my highest recommendation'; 'Would like applicant to stay at our institution'; and 'Exceeded expectations'. The three most negative were: 'Solid performance'; 'Showed improvement' and 'Performed at expected level'.

One persistent problem is that referees are consciously or unconsciously biased when writing references (see Chapter 2). One study investigated whether men were described more in agentic terms and women more in communal terms.

Madera et al. (2009) noted that:

> Historically, men have been more likely to engage in tasks that require speed, strength, and the ability to be away from home for expanded periods of time, whereas women were more likely to stay home and engage in family tasks, such as child rearing. Accordingly, men are perceived and expected to be agentic, and women are perceived and expected to be communal. Agency includes descriptions of aggressiveness, assertiveness, independence, and self-confidence. Agentic behaviors at work include speaking assertively, influencing others, and initiating tasks. Communal behaviors at work include being concerned with the welfare of others (i.e., descriptions of kindness, sympathy, sensitivity, and nurturance), helping others, accepting others' direction, and maintaining relationships.
>
> *(p. 1592)*

In their study they confirmed their hypotheses: women were more likely to be described in communal and men in agentic terms, and that agentic descriptions were more likely to lead to more positive hiring ratings.

5.1.2 Structured vs Unstructured References

References can be classified on the basis of how structured/standardised they are, ranging from completely unstructured ('What do you think of X?') to totally structured (e.g., standardised multiple-choice questions, checklists and ratings). The latter require referees to address predefined areas and often merely tick boxes. Thus, one might be asked to rate:

How well does the candidate work in teams: Poorly 1 ... 7 Very Well

How would you rate the candidates EQ: Below Average 1 ... 7 Above Average

Was their absenteeism rate, compared to peers: Very High 1 ... 7 Very low

Some are more open ended like: *Why did X leave your organisation? What are/were their principal strengths and weaknesses?*

Others might have binary answers like: *Would you rehire the candidate? Yes / No*

Were they involved in any major or minor injury claim accidents? Yes / No

One major problem for many references is there is no option to respond with 'Don't know' or 'Not sure', and not responding may be interpreted as carelessness or, worse, desire to hide something.

One of the most well-known structured references is the US *Employment Recommendation Questionnaire* (ERQ), developed for the US civil service and investigated in many psychological studies. The ERQ covers five core areas, referring to the candidate's (a) competence or ability, (b) reputation or character, (c) special qualifications (relevant to the job offered), (d) employability by the referee and (e) previous record of problems at work.

McCarthy and Goffin (2001) tested three different rating items (like rating on multi-item scales or making global trait ratings) and found the relative percentile method the best: that is, where people rate individuals compared to their peer group. They gave a rating (percentage) which refers to the percentage of people in the applicant's peer group who would score lower than the applicant. The latter is very common in academic research where the referee is asked whether a person is in the top 5%/10%/25%/50% of their peer group in terms of ability.

Researchers in the area would recommend that referees be asked specific questions about a candidate so they can indicate their confidence in their ratings (i.e. whether or not they had enough data to answer the question). Unstructured references may say more about the referee than the candidate.

One of the problems with referees is essentially the same as with interviewers. It is the impact of the personality of the referee on the reference. How insightful, honest and literate is the referee? Not all referees are equally perceptive about people. Technical types can find (all) people problematic. Because of their rigid nature, they may have little insight into others' emotions and motivations; hence their references would be worthless.

Referees can have a very different 'take' on the same person even when given the same 'data'. Some have a shrewd, clinical assessment, soon getting below the surface acting. Others seem impervious to the beliefs, values and motives of people they work with and for.

Next there is the problem of literacy. References are written or spoken. But no matter how insightful a person, if they have a restricted, limited or amateur vocabulary they may never really be able to communicate their impressions.

Third, their mood. Indeed their moodiness can have an effect. Get them on the wrong day and their 'negative affectivity' is projected onto others. Find them after a morale-boosting success and this spills over onto the candidate reference.

References are meant to describe behaviours, but of course they can be just as much an index of liking and 'fit'. By and large we are attracted to people like us. Extraverts seek out fun-loving, optimistic partygoers. The tender-minded, empathic, agreeable types search for like-minded companions.

Thus, the personality of the referee has a powerful impact on the style, tone and, indeed, encoded messages in the reference. For easy proof, compare half a dozen references for the same person and note the differences.

In a funny and sceptical paper, three American academics provide a typology of referees (Guduguntla et al., 2020), such as the following:

> The Cookie Cutter takes the all too familiar approach to writing: copy and paste. Here, standardized forms and templates are used to compose letters of recommendation. The result is often a generic, vague product riddled with typos. Errors such as switched pronouns, incorrect names, and remainders of templated phrasing abound. Such writers are also the most prone to using stereotyped adjectives for men and women. Often, men are described by their ability, and women are described by their effort, propagating unconscious gender bias in reference writing. Some programs may begin to doubt the authenticity of the applicant's entire portfolio as many such letters have been recognized as plagiarized or otherwise questionable. If you have seen one Cookie-Cutter letter, you have seen them all.

5.1.3   Reliability of References

Early research on the reliability of the employment reference produced pessimistic results: referees do not agree in their evaluations (Muchinsky, 1979). A study examining letters of recommendation in the US civil service found that different ratings from different referees correlated only at .40 (Mosel & Goheen, 1959). This value is somewhat lower than – but still comparable to – that obtained in multi-source or '360-degree' feedback settings (see next section), where the inter-rater reliability can approach .60 (Murphy & Cleveland, 1995).

To some extent this is to be expected as people may show 'different aspects of themselves' to different people. Therefore, there is little point in using multiple sources if we expected all of them to provide the same information. This is a well-known contradiction in academic grading where exams are frequently double-marked by faculty only to agree with similar marks in the end (Baird et al., 2004) However, inter-rater agreements of .40 are low and mean that only

20% of the variance in candidates' attributes is accounted for, leaving a substantial percentage of variance unexplained.

The low reliability of references has in part been explained in terms of evaluative biases (Feldman, 1981) attributable to personality characteristics of the referee. Referees' mood states when writing the references will influence whether the reference is more or less positive (Judge & Higgins, 1998). Thus, when referees retrieve information about candidates, their judgement is already clouded by emotional information (often as simple and general as 'good' or 'bad'). Some of the sources of such mood states are arguably dispositional (e.g. emotionally stable and extraverted individuals more frequently experience positive affect states, whereas the opposite applies to neurotic introverted people), and personality characteristics can have other (non-affective) effects on evaluations too.

More reliable information from reference letters can be obtained if different raters base their ratings and conclusions on the same information such as exam results or speed of promotion. For instance, as early as the 1940s the UK Civil Service Selection Board (CSSB) examined multiple references for the same candidates (e.g. from school, university, army and previous employment), written by different referees. Results showed that inter-reliabilities for a panel of five or six people can be as high as .73 (Wilson, 1948). However few employers can afford to examine such detailed information. Furthermore, even if internal consistencies such as inter-rater reliabilities are adequate, that does not mean that employment references will be valid predictors of job-related outcomes. Indeed, the validity of references has been an equally important topic of concern when assessing the utility of this method in personnel selection.

5.1.4 Validity of References

How valid are letters of recommendation in predicting relevant job outcomes? Do they predict how well a candidate will do on a course or in a specific job? This is no doubt partly because it is unclear what the criterion variable is. Most of this research has focused on structured references, not least because it is easier to quantify the validity of these references (particularly compared to the highly variable and, by definition, hard to standardise, unstructured letters of recommendation).

Early studies on the ERQ showed that reference checks correlated in the range of .00 and .30 with subsequent performance. In a meta-analysis, Reilly et al. reported a mean correlation of .18 with supervisory ratings, .08 with turnover and .14 with a global criterion (Reilly & Chao, 1982). A more generous (corrected for unreliability and restriction of range) estimate was provided by Hunter and Hunter's meta-analysis, namely .26 (Hunter & Hunter, 1984), and one of the largest validities was (again, corrected) .36 for head teachers' references and training success in the Navy (Jones & Harrison, 1982). It has been pointed out by Jones et al. that teachers' (or, for that matter, professors') references tend to be more accurate because they are more motivated (than past employers) to maintain credibility as they are likely to write more references in the future.

In an important meta-analysis of letters of recommendation in academia, Kuncel et al. (2014) asked whether these letters add anything extra (incremental validity) above measures of intelligence and their previous performance (Grade point average). They found that the scored references did correlate with the candidates' personal statements, their grade point average, as well as rated personal statements and interviews. Moreover, they did add small but significant incremental variance suggesting as the authors put it 'reasons for hope' as they can provide useful measures of interest, persistence and motivation.

On one hand, it would be unwise to expect higher validities from the reference letter if it is not reliable in the first place. Yet, there are several other converging factors that threaten the validity of this assessment and selection method, namely:

1. References tend to be very *lenient*, which produces highly skewed data. This effect, often referred to as the *Pollyanna Effect*, reduces the real variance

between candidates and means that 'most applicants are characterised as somewhat desirable' (Paunonen et al., 1987, p. 97). This is hardly surprising since referees are nominated by the candidates themselves. Referees who are asked to provide a reference have no incentives to be harsh and may indeed be afraid of being too harsh as they may be sued by the candidates. Moreover, given that harsh comments are so rare and seen as a 'kiss of death' (typically, negative points are given more weight than positive ones), referees are even more sensitive to make them, though research suggests that *mixing up* negative and positive comments makes references to be perceived as more genuine and even results in positive hiring decisions (Knouse, 1983). It is also likely that referees abstain from providing a reference if they cannot be too positive about the applicant, which would explain the poor response rates found (Schneider & Schmitt, 1986).

2. Referees tend to write *similar references* for all candidates. In fact it has been pointed out that references – particularly unstructured ones – provide more information about the referee than the candidate (Baxter et al., 1981). Moreover, and as mentioned earlier, dispositional traits (personality factors) and affective states (mood) distort references significantly (Judge & Higgins, 1998). This leads not only to low reliability but also lower criterion-related validities.

3. Referees (often acting in benefit of the organisation) may wish to *retain good employees* and know that a positive reference may have just the opposite effect. Moreover, for the same reasons they may choose to write overly positive references for staff they are eager to see off. These 'hidden agendas' are hard to evidence but indicate that employers' motivations can have a huge effect on the type of reference provided.

There are now many serious legal issues associated with references, so much so that some organisations refuse to give them. People are directed only to say that the candidate was employed for the specified time they worked there and nothing else. Litigation has followed where a person has been hired partly on the basis of a reference only to discover the person was extremely poor at the job. In this instance it appears references have been over-positive to 'get rid' of the employee. However, what has more recently occurred is that people and organisations have been sued if they refused to give a reference knowing the candidate is in some sense problematic (e.g. has criminal or anti-social tendencies). In this sense some employers claim with respect to references you are 'damned if you do; and damned if you don't'.

Gatewood et al. (2015) list six problems with letters of recommendation:

> - Referees have difficulty in deciding what to include.
> - Reference quality depends on the ability and effort of the writers.
> - References are usually too positive and general.
> - References are difficult to compare.
> - Important and relevant information is ignored.
> - Scoring of letters is very problematic.

5.1.5   How to Improve the Validity of References

Some attempts to improve the quality of data in references use different methods (Cook, 2016):

> *Forced-choice*: This ipsative method reduces leniency like 'Was this candidate more likely to (a) offer help to colleagues (b) complete their work on time' or 'Did this person (a) have a poor attendance/high absentee record (b) gossip a lot in the office.
>
> *Competency based*: Resilience – Was the person able to cope with stress well? Time management – How time-efficient was the person?
>
> *Relative percentiles*: Compared to other workers in similar jobs, what % of your staff scored lower on creativity (or another personality trait).
>
> *Personality-based structured interviews*: Specific questions are asked about specific traits like neuroticism perhaps even using established questionnaire items ('Are they a worrier?')

Research in this area provides some useful guidelines to improve on the validity of recommendation letters: Employers should count 'keywords' (e.g. able, creative, reliable), which are to be previously determined on the basis of job analysis. This technique provides some order to unstructured references, though it is certainly not immune to the referee style. Neary 60 years ago Peres and Garcia (1962) scrutinised over 600 references and identified five key areas that could be used to organise the keyword count: co-operation, intelligence, Extraversion ('urbanity'), vigour, and Conscientiousness ('dependability'). Thus, these days we could simply devise a programme that scored all synonyms and antonyms for

> Co-operative/helpful/supportive
> Intelligent/bright/smart/quick
> Extraverted/sociable/lively
> Vigor/energy/enthusiasm
> Conscientiousness/work ethic/hardworking

Aamodt and colleagues analysed students' references and found support for these categories (Aamodt et al., 1993). Although it is questionable whether these categories truly represent the best way to organise and classify the content of references – notably because established personality taxonomies, such as the Big Five, and cognitive ability models (see Chapters 7 and 6, respectively) have a stronger and more generalisable theoretical basis – it is clear that having a taxonomy or framework to assess unstructured references does help.

There are now many programmes that do Linguistic Inquiry and Word Count which can be programmed to look for themes like 'positive emotions' or agency.

The predictive validity of references tends to increase when referees are asked to use 'relative percentiles', i.e. comparative rankings of how well the candidate does in any given area relative to the group the referee uses as frame of reference. Although percentiles are not normally distributed and inflated (80th percentiles being the average; McCarthy & Goffin, 2001), they still force referees to distinguish between candidates.

Last, but not least, it has been argued that if the anonymity of the referees were preserved, references would be less lenient, more heterogeneous and more accurate/valid (Ceci & Peters, 1984).

Research also indicates that using concrete examples to back up statements about the candidate's attributes and including both positive *and* negative information about the candidate leads to improved references. This was the conclusion of a study by Knouse (1983). The worst-case scenario on the other hand was for references that had no examples and included some negative information.

Gatewood et al. (2015) note:

---

1. Reference data is best when it is strictly job related.
2. One needs very specific application forms for different jobs (i.e. 'One size fits all' does not work).
3. Reference checks are subject to discrimination guidelines.
4. Well-planned structured reference checks are less open to charges of discrimination.
5. Applicants need to give written permission for their referees to be contacted.
6. Those doing face-to-face or telephone interviewing need to be trained.
7. All reference check information needs to be recorded in writing.
8. If the applicant-nominated referees did not provide references, others should be provided.
9. Where possible, check all application form information.
10. Be very sensitive to negative information, which needs to be verified and relevant to the job.

5.1.6   An Evolutionary Perspective

Given the unreliability and poor validity of letters of references, it seems hard to understand why this method of assessment is used so widely. One reason may be that employers are unaware of the problems associated, though given that references are used even in business and psychology schools (where employers have access to this literature and tend to be aware of the low validity and reliability of recommendation letters), there may be other reasons.

Colarelli et al. (2002) explained the widespread use of references in terms of what evolutionary theory calls 'reciprocal altruism' (quid pro quo), which is the basis of cooperation among non-kin (Buss, 1995). They applied the principle of reciprocal altruism to the relationship between the applicant and candidate, specifically how closeness between them determines the favourability of the references. They argued that 'a recommender will be inclined to write favourably if the applicant is perceived as a valuable resource or if there has been a history of mutually beneficial social exchange. An evolutionary psychological perspective suggests that cooperation, status competition and mating interests should affect the tone of letters of recommendation' (p. 325).

A second hypothesis derived from evolutionary theory is that men's preference for younger females should be reflected in more favourable references. Specifically, the authors explained that 'males typically desire attractive, younger females as mating partners because youth and beauty are cues of health and fertility ... As such, males are likely to be most solicitous towards younger females and regard them in a positive way. This positive regard, in turn, is likely to be reflected in letters of recommendation' (p. 328).

5.1.7 Compliance with Request

What does it mean if a referees ignores a request for a reference or says that he or she prefers not to provide it? This is the question Hedricks et al. (2019) asked, supposing it may be due to the candidates actual (probably poor) job performance, their relationship with the candidate or the method of requesting the letter. All three factors were important, and they provided some practical implications:

> First, our study revealed that employers are not necessarily consistent when asking questions of reference providers that will help them make reasoned hiring decisions on candidates. For example, the majority of

employers (73.7%) did not ask about a candidate's work-related areas for improvement (or weaknesses). Employers who ask such questions may thus benefit from competitive advantage in the war for talent.

Second, a minority of participants reported being contacted through an email link to an online survey for a reference check. Online methods of reference checking have proven to be faster and more efficient than phone or written LORs. Using slower and less efficient methods of reference checking will necessarily prolong the selection process and likely lead to a loss of top prospects.

Third, our study and previous data show that the rates of reference provider compliance are likely to range from 85% to 100% and if one captures a measure of this compliance, it can be used as a variable in and of itself in addition to the reference feedback to predict possible relevant work outcomes.

Fourth, employers should consider providing their candidates with guidelines such as: (a) ensure the potential reference provider has had enough opportunity to observe your work behavior; (b) opt for potential reference providers with whom you have more recently worked; and (c) contact your potential reference provider ahead of time and provide them with some useful information on the position for which you are applying. Fifth and finally, if employers are concerned about reference provider compliance, they should avoid the use of LORs. Overall, reference provider compliance was lowest for LORs among all the three methods studied.

(p. 149)

5.1.8   Conclusion

References are only useful if three criteria are met:

First, if the right people are asked to give them. It is those 'in the know'. It is often the boss who is asked to write the reference. But what does he/she know? What do colleagues, reports and customers know? Subordinates always know more than bosses. They know about management style, and foibles, preferences and peccadillos. They usually have 10 times as much contact as bosses. Colleagues (peers) know about abilities and ambitions. Customers know about keeping promises. This is why multi-source (360-degree) feedback and ratings are so interesting. Lecturers are often asked to write references on students they taught 10 years ago in classes of over 100. And, in many universities, lectures are voluntary. So first establish how well the referees know the candidate. In what context (at work, out of work) and for how long? What was the nature of their relationship? In short, what is their data bank? The more they know about all aspects of the person (personality, ability, work style, values) the better.

Second, are they prepared to tell you the *truth*? Are they prepared to talk/ write what they believe and know? For many there is little or no incentive to do so; and if there is indeed an incentive (help get rid of a poor worker; help a relative; knife a talented colleague; get revenge on a person) it may be seriously counterproductive. Referees, quite rightly, get nervous about writing references which can later turn out to be exhibit A. It is for the referee, less effortful, and given they believe they are not being recorded, probably leads to much more disclosure. They should be encouraged to say 'I don't know' if indeed they don't. They may be asked to say how confident they are in their answers and/or what is their source of information.

Third, ask direct, specific questions regarding behaviours and values you want to know about. And be clear what you want to know and why. So, if you want to know about their abilities, ask about how fast and accurate they were; the quality of their written work; their capacity for learning and their general knowledge. If you want to (and you should) know about their work ethic, ask about their achievement striving and how well organised they are. Find out how well prepared they were for important things and whether they had a reputation for hard work. And ask how they coped with stress. Ask about illnesses, absenteeism, moodiness.

Moustafa (2018) notes:

Disqualifying people on the basis of reference letters or any subjective personal judgments is counterproductive for scientists and for the scientific knowledge more generally. Should it be kept at all, the letter of recommendation should be written jointly between the mentors or advisors and the trainees to prevent any potential errors and biased language and to serve as a good mentoring opportunity promoting self-reflection. Even though, this would not remove its deficiencies mentioned above, so it should be better to remove such educational accessories from academia to reduce their pull string effects and to keep academia as an objective field as possible.

(pp. 3–4)

REFERENCES

Aamodt, M. G., Bryan, D. A., & Whitcomb, A. J. (1993). Predicting performance with letters of recommendation. *Public Personnel Management, 22*(1), 81–90.

Aamodt, M. G., Nagy, M. S., & Thompson, N. (1998, June). *Employment references: Who are we talking about.* Paper presented at the annual meeting of the International Personnel Management Association Assessment Council, Chicago, IL.

Baird, J.-A., Greatorex, J., & Bell, J. F. (2004). What makes marking reliable? Experiments with UK examinations. *Assessment in Education: Principles, Policy & Practice, 11*(3), 331–348.

Baxter, J. C., Brock, B., Hill, P. C., & Rozelle, R. M. (1981). Letters of recommendation: a question of value. *Journal of Applied Psychology, 66*(3), 296–301.

Buss, D. M. (1995). Evolutionary psychology: a new paradigm for psychological science. *Psychological Inquiry, 6*(1), 1–30.

Ceci, S. J., & Peters, D. (1984). Letters of reference: a naturalistic study of the effects of confidentiality. *American Psychologist, 39*(1), 29–31.

Colarelli, S. M., Hechanova-Alampay, R., & Canali, K. G. (2002). Letters of recommendation: an evolutionary psychological perspective. *Human Relations, 55*(3), 315–344.

Cook, M. (2016). *Personnel selection: Adding value through people – A changing picture* (6th ed.). Chichester, UK: John Wiley & Sons.

Gatewood, R., Feild, H. S., & Barrick, M. (2015). *Human resource selection* (8th ed.). Boston, MA: Cengage Learning.

Guduguntla, V., Adzemovic, T., & Chopra, V. (2020). Writing Wrongs. *The American Journal of Medicine, 133*(1), 14–16.

Hedricks, C. A., Rupayana, D. D., Fisher, P. A., & Robie, C. (2019). Factors affecting compliance with reference check requests. *International Journal of Selection and Assessment, 27*(2), 139–151.

Hunter, J. E., & Hunter, R. F. (1984). Validity and utility of alternative predictors of job performance. *Psychological Bulletin, 96*(1), 72–98.

Jones, A., & Harrison, E. (1982). Prediction of performance in initial officer training using reference reports. *Journal of Occupational Psychology, 55*(1), 35–42.

Judge, T. A., & Higgins, C. A. (1998). Affective disposition and the letter of reference. *Organizational Behavior and Human Decision Processes, 75*(3), 207–221.

Knouse, S. B. (1983). The letter of recommendation: specificity and favorability of information. *Personnel Psychology, 36*(2), 331–341.

Kuncel, N. R., Kochevar, R. J., & Ones, D. S. (2014). A meta-analysis of letters of recommendation in college and graduate admissions: reasons for hope. *International Journal of Selection and Assessment, 22*(1), 101–107.

Madera, J. M., Hebl, M. R., & Martin, R. C. (2009). Gender and letters of recommendation for academia: agentic and communal differences. *Journal of Applied Psychology, 94*(6), 1591–1599.

McCarthy, J. M., & Goffin, R. D. (2001). Improving the validity of letters of recommendation: an investigation of three standardized reference forms. *Military Psychology, 13*(4), 199–222.

Mosel, J. N., & Goheen, H. W. (1959). The employment recommendation questionnaire: III. Validity of different types of references. *Personnel Psychology, 12*, 469–477.

Murphy, K. R., & Cleveland, J. N. (1995*). Understanding performance appraisal: Social, organizational, and goal based perspectives.* Thousand Oaks, CA: Sage.

Moustafa, K. (2018). Recommendation letters and contacts: an implicit pull string to end within academia. *Arabic Science Archive, 14*, 1–4.

Muchinsky, P. M. (1979). The use of reference reports in personnel selection: a review and evaluation. *Journal of Occupational Psychology, 52*(4), 287–297.

Nicklin, J. M., & Roch, S. G. (2008). Biases influencing recommendation letter contents: physical attractiveness and gender 1. *Journal of Applied Social Psychology, 38*(12), 3053–3074.

Nicklin, J. M., & Roch, S. G. (2009). Letters of recommendation: controversy and consensus from expert perspectives. *International Journal of Selection and Assessment, 17*(1), 76–91.

Paunonen, S. V., Jackson, D. N., & Oberman, S. M. (1987). Personnel selection decisions: effects of applicant personality and the letter of reference. *Organizational Behavior and Human Decision Processes, 40*(1), 96–114.

Peres, S. H., & Garcia, J. R. (1962). Validity and dimensions of descriptive adjectives used in reference letters for engineering applicants. *Personnel Psychology, 15*(3), 279–286.

Reilly, R. R., & Chao, G. R. (1982). Validity and fairness of some alternative employee selection procedures. *Personnel Psychology, 35*(1), 1–62.

Saudek, K., Saudek, D., Treat, R., Bartz, P., Weigert, R., & Weisgerber, M. (2018). Dear program director: deciphering letters of recommendation. *Journal of Graduate Medical Education, 10*(3), 261–266.

Schneider, B. & Schmitt, N. (1986). *Staffing Organizations* (2nd ed.). Glenview, IL: Scott Foresman.

5.2 MULTI-SOURCE (360-DEGREE) RATINGS

What is it?

It is based on the idea that because people know different things about an individual it is more reliable to get multiple ratings of their ability, motivation, personality and performance from a range of people they work with, including their boss, colleagues, subordinates and clients.

How does it work?

Staff are given, hopefully, a well-designed and salient rating form that they are asked to complete on a person they know relatively well at work. These ratings are collated, differences and disagreements noted and fed back to the target person as a developmental exercise.

What of the evidence?

There are four factors which have to be fulfilled for the exercise to work: the rating form needs to be well designed (see questionnaires); the ratings need to be salient and job analysis derived; the raters need to know the person well; they have to be scrupulously honest in their ratings.

Practical problems: cost, ethics, politics

It can be an expensive exercise if led by consultancy firms (who design the process, including training raters), but has become very popular over the past 40 years. The major ethical and political issues revolve around assurances to the raters that their identity will not (even cannot) be disclosed and that therefore they are quite candid (as well as accurate) in those ratings.

Recommendations for use

If done well it can be a very useful way of getting data on an individual but from a developmental point of view the effect wears off rather quickly.

5.2.1 *Introduction*

Ask an individual: Who knows you best? Most respond their partner. The reason is obvious: they have usually spent a very long time with their partner who they have seen in a very wide variety of situations. Furthermore, they have talked to them at length about hopes and dreams, worries and concerns, strengths and weaknesses.

Surely the best people to assess and evaluate a person are those who know him/her best in the workplace. Those who have most data should do ratings. The premise of multi-source ratings is that the reliability of assessment is greatly increased by using multiple raters.

This is similar to the assumption made by those who favour letters of recommendation. People have very different experiences of an individual, depending on whether they are colleagues, subordinates or clients. You interact with, and disclose to, people in the workplace quite differently. So, who has the best data to make assessment ratings? Bosses tend to know about performance outcomes (productivity, profit); peers about abilities, ambitions and values; subordinates about working style and personality; and clients about social skills. Therefore, would it not be prudent to get them all to rate the individual, as well as let him/her rate themselves? Surely combining the ratings would add to inter-rater reliability.

Interest in multi-source ratings, also called 360-degree feedback, has its origins in two areas of psychology. Psychometricians have always been interested in rater bias and rater reliability. The central question is why *two* people rating the *same* person, behaviour or performance differ and whether they can (or should) be trained to be more similar and accurate. Similarity or rater agreement does not necessarily mean accuracy however, though it is not always possible to have a clear, objective behavioural measure against which to compare individual ratings.

Interest concerns primarily how individuals combine, discount or emphasise certain information in order to come up with a particular impression. This used to be called the *person perception* literature which dominated social psychology in the 1960s. It can also be relevant to how professional assessors or selectors rate people in interviews or at assessment centres.

The second issue is whether rater differences are a function of different information they have on an individual. Are differences explained in terms of a different 'database'? Who knows you best? What do they actually know about you? What do your reports/subordinates know that your boss doesn't? How much have you interacted with them? Is your data purely observational or supplemented by self-report? What sort of data do people have to complete the rating. Clearly, if they have radically different data, qualitatively and quantitatively this will impact on their ratings and possibly be the major cause of the differences or incongruity.

There is an extensive literature in applied psychology on the *use* of different ratings for performance management and developmental processes. (Church et al., 2019; Furnham, 2019). The early research looked at the usefulness of self-ratings of performance. Are people honest and insightful enough to accurately report on their aptitudes, behaviours and skills?

This research then moved on to investigate the causes and consequences of difference between a person's self-ratings and those of his/her boss/supervisor. This, in turn, led to an interest in differences in the evaluation of peers, subordinates and clients (as well as self- and boss ratings) and hence the concept of 360-degree evaluation. However, at much the same time, the use of these ratings as a potential development training tool become popular. Papers published from around 1990 onwards reflects this interest.

Here is an example.

Imagine you were asked to rate your boss on the following dimensions from Extremely (10) to Not at all (1). If you do not know or are unsure, score 0.

Clarity of thought: Logical, coherent, clear and economical narrative

Intellectual curiosity. The desire to engage in, and enjoy, effortful cognitive activity at work.

Productivity: Being well organised, prepared and systematic in workstyle (conscientiousness, planful).

Detail orientation: An inclination for consistent granular analysis and recording of salient information.

Adaptability and flexibility: Able and willing to give up preferred ideas and ways of behaving.

Risk appetite: The level of risk the individual is prepared to accept after full assessment of up- and downsides cases.

Comfort with uncertainty: Being sufficiently tolerant of ambiguity and a lack of clarity.

Emotional regulation: Ability to manage and respond to emotional experiences (stable, retaining conviction).

Interpersonal sensitivity: The ability to accurately assess and handle the motivations and beliefs of others.

Persuasiveness: The ability to charm, influence and persuade others to their way of thinking.

Self-confidence: Having appropriate and realistic confidence in one's own abilities.

Unconventional and maverick: Tendency to be bold, rebellious and displaying norm-violating behaviour.

Honesty and integrity: Having a sound and developed moral compass.

Self-awareness: Ability to articulate and observe one's own motivations, thought patterns and behaviours.

There are literally hundreds of these ratings which are often unique to an organisation and based on their particular competency model. Much depends on the clarity of these ratings and there are many reasons why they are important. Sometimes people are asked to rate how important each trait is for the target person to succeed.

5.2.2 Pros and Cons

It is argued that this measures in detail the behaviours and competencies shown by the individual or group in achieving goals. Participants can be accurately and confidentially assessed by themselves, their boss, their staff, team members, internal/external customers, suppliers, family and friends. The raters judge what they perceive, that is actual behaviour and not the intentions behind it. The aggregated feedback data has many uses, including development, appraisal, teambuilding, validation of training, organisation development and remuneration. The results are a mixture of strengths and areas for development, some expected and some unexpected. 360-degree feedback has become popular recently because of changes in what organisations expect of their employees, increasing emphasis on performance measurement, changing management concepts and more receptive attitudes.

Edwards and Ewen (1996, p. 52) presented the pros and cons for using it in assessment (Tables 5.1 and 5.2).

Later (p. 59) they present guidelines for organisations that want to use an existing system used in development to use it for pay/appraisal methods.

5.2.3   The Nature of Feedback

The major idea in 360-degree ratings is showing the ratee the feedback. Indeed the very fact that others, including the target person,

Table 5.1 *Arguments for and against using 360-degree feedback for appraisal and pay*

Argument Against	Solution
Ruins development	Provide a non-performance affecting section
Inflates ratings	Use intelligent scoring and respondent accountability
Users manipulate the system	Use intelligent scoring and respondent accountability
Arguments For	**Explanation**
Already being used	Many organisations are already using the information
Market driven	Users spontaneously are developing home-grown systems
Credibility and validity	Experience and research show process validity
Employee driven	Employees are asking for the use of 360° feedback systems

Table 5.2 *Guidelines for moving 360-degree feedback from development to pay and appraisal*

User surveys: Users support from satisfaction surveys should exceed 75 percent.

Anonymity: Users must have confidence that their individual ratings will be *absolutely* confidential.

Distinction: The spread of scores should clearly differentiate high, medium, and low performance.

Valid difference: The distinctions must represent truly high, medium, and low performance.

Response rates: Responses from those who provide feedback should be above 75 percent.

Administrative overhead: The time required for respondents and for process administration must be minimised and reasonable.

Invalid respondents: Respondents must be accountable for honest ratings; invalid responses – those 40 percent different from the consensus of others – should be below 5 percent.

Diversity fairness: Respondents do not systematically discriminate unfairly against protected status groups, and members of such groups should receive performance scores similar to others.

Training: Users should be trained in both providing and receiving behaviour feedback.

Safeguards: Safeguards to process fairness, such as intelligent scoring which minimises known sources of bias, are understood and supported by users.

---

may see your ratings (albeit supposedly anonymised) can and does have a big impact on them. Often people are far less likely to be as 'negative' as they might be, fearing reprisals. That is the purpose of the rating and its consequences have a very large impact on the rating itself. Often, these multi-source ratings are used for different purposes but mainly as developmental/coaching material, but also the fundamental data is used in any performance management system.

Also, at the most fundamental level is the simple question – Does giving anyone feedback (whatever its quality) have any effect on performance? This is taken on trust and is crucial to the whole enterprise. Fletcher et al. (1998) argued that if any of the ratings used in multi-rater feedback are filled with biases, errors and distortions irrespective of whether they are used for development or appraisal, they are likely to provide assessments that are seriously misleading.

Multiple rater feedback (MRF) has been used for executive development, team-building and coaching. It has 'travelled' from the English-speaking world to many other countries. Hence, there are issues around translation and cultural appropriateness. Thus, in some countries it is 'preposterous' to expect subordinates/reports to rate their superiors/boss: it is culturally quite unacceptable and if done so will lead to considerable difficulty and bias.

Bracken et al. (2001) specify eight characteristics of feedback itself that are essential to the effective working of the system:

> *Credibility.* The feedback should come from credible sources, in this case individuals who have had sufficient opportunity to observe job-relevant behaviour and are motivated to present the feedback honestly.
>
> *Timeliness.* The feedback should, as much as possible, occur without significant delay that might reduce its accuracy. Timeliness speaks to the need, at a minimum, to specifically inform the rater as to the time frame that is relevant (for example, the last year).
>
> *Fairness.* In this context, the perception (and reality) that the feedback is fair begins with the common standard that is applied to all participants, as defined by the content of the instrument and consistent administration.
>
> *Clarity.* Ambiguity regarding feedback causes hesitation and misdirected actions. Clear, behavioural items presented (in feedback reports) in a manner to promote full understanding of the feedback help advance acceptance.
>
> *Relevance.* The feedback should be restricted to behaviours that are job-relevant and clearly communicated as being important to individual and ultimately organisational effectiveness.
>
> *Consensus.* A major rationale for multiple source feedback (MSF) as a cause of behaviour change is in the power found in consistent feedback from multiple

sources. It is certainly difficult to discount feedback that sends a common message from many reliable observers.

Actionability. The feedback must indicate behaviours that the participant can address through constructive actions.

Specificity. The MSF process should encourage specific behavioural feedback from raters, supported both by behavioural items and by training raters to write in comments that offer insight as to the basis of the ratings.

(p. 489)

In their paper they point out various 'fatal errors' in introducing a 360-degree assessment system: insufficient communication to those involved; no or insufficient training; an autocratic, hierarchical organisation that attempts to kill the project; feedback that is untimely (late); clear data errors; cost-benefit analysis being poor or too long; taking up too much respondent time and supervisor time; and errors because of people playing games or trying to sabotage the system.

Equally, they point out characteristics of a 'successful system' which includes participants and users being involved in both the design and assessment of the instrument; that the process is seen to be fair, accurate, simple, credible and time efficient; that users are trained; that complete anonymity is ensured; that the system is automated; that various safeguards are put in place; and that expectations are properly managed throughout the whole process.

The 360/MRF enterprise has now been popular for over 30 years. It has been widely adopted by companies who have been impressed by ever easier ways to administer the questionnaires and the increasing sophistication of reports. Similarly, academic research has continued to investigate serious puzzles in the area, the most fundamental of which is rater incongruence.

5.2.4 Rater Congruence: A Crucial Academic Question

Earlier, researchers were interested in the issues of *self-appraisal* or self-rating. This essentially concerned an individual's supposedly honest and accurate appraisal of their own behaviour. Researchers agreed on two things:

1. Self-ratings tend to have systematic problems: *Leniency Error* (people are not hard on themselves); *Restriction of Range* (they rarely use the full scale) and *Halo Effect* (they tend not to differentiate or discriminate their strengths and weaknesses).
2. Self-ratings/evaluations are really only useful under very specific conditions.

In their still often-quoted, classic review of the self-evaluation literature, Mabe and West (1982) found that self-evaluations predict performance outcomes only when specific criteria are met, that is only under certain conditions. Failure to fully consider the conditions, therefore, can lead to the erroneous conclusion that self-rated job performance fares poorly in relation to supervisory ratings when, in fact, it is the conditions under which self-ratings were obtained (and not the ratings themselves) that lead to a lock of convergence.

Five of Mabe and West's nine criteria seem particularly relevant to self-appraised job performance and include: (1) the degree of matching between the self-evaluation and the criterion, i.e. supervisory rating, such that similar abilities are measured; (2) measures of skills tied to actual performance rather than to general abilities; (3) temporal contiguity between the self-evaluation and the criterion so that they refer to the same time period, i.e. past, present or future performance; (4) use of individuals who have experience with self-evaluation; and (5) relative self-evaluations that are tied to a criterion group, i.e. co-workers.

Over the years, the data on congruency is mixed. Some studies found little evidence of major disagreement (i.e. lack of congruence) between self- and supervisor ratings. Inevitably, however, those that do attract most attention concern findings where there is much disagreement between raters

Studies then moved on to look quite specifically at differences between self-ratings and boss's ratings, no doubt because of the way some organisations encouraged self-ratings in appraisal, but also because of sex differences. There are now reviews of the whole area (Bracken et al., 2016; Good & Coombe, 2009; Valle & Bozeman, 2002).

Because raters at different organisational levels probably observe different facets of ratees' job performances, their ratings ought to reflect these differences, and therefore *high agreement may be an erroneous requirement.* Thus, raters should be subgrouped by organisational level, with each providing performance evaluations using only dimensions appropriate to the level of the position they are asked to rate.

Harris and Schaubroeck (1988), in an early meta-analysis, found a relatively high correlation between peer and supervisor ratings, but only a moderate correlation between self-supervisor and self-peer ratings. They also found that, while rating format (dimensional vs global) and rating scale (trait vs behavioural) had little impact as moderator variables, job type (managerial/professional vs blue-collar/service) did seem to moderate self-peer and self-supervisor ratings. Their analysis showed a higher convergence between observer (peer and supervisor) ratings than self and observer and that self-peer and self-supervisor ratings are particularly lower correlations for managerial/professional staff.

Some studies looked at self- vs supervisor rating differences compared to looking specifically at self- vs subordinate ratings as well as the congruence between all five constituent parties in the 360-degree circle: supervisor, colleague, subordinates, clients and self. Furnham and Stringfield (1994), in a study of three rating groups (supervisory, self and subordinate), found that there was greater similarity between subordinate and supervisor than between self-ratings with either. This finding was confirmed in a second study, this time adding the effects of consultant ratings (Furnham & Stringfield, 1998). In other words, observers from whichever level agree more with each other than the person rating themselves.

The whole business of rater agreement/congruence is neither merely academic nor trivial (Atkins & Wood, 2002; Carless & Roberts-Thompson, 2001). The question is central to the whole enterprise. If feedback per se is behaviourally or cognitively useful (i.e. it leads to change), then it should be accurate. If feedback from different sources is very different, it reflects on the accuracy of that feedback. Whilst it is quite possible that feedback can be quite different, even contradictory, from different sources and yet remain accurate, it should be acknowledged that the situation is rather rare.

5.2.5   Does Agreement Matter?

Atwater et al. (1998) addressed the central controversy about congruence: Does it matter? On the other hand, it could be argued that although self-other agreement may be useful and desirable for training purposes it does not relate to understanding individual performance or effectiveness. In their complex and sophisticated study, they showed that agreement/congruence was important and did matter but that the relationship was complex.

One obvious issue is whether the ratings are complementary or contradictory. Problems arise where people on the same level (i.e. reports or peers) give radically different ratings of the same behaviour. Thus, one may rate the boss in terms of 'being planful and organised' as weak (2/7) while another thinks they are very strong (6/7)

There can be many explanations for the lack of agreement:

1. They have different data bases in the sense that they interact with the boss in different contexts and tasks which have different requirements. Both are accurate but different.
2. They have different definitions about what being planful and organised means: though they may have the same observational data, one person's planful is another's disorganised.
3. The have radically different rating styles and criteria: one is very lenient the other harsh.
4. The rating reflects more their relationship with, and liking for, the boss and has little to do with his or her actual behaviour.
5. The raters are trying to influence the consequences of the ratings: that is, if they know what the ratings are going to be used for (i.e. salary bonus) they will systematically alter their ratings to achieve that end.

Yammarino and Atwater (2001) noted there are important implications for development when people self-rate much more highly (over-estimator) or low (under-estimator) compared to others where agreement is good with high ratings or good with low ratings.

They note:

These self-other rating types and their differential individual and organisational outcomes suggest several implications for leadership training and development.

First, most of the issues we have noted can be addressed by training and education program.

Second, using feedback in leadership training and development programs to enhance self-perception accuracy and self-other agreement is likewise critical.

Third, high self-other rating agreement should be a goal of all leadership training programs that use feedback as a developmental tool.

Fourth, over time, in both leadership training programs and tracking of employee career paths, declining self-other rating discrepancy can be used as an indicator of improved self-perception accuracy.

Fifth, using MSF with the intention of changing self-ratings and behaviours must be approached cautiously.

Sixth, individuals receiving feedback that is more negative than expected (over-estimators) may need some special attention.

(pp. 218–220)

One of the major problems of this area is the lack of objective measures in the sense that all the ratings are subjective. Thus, whilst two or more raters might show high agreement, it does not necessarily mean that the ratings are accurate. Consider, for example, issues about time where raters are required to assess how time efficient a person is in completing an assignment. Unless the raters have some good normative data about the speed the average person completes the task they could be in complete agreement, but also erroneous in their judgements.

5.2.6 *Rater Training*

One obvious and practical issue refers to selecting and training raters. Learning to become what is effectively a judge is not easy. This can be illustrated by the amount of training and effort that goes into training people like sports referees, tea and wine tasters and other human endeavours. A judge/rater needs to understand and recognise *what* they are rating. They need sufficient reliable evidence upon which to make judgements. They need to understand the criteria they are rating and use any rating scale sensitivity judiciously and above all differentially to distinguish within and between individuals. They need to avoid rating when they do not have the data. They need to avoid being overly lenient or harsh or undifferentiating. This is a tall order. It takes considerable effort to achieve reliable ratings as any judge knows.

Very few organisations are prepared to put the necessary effort and money into this training which may be fundamental to the whole enterprise. Who will best ensure accurate, fair and acceptable ratings?

Obviously, raters need training. According to Antonioni and Woehr (2001, p. 121):

> A great deal of research indicates that rater training has tremendous potential for improving the effectiveness and utility of performance ratings. Rater training is critical because many of the individuals participating in the MSF process are rating work behaviours or competencies for the first time. The process of rating others should not be taken lightly; raters need to understand their responsibility. This means that raters must provide bias-free ratings based on actual behaviours and results, not ratings based on how much they like a ratee or on very limited observations. Organisations must offer training and support to increase rater responsibility. Rater training needs to address five areas:
>
> 1. Familiarising raters with each of the performance dimensions.
> 2. Establishing standards pertaining to each of the dimensions to be rated.

3. Improving behavioural observation skills.
4. Preventing common rating errors.
5. Writing descriptive not evaluative comments to support ratings.
6. Finally, the training should include time for individuals to practice giving ratings and an opportunity to get feedback on the practice ratings.

Can one increase agreement/congruence between self- and supervisor ratings? Schrader and Steiner (1996) showed that the more explicit and objective the comparative standards, the higher the level of inter-rater agreement.

The instructions they gave to improve matters are given in Table 5.3.

Some organisations have rater training sessions to help people make similar judgements. The rating behaviours are explained, and people are given feedback on their rating style. Furnham (2019) noted three distinct types of raters:

1. *Manager Softy (everyone wins/too lenient)*

Manager Softy likes to see the good in people. He/she believes that giving everyone high marks on all the ratings avoids conflict and getting upset and motivates them all. He/she tries to stay popular by giving all subordinates high marks. It is not necessarily that he/she always prefers to see the good in people but that he/she is usually a cowardly or weak manager.

This rating strategy fails because: It lets down and demotivates really good performers; it may make poor ratees complacent believing their performance is excellent; an indirect/senior rater spots Manager Softy and confronts him/her as an inaccurate rater; Manager Softy is vulnerable to assertive demanding ratees who exploit his/her good nature to give inflationary ratings; staff become demotivated as they expect rewards but don't get them because are later adjusted or normalised.

Table 5.3 *Instructions to improve self and supervisor agreement*

Comparison standard	Instructions
Internal	Use your *own personal, internal values and standards* as criteria. That is, base your ratings on how well you personally feel you have done over the past six months relative to your abilities and past performance. DO NOT give consideration to any other criteria beyond your own beliefs as to how well you performed.
Absolute	Use your company's *minimum requirement for adequate performance* of [a number was supplied as defined by the organisation for the dimension] as the criterion. That is, for each dimension rate yourself in comparison to the minimal level of performance as defined by your company or group's policy. DO NOT give consideration to any other criteria beyond your own belief as to whether or not you met this minimum requirement.
Relative	Use your *co-workers' performance* as a criterion. That is, think about how your co-workers have performed and compare yourself to them. DO NOT give consideration to any other criteria beyond your own belief as to how well you performed in direct comparison to your co-workers.
Multiple	Use *your own personal standards, your attainment of the minimum requirements and goals* and *your comparison with fellow co-workers* as the criteria. That is, consider all three standards as defined in the previous pages. Give equal consideration to all three of the criteria.

2. Manager Midway (everyone is mediocre/central tendency)

Manager Midway takes the concept of average too seriously. He/she believes that *all* their ratees are pretty average on everything (KPIs/KRAs). They think that giving nearly everyone average scores is the best strategy because then they won't have to deal with the problems of high expectations of those rated highly or disappointment of those rated lowly. So, Manager Midway sits on the fence and gives average scores for everything. In essence then, they do not differentiate either within or between people and hence provide feedback of little use.

This rating strategy fails because: Staff get no feedback on their performance as every practice is rated as average; staff believe their manager neither appreciates nor understands their strengths and weaknesses or those of peers; the indirect rater may believe Manager Midway does not really know his/her staff; data generated tells HR nothing about who should be promoted, etc.

3. *Manager Nasty (nobody is any good/too tough)*

Manager Nasty comes from the hard school believing that 'if you give people an inch, they take a yard'. He/she thinks that sticks work better than carrots and people respond better to threats of punishment than the promise of reward. So, Manager Nasty gives low marks on most KRAs irrespective of actual performance.

This technique fails badly because: All staff need encouragement as well as chastisement. If they believe their ability and effort are not rewarded or recognised they are likely to reduce their motivation. Managers who only punish are neither liked or respected – they may be feared but rarely are they thought of as fair. Manager Nasty's staff will probably get the minimum (zero) performance-related pay, which is deeply demotivating. Another/indirect rater may be lead to believe that the department or section led by Manager Nasty is overall weak and incompetent.

5.2.7 The Consequences of Congruence

Bass and Yammarino (1991) looked specifically at the congruence of self and other leadership ratings among American naval officers. One interesting finding was that, though self-ratings of leadership behaviour tended to be inflated in comparison to subordinates' ratings, *the more successful officers were less likely to inflate their self-described leadership behaviour.*

This finding was partly confirmed by Furnham and Stringfield (1993). Bass and Yammarino (1991) believe this could be due to the fact that subordinates' descriptions of leadership were significantly related to superiors' ratings of performance and promotion, but self-ratings of leadership were not associated with these measures. They note more accurate self-ratings of leadership were associated with successful job performance. But the authors also suggest abandoning the use of self-assessments of leadership behaviour for screening of job applicants, because they do not appear to contribute to the understanding of leadership success, nor to a maximal explanation of success even when optimally combined with subordinates' ratings.

What difference does the rater have on the ratings? Antonioni and Park (2001) looked at whether rater and ratee age, gender and job tenure affected the ratings. More unusually they also looked at affect: simply whether the rater liked the ratee. They found a dramatic effect for liking, which showed the influence of rater affect (how much they liked the person they were rating) on the leniency of ratings was significantly greater in upward and peer feedback than in downward feedback.

The central issue at the heart of this whole area is surely the reliability, validity, meaningfulness and usefulness of ratings. Few address the most fundamental question of all: How should we measure the impact of MSF? Smither and Walker (2001) point out the well-known problems of measuring change after interventions. Seifert et al. (2003) asked two simple but important questions: Does feedback facilitate management improvement? Does it matter how the feedback is received? First, they reviewed 14 studies, all of which measured change over time in performance (from 3 to 48 months). Five showed *Yes* (an improvement), four *No* (none) and five *Inconclusive* results. Because of the problems with those studies, the authors did their own study. There were three conditions: no feedback control group; a feedback report; a feedback workshop.

Managers in the feedback workshop increased their use of some core influence tactics with subordinates, whereas there was no change in behaviour for the control group or for the comparison group. The feedback was perceived to be more useful by managers who received it in a workshop with a facilitator than by managers who received only a printed feedback report.

They note:

> In summary, we found that a multisource feedback workshop can improve managerial behaviour even when there is little skill training, a non-supportive climate, and no extrinsic inducements. Increasing the effectiveness of the feedback beyond the level achieved in our study would probably require more of the facilitating conditions. Learning how to create these conditions should be a primary objective of future research on behavioural feedback programmes.
>
> (p. 568)

The central question as to whether 360-degree feedback 'works' must refer to the aims in using it. There may be many difficult-to-measure criteria of success: increased self-awareness, better within-team relationships, more acceptance of an appraisal system, measurable individual behavioural change and, perhaps most desirable and important of all, increase in organisational efficiency measured by increased revenue and profit or decreased costs. These are notoriously difficult to measure as well as to attribute to a single factor. Indeed, just as some marketing specialists believe, it is essentially impossible to demonstrate the efficacy of 360-degree feedback any more than training programme feedback.

5.2.8   Conclusion

Self- and other ratings of behaviours are often very subjective. The more observable and specific the behaviour rated (i.e. 'is smartly dressed' vs 'has leadership potential') the more congruent the ratings. Academics often note that their 'gold standard' of the peer-review of academic papers is characterised by surprisingly low inter-rater reliability, which is disappointing given that supposedly highly trained experts are rating the same technical manuscript.

This chapter considers why there may be important and consequential differences between raters of the same behaviour. There are many possible explanations ranging from the self-awareness of managers who rate themselves to the fact that people have never been trained to use the rating scale. Perhaps the most common causes of incongruity are the poorly worded rating scales, the fact that raters have widely different data/information on the person they are rating and knowing what is to be done with the ratings so they can adjust them to fulfil their own ends.

REFERENCES

Antonioni, D., & Park, H. (2001). The relationship between rater affect and three sources of 360-degree feedback ratings. *Journal of Management, 27*(4), 479–495.

Antonioni, D., & Woehr, D. J. (2001). Improving the quality of multi-source rater performance. In D. W. Bracken, C. W. Timmreck, & A. H. Church (Eds.), *The handbook of multi-source feedback* (pp. 114–130). San Francisco, CA: Jossey-Bass Inc.

Atkins, P. W., & Wood, R. E. (2002). Self-versus others' ratings as predictors of assessment center ratings: validation evidence for 360-degree feedback programs. *Personnel Psychology, 55*(4), 871–904.

Atwater, L. E., Ostroff, C., Yammarino, F. J., & Fleenor, J. W. (1998). Self-other agreement: does it really matter?. *Personnel Psychology, 51*(3), 577–598.

Bass, B. M., & Yammarino, F. J. (1991). Congruence of self and others' leadership ratings of naval officers for understanding successful performance. *Applied Psychology, 40*(4), 437–454.

Bracken, D. W., Rose, D. S., & Church, A. H. (2016). The evolution and devolution of 360 feedback. *Industrial and Organizational Psychology, 9*(4), 761–794.

Bracken, D. W., Timmreck, C. W., & Church, A. H. (2001). *The handbook of multi-source feedback*. San Francisco, CA: Jossey-Bass Inc.

Carless, S. A., & Roberts-Thompson, G. P. (2001). Self-ratings in training programs: an examination of level of performance and the effects of feedback. *International Journal of Selection and Assessment, 9*(3), 217–225.

Church, A. H., Bracken, D. W., Fleenor, J. W., & Rose, D. S. (2019). *Handbook of strategic 360 feedback*. Oxford, UK: Oxford University Press.

Edwards, M. R., & Ewen, A. J. (1996). 360-degree feedback: royal fail or holy grail?. *Career Development International, 1*(3), 28–31.

Fletcher, C., Baldry, C., & Cunningham-Snell, N. (1998). The psychometric properties of 360 degree feedback: an empirical study and a cautionary tale. *International Journal of Selection and Assessment, 6*(1), 19–34.

Furnham, A. (2019). Rater congruency: why ratings of the same person differ. In A. H. Church, D. W. Bracken, J. W. Fleenor, & D. S. Rose (Eds.), *Handbook of strategic 360 feedback* (pp. 291–308). Oxford, UK: Oxford University Press.

Furnham, A., & Stringfield, P. (1993). Personality and occupational behavior: Myers–Briggs type indicator correlates of managerial practices in two cultures. *Human Relations, 46*(7), 827–848.

Furnham, A., & Stringfield, P. (1994). Congruence of self and subordinate ratings of managerial practices as a correlate of supervisor evaluation. *Journal of Occupational and Organizational Psychology, 67*(1), 57–67.

Furnham, A., & Stringfield, P. (1998). Congruence in job-performance ratings: a study of 360 feedback examining self, manager, peers, and consultant ratings. *Human Relations, 51*(4), 517–530.

Good, D., & Coombe, D. (2009). Giving multisource feedback a facelift. *Journal of Change Management, 9*(1), 109–126.

Harris, M. M., & Schaubroeck, J. (1988). A meta-analysis of self-supervisor, self-peer, and peer-supervisor ratings. *Personnel Psychology, 41*(1), 43–62.

Mabe, P. A., & West, S. G. (1982). Validity of self-evaluation of ability: a review and meta-analysis. *Journal of applied Psychology, 67*(3), 280–296.

Schrader, B. W., & Steiner, D. D. (1996). Common comparison standards: an approach to improving agreement between self and supervisory performance ratings. *Journal of Applied Psychology, 81*(6), 813–820.

Seifert, C. F., Yukl, G., & McDonald, R. A. (2003). Effects of multisource feedback and a feedback facilitator on the influence behavior of managers toward subordinates. *Journal of Applied Psychology, 88*(3), 561–565.

Smither, J. & Walker, A. (2001) Measuring the impact of multisource feedback. In D. W. Bracken, C. W. Timmreck, & A. H. Church (Eds.), *The handbook of multi-source feedback* (pp. 256–271). San Francisco, CA: Jossey-Bass Inc.

Valle, M., & Bozeman, D. P. (2002). Interrater agreement on employees' job performance: review and directions. *Psychological Reports, 90*(3), 975–985.

Yammarino, F. J., & Atwater, L. E. (2001). Understanding agreement in multisource feedback. In D. W. Bracken, C. W. Timmreck, & A. H. Church (Eds.), *The handbook of multi-source feedback* (pp. 205–220). San Francisco, CA: Jossey-Bass Inc.

5.3 SURVEILLANCE, TRACKING AND WEARABLES

What is it?

It can be a number of different techniques which monitor a person's behaviour both at, and outside, work. It may include being observed, recorded by camera, or by requiring people to wear various sensors while at work. These techniques provide behavioural and physiological evidence over time.

How does it work?

The idea is that we get a purer/better measure of a person's motivation and personality from what they do, and how they respond to situations, rather than what they say. The very varied physiological data can be combined to try to understand a person's lifestyle and also their workstyle.

What of the evidence?

There is not a lot of evidence that this type of physiological data measures either personality or ability. Furthermore, many people are very unhappy about its use and abuse.

Practical problems: cost, ethics, politics

The cost of surveillance devices is rapidly coming down. There are, however, ethical concerns of how, when and why people are under surveillance; whether people know or approve that they are being watched; and what is done with the data that is collected.

Recommendations for use

It could be dangerous, unwise and unethical to rely on surveillance data for assessment or selection.

5.3.1 *Introduction*

It is quite probable that you are 'under surveillance' for a large part of your journey to and from work, as well as when you are at work. Your behaviour is being monitored by a range of technologies from cameras, heat sensors, face-recognition devices and computer tracking.

New technology has produced many cost-effective and easily available ways of monitoring employees and putting them under overt and covert surveillance. Once the exclusive toys of private investigators and the secret service, they are now abundantly available online.

Heat or weight sensors can detect precisely how long you sit at your chair. Furthermore, there are now a very large number of devices that can track, in detail, precisely how you use your computer from simple key depressions to the websites you scan and the frequency of words that you use.

Twenty years ago, researchers listed eight methods of computer-assisted electronic monitoring at work: video cameras (such as CCTV), computer sampling, email interception, access codes, expert systems, transaction audits, phone taps and hidden microphones. The growth in surveillance has ignited controversy over ethical issues involved in surveillance at work.

It is difficult to get accurate figures on the number and growth of CCTV cameras in any town or country. They are in both private and public hands, and both inside and outside buildings.

Traditionally (electronic) surveillance has been used by civic authorities mainly for crime prevention but developments in the field have led to its widespread use. This may involve cameras, light detection devices or heat monitors on seats. Estimates say that there may be over 400 million surveillance cameras worldwide. Previously they were sometimes 'manned', making them very expensive, but now *face-recognition technology* has really made a big difference to how they can be used. How would you feel if the security people or indeed 'front-desk' staff were replaced by 24-hour surveillance, face-recognition cameras?

From the moment you arrive at work it is possible that you are being watched and recorded: where you go, who you speak to and who you email. Employees may or may not know when, how and why they are under surveillance. Furthermore, they may or may not believe the reasons given for the surveillance by those who install it. Indeed, there are a number of celebrated court cases where employees have taken their employers to court on matters of surveillance. This will no doubt increase.

As a consequence, we have people interested in counter-surveillance and inverse surveillance. This amounts to attempts to avoid surveillance or actually 'spying on' those who are spying on you. It is the equivalent of buying and using devices in your car which detect speed cameras ahead or other public monitoring devices.

There are many concerns with privacy and the violation of rights. Many people refute the 'for your own protection' argument as they are filmed in buildings and public transport. They feel uncomfortable that 'big brother' is always watching. Most of us have things we do not want others to know about: where we shop and go for entertainment. We don't necessarily want to tell our boss that we are actively looking for a new job.

Indeed, it has been argued that with the growth of online technology, we are all watching each other. That is, there is now as much horizontal (peer to peer) as opposed to vertical surveillance. For some it seems like the old East German STASI philosophy and methodology is alive and well and 'operating in your area'.

People can effectively be tracked everywhere they go in the street, in big hotels and departmental stores. The most common methods include closed-circuit television (CCTV cameras) or interception of electronically transmitted information (such as internet traffic or phone calls). Perhaps the most common is automated internet surveillance through computers. They work by signaling certain 'trigger words or phrases, visiting particular websites or communicating via email or online chat with certain individuals or groups. Thus, it is possible to install software, both directly and remotely to monitor many aspects of a person's computer usage. The same can be done with telephones that can be programmed to search for words, phrases, codes that are deemed to be interesting to those who monitor them. We have long been able to trace calls, now we can gather the location data of speakers very easily. This used to be called wiretapping.

5.3.2   Types of Surveillance

1. *Social network analysis*: This usually requires a worker wearing a badge at work which has (whether they know it or not) the technology to track who

they contact on a daily or monthly basis. That is, badges alert each other, when in a certain range. In due course this data provides a very important network analysis of the whole organisation. Although one cannot be sure why people contact each other or what they actually communicate, this surveillance method builds up a very interesting picture of the whole organisation. The technology has been used in tracing viruses.

2. *Biometric*: These include fingerprints, facial patterns, walking gait, DNA and voice patterns. This is now used widely in airports, malls and well-known public places to detect unusual behaviour such as signs of nervousness or having unusual interests in particular things. Video pictures can be used to attempt to detect well-known signs of anxiety or anger or other extreme emotions. Facial recognition technology has 'zoomed ahead' and is now used in many settings, though there remain very serious concerns about inaccuracies and mis-identifications.

3. *Data mining and profiling*: This involves forming a profile of an individual through publicly available data – credit card usage, email and telephone calls and, most common, social media. It is not so much a paper trail as an electronic trail. Furthermore, this can be combined with demographic data (age, address, place of birth). It is becoming easier to collect and integrate this information, and given some sophisticated algorithms create a 'rich picture' of the values and habits of an individual. There are enough scandals surrounding this type of data and the way it can be misused.

4. *Work surveillance*. It has been estimated that more than 40% of the companies monitor email traffic of their workers. We read about people being fired because of 'inappropriate or offensive language' and 'viewing, downloading, or uploading inappropriate/offensive content'. There are cameras in public areas and car parks. Heat and light detectors can determine whether someone is in a particular space.

5. *Spies and detectives*: Some organisations employ private detectives or those who infiltrate organisations to get very unique and special data. This is rare and expensive but has been done many times to infiltrate certain political groups, or in business those who belong to societies or 'shadowy' organisations with very specific goals (like world domination!)

6. *Satellite imagery*. These can be used to detect when people move outdoors and is being supplemented by much cheaper drones. People in the security world and business can offer a wide range of very expensive technologies which can track any individual's movements outside.

7. *Machine-readable identification.* One of the simplest forms of identification is the carrying of documents (passports), cards and other identification symbols. Some nations have an identity card system to aid identification, whilst others are considering it but face public opposition. Other documents, such as passports, driver's licenses, library cards and banking or credit cards are also used to verify identity, particularly if there are photographs attached.

    If the form of the identity card is 'machine-readable', usually using an encoded magnetic stripe or identification number (such as a social security number), it corroborates the subject's identifying data. In this case it may create an electronic trail when it is checked and scanned, which can be used in profiling, as mentioned above.

8. *Mobile phones.* Mobile phones are also commonly used to collect geolocation data. The geographical location of a powered mobile phone (and thus the person carrying it) can be determined easily (whether it is being used or not). It is not unusual for people at airports to (legally) demand to see your mobile phone with all details of who you have recently contacted.

9. *Human microchips.* A human microchip can be implanted in the body which contains a unique ID number that can be linked to information contained in an external database to monitor heath issues, medical history, medications, allergies and certain types of people, such as criminals.

10. *Bugs and devices.* Covert listening devices and video devices, or 'bugs', are hidden electronic devices which are used to capture, record and/or transmit data to a receiving party such as a law enforcement agency.

The advance in technology, the reduction in its costs and increasing concerns about illegal and 'inappropriate' behaviour have led to a corporate surveillance culture. This is rarely done for selection but much more commonly for those at work.

5.3.3   Attitudes and Reactions to Surveillance

More than 20 years ago Oz et al. (1999) listed eight methods of computer-assisted electronic monitoring and noted that of these the most technologically advanced are expert systems, which are more commonly referred to as EPM – 'electronic performance monitoring'.

The Office of Technological Assessment described EPM as the 'computerized collection, storage, analysis and reporting of information about employees' activities'. EPM can be used to monitor a variety of mostly quantitative variables, such as the punctuality of employees, the amount of break time taken, the amount of idle time, the number of words written per minute, transactions completed, number of telephone calls made (time per call, revenue per call), just to name a few. In effect, this now means that there is a potential to monitor employees' specific daily behaviours, which has not been possible through traditional methods.

As these newer methods of surveillance offer continuous monitoring over an employees' time at work, this has unsurprisingly ignited much debate over whether it is morally right or even organisationally wise to implement such control. So far there have been numerous studies conducted looking into the possible effects of EPM, by comparing EPM and non-EPM scenarios and measuring factors such as stress, productivity, job satisfaction, turnover, etc. These have mainly used cross-sectional studies, observational studies and a few laboratory studies. However, less research has been conducted into looking at people's attitudes towards surveillance and what factors and traits may correlate with them.

Kolb and Aiello (1996) looked specifically at examining how monitoring affected the stress levels of participants split into two groups, depending on whether they were assessed to have an internal or external locus of control, based on a questionnaire. Neither the monitored nor non-monitored group felt an increase in stress, going against previous research showing that monitoring tends to increase stress (Amick & Smith, 1992). However, it was found that in those participants with an external locus of control, monitoring decreased the levels of stress, while the opposite effect was demonstrated in those with an internal locus of control (Kolb & Aiello, 1996).

Oz et al. (1999) examined the responses of 823 part-time students who were in full time employment, mainly looking for differences between the attitudes of supervisors and their subordinates, but also for any gender differences. Supervisors were more likely to support the idea of electronic monitoring, while also suggesting that it would be a good tool in reducing theft. Meanwhile, subordinates (non-supervisors) expressed greater agreement with the idea that electronic monitoring would have a negative impact and create tensions in the workplace, as well as agreeing that employees should be made aware of when monitoring is taking place. In terms of gender differences, it was found that women were more likely than men to think that monitoring would reduce theft (Oz et al., 1999).

Samaranayake and Gamage (2012) looked at how electronic monitoring affected employees' satisfaction. They gathered data from 380 employees of a software company, using a questionnaire containing 75 questions, each answered on a five-point Likert scale, in order to assess their job satisfaction as well as the employees' perception of task satisfaction, relevance to work, invasion of privacy, level of infringement, rationale of employer and judgement of effectiveness. It was found that job satisfaction was positively correlated with those workers who had a positive opinion of electronic monitoring. This supports the idea that monitoring is fair, unbiased and provides a fuller image of the employee. However, it did also show that the greater the perception of invasion of privacy, the lower the job satisfaction was, and this was also true in those that felt that monitoring made their work more complex. Interestingly, by looking at subgroups it was found that the effect that monitoring had on job satisfaction was much weaker in those employees with a higher professional experience.

Furnham and Swami (2015) got a large British sample to complete a new 16-item 'surveillance at work' measure which resolved statistically into two clear factors which reflected positive and negative attitudes to surveillance. Higher scores on Negative Aspects of Surveillance were significantly associated with lower job satisfaction, lower job autonomy, greater perceived discrimination at work, more negative attitudes to authority and greater left-wing orientation, while higher scores on Positive Aspects of Surveillance were significantly associated with greater job satisfaction and more positive attitudes towards authority.

A very similar result was found by Jacobs et al. (2019), who asked 1,273 American workers their experience of and beliefs about wearables and their willingness to wear them. They found if people were told the aim was to improve safety, they were happier than if they thought they were simply to provide tracking information for someone at work. They note:

> Organizations intending to implement wearable technology should (a) focus its use on improving workplace safety, (b) advance a positive safety climate, (c) ensure sufficient evidence to support employees' beliefs that the wearable will meet its objective, and (d) involve and inform employees in the process of selecting and implementing wearable technology.
>
> *(p. 148)*

The results suggest three things: people remain sceptical and suspicious on surveillance at work; the more alienated, disenchanted and unhappy people are in general, the more negative they are about surveillance; the more thoroughly, honestly and clearly the organisation communicates about the nature and purpose of surveillance, the better it is received.

5.3.4 Wearable Technology

Imagine a candidate were asked to wear a 'smart watch' or a fitness tracker for a month before they came to an interview. Wearable technology goes back at least 25 years and was originally called affective computing because it was the use of computers to measure emotional states.

In the workplace, employees have wearables such as smart watches and fitness trackers that have sensors and are leaving large digital footprints that can be analysed to understand patterns of behaviour.

Wearables can be embedded in clothes, watches and other accessories. They are often marketed as effective health behaviour change tools that give useful feedback to impact on psychological well-being and affect. In this sense people volunteer to use and monitor the data from wearables and are consequently positively disposed towards them (Ryan et al., 2019).

As Al-Eidan et al. (2018) note the term 'wearables', wearable technology and wearable devices, is a form of consumer electronics technology that is based on embedded computer hardware that is built into products that are worn on the outside of one's body. They claimed that the most investigated wearable devices are as follows: (i) smart watch; (ii) smart eyewear (e.g. smart glasses and head-mounted displays); (iii) egocentric vision devices; (iv) light-based devices; (v) fabrics, textiles and skin-based devices; (vi) tactile gloves; (vii) hair- and nail-based devices; and (viii) magnetic inputs (e.g. Google cardboard).

They noted that these techniques have been researched many times and in different domains, such as sport, health, education and security. They concluded in their descriptive review that the main challenges for the use of wearable technology are: battery life, user acceptance, safety, weight, fault tolerance and privacy concerns.

There have been a number of studies that have attempted to determine whether wearable sensors can be used to assess individual differences and group behaviour. Thus, Olguin et al. (2009), in an early study, instrumented a group of 67 nurses with sociometric badges capable of measuring physical activity, speech activity, face-to-face interaction and physical proximity. The data measured physical and speech activity, face-to-face interactions proximity to others and social network data. Using the data collected they tried to identify different personality traits and estimate the overall group's perception of workload, difficulty to obtain information, quality of group interaction, productivity and stress, as well as average patient recovery time and daily number of delays. They found Neuroticism was related to face-to-face measures, Extraversion to measures of proximity, Agreeableness to speech activity and Conscientiousness to social networking. Correlations were modest. They concluded: 'We presented experimental results that show that it is possible to identify individual personality traits as well as subjective and objective group performance metrics from low level sensor data' (p. 73).

In a study monitoring 66 people for 30 days and collecting data using mobile phones and wearable sensors and questionnaires, Sano et al. (2015) assessed things like academic performance, sleep quality, stress levels and mental health. Wearable sensors capture mainly how we move, sleep and exercise, while phones capture mainly how we communicate with others. They had 1,980 days of data and found they could classify people into personality and other groups on the basis of this data.

In another study, Cai (2019) tested 50 students to examine how personality traits were associated with personal behaviours under specific emotional states based on physiological data collected from three wearable devices: Emotive Insight, Spire Stone and Huawei Fit Watch. They were tested before a crowd and/or when watching a movie where physiological data was measured by wearables. Behaviours like blink, wink, surprise, furrow, smile and clench were correlated with personality traits under emotion states of excitement, relaxation, stress, engagement, interest and focus. Again, they showed modest, but some significant correlations (i.e. Agreeableness is very related to blinking) and concluded that emotions mediate the relationship between personality and their measured behaviours.

Experimental data was gathered from 50 participants subjected to a Big Five Inventory (BFI) questionnaire to get their personality traits, presenting before a crowd and/or watching a movie where physiological data was measured by wearables. They found that correlations between the personality traits and the personal behaviors greatly depended on the emotional states.

A growing trend is the use of tracking badges in the workplace. These allow employers to follow employees' behaviours at work and record the frequency of talking, turn taking and where in the office they are the most. The MIT laboratory has developed a new technology called SocioMeter, a wearable sensor to measure face-to-face inter-actions between people with an IR transceiver, a microphone and two accelerometers (Choudhury & Pentland, 2010). The data that can be gathered from these emerging technologies have been demonstrated to be extremely useful in social network analysis by identifying a central node in a network (Woolley et al., 2010). It has also shown where people go for advice and how ideas and information spread within an organisa-tion, which has in turn predicted team effectiveness.

One important issue here is how and when employees provide consent for the use of their wearable data to be collected, analysed and stored. For instance, consent may be buried in lengthy and complex legal documents which employees are asked to sign at the beginning of their employment period. Many employees may not read or fully understand these documents and click to accept without compre-hending their implications. Few people have considered the ethics of these techniques and employee attitudes to surveillance (Furnham & Swami, 2015).

5.3.5   Conclusion

The wearables idea is that we can gather a wide range of physiological data from individuals which give us a profound insight into their personality and motivation, though possibly less about their intelligence. This idea is not new and found perhaps its most contro-versial manifestation in the lie detector (see Chapter 18).

This issue is important for the 'wearables debate' in selection and monitoring. It is the familiar problem of psychometric reliability and validity. What is the relationship between the physiological evidence provided by wearable technology and the personality and motivation of the wearer? Again, we have the Scottish verdict of 'not proven'. More simply, and more importantly perhaps, the question is: it is possible to assess/measure what ever is of interest (ability, motivation, personality) by different, cheaper but still equally valid measures, free of ethical issues?

REFERENCES

Al-Eidan, R., Al-Khalifa, H., & Al-Salman, A. (2018). A review of wrist-worn wearables. *Journal of Sensors, 2018*, 1–20.

Amick, B. C., & Smith, M. J. (1992). Stress, computer-based work monitoring and measurement systems: a conceptual overview. *Applied Ergonomics, 23*(1), 6–16.

Cai, R. (2019). Correlation analyses between personality traits and personal behaviours under specific emotion states using physiological data from wearable devices. *Hosei University Graduate School of Information Science, 14*, 1–6.

Choudhury, T., & Pentland, A. (2010). *The sociometer: A wearable device for understanding human networks*. Cambridge, MA: Human Design Group.

Furnham, A., & Swami, V. (2015). An investigation of attitudes toward surveillance at work and its correlates. *Psychology, 6*(13), 1668–1675.

Jacobs, J. V., Hettinger, L. J., Huang, Y. H., Jeffries, S., Lesch, M. F., Simmons, L. A., Verma, S. K., & Willetts, J. L. (2019). Employee acceptance of wearable technology in the workplace. *Applied Ergonomics, 78*, 148–156.

Kolb, K. J., & Aiello, J. R. (1996). The effects of electronic performance monitoring on stress: locus of control as a moderator variable. *Computers in Human Behavior, 12*(3), 407–423.

Olguin, D. O., Gloor, P. A., & Pentland, A. S. (2009). *Capturing individual and group behaviour with wearable sensors* (pp. 68–74). Palo Alto, CA: Spring Symposium on Human Behaviour Modelling at Association for the Advancement of Artificial Intelligence.

Oz, E., Glass, R., & Behling, R. (1999). Electronic workplace monitoring: what employees think. *International Journal of Management Science, 27*(2), 167–177.

Ryan, J., Edney, S., & Maher, C. (2019). Anxious or empowered? A cross-sectional study exploring how wearable activity trackers make their owners feel. *BMC Psychology, 7*(42), 1–8.

Samaranayake, V., & Gamage, C. (2012). Employee perception towards electronic monitoring at work place and its impact on job satisfaction of software professionals in Sri Lanka. *Telematics and Informatics, 29*(2), 233–244.

Sano, A., Phillips, A. J., Amy, Z. Y., McHill, A. W., Taylor, S., Jaques, N., Czeisler, C. A., Klerman, E. B., & Picard, R. W. (2015). Recognizing academic performance, sleep quality, stress level, and mental health using personality traits, wearable sensors and mobile phones. In *Proceedings of the 12th International Conference on Wearable and Implantable Body Sensor Networks* (pp. 1–6). Cambridge, MA: Institute of Electrical and Electronics Engineers.

Woolley, A. W., Chabris, C. F., Pentland, A., Hashmi, N., & Malone, T. W. (2010). Evidence for a collective intelligence factor in the performance of human groups. *Science, 330*(6004), 686–688.

5.4 ASSESSMENT CENTRES

What are they?

Assessment centres (ACs) are arranged testing sessions where candidates are assessed on a number of specified job competencies, by a combination of different tests/methods, and recorded/evaluated by a team of observers and assessors. They may range from three hours to three days of assessment.

How do they work?

They are based on the multi-trait, multi-method approach, which argues that to improve both the reliability and validity of an assessment it is best to use various methods (see Chapter 1) and various assessors and have different tests to measure the same things.

What of the evidence?

There is a lot of evidence for them being one of the best methods of assessment because they collect so much data using different methods.

Practical problems: cost, ethics, politics

The major problem is cost rather than ethics or politics. The question is the cost to benefit ratio given the possibility of using other methods.

Recommendations for use

It is always a good idea to spend money proportionate to the nature and importance of the job. Investing and updating AC methodology for a big organisation could be seen to show benefits in the end.

5.4.1 Introduction

Assessment centers are widely used both for development and selection processes (Woodruffe, 1995). When reviewers have compared the predictive validity of various assessment methods from references, work samples, personality tests, cognitive ability tests, assessment center scores, etc., most have found ACs have among the best validity statistics (see Chapter 1).

Most assessment centres are designed to measure highly specified, and often unique, organisational 'competencies' by a variety of methods: e.g. subjective self-reports, objective performance tests, and observational data. These use the famous multi-trait, multi-method approach in that they try to measure *different* traits and competencies by *different* methods. They use all sorts of exercises and data (self-report via review or questionnaire; observational data by peers and assessors; test data of all sorts) to attempt to accurately and sensitively measure different criteria.

The design nearly always involves planning a grid with the rows being competencies (i.e. social influence, numeracy, delegation) and the columns being exercises (i.e. role-play, presentation, business simulation). Assessors have a 'conference' after the centre to agree marks. The results can mean that candidates can be assessed and ranked on a competency by competency basis, as well as given an overall ranking.

ACs are tailor made, so they can assess a range of attributes by a range of methods. However, as Cook (2016) has noted, AC validity may have an element of circularity, because it tends to assess what management think of the applicants during the AC with what management think of the candidate subsequently 'on the job'. ACs are intended to assess competences as exhibited in a number of exercises (convergent validity). Their construct validity has been researched, showing that ACs correlate quite strongly with other methods. Also, ACs create less adverse impact and encounter fewer legal problems, which makes them increasingly attractive to employers.

Traditionally they are expensive in terms of time, effort and money but given their predictive validity they are usually considered worth the effort (Krause et al., 2006). A good deal has been written about the history and philosophy of assessment centres (Woodruffe, 1995). Whilst they have changed somewhat over the years, they have tended to maintain their original purpose and processes (Howard, 1997; Moerdyk, 2014).

5.4.2 Evaluation or Selection

A big issue for the AC world is whether an AC is the same as a development centre or not. Some argue that most developmental centres are disguised ACs. It is possible to distinguish between the two on various dimensions.

The following table compares development- to selection-focused ACs.

	Development-focused	Mixed	Selection-focused
Purpose	Development career planning	Promotion development	Selection centre
Label	Development centre		Selection centre
Philosophy	Done for the participant	Done with the participant	Done to candidate
Method	Self-assessment/peer assessor plus assessor's view	Assessment with feedback	Testing/no feedback
Assessor's role	Facilitator		Judge
Includes	Self-insight materials		Cognitive test
Output	Personal development plan	Report	Selection decision
Information exercises	Open		Secret
Feedback given	After each exercise	After centre	Not given
Owner of information	Participant	Owner of information	Organisation
Duration	One week		One day

The reason for the confusion is twofold. First, development usually follows from assessment and diagnosis: what needs to be developed and can a before-and-after improvement be shown? Attending an AC can make a person anxious and eager to create a good impression and thus not manifest 'natural' behaviour, which leads some groups to present an AC as a development centre (DC).

The time and cost involved in planning, running and then analysing AC data means that using them represents a serious commitment on the part of many organisations. However, again and again these are seen as the most efficient and effective of *all* assessment methods. This is because of the quantity and quality of the data gathered on each individual and the way in which the assessors are traditionally trained.

5.4.3 What Do They Measure?

ACs are designed to measure characteristics of an individual, often called competencies that are specifically relevant to a job, and possibly particular to the organisation. There are usually two types of competencies: general or specific. In the former case it is argued that nearly all jobs require similar competencies and these are worth measuring. Furthermore, it means the same data can be used to place people in all sorts of jobs.

Probably the best known model is the *Great Eight*.

The Great Eight competencies are

Leading and deciding. Takes control and exercises leadership. Initiates action, gives direction and takes responsibility.
Supporting and cooperating. Supports others and shows respect and positive regard for them in social situations. Puts people first, working effectively with individuals and teams, clients and staff.
Interacting and presenting. Communicates and networks effectively. Successfully persuades and influences others. Relates to others in a confident, relaxed manner.
Analysing and interpreting. Shows evidence of clear analytical thinking. Gets to the heart of complex problems and issues. Applies own expertise effectively. Quickly takes on new technology.
Creating and conceptualising. Works well in situations requiring openness to new ideas and experiences. Seeks out learning opportunities. Handles situations and problems with innovation and creativity.
Organising and executing. Plans ahead and works in a systematic and organised way. Follows directions and procedures. Focuses on customer satisfaction and delivers a quality service to the agreed standard.
Adapting and coping. Adapts and responds well to change. Manages pressure effectively and copes well with setbacks.

(cont.)

Enterprising and performing. Focuses on results and achieving personal work objectives. Works best when work is closely related to the results, and the impact of personal effort is obvious. Shows an understanding of business, commerce and finance.

Bartram and colleagues conducted factor analyses of self- and manager-rated performance ratings on a huge amount of data to derive the *Universal Competency Framework* (UCF) for performance (Bartram et al., 2002; Kurz & Bartram, 2002). At the lowest level of the framework, 112 component competencies (defined as basic units for higher-level performance competencies) were identified through a content analysis of existing performance models. These components were ultimately aggregated into eight factors known as the Great Eight competency framework.

The Great Eight factors were argued to occupy the same hierarchical level in the performance domain as the Five Factor Model (FFM) in personality (Bartram, 2005), and have been corroborated through factor analyses of other competency ratings and models (Kurz et al., 2004).Various studies have been published using the Great Eight (Furnham et al., 2012).

The question for the AC designer becomes to choose or devise instruments which reliably measure all eight. It is not clear whether this has been done but remains an important challenge.

Inevitably this is not the only generic list of competencies. Thus, business psychology consulting companies often devise their own set of competencies and ACs to go with them, which they sell to all their client organisations. The following list was used by a British consulting company called KAISEN, which attracted validation research (Furnham et al., 1997):

Drive to achieve: Concern to do things better or more efficiently than they have been done previously or better than they are done elsewhere.

Drive to lead: Desire to have the responsibility and authority of position to
make an impact on others. Concerned to be involved in work that seems to
have status and importance.

Conceptual ability: Ability to conceptualise the main themes and issues from
factual or abstract information. Ability to identify key patterns of
principles from complex information. Interested in generating and using
'maps' or models.

Intuition: Confidence in own intuitions when making judgements. Draw
strongly on past learning, consciously or unconsciously.

Interpersonal sensitivity: Interest in, and open attitude to, other people's
opinions, values, perspective, behaviour and personality.

Social adaptability: Ability to relate competently with a wide range of
different people in different social situations, using a broad repertoire of
influence styles.

Optimism: Belief that things will turn out well. Generally positive and
enthusiastic about life.

Resilience: Ability to cope with stress and adjust to unsatisfactory conditions.
Ability to retain emotional balance when under pressure and to 'bounce
back' after setbacks.

Interest in business: Fascination for how businesses work. Interest in facts,
figures, events and stories that help to explain things. 'Passive' attention to
things that might be relevant, 'active' investigation to find out
missing information.

Internal locus of control: Possession of a clear internal framework of
principles and beliefs that guide the individual's judgement.

Some organisations have their own, supposedly unique, competencies, for which they then commission AC experts to devise measures to assess. Because of the problems associated with each and every competency concept, one advantage of ACs is that the same competency is assessed by more than one person using more than one method. These competencies make up the 'rows' in the assessment grid (see below).

5.4.4   Typical Exercises

The whole point of an AC is that people undergo extensive assessment with many different exercises. This is why they take such a long time and are so expensive. They are also often a 'logistic nightmare' as so many people are involved.

There is no agreed list of what sort of things are assessed. Moerdyk (2014) suggests the following:

1. *Personality assessment:* This can be done online before they arrive or while they are there. There are a huge variety of tests to choose from yet, in effect, around 10 of the most marketed tests are used.

2. *General aptitude:* A widely used measure is the Ravens Standard Progressive Matrices (RPM), because it is considered a culture fair measure of general intellectual ability. Again there are many different tests to choose from. Sometimes a very specific battery is used to measure particular facets of intelligence (mathematical, spatial).

3. *In-basket exercises:* This is a simulation in which each candidate is required to work through a typical manager's in tray and to make various decisions . For instance, the candidate may be told they have just taken over the department/organisation. The exercise can have as many as 20 or 30 different tasks of varying complexity, many of them linked some complex algorithm. This exercise allows the assessor(s) to evaluate various cognitive, decision-making and managerial competencies in a realistic job situation.

4. *Leaderless group technique:* In this kind of exercise, groups of four to six people are given a task to do with competing interests and limited resources. The candidates have to charm, influence and persuade the others to get the resources allocated to his/her needs. The tasks are best when they are representative of the job actually being assessed.

5. *Role-play:* These are used to identify the person's interpersonal skills. A typical situation is one where a subordinate has to be counselled or disciplined, or a problem client/customer dealt with. The other role-player is often a skilled and experienced actor, which can significantly increase costs.

6. *Written exercises:* These are used to determine a person's ability to think strategically or construct a document in a logical manner, language skills and tact. Some jobs are heavily reliant on writing skills and therefore the ACs have a variety of exercises that test fluency, vocabulary and logic.

7. *Oral presentations:* The candidate is required to make an oral presentation of varying lengths, with and without PowerPoint and with

different types of preparation features, such as the person's creativity, coherence, self-confidence, and impact can be assessed.

8. *Interviews*: In almost all cases, the person being assessed is given a structured interview in which various aspects of cognitive, interpersonal and other competencies are assessed. It is quite common to have multiple interviews with different interviewers to check reliability.

9. *Social interaction*: In many ACs, the people being assessed are observed as they interact with each other and/or the observers over a meal or during a social occasion such as a cocktail party. This may or may not be recorded electronically or by evaluators who are at the event. They are usually trying to assess emotional intelligence, apparent sincerity and tact.

10. *Analysis problem*: This is usually a group of exercises that involves the in-depth analysis of a particular problem situation, such as the development of a new product, relocation of a plant, integrating product lines, etc. These can be of a divergent (i.e. brainstorming) or convergent (problem solving) nature.

11. *Team roles, preferences and interaction*: This refers to attempts to see how people work in teams and the sort of roles that they prefer, like team leader, creative ideas person and resource investigator. This can be done using a mixture of questionnaires and simulated group activities.

The exercises should, as far as possible, reflect the realities of the job. It is therefore necessary to tune each exercise to the job and corporate culture.

Here is an example of a relative short AC that was run after candidates completed a personality test, an intelligence test and two interviews:

In tray. Candidates were given 15 fairly typical managerial problems that may be encountered by people in that job. The situations were targeted at testing managerial skills such as delegation, performance management, team building, etc. Candidates were given 45 minutes to write down solutions for each. A single efficiency score was the overall result.

Prioritise. Candidates were also asked to go through 15 situations and prioritise them for their attention. That is, they were to rank order them according to the effort, energy and resources that they should dedicate to each. They were given 5 minutes to complete this task after solving the previous problems. This was measured against a 'correct' order list.

Problem solving. Candidates were each given a file with 30–35 papers relating to a particular tricky and complex business problem. They were asked to provide a written report summarising the nature of the problem as well as recommendations for a solution. The task attempted to measure analytical skills. Candidates were given 45 minutes for this task.

Document drafting. The problem-solving exercise was concerned with the quality of solutions. This exercise was concerned with drafting/writing skills. The task was to write a clear, succinct account of the candidates understanding of the problem and the solution. They had 25 minutes to complete this task. An overall judgement was made on the draft provided.

Proof-reading. Candidates were given a four hundred word paper that contained 25 grammatical and spelling mistakes. They had five minutes to identify and correct as many errors as they spotted.

Press response. Candidates were told of a number of serious PR disasters, such as a whistle-blowers report, and they were asked to devise a response within 300 words. These were evaluated by three judges.

Agenda hiding. Candidates were paired up and given a simple question on a card (e.g. Do you prefer dogs or cats? Are you a saver or a spender? What was your greatest achievement at school?). Their task was to get the answer to their question without the other person knowing what the question was. They also have to try to hear what the other person's question was. They get scored on hiding the question, getting their answer and hearing the other person's question.

All evaluations were made by the same assessors, and a reliability check was undertaken to ensure scoring was consistent. The main assessor was the person who designed the exercises. Around 80% of the completed exercises were independently rated by a second or third expert in this area to ensure reliability. There was little or no disagreement with extreme score (i.e. 1 or 5) and overall levels of reliability exceeded .90. Each task was evaluated on a five-point scale, where 1 was excellent and 5 poor, to indicate overall performance on that task.

5.4.4.1 The Scoring

Most ACs have a grid scoring system such as the following, which is based on an actual grid used in organisations. The rows represent the competencies that the AC was designed to assess and the columns the assessment methods. The idea is that each competency is assessed by at least one, preferably two or three different methods.

In this example, 19 competencies are being evaluated

Competencies	Interview	Group exercise	One to one business meeting	Case study presentation	Personal development planning exercise
Drive	X		X		X
Ability to build a strong team	X				
Commerciality and growth focus			X	X	
Confidence and resilience			X	X	
Influence				X	
Action orientation	X				X
Incisiveness				X	
Customer focus	X			X	
Strategic business understanding			X	X	
Clarity of thought			X	X	X
Creativity Inventiveness and innovation				X	X
Probing questioning			X		
Listening and interpretation			X		

(*cont.*)

Competencies	Interview	Group exercise	One to one business meeting	Case study presentation	Personal development planning exercise
Positive contributions to a group debate	X				
Self- and other awareness	X				
Soliciting other's points of view	X				
Conceptual thinking	X	X			
Presentation skills				X	
Analysis of written information	X				

Moerdyk (2014) gives an example of a numerical rating scale for a typical competency. It is obvious that by using scales as these it is relatively easy to assess the agreement/reliability of different raters.

Score	Interpretation
0	Does not exist, could not be detected
1	Poor, underdeveloped, inadequate for current position
2	Minimum required for adequate performance
3	Adequate – further development required for good performance
4	Good – meets requirements for good performance
5	Very good – good performance almost guaranteed
6	Excellent – will succeed at the next level of promotion
6+	Excessive – too much of a good thing –unbalanced, will interfere with good performance

He also provides an example of the scoring sheet of an assessor

Positive	4	Negative
☑ Breaks problem down into logical elements		[ ] Deals with large/ inappropriate elements
☑ Probes for information		[ ] Accepts information at face value
☑ Asks diagnostic questions		
☑ Identifies cause and effect relationships		[ ] Asks rhetorical/closed questions only
[ ] Prioritises		[ ] Focuses on symptoms
		☑ Lists
Asked person when problem first occurred		On Monday he told me this
What did you do next?		and on Tues he did that and
Why do you think this happened?		on Thursday he did . . .
First you said they were useless, and then what did you do?		

This is interesting and important because it gives some idea of the difficulty in scoring each exercise. Raters are often given descriptions of typical behaviour and a way of scoring them so that they each derive a reliable score. Inevitably some are much easier to rate than others. This gives an indication also of the amount of rater training that is necessary to achieve reliability on an exercise-by-exercise basis.

5.4.5   *Validity*

Inevitably there has been a great deal of interest in the construct, predictive and incremental validity of assessment centres (Donahue et al., 1997; Kleinmann & Koller, 1997; Kudisch et al., 1997; Thornton et al., 1997).

Whilst some of these centres used established, validated tests, most in fact celebrate the fact that the tests/tasks devised for the centre are particularly relevant or salient to the group of individuals tested and the job being advertised. That is, they are *tailor made*, or bespoke, to assess a range of competencies. This also means that until established by empirical research, they only have *face* validity and not *predictive* validity, which is why indeed they are constructed. To do this research a robust, sensitive and salient criterion, or better multiple salient criteria, needs to be found, measured and related to assessment centre task scores to demonstrate their validity.

Over the past 20 years various reviewers have tried to compare the validity of different assessment methods, such as cognitive ability tests, interviews, work samples, etc. (Anderson & Cunningham-Snell, 2000; Cook, 2016; Schmitt, 1989). Many reviewers place assessment centres above most other methods (like personality tests) in terms of their validity. However, it is not always possible to separate out different methods because more complex assessment centres tend to use cognitive ability and personality tests (as well as interviews, etc.) as part of the process to derive data.

There have been many studies that have examined personality, cognitive ability and assessment centre ratings. Some have looked very specifically at the relationship between personality trait scores and assessment centre ratings (Craik et al., 2002; Furnham & Crump, 2005; Haaland & Christiansen, 2002; Kolk et al., 2004; Lievens et al., 2001; Riggio et al., 2003; Waldman & Korbar, 2004). They have tended to show significant, but low and predictable, correlations between self-report-derived trait scores and observer ratings on assessment centre tasks.

Other studies have looked at the combined relationships of cognitive ability and personality trait scores on assessment centre ratings (Carless & Allwood, 1997; Dayan et al., 2002; Hardison, 2006; Krajewski et al., 2006; Lievens et al., 2003; de Meijer et al., 2006). Most have been concerned with the relationship between the individual difference measures and the assessment ratings, but also the incremental validity of the latter over the former in predicting work outcomes.

Hermalin et al. (2017) performed a meta-analysis of the selection validity of assessment centres. They examined 26 studies and 27 validity coefficients relating the *Overall Assessment Rating* to supervisory performance ratings. They obtained a corrected correlation of $r = .28$ between the Overall Rating and Supervisory Job Performance ratings. They also suggest that this validity estimate is likely to be conservative given that assessment centre validities tend to be affected by indirect range restriction.

The *criterion-related validity* of ACs has been well documented (Gaugler et al., 1987; Klimoski & Brickner, 1987; Lance, 2008; Lievens & Thornton, 2005). Criterion-related validity is essentially the relationship between various scores derived from an AC, and *actual*, behavioural work-based criteria collected by the organisation. Dayan et al. (2002) reported criterion-related validity ratings from earlier meta-analyses; Schmitt et al. (1984) found an average validity of .41; while Gaugler et al. (1987) cited an average validity of .37. Overall these are very high scores, which is why ACs are so highly valued.

Despite the strong criterion-related validity of ACs, their *construct validity* has not been well established, based on the use of competencies as the intended construct dimensions (Lance, 2008; Lievens & Thornton, 2005). Research has (Lance, 2008; Lievens, 2009; Lievens & Thornton, 2005) indicated that ACs do not always work as they are intended, due to the possible misapplication of multitrait–multimethod design. ACs are designed to evaluate behaviours according to content-valid simulated performance situations, hence behavioural outcomes are meant to be situation specific, and not cross-exercise consistent. In one study that corrected for typical methodological constraints found in construct validation, exercises were found to account for most of the variance (33%) followed by dimensions (22%) (Bowler & Woehr, 2006).

Convergence between exercises is expected to be stronger when the exercises provided opportunity to observe behaviours relating to the same trait. Furthermore, discrimination among dimensions within the exercises is expected to be stronger when the dimensions were measuring differing underlying traits (Lievens, 2009). In line with the theory, Haaland and Christiansen (2002) found that convergence between dimension ratings in exercises was positively dependent on the trait activation potential of the exercises. A re-analysis of existing AC studies had also confirmed the propositions of the theory (Lievens, 2009).

There have also been a few studies on the *incremental validity* of the AC over and above other aptitude tests (Lievens & Thornton, 2005). This refers to whether AC scores predict behavioural criteria incrementally over other measures which are also known to be related to those criteria. These limited studies have demonstrated the incremental validities of the ACs over cognitive ability tests (Dayan et al., 2002; Schmidt & Hunter, 1998; Schmitt et al., 1984, as cited in Dayan et al., 2002), and over behaviour description interviews (Lievens & Thornton, 2005). Despite the encouraging research, the incremental validities found from these studies were relatively modest and generally not well established.

Hoffman et al. (2015), in a recent review, noted the nomological network analyses suggested that the AC exercises tend to be modestly associated with intelligence (GMA), the trait Extraversion and, to a lesser extent, Openness to Experience, but largely unrelated to Agreeableness, Conscientiousness and Emotional Stability. Also, a content analysis of exercise descriptions yielded some evidence of accurately measuring complexity, ambiguity, interpersonal interaction and fidelity, but not interdependence.

As noted in Chapter 1, the overall psychometric properties of well-designed and run ACs are impressively high compared to most other methods, many of which are also used in ACs.

5.4.6   Conclusion

According to Moerdyk (2014), ACs have numerous advantages: Most are competency based, job related and organisationally relevant because exercises are tailored to meet organisation and industry needs. Most are based on real-life situations typical of those likely to be faced in the work situation (and therefore have face validity). They do (or should) use properly trained observers, some of whom are actual line managers, under the direction of a trained psychologist. Indeed, the use of line managers helps ensure that the decisions arrived at are acceptable to other line managers. Equally different exercises are scored for different competencies by different assessors and the scores combined to give a single score. This process of triangulation hopefully strengthens predictive validity.

Ideally, ACs provide further training for both participants and observers. More importantly they are defensible in court as they are based on specific job needs and are competency based.

Finally, an important finding from this research is that candidates who attend ACs generally have a positive view of the organisation even when they are not selected.

Moerdyk (2014) also notes some of the disadvantages associated with ACs. They are labour intensive and time consuming. Because they require specially trained assessors, they are expensive to develop and validate and costly to implement. Also, they require participants and observers to be removed from the workplace for several days, requiring substitutes to be found for this period.

REFERENCES

Anderson, N., & Cunningham-Snell, N. (2000). Personnel selection. In N. Chmiel (Ed.), *Introduction to work and organizational psychology* (pp. 69–99). Oxford, UK: Blackwell.

Bartram, D. (2005). The great eight competencies: a criterion-centric approach to validation. *Journal of Applied Psychology, 90*(6), 1185–1203.

Bartram, D., Robertson, I. T., & Callinan, M. (2002). Introduction: a framework for examining organisational effectiveness. In I. T. Robertson, M. Callinan, & D. Bartram (Eds.), *Organisational effectiveness: The role of psychology* (pp. 1–10). Chichester, UK: Wiley.

Bowler, M. C., & Woehr, D. J. (2006). A meta-analytic evaluation of the impact of dimension and exercise factors on assessment center ratings. *Journal of Applied Psychology, 91*, 1114–1124.

Carless, S. A., & Allwood, V. E. (1997). Managerial assessment centres: what is being rated? *Australian Psychologist, 32*, 101–105.

Cook, M. (2016). *Personnel selection: Adding value through people.* Chichester, UK: Wiley.

Craik, K. H., Ware, A. P., Kamp, J., O'Reilly, C., Staw, B., & Zedeck, A. (2002). Exploration of construct validity in a combined managerial and personality assessment programme. *Journal of Occupational and Organizational Psychology*, 75, 171–193.

Dayan, K., Kasten, R., & Fox, S. (2002). Entry-level police candidate assessment centre: an efficient tool or a hammer to kill a fly? *Personnel Psychology*, 55, 827–829.

de Meijer, L. A.L., Born, M. P., Terlouw, G., & van der Molen, H. T. (2006). Applicant and method factors related to ethnic score differences in personnel selection: a Study at the Dutch Police. *Human Performance*, 19(3), 219–251.

Donahue, L., Truxillo, D., Cornwell, J., & Gerrity, M. (1997). Assessment centre construct validity and behavioural checklists. *Journal of Social Behavior and Personality*, 12, 85–107.

Furnham, A., & Crump, J. (2005). Personality traits, types, and disorders: an examination of the relationship between three self-report measures. *European Journal of Personality*, 19(3), 167–184.

Furnham, A., Crump, J., & Whelan, J. (1997). Validating the NEO Personality Inventory using assessor's ratings. *Personality and Individual Differences*, 22, 669–675.

Furnham, A., Miller, T., Batey, M., & Johnson, S. (2012). Demographic and individual correlates of self-rated competency. *Imagination, Cognition and Personality*, 31, 247–265.

Furnham, A., Taylor, J., & Chamorro-Premuzic, T. (2008). Personality and intelligence correlates of assessment center exercises. *Individual Differences Research*, 6, 181–192.

Gaugler, B.B., Rosenthal, D.B., Thornton, G. C. III, & Benson, C. (1987). Meta-analysis of assessment centre validity. *Journal of Applied Psychology*, 72(3), 493–511.

Goldstein, H. W., Yusko, K. P., Braverman, E. P., Smith, D. B., & Chung, B. (1998). The role of cognitive ability in the subgroup differences and incremental validity of assessment center exercises. *Personnel Psychology*, 51, 357–374.

Haaland, S., & Christiansen, N. D. (2002). Implications of trait-activation theory for evaluating the construct validity of assessment center ratings. *Personnel Psychology*, 55, 137–163.

Hardison, C. M. (2006). Construct validity of assessment center overall ratings: an investigation of relationships with and incremental criterion related validity over big 5 personality traits and cognitive ability. *Dissertation Abstracts International: Section BL: The Sciences and Engineering*, 66, 6959.

Hermelin, E., Lievens, F., & Robertson, I. T. (2007). The validity of assessment centres for the prediction of supervisory performance. *International Journal of Selection and Assessment*, 15, 405–411.

Hermalin, B. E., & Weisbach, M. S. (2017). Assessing managerial ability: implications for corporate governance. In B. E. Hermalin, & M. S. Weisbach (Eds.), *The Handbook of the Economics of Corporate Governance* (vol. 1, pp. 93–176). Amsterdam, The Netherlands: Elsevier.

Hoffman, B. J., Kennedy, C. L., LoPilato, A. C., Monahan, E. L., & Lance, C. E. (2015). A review of the content, criterion-related, and construct-related validity of assessment center exercises. *Journal of Applied Psychology, 100*(4), 1143–1168.

Howard, A. (1997). A reassessment of assessment centres. *Journal of Social Behavior and Personality, 12*, 13–52.

Kleinmann, M., & Koller, O. (1997). Construct validity and assessment centres. *Journal of Social Behavior and Personality, 12*, 65–83.

Klimoski, R., & Brickner, M. (1987). Why do assessment centers work? the puzzle of assessment center validity. *Personnel Psychology, 40*, 243–260.

Kline, P. (1994). *The handbook of psychological testing*. London, UK: Routledge.

Kolk, N. J., Born, M. P., & Van Der Flier, H. (2004). Three method factors explaining the low correlations between assessment center dimension ratings and scores on personality inventories. *European Journal of Personality, 18*, 127–141.

Krajewski, H. T., Goffin, R. D., McCarthy, J. M., Rothstein, G., & Johnston, N. (2006) Comparing the validity of structured interviews for managerial-level employees: should we look to the past or focus on the future? *Journal of Occupational and Organizational Psychology, 79*, 411–432.

Krause, D. E., Kersting, M., Heggestad, E., & Thornton, G. (2006). Incremental validity of assessment centre ratings over cognitive ability tests. *International Journal of Selection and Assessment, 14*, 360.

Kudisch, J., Ladd, R., & Dobbins, G. (1997). New evidence on the construct validity of diagnostic assessment centres. *Journal of Social Behavior and Personality, 12*, 129–144.

Kurz, R., & Bartram, D. (2002). Competency and individual performance: Modeling the world of work. In I. T. Robertson, M. Callinan, & D. Bartram (Eds.), *Organizational effectiveness: The role of psychology* (pp. 227–255). Chichester, UK: Wiley.

Kurz, R., Bartram, D., & Baron, H. (2004). Assessing potential and performance at work: The Great Eight competencies. In *Proceedings of the British Psychological Society Occupational Conference* (pp. 91–95). Leicester, UK: British Psychological Society.

Lance, C. E. (2008). Why assessment centres do not work the way they are supposed to. *Industrial and Organisational Psychology, 1*(1), 84–97.

Lievens, F. & Thornton, G. C. III (2005). Assessment centres: recent developments in practice and research. In A. Evers, O. Smit-Voskuijl, & N. Anderson (Ed.), *Handbook of selection* (pp. 243–264). New York: Blackwell Publishing.

Lievens, F. (2009). Assessment centers: a tale about dimensions, exercises, and dancing bears. *European Journal of Work and Organisational Psychology, 18* (1), 102–121.

Lievens, F., De Fruyt, F., & Van Dam, K. (2001). Assessors' use of personality traits in descriptions of assessment centre candidates: a five-factor model perspective. *Journal of Occupational & Organizational Psychology, 74*, 623–636.

Lievens, F., Harris, M. M., & Van Keer, E. (2003). Predicting cross-cultural training performance: the validity of personality, cognitive ability and dimensions measured by an assessment center and a behavior description interview. *Journal of Applied Psychology, 88*, 476–489.

Livens, F. and Klimoski, R. J. (2001) Understanding the assessment centre process: where are we now? In C. L. Cooper, & I. T. Robertson (Eds.), *International review of industrial and organisational psychology*, vol. 16. Chichester, UK: Wiley.

Moerdyk, A. (2014). *The principles and practice of psychological assessment* (2nd ed.). Pretoria, South Africa: Van Schaik Publishers.

Murray, M. (2005) How to design a successful assessment centre. *People Management (UK), 11*(4) 24–45.

Petrides, K. V., Weinstein, Y., Chou, J., Furnham, A., & Swami, V. (2010). An investigation into assessment centre validity, fairness, and selection drivers. *Australian Journal of Psychology, 62*, 227–235.

Riggio, R. E., Mayes, B. T., & Schleicher, D. J. (2003). Using assessment center methods for measuring undergraduate business student outcomes. *Journal of Management Inquiry, 12*, 68–78.

Schmitt, N. (1989). Construct validity in personnel selection. In B. J. Fullon, H. P. Pfister, & J. Brebner (Eds), *Advances in industrial and organizational psychology* (pp. 331–341). New York, NY: Elsevier Science.

Schmitt, N., Gooding, R. Z., Noe, R. A., & Kirsch, M. (1984). Meta-analyses of validity studies published between 1964 and 1982 and the investigation of study characteristics. *Personnel Psychology, 37*, 407–422.

Schuler, H., & Funke, U. (1999). The moderating effect of raters' opportunities to observe ratees' job performance on the validity of an assessment centre. *International Journal of Selection and Assessment, 7*, 133–141.

Spector, P. E., Vance, C. A., Schneider, J. R., & Hezlett, S. A. (2000). The relation of cognitive ability and personality traits to assessment center performance. *Journal of Applied Social Psychology, 30*, 1474–1491.

Thornton, G. C., & Gibbons, A. M. (2009). Validity of assessment centers for personnel selection. *Human Resources Management Review, 19*, 169–187.

Thornton, G. C, Tziner, A., Dahan, M., Clevenger, J., & Meir, E. (1997). Construct validity of assessment centre judgements. *Journal of Social Behavior and Personality*, 12, 109–127.

Toh, S. M., & Furnham, A. (2015). The validation of assessment centres in Asia. *Asia-Pacific Journal of Business Administration*, 7, 20–33.

Waldman, D. A., & Korbar, T. (2004). Student assessment center performance in the prediction of early career success. *Academy of Management Learning and Education*, 3, 151–167.

Woodruffe, C. (1995). *Assessment Centres*. London, UK: IP.

6   Behavioural Tests

6.1   INTELLIGENCE, COGNITIVE ABILITY, ACHIEVEMENT AND APTITUDE TESTS

What are they?

Tests of many kinds that purport to measure general intelligence ('g') or a specific type of intelligence/ability such as spatial intelligence or general knowledge. They differ very widely but surprisingly appear to intercorrelate fairly highly, suggesting they are all measuring information processing capacity.

How do they work?

Almost all IQ tests are 'power tests', meaning that they are strictly timed and there are very clear right and wrong answers. Scores are usually normally distributed in the population. Tests batteries can measure specific abilities (verbal, spatial, mathematical) as well as an overall score usually on a standard scale with M = 100 and SD = 15 points.

What of the evidence?

There is considerable evidence of their reliability and validity. Hence, they are often regarded as some of the best tests in the entire field of psychometrics. Most importantly they show impressive predictive validity in the workplace, particularly for complex and leadership jobs.

Practical problems: cost, ethics, politics

There are a few problems of availability and cost, but considerable problems with ethics and politics because of established group (age, race, sex) differences. Despite their validity, legal, moral and political issues inhibit many selectors from using them.

Recommendations for use

Even though they have considerable predictive validity in educational and work settings there can be many difficult and sensitive 'political' issues to be overcome before they are used advisably. Because of their efficacy, such issues should, where possible, be addressed so that these tests can be used, particularly in the assessment of professional jobs and senior leadership positions.

6.1.1   Introduction

Intelligence tests refer to achievement, aptitude or general mental ability (GMA) tests. Many terms cover the same areas: ability, achievement, cognitive ability, mental ability and intelligence tests. These are also distinct from social intelligence tests, creativity or divergent thinking tests, which are about style of thinking and social skills.

What is intelligence, and can it be measured? It has been said 'Intelligence is what an intelligence test measures and that is all.' Many laypeople are deeply sceptical about the use of intelligence tests. But are laypeople correct? Could and should such tests be used in job and educational selection.

A hundred years ago, Thorndike et al. (1921) asked 14 experts to define intelligence. Here are some of their answers:

- The ability to carry out abstract thinking.
- The ability to adjust to one's environment.
- The ability to adapt to new situations of life.
- The capacity to acquire knowledge.
- The capacity to learn or to profit from experience.
- Good responses from the point of view of psychological truth or fact.

Probably the most famous study of experts' definitions was done by the editors of the *Journal of Educational Psychology* ('Intelligence and its measurement' 1921). Contributors to this issue provided several different definitions as follows:

1. The power of good responses from the point of view of truth or facts.
2. The ability to carry on abstract thinking.
3. Sensory capacity, capacity for perceptual recognition, quickness, range or flexibility of association, facility and imagination, span of attention, quickness or alertness in response.

4. Ability to learn or having learned to adjust oneself to the environment.
5. Ability to adapt oneself adequately to relatively new situations in life.
6. The capacity for knowledge and knowledge possessed.
7. A biological mechanism by which the effects of a complexity of stimuli are brought together and given a somewhat unified effect in behaviour.
8. The capacity to inhibit an instinctive adjustment, the capacity to redefine the inhibited instinctive adjustment in the light of imaginably experienced trial and error, and the capacity to realise the modified instinctive adjustment in overt behaviour to the advantage of the individual as a social animal.
9. The capacity to acquire capacity.
10. The capacity to learn or to profit by experience.
11. Sensation, perception, association, memory, discrimination, judgement and reasoning.

Laypeople use the term to describe others, although they do not always understand the mechanism or process by which it is possible to deduce significant interpersonal differences. A lot of focus has been on the use of tests and the meaning of scores. However, it is difficult to deny the accumulated evidence that intelligence scores do have predictive significance: that is, for tests administered and scored at time 1; there is a positive significant correlation with predicted educational and work achievement at time 2 (Deary, 2000, 2001; Mackintosh, 1998).

Academic research has shown that, quite consistently, cognitive ability accurately predicts job performance across *all* jobs, but particularly in *complex* jobs. Many psychologists working in the area believe that intelligence is the *single best* predictor of (senior, managerial) work performance. Nearly all recent research points to the predictive power of cognitive ability and hence the importance of using these tests in selection.

Intelligence tests measure different, but related, variables like memory, verbal comprehension, reasoning and spatial orientation. As well as cognitive ability tests there are mechanical ability tests, clerical ability tests and physical ability tests which measure different but related variables.

The publication of a highly controversial book on intelligence over 25 years ago – *The Bell Curve* by Hernstein et al. – led more than 50 of the world's experts on intelligence to write to the *Wall Street Journal* on 15 December 1994. Their summary is an excellent and clear statement on what psychologists (probably still) think about intelligence.

They do note five points of what they call 'practical importance':

1. IQ is strongly related, probably more so than any other single measurable human trait, to many important educational, occupational, economic and social outcomes. Its relation to the welfare and performance of individuals is very strong in some arenas in life (education, military training), moderate but robust in others (social competence), and modest but consistent in others (law-abidingness). Whatever IQ tests measure, it is of great practical and social importance.

2. A high IQ is an advantage in life because virtually all activities require some reasoning and decision-making. Conversely, a low IQ is often a disadvantage, especially in disorganised environments. Of course, a high IQ no more guarantees success than a low IQ guarantees failure in life. There are many exceptions, but the odds for success in our society greatly favour individuals with higher IQs.

3. The practical advantages of having a higher IQ increase as life settings become more complex (novel, ambiguous, changing, unpredictable or multifaceted). For example, a high IQ is generally necessary to perform well in highly complex or fluid jobs (the professions, management); it is a considerable advantage in moderately complex jobs (crafts, clerical and police work); but it provides less advantage in settings that require only routine decision-making or simple problem solving (unskilled work).

4. Differences in intelligence are certainly not the only factor affecting performance in education, training and highly complex jobs (no one claims they are), but intelligence is often the most important. When individuals have already been selected for high (or low) intelligence – and so do not differ much in IQ – as in graduate school (or special education), other influences on performance loom larger in comparison.

5. Certain personality traits, special talents, aptitudes, physical capabilities, experience and the like are important (sometimes essential) for successful performance in many jobs, but they have narrower (or unknown) applicability

> or 'transferability' across tasks and settings compared with general
> intelligence. Some scholars choose to refer to these other human traits
> as 'intelligences'.

The recent research evidence is very clear. The single best predictor of success in complex, changing managerial jobs is intelligence.
Brighter people learn faster, they have a greater store of knowledge and
they tend to be intellectually more self-confident. They analyse problems more efficiently and are less threatened by change. Moreover, the
experts on selection argue that tests are useful, cheap, fast, easy, versa-
tile, scorable and understandable (Gatewood et al., 2016).

Yet we know, from extensive American research, that mental ability tests create a large adverse impact on some ethnic minorities, yet there
is less information on this issue elsewhere. Attempts to solve the adverse
impact problem in the USA include trying to identify features of mental
ability testing that will reduce adverse impact. Attempts to deal with the
adverse impact problem in the USA include score banding, which defines
a range of scores as equivalent, thus allowing selection within the band to
be based on achieving diversity (see Chapter 2).

Furnham (2008) considered some of the more controversial
issues and noted:

- Do intelligence tests have adequate validity? Yes. They predict school
  success (around $r = .50$) and how long people remain in school ($r = .70$), and
  many other educational or organisational and social variables.
- Do intelligence tests predict job performance and academic success? Yes.
  There are various caveats to this question, which is central to this chapter
  and this book which will be discussed later in detail.
- But are there not multiple intelligences? No. Not in the sense that most
  people are very good at some cognitive tasks and very bad at others.
  Generally, we find that scores on all sorts of (good) IQ tests correlate
  positively and significantly with one another. That is, people perform at a
  broadly similar level across all tasks (vocabulary, maths, etc.).
- Are all IQ tests equally good? No. It takes quite some effort to develop,
  refine and produce a test that gives an all-round picture of a person's
  cognitive functioning.

Most people are familiar with the many and frequent objections to tests. Consider the following, *all of which are erroneous:*

> All tests are very culture bound – devised for, and by, white middle class (males) to their advantage.
>
> All they measure is how rich a person's parents are/were and how much education they had.
>
> There are many very different types of intelligence and no one test (or even battery) can properly measure them.
>
> The more you practice the higher your score. They therefore measure only effort not ability.
>
> We all know seriously bright people who never excel at school or in jobs. Test scores predict nothing.
>
> Test scores change. You can increase your intelligence. Scores should measure potential, not how well you do today.

Other questions refer to issues around *practice and coaching*: that is could one significantly increase one's score by being coached or practicing. Most studies have shown that practicing and coaching have very little effect raising scores by less than a 1/3 of a standard deviation (i.e. around 5 IQ points). The question is why scores go up: a better understanding of the test format, reduced test anxiety, picking up very specific skills in vocabulary in particular. Practice and coaching have the most effect on those groups who have the least IQ test experience, but even then it is not very large (Gatewood et al., 2016).

Hough et al. (2001), in an important and extensive review, looked at all the issues, evidence and lessons learned around the issue of adverse impact. They note that the setting, the sample and the construct measured often individually or in combination *moderate* the magnitude of differences between groups. The more the nature of work is specified, and the more salient and valid instruments are chosen, the better. The data looking at both crystallised intelligence (namely verbal ability, quantitative ability, science achievement) as well as fluid ability (spatial ability, memory, mental processing speed) reveal systematic and replicable race, gender and age differences. There are also personality and physiological differences between these groups. They suggest various possible ways to reduce negative impact, including test coaching for applicants, improving test-taking, motivation of applicants, using different criteria for different groups distinguishing between task and contextual performance. They also consider, in detail, statistical methods for detecting and reducing adverse impacts like test score banding and predictor/criterion weighting.

It is indeed these applied and practical quandaries rather than the science behind intelligence testing that has led it to be such a controversial topic in organisational psychology.

6.1.2 Distinctions, Differences and Disagreements

There are all sorts of passionate debates in the world of intelligence testing. These refer, particularly, to bias against certain groups as well as possible practice effects. There are other important issues: Are they equally valid predictors of work outcome in different jobs, and in different countries? Is there evidence of incremental validity above other techniques (Cook, 2016)?

6.1.2.1 Nature vs Nurture

One of the most controversial aspects of intelligence is the nature/nurture issue; how much of intelligence is due to genetics? This is an ongoing war, which is beyond the scope of this book. Suffice it to say that the latest book in this field has the following quotes (Plomin, 2018):

> In the Nature-Nurture War, Nature Wins ... We would essentially be the same person if we had been adopted at birth and raised in a different family. Environmental influences are important, accounting for about half of the differences between us, but they are largely unsystematic, unstable and idiosyncratic ... The environment can alter this plan [of development] temporarily, but after these environmental bumps we bounce back to our genetic trajectory. DNA isn't all that matters, but it matters more than everything else put together in terms of the stable psychological traits that make us who we are.

These thoughts were used in an attack by Kaufman (2019), which gives some sense of the nature of this argument.

Eysenck earlier traces the link between the genetics and the outcomes. The idea is that genetics informs biology, which relates to performance on IQ tests which have social consequences.

6.1.2.2   Sex, Race and Generational Effects

Again, this a massive and highly debateable topic. The 'bottom-line' is this (though of course this is disputable): There are small subscale differences between the sexes (i.e. males score higher on visuo-spatial tests) but overall there are very small, indeed almost no sex differences in intelligence. There are clearly replicable race differences, though unclear why that occurs. Fluid intelligence (see below) declines with age, particularly over 40 years; hence there are clear age differences. Knowing and accepting these differences means that various 'corrections' can be made, and they can be used in selection (see Chapter 2).

6.1.2.3   Lumpers and Splitters

More relevant to this work is that on the facets or domains of intelligence. According to Sternberg, researchers in the controversial field of intelligence tend either to be *lumpers* or *splitters*. The former emphasises that people who tend to do well on one sort of IQ test do well on practically all others. They talk of general intelligence (g) and see the IQ score (derived, of course, from a good test) as highly predictive of educational, business and life success. Some lumpers are happy to see and agree that there are identifiable facets of g: that is, that we can assess different aspects of intelligence but that they are all highly related. These include crystallised/general knowledge, visual and hearing accuracy and memory and efficiency of information processing (fluid ability).

Splitters, on the other hand, are advocates of multiple intelligence (see Table 6.1). Sternberg himself is a splitter and a well-known advocate of practical or successful intelligence (Sternberg, 1997). Without doubt,

Table 6.1 *Gardner's multiple intelligences model and definitions (Gardner, 1983, 1999)*

Gardner's multiple intelligences	Gardner's definitions (1983, 1999)	Measure definitions
Verbal/ Linguistic	This area has to do with words, spoken or written. People with high verbal-linguistic intelligence display a facility with words and languages. They are typically good at reading, writing, telling stories and memorizing words along with dates. They tend to learn best by reading, taking notes, listening to lectures, and discussion and debate. Those with verbal-linguistic intelligence learn foreign languages very easily as they have high verbal memory and recall, and an ability to understand and manipulate syntax and structure. Careers that suit those with this intelligence include writers, lawyers, policemen, philosophers, journalists, politicians, poets, and teachers.	Ability to use words
Mathematical/ Logical	This area has to do with logic, abstractions, reasoning, and numbers. While it is often assumed that those with this intelligence naturally excel in mathematics, chess, computer programming and other logical or numerical activities, a more accurate definition places less emphasis on traditional mathematical ability and more on reasoning capabilities, abstract patterns of recognition, scientific thinking and investigation, and the ability to perform complex calculations. It correlates strongly with traditional concepts of 'intelligence' or IQ. Careers which suit those with this intelligence include scientists, physicists, mathematicians, logicians, engineers, doctors, economists and philosophers.	Ability to reason logically, solve a number problem
Spatial	This area deals with spatial judgment and the ability to visualize with the mind's eye. Careers which suit those with this type of intelligence include artists, designers and architects. A spatial person is also good with puzzles.	Ability to find your way around in the environment and form mental images
Musical	This area has to do with sensitivity to sounds, rhythms, tones, and music. People with a high musical intelligence normally have good pitch and may even have absolute pitch, and are able to sing, play musical instruments, and compose music. Since there is a strong auditory component to this intelligence, those who are strongest in it may learn best via lecture. Language skills are typically	Ability to perceive and create pitch and rhythm

	highly developed in those whose base intelligence is musical. In addition, they will sometimes use songs or rhythms to learn. They have sensitivity to rhythm, pitch, meter, tone, melody or timbre. Careers that suit those with this intelligence include instrumentalists, singers, conductors, disc-jockeys, orators, writers and composers.	
Body-Kinaesthetic	The core elements of the bodily-kinaesthetic intelligence are control of one's bodily motions and the capacity to handle objects skilfully (206). Gardner elaborates to say that this intelligence also includes a sense of timing, a clear sense of the goal of a physical action, along with the ability to train responses so they become like reflexes. In theory, people who have bodily-kinaesthetic intelligence should learn better by involving muscular movement (e.g. getting up and moving around into the learning experience), and are generally good at physical activities such as sports or dance. They may enjoy acting or performing, and in general they are good at building and making things. They often learn best by doing something physically, rather than [by] reading or hearing about it. Those with strong bodily-kinaesthetic intelligence seem to use what might be termed muscle memory – they remember things through their body such as verbal memory. Careers that suit those with this intelligence include: athletes, dancers, musicians, actors, surgeons, doctors, builders, police officers, and soldiers...	Ability to use bodily functions or motor movements
Inter-personal	This area has to do with interaction with others. In theory, people who have a high interpersonal intelligence tend to be extroverts, characterized by their sensitivity to others' moods, feelings, temperaments and motivations, and their ability to cooperate in order to work as part of a group. They communicate effectively and empathize easily with others, and may be either leaders or followers. They typically learn best by working with others and often enjoy discussion and debate. Careers that suit those with this intelligence include sales, politicians, managers, teachers, and social workers.	Ability to understand other people
Intra-personal	This area has to do with introspective and self-reflective capacities. People with intrapersonal intelligence are intuitive and typically introverted. They are skilful at deciphering their own feelings and motivations. This refers to having a deep understanding of the self; what are your strengths/ weaknesses, what makes you unique, you can predicts your own reactions/ emotions. Careers which suit those with this intelligence include philosophers, psychologists, theologians, lawyers, and writers. People with intrapersonal intelligence also prefer to work alone.	Ability to understand yourself and develop sense of your own identity

Table 6.1 (*cont.*)

Gardner's multiple intelligences	Gardner's definitions (1983, 1999)	Measure definitions
Naturalistic	This area has to do with nature, nurturing and relating information to one's natural surroundings. Careers which suit those with this intelligence include naturalists, farmers and gardeners.	Ability to identify and employ many dimensions in the natural world, e.g. classifying animals and plants
Existential	Ability to contemplate phenomena or questions beyond sensory data, such as the infinite and infinitesimal. Ideal careers: cosmologist, philosopher.	Ability to understand the significance of life, the meaning of death, and the experience of love
[Spiritual]	This ability has to do with understanding aspects of the meta-physical and spiritual world.	[Ability to engage in thinking about cosmic issues, the achievement of a state of being and the ability to have spiritual effects on others]

however, the most famous splitter is Gardner, who initially claimed there were seven intelligences that were distinct and not closely related. This claim has, however, been challenged by many.

The idea that there are multiple and distinct intelligences has given rise to the idea that different professions require different types of intelligence. Whilst this seems a reasonable and common-sense assumption, the evidence that these intelligences are unique and unrelated does not exist.

Disputes with lumpers (who believe in general intelligence) and splitters (who believe in multiple intelligences) go on, but it is probably fair to say that all those working in the field of intelligence (as opposed to education) find the evidence for general intelligence most compelling.

6.1.2.4   Fluid and Crystallised

Since the turn of the century, another, a more important and widely accepted, distinction has been made between *fluid* and *crystallised* intelligence by Cattell (1987). The analogy is to water – fluid water can take any shape, whereas ice crystals are rigid. Fluid intelligence is effectively the power of reasoning and processing information. It includes the ability to perceive relationships, deal with unfamiliar problems and gain new types of knowledge. Crystallised intelligence consists of acquired skills and specific knowledge in a person's experience. Crystallised intelligence thus includes the skills of an accountant and a lawyer, as well as a mechanic and a salesperson.

Fluid intelligence peaks before 20 and remains constant, with some often declining in later years, starting in middle age (around 40 years). Crystallised intelligence, on the other hand, continues to increase. Thus, a schoolchild is quicker than a retired citizen at solving a problem that is unfamiliar to both of them, but even the most average older person will excel at solving problems in his/her previous area of occupational specialisation. Children do well at Sudoku and adults at crosswords.

In some cases, people try to solve problems by thinking about them in familiar terms – that is by using crystallised intelligence. Most intelligence tests use both types of intelligence, though there is a clear preference for fluid intelligence tests. Thus, consider the following:

1. Which of these numbers does not belong with the others?
   625, 361, 256, 193, 144
2. Which of the following towns is the odd one out?
   Oslo, London, New York, Cairo, Bombay, Caracas, Madrid.

The former is a measure of fluid and the latter of crystallised intelligence.

These two types of intelligence are highly correlated, although they are conceptually different. Usually *what* you have learned (crystallised intelligence) is determined by *how well* you learn (fluid intelligence). Thus, one good reason to have a measure of crystallised ability is that a tendency to work hard is a good measure of scholastic and business success – and hard work results in better scores in tests of crystallised ability. Another reason is that even short *vocabulary tests* give very reliable scores.

With changing technology, the value of crystallised intelligence may be dropping. Crystallised intelligence comes with age and experience. If that knowledge can be cheaply, accurately and efficiently stored and accessed by computers, the value of crystallised intelligence may decline.

Sceptics may argue that computers could also assist in fluid intelligence problems, thus making that sort of intelligence equally less valuable.

Furnham (2008) has argued that it is business CEO's fluid intelligence, personality and motivation that appear to be the key to success. In a different age, when education came through the apprenticeship system, the value of crystallised intelligence was particularly great. It still is in some sectors. Being a wine buff, an antiques expert or a skilled musical performer all mean long hours of attempts to accumulate wisdom.

6.1.2.5   Intelligence and Thinking/Cognitive Styles

Although it may seem surprising to many, there are comparatively few studies that look at the relationship between cognitive ability (intelligence), cognitive (intellectual) style (see next paragraph) and motivation (Furnham, 2008). However, it seems quite reasonable to assume that intellectual style is more closely related to measures of crystallised rather than fluid intelligence.

The oldest literature in this area is on cognitive style which is how (rather than how efficiently or how much) an individual thinks, processes information or attempts to understand the world around them. The list of cognitive styles is extensive. Messick (1984) listed 19 cognitive style variables, which could be grouped under 8 dimensions: broad vs narrow categorising, cognitive complexity vs simplicity, field dependence and independence, levelling vs sharpening, scanning vs focusing, converging vs diverging, automatisation vs restructuring and reflection vs impulsivity. It is a confusing area.

Indeed, it may be possible to develop a model which explains a process whereby styles influence intelligence. Thus, for instance, a bright (high fluid intelligent) stable, ambivert from a middle-class home which provides and values education may be encouraged to develop a deep approach to learning and an analytic, or legislative, thinking style. In doing so they acquire a wide vocabulary and an extensive general knowledge. In this sense the less 'g' loaded IQ tests may be more strongly correlated with intellectual styles.

There are individual differences in cognitive strategy preferences associated with these styles. One example is the Assimilator–Explorer (A-E) cognitive style. *Assimilators are seen as more rule bound in problem solving* behaviour and interpreting new events in terms of existing knowledge. *Explorers have a disposition towards novelty seeking* as manifest by searching for new types of solutions and new ways of solving problems without any external pressure to do so. Consequently, the A-E styles have been operationalised as a continuum where higher scores describe Explorers and lower scores describe Assimilators. These have been placed in the Wholist–Analyst category of style constructs. Like several other style constructs in this category, the A-E styles correlates with all the factors in the five-factor model of personality, but not extensively so, and does not correlate with general intelligence (Martinsen & Kaufmann, 2000). Moreover, Martinsen and Furnham (2016) found that there were significant but not strong correlations between the A-E styles and scores on a creative activities' checklist and with fluency (explorers had higher creativity and fluency scores).

Much depends on which measure of style is used. Though they do overlap, it does seem that some style measures are more psychometrically valid than others. Furthermore, most but not all are multidimensional. It is likely that some dimensions would be more closely related to intelligence than others. Thus, for instance, it is possible that convergent–divergent thinking is only modestly correlated with intelligence (though not creativity) while a deep learning style is correlated with intelligence

Of particular interest and importance is the issue of the development and change of both intelligence and intellectual style over time. There appear to be no longitudinal studies of changes in style over time whilst there are studies of both changes in personality and intelligence over time. Overall, it seems the changes are small but predictable. While entity or essentialist researchers would no doubt argue that after adolescents' intelligence (and to some extent personality traits) are fixed and immutable, incremental theorists would argue that it is possible to increase intelligence (and test scores) and no doubt change.

There are some differences in thinking styles: see the distinction between convergent and divergent thinking in creativity (see Section 6.3). However, whilst that may be true there is less evidence there are actual cognitive difference variables between them: that is weak relationships between IQ and cognitive/thinking style.

6.1.3   Different Tests

Just as with personality tests there are many tests available. Unlike personality tests, however, scores on nearly all of these tests tend to correlate with each other positively.

6.1.3.1 Test Batteries

There are various well-known IQ test batteries. Most of these were developed in educational settings to get a comprehensive idea of an individual's all-round intelligence and capacity to learn. Thus, each battery may have been 10 and 20 tests. Perhaps the three most famous intelligence tests in the world are Raven's Progress Matrices (1965), which is a nonverbal test of fluid ability; the Wechsler Adult Intelligence Scale–Revised (WAIS-R; Wechsler, 1958); and the Stanford-Binet test (Terman & Merrill, 1960), which has been updated. Kline (1996) has argued that these two tests 'stand out as benchmarks in the measurement of intelligence' (p. 49). Both tests have multiple scales.

The WAIS-R has 11 tests that are divided into verbal and performance measures (see Table 6.2); the Stanford Binet is divided into 12 subscales, many of which are very similar to those of the WAIS-R. Recent studies have shown that various population groups react favourably to the WAIS-R, believing that most of the subscales are fair tests of intelligence (Beglinger et al., 2000).

The latest WAIS has 10 tests measuring four scores.

> *Verbal comprehension*: the ability to listen to a question, draw upon learned information from both formal and informal education, reason through an answer and express thoughts aloud.
> *Perceptual reasoning*: the ability to examine a problem, use visual-motor and visual-spatial skills, organise thoughts, create solutions and then test them.
> *Working memory*: the ability to memorise new information in short-term memory, concentrate and manipulate information which is important in higher-order thinking, learning and achievement.
> *Processing speed index*: the ability to focus attention and scan, discriminate between and sequentially order visual information.

Thus, one can derive subscale or total scale scores. The test has usually to be administered individually and takes over an hour. It has been subject to some of the most consistent and rigorous of validations of tests in psychology.

Table 6.2 *Wechsler Adult Intelligence Scale (WAIS)*

Test	Description
Verbal scale	
Information	Taps general range of information
Comprehension	Tests understanding of social conventions and ability to evaluate past experience
Arithmetic	Tests arithmetic reasoning through verbal problems
Similarities	Asks in what way certain objects or concepts are similar; measures abstract thinking
Digit span	Tests attention and rote memory by orally presenting series of digits to be repeated forward or backward
Vocabulary	Tests ability to define increasingly difficult words
Performance scale	
Digit symbol	Tests speed of learning through timed coding tasks in which numbers must be associated with marks of various shapes
Picture completion	Tests visual alertness and visual memory through presentation of an incompletely drawn picture; the missing part must be discovered and named
Block design	Tests ability to perceive and analyse patterns by presenting designs that must be copied with blocks
Picture arrangement	Tests understanding of social situations through a series of comic-strip-type pictures that must be arranged in the right sequence to tell a story
Object assembly	Tests ability to deal with part/whole relationships by presenting puzzle pieces that must be assembled to form a complete object

There are other tests which attempt to measure general intelligence in less time. One of the best known is *The Wonderlic Personnel Test* (Wonderlic, 1992). This 50-item test can be administered in 12 minutes and measures general intelligence. Scores can range from 0 to 50. Items include word and number comparisons, disarranged sentences, serial analysis of geometric figures and story problems that require mathematical and logical solutions. The test has impressive norms and correlates very highly ($r = .92$) with the WAIS-R.

The test has questions about geometry and maths as well as language. The types of questions that have appeared in the oldest versions of the Wonderlic test include: analogies, analysis of geometric figures, arithmetic, direction following, disarranged sentences, judgement, logic, proverb matching, similarities and word definitions. Practice questions example: 'If a piece of rope cost 20 cents per 2 feet, how many feet can you buy for 30 dollars?' 'Which of the numbers in this group represents the smallest amount? (a) 0.3 (b) 0.08 (c) 1 (d) 0.33'. 'A clock lost 2 minutes and 36 seconds in 78 days. How many seconds did it lose per day?'

For the researcher the Wonderlic gives a good indication of the IQ of anyone taking the test, it also has two versions so that it is possible to measure how IQ changes over time.

6.1.3.2   Self-Estimates/Assessments of Intelligence

6.1.3.2.1   Do people know how bright they are? Will they give fair assessment? Could these be used instead of giving them tests? Research in this area has shown that the correlation between actual test and self-estimated scores is around $r = .30$, though this can get higher, but rarely above $r = .50$, which suggests they cannot be proxy for actual tests. Importantly, studies focusing on sex differences have shown systematic differences.

How Intelligent Are You? IQ tests measure a person's intelligence. The average or the mean score on these tests is 100. Most of the population (about two thirds of people) score between 85 and 115. Very bright people score around 130 and scores have been known to go over 145. You might score 118 or 97 or 123. We want you to estimate your overall IQ and your score on 10 basic types of intelligence (see Table 6.3).

Table 6.3 *Measuring self-estimated intelligence*

	Estimate
1. **Overall intelligence**	
2. **Crystallised intelligence** (depth and breadth of acquired knowledge, ability to communicate this knowledge and ability to reason using previously learned knowledge and experience)	
3. **Fluid intelligence** (the broad ability to reason, form concepts and solve problems)	
4. **Quantitative reasoning** (the ability to comprehend quantitative concepts and relationships)	
5. **Reading and writing ability** (basic reading and writing skills)	
6. **Short-term memory** (ability to apprehend and hold information in immediate awareness and then use it quickly)	
7. **Long-term storage and retrieval** (the ability to store information and easily retrieve it later)	
8. **Visual processing** (the ability to think with visual patterns, including the ability to store and recall visual representations)	
9. **Auditory processing** (the ability to analyse auditory stimuli)	
10. **Processing speed** (the ability to perform automatic cognitive tasks, particularly when measured under pressure)	
11. **Decision/reaction time/speed** (reflects the immediacy with which an individual can react to stimuli or a task)	

Furnham (2017) summarised the research in the area thus:

First, males of all ages and backgrounds tend to estimate their (overall) general intelligence about 5–15 IQ points higher than do females. Always those estimates are above average and usually around one standard deviation above the norm.

Second, when judging 'multiple intelligences', males estimate their spatial and mathematical (numerical) intelligence higher but emotional intelligence lower than do females. On some multiple intelligences (verbal, musical, body-kinaesthetic), there is little or no sex difference.

Third, people believe these sex differences occur across generations: people believe their grandfather was/is more intelligent than their grandmother;

their father more than their mother; their brothers more than their sisters; and their sons more than their daughters. That is, throughout the generations in one's family, males are judged more intelligent than females. Fourth, sex differences are cross-culturally consistent. While Africans tend to give higher estimates, and Asians lower estimates, there remains a sex difference across all cultures. Differences seem to lie in cultural definitions of intelligence as well as norms associated with humility and hubris.

Fifth, the correlation between self-estimated and test-generated IQ is positive and low in the range of $r = .2$ to $r = .5$, suggesting that you cannot use estimated scores as proxy for actually scores.

Sixth, with regard to outliers, those who score high on IQ but give low self-estimates tend nearly always to be female, while those with the opposite pattern (high estimates, low scores) tend to be male.

6.1.3.3 *Crystallised Intelligence*

6.1.3.3.1 General Knowledge The measurement of crystalised Intelligence (Gc) usually includes tests of vocabulary and general knowledge (GK). The domain of GK as a central component of intelligence, and a reliable metric of it, however, remains controversial in the literature (Chamorro-Premuzic et al., 2006a,b). The major controversy concerns what might be considered as *general* knowledge for different groups of participants. Other issues concern how 'g-loaded' GK tests are.

Not all of the major IQ tests have a GK subscale. Thus, while the WAIS (Wechsler, 1981) has an *Information* subscale, which is similar to a GK test, the Stanford-Binet (Terman & Merrill, 1960) does not. However, the relationship between GK and intelligence has been reasonably well documented, as early as Vernon's (1969) work on scholastic and educational ability.

One test of GK that is increasing in usage is the 216-item (and the shorter 72-item) test developed by Irwing et al. (2001). It has a total score and six subscale scores assessing knowledge in specific areas. The GK test possesses good psychometric qualities and is reasonably up to date. The shortened 72-item GK test with comparable qualities has been used by Furnham and Chamorro-Premuzic (2006).

The GK test (Irwing et al., 2001) is a 72 open-answer item questionnaire (Batey et al., 2009). It consists of 6 different topic areas assessed by 12 questions each: including literature, general science, medicine, games, fashion and finance. Most studies gave people 20 minutes to complete the task. Scores are either correct (1) or incorrect (0) and are aggregated. Some examples of these items are:

---

1. Who wrote *1984*?
2. Who wrote *The Shining*?
3. What character appears in 'Homer and James Joyce?'
4. Who wrote *The Catcher in the Rye*?
5. Which is the lightest of all the gases?
6. How many chromosomes are there in normal human cells?
7. What law states that the volume and pressure of a gas are inversely proportional?
8. What are the chemical constituents of water?
9. What disease stops blood clotting?
10. What insect spreads malaria?
11. What disease is caused by insufficient production of insulin?
12. What organ is impaired by glaucoma?
13. In what game can a pawn become a queen?
14. In what game can a piece be crowned?
15. In what game can you bid a grand slam?
16. What is the name of the poker hand where all the cards are of the same suit?
17. Which Italian designer was shot in Miami in 1997?
18. Which is the leading American maker of trainers?
19. In which London street are the leading men's tailors?
20. In which decade were flared trousers fashionable?
21. What is the currency of Japan?
22. What is the index of the value of shares in the USA?
23. Which is the second largest world economy?
24. Where is the largest financial centre in Europe?

Many studies have shown that general knowledge or crystallised intelligence is correlated with many other intelligence tests.

Another relatively simple way of measuring intelligence is the depth of an individual's vocabulary. Here is an example:

VOCABULARY In each of the following groups all the words except one have approximately the same meaning (are synonymous).

Which is the odd one out in each group? Circle the one (of the four) words which has a different meaning.

1. Languor, quiescence, lassitude, lethargy
2. Phlegmatic, stolid, stupid, sluggish
3. Dolorous, dismal, mournful, unmusical
4. Obstinate, assiduous, diligent, persevering
5. Astringent, ruthless, severe, austere
6. Incongruous, inconvenient, incompatible, discrepant
7. Punctilious, scrupulous, consistent, conscientious
8. Protuberant, distended, tumid, demented
9. Virulent, malignant, jejune, toxic
10. Oppressive, ravenous, rapacious, voracious
11. Debonair, modish, urbane, suave
12. Mendacious, fickle, untruthful, fictitious
13. Germane, apposite, pertinent, conducive
14. Mephitic, noxious, salacious, insalubrious
15. Precocious, naughty, premature, advanced
16. Perspicuous, discriminating, lucid, explicit
17. Desultory, refractory, contumacious, recalcitrant
18. Cacophonous, discordant, indecorous, dissonant
19. Specious, convincing, plausible, ostensible
20. Insouciant, egregious, prodigious, monstrous
21. Imply, insinuate, correspond, hint
22. Incipient, inchoate, incoherent, rudimentary
23. Concurrent, co-existent, concomitant, contingent
24. Exculpate, sequestrate, exonerate, acquit

The major issue with measures of crystallised intelligence is that they are highly culture and language specific, and in that sense not culture fair. They are also to a large degree related to a person's education, rather than their information processing (as opposed to storage) capacity.

6.1.3.4 Fluid Intelligence
Fluid intelligence is about the efficiency (speed and accuracy) of information processing. Again, there are many tests in this area. Consider two:

1. *Baddeley's reasoning test (BRT)* (Baddeley, 1968)(see Table 6.4): This 64-item test can be administered in 3 minutes and measures GK through logical reasoning. Numerous studies over the years have provided evidence of the test's predictive and concurrent validity (Chamorro-Premuzic et al., 2004). Thus, for instance, Batey et al. (2009) found the BRT was positively correlated with General Knowledge ($r = .40$, $N = 72$), while Furnham et al. (2006) found it correlated significantly with the Wonderlic measure ($r = .56$, $N = 70$). Earlier, Furnham and Chamorro-Premuzic (2006) found that BRT correlated with the Wonderlic ($r = .40$, $N = 112$) and General Knowledge ($r = .29$, $N = 110$).

2. *Mental arithmetic* (Lock, 2008)(see Table 6.5): This is a 30-item test requiring a person to make 10 arithmetic calculations (multiply, divide, add, subtract) per item. It is meant to be a mental test, though some people do attempt written calculations. Ten minutes are allowed for the administration for the full test of 20 items.

6.1.4 Intelligence Research and Testing at Work

Do tests predict behaviour at work? If they do, how do we explain this? And what else predicts work-related behaviour and success? There is a very long and important literature on IQ and education which of course informs the concept of training at work. The efficiency, speed and generalisability of learning via training is indeed related to intelligence. Estimates differ between about $r = .30$ to $r = .60$ (Ree & Carretta, 1998).

Studies on the predictive validity of intelligence tests go back a long way. Harrell and Harrell (1945) showed that individuals with low IQs were unlikely to be found in higher status, 'white collar', jobs that appeared to require high levels of education as a condition of entry. They found more variability at the bottom than the top: that is, there is a greater range in the IQs of people in less prestigious, skilled and unskilled professions than those in higher professions. However, studies and reviews by Ghiselli (1966) suggested that IQ scores were modest (even mediocre) predictors of job performance over time in a particular occupation.

The armed services have always been a good source of data on intelligence and job performance. Indeed, many have developed

Table 6.4 *Baddeley's reasoning test*

Instructions

In the following test there are a number of short sentences each followed by a pair of letters (AB or BA). The sentences claim to describe the order of the two letters, i.e. to say which comes first.

They can do this in several different ways. Thus, the order AB can be correctly described by saying either (1) A precedes B, or (2) B follows A, or (3) B does not precede A or (4) A does not follow B. All these are correct descriptions of the pair AB but are incorrect when applied to the other pair, BA.

Your job is to read each sentence and to decide whether it is a true or false description of the letter pair which follows it. If you think that the sentence describes the letter pair correctly put a tick in the first column (labelled **Tr** for True). If you think the sentence does not give a true description of the letter order, put a tick in the second (labelled **Fa** for False) column.

When you start the main test, work as quickly as you can without making mistakes. Start with sentence 1 and work systematically through the test leaving no blank spaces. Do not begin the test until you are given the start signal. You have 3 minutes to complete as many as you can; BUT DO NOT miss any out.

	Tr	Fa			Tr	Fa
1. A is preceded by B – BA			13. B is not followed by			
2. B does not precede			A – BA			
A – AB			14. B is preceded by A – AB			
3. A is not followed by			15. B is followed by A – BA			
B – BA			16. B precedes A – BA			
4. B is preceded by A – BA			17. A is not followed by			
5. A is followed by B – AB			B – AB			
6. A does not follow B – AB			18. A is followed by B – BA			
7. B is not preceded by			19. B is not preceded by			
A – AB			A – BA			
8. B follows A – AB			20. B is followed by A – AB			
9. A precedes B – BA			21. A is not followed by			
10. B does not follow			B – BA			
A – BA			22. A is preceded by			
11. B precedes A – AB			B – AB			
12. B is followed by A – AB			23. B does not follow A – AB			

Table 6.4 (*cont.*)

Tr	Fa	Tr	Fa
24. A is not preceded by B – BA		29. A precedes B – AB	
25. A follows B – BA		30. B follows A – BA	
26. A is not preceded by B – AB		31. B does not precede A – BA	
27. A follows B – AB		32. A does not precede B – BA	
28. A does not precede B – AB			

their own intelligence tests like the American Armed Services Vocational Aptitude Battery (ASVAB). Because of the number of recruits into the army and because of the necessity of technical training it has been relatively easy for psychologists to relate test to job performance on large numbers of recruits (Campbell et al., 1990).

Thus Jones (1988) looked at an overall g score and training outcomes for various courses (mechanical, administrative, technical and electronics) for nearly 25,000 soldiers. The correlation was $r = .75$. Ree and Earles (1992) did a similar analysis across 89 military jobs with big samples (between 274 and 3,939) and found a correlation of $r = .76$. McHenry et al. (1990) looked at nine army jobs and found correlations of around $r = .64$ between IQ test scores and 'core technical proficiency' and 'general soldiering proficiency'.

Ree and Earles (1992) looked at seven army jobs: air traffic controller, laboratory scientist, armories communication specialist, ground equipment mechanic, jet engine mechanic, radio operator and personnel specialist. In each case they were given the IQ subtest ASVAB. When the overall g score was correlated with good criteria measure, the r varied between .21 (air traffic) and .72 with an average of .44. In accordance with previous research, the study showed quite

Table 6.5 A mental arithmetic test

Mental   Arithmetic   1 NAME

This test has 30 simple arithmetic questions. Each has the same format. You are asked to make 10 simple calculations per question to get a correct answer. *You have only 10 minutes, so work as quickly and accurately as possible.*

1	24	½ of it	×3	÷4	Times by itself	+3	½ of it	÷6	×4	−9	=
2	8	×4	Double it	−1	÷7	×3	+3	Half of it	÷3	Times by itself	=
3	Ten	Times by itself	−1	÷3	Minus 1	Half of it	÷4	×9	+4	÷8	=
4	7	Times by itself	+5	÷6	×5	+3	÷4	+1	×3	+9	=
5	70	Half of it	+1	÷4	Times by itself	−9	Half of it	−9	Double it	÷9	=
6	28	¼ of it	×8	−2	÷6	×11	−4	÷5	+2	÷3	=
7	29	+7	½ of it	÷3	×9	+2	÷7	Double it	Double it	×4	=
8	8	×6	+1	÷7	×5	Double it	+2	÷9	Times by itself	−9	=
9	34	Half of it	+8	÷5	×11	Plus 1	÷8	Times by itself	−1	÷6	=
10	77	+4	÷9	×7	+1	÷8	×9	Double it	÷12	+9	=

simply that general (rather than specific) intelligence was the best predictor of all the work outcomes.

Reviewers have pointed out there are many correlates of IQ scores. Ree and Earles (1992) listed 10 categories of psychological outcomes:

- Abilities (reaction time, analytic style, eminence)
- Creativity/artistic (craftwork, musical ability)
- Health and fitness (infant mortality, dietary preference, longevity)
- Interests/choice (marital partner, sports participation, breadth and depth of interest)
- Moral (delinquency (−), racial prejudice (−) values)
- Occupational (SES, occupational status, income)
- Perceptual (myopia, field-independence, ability to perceive brief stimuli)
- Personality (achievement motivation, altruism, dogmatism) (−)
- Practical (social skills, practical knowledge) and other (motor skills)
- Talking speed, accident proneness (−)

Various reviews published in the 1960s and 1970s suggested that intelligence (and personality) tests did not predict organisational outcomes very well. Furthermore, the socio-political zeitgeist of these times discouraged many businesspeople from trying to measure intelligence. Major controversies about intelligence and race suggested that tests were significantly biased as well as lacking in predictive validity.

However, things were to change dramatically with the paper by Hunter and Hunter (1984), who presented a re-analysis of earlier plus other databases. In their analysis they took into account various statistical factors that impact on the size of correlations: size of sample, restriction of range and reliability of data. Based on data from 30,000 people and 425 correlations, their 'bottom-line' figure for the correlation between supervisor-rated job performance and IQ was $r = .53$. They broke this down for various job families. The highest correlation was for salespeople ($r = .62$) and nearly all were over $r = .40$; for service workers it was $r = .49$, trades and crafts workers $r = .50$ and vehicle operators $r = .46$.

As Brody (1992) noted, despite some criticisms of their methods, Hunter and Hunter (1984) demonstrated quite clearly that IQ scores related logically and consistently with many kinds of job perform-ances. By the end of the century, reviewers like Ree and Carretta (1998) felt able to conclude: 'Occupational performance begins with learning the knowledge and skills required for the job and continues into on-the-job performance and beyond. We and other investigators have demonstrated that g predicts training performance, job perform-ance, lifetime productivity, and finally, early mortality' (p. 179). More recent reviews (see point 6.5) are even more positive about the role of intelligence in all aspects of life.

A central, often unanswered question is *how* intelligence pre-dicts overall or specific job performance. This, in the first instance, can best be done via path analysis. Hunter (1986) showed that intelli-gence strongly predicted job knowledge, which predicted both 'object-ive' job performance and supervisors' ratings. Borman et al. (1993) tested a model which went thus: IQ (ability) results in a person having an opportunity to acquire job experience as a supervisor. It also pre-dicts an increase in job knowledge. Experience in turn leads to a further increase in job knowledge. Experience, ability and knowledge predict proficiency. Thus, intelligence predicts job performance.

Thus, it seems that intelligence predicts learning, knowledge and proficiency, which in turn usually predict learning from experience. That is, bright people learn faster, demonstrate salient skills and get promoted. This adds to their knowledge and experience, all of which influence supervisor ratings or any other measure of job performance.

Whilst these analyses used different tests, they were all reliable and highly inter-correlated (Hulsheger et al., 2007). However, it is possible to divide the tests essentially into those that measure general mental ability rather than specific cognitive abilities.

The best known meta analyses from the 1980s were those by Hunter and Hunter (1984) and Hunter (1986), though there were others before. Although there were some trends, what was noticeable was the variability in the correlations between IQ test scores and job performance: some very high, others very low. This led to the 'doc-trine of situational specificity' which argued that the relationship was dependent on the particular job, job performance criteria and IQ test itself. However this, in turn, led to the development of meta-analysis which through various statistical and 'corrective' techniques aims to show the true operational validity between GMA and work outcomes (Hunter, 1986; Hunter & Hunter 1984; Hunter & Schmidt, 1990; Schmidt & Hunter, 1998).

Ones, Viswesvaran and Dilchert (2006) provided an excellent comprehensive and up-to-date review of meta-analyses that were concerned with cognitive ability, selection decisions and success at work. In doing so they examined many different areas and came to clear conclusions:

- Based on data of well over a million students, they note GMA is a strong, valid predictor of exam success, learning and outcome at school and university, regardless of the speciality or subject considered.
- Training success at work, as measured by such things as supervisor ratings or job knowledge acquired, is predicted by GMA and the more complex the job, the more powerfully it predicts.
- Regarding job performance, cognitive ability tests predict outcomes across jobs, situations and outcomes – i.e. validity is transportable across occupational group and is cross-culturally generalisable.
- Tests of specific ability do *not* have incremental validity over general measures and although they may be more acceptable to job applicants, the relative importance of these abilities alters over time.
- Intelligence predicts job performance well because it is linked to the speed and quality of learning, adaptability and problem-solving ability.
- Cognitive ability tests are predictively fair to minority groups but can have an adverse impact, which is a sensitive political issue.
- In short, GMA is one of the best, if not *the* best predictor of success in applied settings.

Various meta analyses have been done over the last five years that have attempted a critical, comprehensive overview of the role of intelligence (often called general mental ability or cognitive ability test results) in predicting work-related outcomes (see Table 6.6)

Some reviewers have tended to concentrate on data from one country, like America (Schmidt & Hunter, 2004), Britain (Bertua et al., 2005), Germany (Hulsheger et al., 2007) or from wider areas like the European Community (Salgado et al., 2003). Despite these differences the results were essentially the same, and all reviewers argued for the practical use of cognitive ability tests, which are quite clearly good predictors of both overall job performance as well as training success.

Salgado et al. (2003) looked at the predictive validity of GMA as well as specific cognitive abilities like verbal, numerical, spatial-mechanical, perceptual and memory to predict measurable job performance and training success. Different selection and personnel practices could, they argue, lead to difference when comparing American and European data. Following the rigorous demands of meta-analysis found more than 250 studies that tested more than 25,000 Europeans. They found an operational validity of .62, which they note 'means GMA is an excellent predictor of job performance' (p. 585) and that 'GMA is the best predictor of job performance' (p. 585). The validity of the five specific measures varied from .35 for verbal to .56 for memory. The data on training ratings was broadly similar if slightly lower (.54 for GMA; .44 for verbal and .34 for memory).

Their conclusion is that, internationally, GMA measures are the *best predictors* of work performance. That is, despite differences in tests used, measures/conceptualisations of job performance and training, differences in unemployment rates, cultural values, demographics, GMA still wins out as the best individual difference psychometric measure. Indeed, the results are strikingly similar to earlier data coming out of America. They conclude that because of the predictive validity of GMA at work across cultures, one can easily conceive of a scientifically feasible general theory of personnel selection. They also point out: '... tests of specific abilities such as verbal, numerical, spatial-mechanical, perceptual and memory failed to demonstrate higher validity than GMA measures. It is thus prudent to reiterate the main practical implications of this finding that GMA tests predicted these two criteria most successfully' (p. 594).

Table 6.6 *The meta-analytic results of operational validity of overall and specific measures*

	Performance	Training
GMA	.62	.54
Verbal	.35	.44
Numerical	.52	.48
Spatial-mechanical	.51	.40
Perceptual	.52	.25
Memory	.56	.43

Table 6.7 *Correlations between overall and specific IQ measures and job performance and training*

	Performance	Training
GMA	.48	.50
Verbal	.39	.49
Numerical	.42	.54
Perceptual	.50	.50
Spatial	.35	.42
Average	.42	.49

Another meta-analysis focused exclusively on British data. This had 283 samples in total over 13,000 people (Bertua et al., 2005) (see Tables 6.7 and 6.8). This analysis looked at the predictive validity of specific abilities (i.e. verbal, numerical, etc.) as well as GMA over seven main groups (clerical, engineer, professional, driver, operator, manager, sales) (see Table 6.7). As in all meta-analyses, they found GMA and abilities to be valid predictors of job performance and training success (performance rho = .48; training rho = .50). They also found, as one may predict, the greater the job complexity, the higher the operational validities between the different cognitive tests and job performance and training success.

Thus, these results were broadly in line with those from both Europe and America. Once again, the conclusion is that GMA

Table 6.8 *The meta-analytic results for GMA over the eight occupational groups*

	Performance	Training
Clerical	.32	.55
Engineer	.70	.64
Professional	.74	.59
Driver	.37	.47
Operator	.53	.34
Manager	.69	.41
Sales	.55	.49
Miscellaneous	.40	.55

measures may be the best single predictor for personnel selection for all occupations. They recommended the use of psychometrically proven measures of GMA in selection 'regardless of job type, hierarchical seniority, potential future changes in job role composition or whether the tests are principally for general or specific cognitive ability' (p. 403).

In their meta-analysis of German data examining both training success (of 11,969 people) and job performance (746 people), Hulgsheger et al. (2007) found validities of .47 for training success and .53 for job performance. They found also, as they suspected, that job complexity did moderate that relationship. Their results were therefore strikingly similar to that shown in other countries.

The following table was reported by Ones et al. (2017) (see Table 6.9).What is striking about this data is, perhaps with the exception of France, the close similarity between the results from studies in the different countries.

Thus, over the past quarter century there is a 'large and compelling literature' showing that intelligence is a good predictor of both job performance and training proficiency at work (Dragow, 2002). Extensive meta-analytic reviews have shown that intelligence was a good predictor of job performance but particularly in complex jobs. Although debated, researchers suggest the correlation between

Table 6.9 *Validity of cognitive ability tests for predicting job performance in international contexts*

Across European countries	k	N	r	p
High-complexity jobs	14	1,604	.23	.64
Medium-complexity jobs	43	4,744	.27	.53
Low-complexity jobs	12	864	.25	.51
Analyses by country				
Belgium and the Netherlands	15	1,075	.24	.63
France	26	1,445	.48	.64
Germany	8	746	.33	.53
Japan	126	26,095		.20
South Korea	8	1,098		.57
Spain	11	1,182	.35	.64
UK	68	7,725	.26	.56

intelligence and job performance is around $r = .50$ (Schmidt & Hunter, 1998). The central question is what other factors like personality or social/emotional intelligence (sometimes called 'social skills') accounts for the rest of the variance. But referring to g or general intelligence, Dragow (2002) is forced to conclude 'for understanding performance in the workplace, and especially task performance and training performance, g is the key ... g accounts for an overwhelming proportion of the explained variance when predicting training and job performance' (p. 126).

Leading researchers in the area, Schmidt and Hunter (2004), also came to a clear conclusion based on 100 years of work. It is

The research evidence that GMA predicts both occupational level attained and performance within one's chosen occupation and does so better than any other ability, trait, or disposition and better than job experience. The sizes of these relationships with GMA are also larger than most found in psychological research. Evidence is presented that weighted combination of specific aptitudes tailored to individual jobs do not predict job performance

> better than GMA alone, disconfirming specific aptitude theory. A theory of
> job performance is described that explicates the central role of GMA in the
> world of work. These findings support Spearman's proposition that GMA is
> of critical importance in human affairs.
>
> *(p. 162)*

Thus, for complex, senior jobs the correlation between GMA and job performance is around .50. Furthermore, intelligence is a more powerful predictor than personality. It is because people with a higher GMA acquire job knowledge more efficiently that it is such a good marker of career success. Job experience does relate to job performance, but it declines over time, unlike the intelligence–performance relationship, which increases.

Since the turn of the millennium there have been some excellent reviews on the subject of intelligence at work. Here are some quotes from those reviews:

> There is abundant evidence that general cognitive ability is highly relevant
> in a wide range of jobs and settings that measures of general cognitive
> ability represent perhaps the best predictors of performance. Ability–
> performance relations are essentially linear and the correlation between
> general cognitive ability and performance appears similar across jobs that
> differ considerably in content. There is some evidence that ability–
> performance correlations tend to increase as jobs become more complex
> but a few other consistent moderators of the ability–performance
> correlation have been reported. Finally, the incremental contribution of
> specific abilities (defined as ability factors unrelated to the general factor) to
> the prediction of performance or training outcomes may very well be
> minimal. (Murphy, 2002, p. 175)
>
> Given the overwhelming research evidence showing the strong link
> between general cognitive ability (GCA) and job performance, it is not
> logically possible for industrial–organisational (I/O) psychologists to have a
> serious debate over whether GCA is important for job performance.
> However, even if none of this evidence existed in I/O psychology, research
> findings in differential psychology on the nature and correlates of GCA

> provide a sufficient basis for the conclusion that GCA is strongly related to job performance. From the viewpoint of the kind of world we would like to live in – and would like to believe we live in – the research findings on GCA are not what most people would hope for and are not welcome. However, if we want to remain a science-based field, we cannot reject what we know to be true in favour of what we would like to be true. (Schmidt, 2002, p. 187)
>
> ' ... the utility of g', is that g (i.e., possessing a higher level of g) has value across all kinds of work and levels of job-specific experience, but that its value rises with a) the complexity of work, b) the more 'core' the performance criterion being considered (good performance of technical duties rather than 'citizenship'), c) the more objectively performance is measured (e.g. job samples rather than supervisor ratings). Predictive validities, when corrected for various statistical artefacts, range from about .2 to .8 in civilian jobs, with an average near .5. In mid-level military jobs, uncorrected validities tend to range between .3 and .6. These are substantial. To illustrate, tests with these levels of predictive validity would provide 30% to 60% of the gain in aggregate levels of worker performance that would be realised from using tests with perfect validity (there is not rush thing) rather than hiring randomly.
>
> *(Gottfredson, 2003)*

6.1.5   Applications and Implications of Testing at Work

Is it advisable to use cognitive tests to make selection, training and promotion decisions? If so, what tests should be administered to whom for what purpose? Are the potential negative consequences greater than the benefits? Could one make a good economic, as opposed to legal, argument for testing in the workplace?

New intelligence tests are frequently invented, particularly those that can be administered electronically. Selectors are always calling for shorter, more accurate and less biased tests. Nearly always these tests are moderately positively correlated, suggesting they all tap into the same ability, namely the efficiency of information processing.

Nearly all agree that intelligence is necessary but not sufficient to ensure success at work. The bright but unmotivated worker may achieve far less than the highly motivated person of average intelligence.

For many the issue is the linear vs threshold hypothesis (Cook, 2016). The latter is the idea that you need to be 'bright enough' and that scores beyond a particular range (say 120 or 1.5 SD above the norm) is sufficient to ensure work performance in any job. The linear hypothesis suggests 'the more the better': any performance indicator increases as intelligence increases linearly, while the curvilinear hypothesis (inverted U) suggests that performance increases up to a point but drops thereafter suggesting that intelligence could be a handicap at high levels. The data support the threshold/bright-enough hypothesis but, as noted earlier, the cut-off or levelling score is dependent on the complexity of work performance it is related to.

6.1.6 Online Testing

Many forms of assessment are going online (interviewing, personality tests). The same is true of ability tests. The question is, are they equivalent to the usual pen-and-paper, proctored tests? There are differences and potential problems: there is a 'load time' on computers, which may take away some answering time; computer test takers do not read instructions as well; sometimes screens do not produce colours and graphs well; it is harder to 'go-back or make notes on computer versions; older people do not perform as well as younger people. There is also the worry of more cheating in unproctored tests as it is not always possible to know who is actually completing the test.

Over the past decade there has been a significant increase in the use of online assessments, particularly of attitudes and beliefs (Barak & English, 2002; Schroeders et al., 2010). There are a number of different platforms that can be used, each with different advantages and disadvantages. A central concern for those using data from online sources is accuracy as well as representativeness (Buhrmester et al., 2011). One central question is *who is taking the test, for what motive and under what conditions?* Another issue concerns the extent to which people are erratic, careless or simply responding randomly (Furnham et al., 2015).

The problems associated with all self-report data, namely dissimulation and self-awareness, in personality and attitudinal research also remains with this type of data (Arthur et al., 2009). Another major issue concerns cheating: being clear about who is actually taking the test and how they could possibly cheat in other ways (Arnold, 2016). There may be other issues that threaten test validity like familiarity with computers, language competence and general use of the internet.

Some factors can be measured online like item response latency and time taken for the test. Time taken in tests has itself proved an interesting indicator of respondent personality (Furnham et al., 1998, 2013). Nearly all intelligence tests are timed, but this issue is less important in assessing crystallised intelligence (Gc) as it may be argued that the respondent either does or does not know the correct answer. Essentially, there is no processing involved except accessing long and medium-term memory.

Whilst there remain many difficulties and issues in IQ testing online, is it now done and future developments will no doubt reduce the number of current problems (Furnham, 2020).

6.1.7   Conclusion

Few areas of psychology attract as much discussion and debate as the topic of intelligence. More academic researchers have been attacked (physically), hounded, sacked and vilified by what they have written about intelligence. The area that inevitably causes most passion is that of age, sex and race differences in intelligence. There is also still considerable debate about the role of intelligence testing in educational settings.

There are essentially two issues: empirical and social policy issues. Most of the debate is about the latter not the former, though there still remains considerable controversy about the predictive power of intelligence tests in all work settings.

The data on general intelligence as a predictor of work-related behaviours is, however, very clear. There are very few researchers who have inspected recent meta-analyses who could not be impressed by the fact that probably the best single predictor of success at work (particularly in senior, complex jobs) is intelligence. This is not to deny that there are no other important factors nor that it is patently obvious that not all intelligent people do particularly well in the workplace. In this sense intelligence is *necessary but not sufficient*. Intelligence is relatively easy to measure reliably and accurately. Intelligence test scores are influenced by other factors (like personality) but not to any great extent. Intelligence is essentially about cognitive capacity and refers to both efficient problem solving, but also accumulated knowledge.

However, the science and the practice of intelligence testing remain far apart because of the history of misunderstanding, misapplications and political differences. The signs are hopeful for the future where differential psychologists and people at work could benefit from some of the most valid and predictive of all measures in the workplace.

To conclude with Dilchert (2018)

One lesson our field has learned is that organizations and practitioners are not persuaded by criterion-related validity evidence alone. If that were the case, every organization would use a standardized cognitive ability assessment in their admissions or hiring process – for all opportunities, for all jobs. Ultimately, decisions of predictor constructs and assessment methods must consider scientific evidence, organizational values, as well as economic and societal contexts.

It is the responsibility of IWO psychologists to make such evidence available and help organizations make the most responsible decision in a given context. Cognitive ability tests are among the most powerful weapons in the IWO psychology arsenal. The analogy might be crude, but it is apt. We must weigh a variety of factors regarding their deployment: effectiveness, efficiency, and consequences (including applicant reactions and workforce diversity). However, we must also consider the consequences of not deploying a reliable and valid predictor tool at our disposal – including reduced objectivity, lowered productivity, and insufficient societal benefit – especially when resources to be distributed (educational opportunities, jobs) are scarce.

(p. 268)

REFERENCES

Arnold, I. (2016). Cheating at online formative tests. *Internet and Higher Education, 29*, 98–106.

Arthur, W., Glaze, R., Villado, A., & Taylor, J. (2009). Unprotected internet-based tests of cognitive ability and personality. *Industrial and Organizational Psychology, 2*, 39–45.

Baddeley, A. D. (1968). A 3 minute reasoning test based on grammatical transformation. *Journal of Social and Clinical Psychology, 4*, 359–373.

Barak, A., & English, N. (2002). Prospects and limitations of psychological testing on the internet. *Journal of Technology in Human Services, 19*, 65–89.

Batey, M., Chamorro-Premuzic, T., & Furnham, A. (2009). Intelligence and personality as predictors of divergent thinking: the role of general, fluid and crystallised intelligence. *Thinking Skills and Creativity, 4*(1), 60–69.

Beglinger, L. J., Gaydos, B., Tangphao-Daniels, O., Duff, K., Kareken, D. A., Crawford, J. F., et al. (2005). Practice effects and the use of alternate forms in serial neuropsychological testing. *Archives of Clinical Neuropsychology, 20*, 517–529.

Bertua, C., Anderson, N., & Salgado, J. (2005). The predictive validity of cognitive ability tests. A UK meta-analysis. *Journal of Occupational and Organisational Psychology, 78*, 387.

Borman, W., Hanson, M., Oppler, S., Pulakis, E., & White, L. (1993). Role of early supervisory experience in supervisor performance. *Journal of Applied Psychology, 78*, 443–449.

Brody, N. (1992). *Intelligence*. London, UK: Academic Press.

Buhrmester, M., Kwang, T., & Gosling, S. D. (2011). Amazon's Mechanical Turk a new source of inexpensive, yet high-quality, data? *Perspectives on Psychological Science, 6*(1), 3–5.

Campbell, P., McHenry, J., & Wise, L. (1990). Modeling job performance in a population of jobs. *Personnel Psychology, 43,* 313–333.

Carroll, J. (1993). *Human cognitive abilities.* Cambridge, UK: Cambridge University Press.

Cattell, R. (1987). *Intelligence: Its structure, growth and action.* New York: North Holland.

Chamorro-Premuzic, T., Furnham, A., & Ackerman, P. (2006a). Incremental validity of typical intellectual engagement as predictor of different academic performance measures. *Journal of Personality Assessment, 87,* 261–268.

Chamorro-Premuzic, T., Furnham, A., & Ackerman, P. (2006b). Ability and personality correlates of general knowledge. *Personality and Individual Differences, 41,* 419–429.

Chamorro-Premuzic, T., Furnham, A., & Moutafi, J. (2004). The relationship between estimated and psychometric personality and intelligence scores *Journal of Research in Personality, 38,* 505–513.

Deary, I. (2000). *Looking down on human intelligence.* Oxford: Oxford University Press.

Deary, I. (2001). *Intelligence: A very short introduction.* Oxford: Oxford University Press.

Dilchert, S. (2018). Cognitive ability. In D. S. Ones, N. Anderson, C. Viswesvaran, & H. K. Sinangil (Eds.), *The SAGE handbook of industrial, work & organizational psychology: Personnel psychology and employee performance* (pp. 248–276). New York: Sage.

Dragow, F. (2002). Intelligence and the workplace. In W. Borman, D. Ilgen, & R. Klimozki (Eds.), *Handbook of psychology* (Vol. 12, pp. 107–130). New York: Wiley.

Furnham, A. (2008). *Personality and intelligence at work.* London, UK: Routledge.

Furnham, A. (2017). Whether you think you can, or you think you can't – you're right. Differences and consequences of beliefs about your ability. In Robert Sternberg, Susan Fiske, & Don Foss (Eds.), *Scientists making a difference: The greatest living behavioral and brain scientists talk about their most important contributions.* Cambridge, UK: Cambridge University Press.

Furnham, A. (2020). *The Assessment of General Knowledge Online: Two studies using two platforms examining demographic, self-assessment and internet usage correlates.* Paper under review.

Furnham, A., & Chamorro-Premuzic, T. (2006). Personality, intelligence and general knowledge. *Learning and Individual Differences, 16*, 9–90.

Furnham, A., Forde, L., & Cotter, T. (1998). Personality scores and test taking style. *Personality and Individual Differences, 24*(1), 19–23.

Furnham, A., Hyde, G., & Trickey, G. (2013). On-line questionnaire completion time and personality test scores. *Personality and Individual Differences, 54*(6), 716–720.

Furnham, A., Hyde, G., & Trickey, G. (2015). Personality and value correlates of careless and erratic questionnaire responses. *Personality and Individual Differences, 80*, 64–67.

Furnham, A., Rawles, R., & Iqbal, S. (2006). Personality, intelligence and proof-reading. *Personality and Individual Differences, 41*, 1457–1467.

Gardner, H. (1983). *Frames of mind: The theory of multiple intelligences.* New York: Basic Books.

Gardner, H. (1999). *Intelligence reframed.* New York: Basic Books.

Gatewood, R., Feild, H. S., & Barrick, M. (2016). *Human Resource Selection.* Scarborough, ON, Canada: Nelson Education.

Ghiselli, E. (1966). *The validity of occupational aptitude tests.* New York: Wiley.

Gottfredson, L. (2003). g jobs and kife. In J. Nyborg (Ed.), *The science of mental ability* (pp 293–342). Oxford, UK: Pergammon.

Harrell, T., & Harrell, M. (1945). Army general classification test scores for civilian occupations. *Educational and Psychological Measurement, 5*, 229–239.

Hough, L., Oswald, F., & Floghart, R. (2001). Determinants, detection and amelioration of adverse impact in personal selection procedures. *International Journal of Selection and Assessment, 9*, 152–194.

Hulsheger, U., Maier, G., & Stumpp, T. (2007). Validity of general mental ability for the prediction of job performance and training success in Germany. *International Journal of Selection and Assessment, 15*, 3–18.

Hunter, J. (1986). Cognitive ability, cognitive aptitudes, job knowledge and job performance. *Intelligence, 29*, 340–362.

Hunter, J., & Hunter, R. (1984). Validity and utility of alternative predictors of job performance. *Psychological Bulletin, 96*, 72–98.

Hunter, J. E., & Schmidt, F. L. (1990). *Methods of meta-analysis: Correcting for error and bias in research findings.* Newbury Park, CA: Sage.

Jones, G. (1988). Investigation of the efficacy of general ability versus specific abilities as predictors of occupational success. Unpublished thesis. St Mary's University of Texas.

Kaufman, S. (2019). There is no Nature-Nurture War. *Scientific American.*

Kline, P. (1996). *The new psychometrics.* London, UK: Routledge.

Irwing, R., Cammock, T., & Lynn, R. (2001). Some evidence for the existence of a general factor of semantic memory and its components. *Personality and Individual Differences, 30*, 857–871.

Mackintosh, N. (1998). *IQ and human intelligence.* Oxford: Oxford University Press.

Martinsen, Ø. L., & Furnham, A. (2016). The Assimilator–Explorer styles and creativity. *Personality and Individual Differences, 98*, 297–299.

Martinsen, Ø. L., & Kaufmann, G. (2000). The Assimilator–Explorer cognitive styles and their relationship to affective-motivational orientations and cognitive performances. In R. Riding & S. Raynor (Eds.), *International perspectives on individual differences: Vol. 1. New developments in learning/cognitive styles* (pp. 3–41). Stamford, CT: Ablex Publishing Corporation.

McHenry, J., Hough, L., Toquam, J., Hanson, M., & Ashworth, S. (1990). Project A validity results. *Personnel Psychology, 43*, 335–354.

Messick, S. (1984). The nature of cognitive styles: problems and promises in educational practice. *Educational Psychologist, 19*, 59–74.

Murphy, K. (2002). Can conflicting perspectives on the role of g in personnel selection be resolved? *Human Performance, 15*, 173–186.

Ones, D., Dilchert, S., Viswesvaran, C., & Salgado, J. (2017). Cognitive ability: masurement and validity for employee selection. In James Farr, & Nancy Tippins (Eds.), *Handbook of employee selection* (pp. 251–276). New York: Routledge.

Plomin, R. (2018). *Blueprint: How DNA makes us who we are.* London: Allen Lane.

Ree, M. J., & Earles, J. A. (1992). Intelligence is the best predictor of job performance. *Current Directions in Psychological Science, 1*, 86–89.

Ree, M., & Carretta, T. (1998). General cognitive ability and occupational performance. *International Review of Industrial and Organisational Psychology, 13*, 161–189.

Schmidt, F. (2002). The role of general cognitive ability and job performance. *Human Performance, 15*, 187–210.

Schmidt, F. L., & Hunter, J. E. (1998). The validity and utility of selection methods in personnel psychology: practical and theoretical implications of 85 years of research findings. *Psychological Bulletin, 124*, 262–274.

Schmidt, F., & Hunter, J. (2004). General mental ability in the world of work. *Journal of Personality and Social Psychology, 86*, 162–173.

Schroeders, U., Wilhelm, O. & Schipolowski, S. (2010). Internet-based ability testing. In S. D. Gosling, & J. A. Johnson (Eds.), *Advanced methods for behavioral research on the Internet* (pp. 131–148). Washington, DC: American Psychological Association.

Sternberg, R. (1997). *Successful intelligence*. New York: Plume.

Terman, L., & Merrill, M. (1960). *Stanford–Binet intelligence scale*. New York: Houghton Mufflin.

Thorndike, E. L., Henmon, V. A. C., & Buckingham, B. R. (eds.) (1921). *Intelligence and its measurement: A symposium*. Baltimore, MD.

Vernon, P. (1969). *Intelligence and cultural environment*. London, UK: Methuen.

Wechsler, D. (1958). *Measurement of adult intelligence* (4th ed.). Baltimore, MD: William & Wilkins.

Wechsler, D. (1981). *Manual for the adult intelligence scale* (revised). New York: Psychological Corporation.

Wonderlic Personnel Test, Inc. (1992). *Wonderlic Personnel Test and Scholastic Level Exam: User's manual*. Libertyville, IL: Author.

6.2   UNOBTRUSIVE MEASURES

What are they?

They are ways of investigating an individual's writings, behaviour or records that are non-reactive sources of information to infer their motivation, values and personality.

How do they work?

The idea is to find either a 'footprint' of a person's behaviour or set up conditions to experimentally obtain 'non-reactive' data about individuals which give an indication of their 'real' personality and motivation.

What of the evidence?

There is some evidence, depending on the technique and what it supposedly measures, that these methods can provide good data to test particular hypotheses.

Practical problems: cost, ethics, politics

There can be significant and serious ethical problems about the acquisition of data. Also, the cost-benefit analysis suggests it is perhaps wise only to use these techniques to measure very specific issues.

Recommendations for use

They may prove an excellent supplement to other data when trying to assess sensitive issues such as prejudice, altruism, addictions, etc.

6.2.1   Introduction

For many individuals an average day may include travelling to work on public transport which is electronically paid for. They make a number of purchases by credit/debit/store card which is recorded by the bank and the store. Furthermore, it is likely that they go online; especially while using social media more data is recorded; what you 'like', how often you like it and the comments you make show a lot about your own interests, as well as what you post can greatly reflect your own personality and self-image. Most people carry mobile phones, each containing a wealth of data, including photographs, regular contacts, even data on your health condition from fitness apps. Many of us are 'on camera' in the street and in shops. People deliver things to our house and take away rubbish/garbage. In short, there is an ever-increasing amount of data on an individual (see Chapter 9).

In some countries people are required to carry an identity card and or a passport which has in it a great deal of electronically recorded data. All this leaves an amazing data trail that can be analysed.

What if, at selection, you were asked to hand over your passport? Would you be happy if the organisation paid people to go through the web searching every reference to you? Maybe they are trying to establish your taste for risk or your levels of self-confidence or optimism, both highly relevant to certain jobs.

What do your 'store cards' or airline cards indicate about your lifestyle? At a job interview, what can or should people 'read into' the strength and style of a handshake, the fashionableness, or formality, of clothing?

In short, there is an ever-increasing databank, one's digital footprint, which is mostly electronically recorded and stored. Medical people, one's employer, the police and the automobile licencing authorities have a great deal of data on us. They can easily find out about our movements, friends and purchases. Have we ever been bankrupt? How many points do we have on our driver's licence? Which countries have we visited? How much do we spend on alcohol?

It is possible to get data on habits and beliefs. For instance, it should not be difficult to get a record of money spent on alcohol (shops, pubs) as well as to collect and sift through rubbish.

Despite the evidence that they are indeed so, almost nobody admits that they are selfish or racists or deceptively dishonest, either due to fear or self-deception. Furthermore, with a great emphasis on 'virtue signalling' everybody wants to believe that they are kind, considerate, empathic, etc. So how do you measure these things when people are so sensitive to how they 'come across' to an observer, particularly an assessor? It is noted in the bible that 'Ye shall know them by their fruits', but with so much information on an applicant, it may be hard to know what to gather and read into.

There is now a mass of data on most individuals, particularly younger, techno-savvy people; they send text messages, emails in the form of blogs and video blogs. This provides a wealth of data on a person's lifestyle and their language, both of which may be good indicators of their education and intelligence. Computers can accurately do content analysis of themes, vocabulary and personal networks.

It is also possible to examine particular documents by their layout, choice of typeface, use of official titles and use of photographs.

6.2.2 Non-reactivity

What benefit does unobtrusive 'Big Data' have over simply asking an individual or those who know him or her? The answer goes back over 50 years when Webb et al. (1966) wrote a book called *Unobtrusive Measures*, which has traces of behaviour not prone to reactivity. The book is a classic with interesting and unusual ideas.

People may be guilty, embarrassed, clumsy or simply nervous when being questioned or watched/observed in an assessment situation, hence the use of unobtrusive measures. The word unobtrusive means *inconspicuous* or *not attracting attention*. It means that people who are being assessed for some characteristic are unaware that they are being monitored.

When people know they are being observed and assessed it is quite likely that their behaviour changes: they 'put on a good front', monitor and change their behaviour to create a good impression. The potential problem with obtrusive assessment is that it is often react-ive, which refers to the *influence that the assessment procedure exerts on the person's performance.*

Hence unobtrusive measures are devised to get more accurate data. The method does not involve the obvious direct elicitation of data from an individual. It is not a substitute for, but rather a supplement to, traditional assessment methods like interviews and questionnaires. The whole idea is that they reduce biases of many types like those noted in interviews. The idea is that people leave a 'footprint' in what they have written or said or done. The digital world and social media have opened up many new opportun-ities for unobtrusive measures, many of which are considered under Big Data (see Chapter 9).

There have been thoughtful and careful reviews of the use of unobtrusive measures in organisational research, which generally conclude that when used carefully and in conjunction with other methods, unobtrusive measures can yield important and hard-to-get information (Hill et al., 2014).

6.2.3 Early Studies

One of the most famous is the 'lost letter' technique where psycholo-gists 'lose' a letter, perhaps addressed to a local or a foreign person, and count whether prejudice is manifest by the finders 'helpfully' posting it, discarding it or ripping it up. The same is true of any 'lost object', like an identity card: will people hand in or post someone's lost item more when they are of the same racial group? What do people do when they find a lost wallet/purse on the street which has been put there by an observer who watches what they do?

Some psychologists have even advocated 'garbology' – going through people's rubbish to find out what they have thrown away. This can be done at the home as well as in the office to see what food they consume or reading matter they throw away. It gives a great insight into their diet and perhaps their socio-political beliefs around ecology and environmentalism. Journalists have done this with politicians to examine their drinking habits.

Responses to advertisements of different kinds have also been examined. The whole world of computing (see Chapter 9) offers amazing opportunities in this regard.

Studies in this field are inevitably fascinating. In one, a social psychologist tried to measure national prejudice by measuring how quickly people hooted when a car from a foreign country did not drive off when a traffic light changed from red to green (Forgas, 2003). Others have looked at preferences for personal space (Reid & Novak, 1975). Early studies looked at 'wear and tear' as a sign of usage: why some students textbooks seem more battered than others; why the carpets around some desks in the office are more worn than others.

Some have suggested analysis of sewerage/toilet water from male/female, worker/executive toilets for incidence of illegal drugs.

Critics point out that these measures are rarely very reliable. They also note some of the ethical problems in fooling people. There are also no control factors so one cannot be certain what chance events are affecting the behaviour examined. Moreover, they are usually much more about group behaviour than individuals. Thus, in using garbology as a measure, it is not clear, even if a person lived alone, that all discarded objects had been used by him or her.

The major *advantage* of using unobtrusive measures is that they are usually free of the self-conscious manipulation of obtrusive measures. Take the drinking of alcohol: most people underestimate how much they drink, and very heavy drinkers may strenuously deny the extent of their drinking. But actually counting their discarded bottles gives one a very real indication of the extent of their habit.

Some organisations in the liquor business require staff to have an annual liver test which they have to agree to when joining. But does an organisation get data about individuals who are of concern with their alcohol abuse?

The primary *disadvantage* of the use of unobtrusive measures such as measuring the wear on the tyres of a disabled person's wheelchair to measure their mobility is that one cannot be absolutely sure what caused the behaviour to occur. In other words, all sorts of other factors that you may not know about may have affected the thing that you are measuring. Can you rule out alternative explanations for the behaviour?

Also, it is not always clear how reactive some behaviours are. For instance, you notice that a person seems to wear a very limited range of coloured outfits, while another has a wide variety of vivid colours. What is this measuring? Creativity? Narcissism? Colour-blindness? It is impossible to tell reliably without other information on the individual.

6.2.4   Different Techniques

There are essentially three different techniques in this area:

Direct Observation

This involves monitoring and observing the behaviour of an individual in two ways:

> Naturalistic observation: This involves recording people in their homes, institutions, classrooms, etc. This is a bit like being an anthropologist. Observers are often interested in the patterns of social interactions: who talks to who, how often? Does carpet wear in the office indicate which desks are walked about most frequently?
>
> Contrived Situations: This involves setting up a 'contrived' situation to determine how an individual responds to particular stimuli. This is a more traditional 'fun-and-games' social psychology but could be done in assessment situations. Thus a 'stooge' could wait with candidates waiting for an interview and see how they behave: which newspapers they choose to read, signs of anxiety, how they respond to another candidate dropping their wallet/purse.

Content Analysis

This is a content analysis of artefacts, documents and data sets. This essentially means looking for themes in the data which are relevant to what one is measuring. The analysis can be quantitative, qualitative or both. The aim is to identify patterns in text.

It may include:

1. Thematic analysis of text. This is to search for thematic categories.
2. Indexing. This could include a computerised scanning of the text and indexes for specific keywords. It would be possible to search for any word like 'boss', 'friend' 'money'.
3. Quantitative descriptive analysis. This may involve counting words or phrases used most frequently in the text. Again, this type of analysis is most often done directly with computer programs.

This method is limited to the types of information available in text form. Also, document-sampling problems could easily lead to various biases. It is also prone to misinterpreting results of automated content analyses. However, content analysis can be a relatively rapid method for analysing large amounts of text.

Behavioural Data

In many societies it is relatively easy to get hold of data about an individual from the census bureau: crime records, health records, economic and consumer data. Secondary analysis often involves combining information from multiple databases to construct a complex and thorough picture of an individual. It is efficient and cheap. However, it can be difficult to access and link data from large complex databases.

6.2.5   Snooping: More Recent Research and Online Behaviour

Over the last 20 years, there has been a renewed interest in particular aspects on unobtrusive measures. Gosling and colleagues (Gosling, 2009; Gosling et al., 2002) have led this research which is about 'what your stuff says about you'. They were interested in how people 'arranged' their environments like their bedrooms and offices and whether they were valid indicators of the inhabitant's personality. This data is now becoming very much more apparent as people Zoom and Skype each other from their houses.

What if you noticed various religious or national symbols? What does the fact that an individual has a number of well-tended plants inside their house indicate? Why are there so many or so few books, and what are their contents? Who are in photographs? The idea is that our chosen and arranged environments provide 'leakage' about our true personalities.

There are various relatively easy-to-score features of a room/office: how tidy/organised it is; how good is the lighting; how cheerful, artistic, exotic, sparse the decor; how many books are there; what evidence is their preferred possession (photographs, flags, sporting equipment). In one well-quoted study, Gosling et al. (2002) got observers to rate a person's office or bedroom on more than 40 characteristics: strong vs weak odour; noisy vs quiet; well-lit vs dark; drafty vs stuffy; hot vs cold; cluttered vs uncluttered; distinctive vs ordinary; etc. They then got the occupiers to complete personality tests and the observers to make ratings of the occupiers based on their data. They found that the environments (both office and bedroom) gave good clues about some traits more than others: openness and conscientiousness more than agreeableness and neuroticism.

Online activity, specifically on social media has also attracted a lot of attention for personality researchers. Extraversion is the trait that's been linked to social media activity, suggesting that people who are more social offline are more social online too. Extraversion has been notably linked to both self-presentation or posting behaviour (status updates, picture uploads), belong behaviour (tagging friends in posts, commenting) and general volume of use (Keep & Amon, 2017; Ong et al., 2011; Seidman, 2013). Extraverts may post more online simply as they have more to post; they are more active socially and take more photos of themselves, their friends and their environment.

Conversely, conscientiousness has been linked to caution in posting online (Seidman, 2013), and negatively predicted self-presentation behaviours online. A simple justification for this would be that conscientious people are less likely to spend time on social media sites, such as Facebook or Instagram, but more likely so is that highly conscientious individuals understand the consequences of posting on their social and occupational lives, and could be more likely to use social media as a tool to reflect the best version of themselves, knowing how attached their social media footprint is to their identity.

Another of the big five personality traits, Agreeableness has also been linked to belonging behaviour online, as well as a tendency to portray themselves authentically online (Keep & Amon, 2017; Seidman, 2013). Neuroticism has been linked to more frequent self-presenting behaviour, alongside Extraversion, but not to belonging behaviour. Conversely to Agreeableness, Neuroticism has also been linked to posting/portraying an ideal and actual self online (Seidman, 2013). These results seem contradictory coming from the same study, but this could mean, practically, that these individuals post both ideal and authentic depictions of themselves across multiple posts or the same post with multiple pictures. An example of this could be the popular 'Instagram vs Reality' trend, where individuals post at least two photos, one where they are posed specifically to engineer a photo which makes them look the most attractive, and another where they are in a more relaxed pose with the intention to highlight any imperfections they have and relate to the insecurities of their audience or friend groups.

The trait Narcissism, a dark personality trait related to high Extraversion and low Agreeableness, has also been shown to link to social media activity (Paramboukis et al., 2016). Even when Extraversion was controlled for, Narcissism predicted a higher frequency of Facebook status updates and people rating their own attractiveness higher in their profile pictures (Ong et al., 2011). This could both be because higher Narcissism could predict people thinking they are normally more attractive, but also more narcissistic individuals would choose profile pictures where they themselves looked good, and not favour photos where they looked worse by comparison with their friends.

Perhaps the most important are social media websites that are related to employment, the most well known of which being *LinkedIn*. Here, impression management and self-presentation likely fall under more scrutiny, as one's profile is focused around their career/and work achievements; mistakes and deviations are potentially more detriment here than on a typical CV (Paliszkiewicz & Madra-Sawicka, 2016). As a result, there is likely to be greater self-monitoring, which may flatten any personality differences. Objective values on *LinkedIn*, however, like the number of skills and connections a person has, have been linked to personality traits (Conscientiousness and Openness, and Extraversion; Bhardwaj et al., 2016) where the authors suggested using both *Facebook* and *LinkedIn* in most cases to get a more comprehensive estimate of an individual's personality. Overall, however, it might be better to avoid using this approach to guess personality traits, unless you're using predefined statistical model, as guesses of trait Extraversion from only viewing the profile of another only has had weak correlations with actual levels of Extraversion ($r = .24–.29$; van de Ven et al., 2017). Other traits may have similar, if not worse, estimates.

The issue with using social media to identify traits in an individual is not knowing their own preference for using social media. All the conclusions made earlier are based on data from group averages which can avoid individual differences, such as people intentionally avoiding social media for their own personal reasons. In that case, you may conclude, wrongly, that a person/applicant is very introverted as they do not have very many accounts, or that the accounts they do have show little activity. Naturally, these methods should not be used in isolation, as many effects of personality traits may overlap or cancel each other out. A better approach for companies to take, perhaps, would be to check participants' social media footprint after they've measured their personality traits through conventional means. They could look for behaviour that is unusual, in light of current research and worthy of note. For example, if a highly extraverted person has scarce presence online, there could be a pre-meditated reason as to why that is and could be worth asking in an interview to get to know job candidates better.

6.2.6 Conclusion

The argument for using unobtrusive measures is that they allow you to measure behaviours non-reactively or naturalistically, that is where a person or group are unaware of being measured. These include often problems with assessment, and whether the measures are really unobtrusive. The fundamental issues are the same as in all other instruments: first validity and second ethics. In extreme cases, online profiles may give reasons for applicants to be removed from the selection process, but personality assessments based on social media activity are likely not reliable or accurate enough to be of any credit in selection processes, at least before the interview process.

REFERENCES

Bhardwaj, S., Atrey, P. K., Saini, M. K., & El Saddik, A. (2016). Personality assessment using multiple online social networks. *Multimedia Tools and Applications*, 75(21), 13237–13269.

Forgas, J. P. (2003). Affective influences on attitudes and judgments. In R. J. Davidson, K. R. Scherer, & H. H. Goldsmith (Eds.), *Handbook of affective sciences* (pp. 596–618). New York City, NY: Oxford University Press.

Gosling, S. (2009) *Snoop: What your stuff says about you*. London, UK: Profile Books Limited.

Gosling, S. D., Ko, S. J., Mannarelli, T., & Morris, M. E. (2002). A room with a cue: personality judgments based on offices and bedrooms. *Journal of Personality and Social Psychology*, 82(3), 379–398.

Hill, A. D., Kern, D. A., & White, M. A. (2014). Are we overconfident in executive overconfidence research? An examination of the convergent and content validity of extant unobtrusive measures. *Journal of Business Research*, 67(7), 1414–1420.

Keep, M., & Amon, K. L. (2017). Follow me: exploring the effect of personality and stranger connections on Instagram use. *International Journal of Virtual Communities and Social Networking*, 9(1), 1–16.

Ong, E. Y. L., Ang, R. P., Ho, J. C. M., Lim, J. C. Y., Goh, D. H., Lee, C. S., & Chua, A. Y. K. (2011). Narcissism, extraversion, and adolescents' self-presentation on Facebook. *Personality and Individual Differences*, 50(2), 180–185.

Paliszkiewicz, J. & Madra-Sawicka, M. (2016) Impression management in social media: the example of LinkedIn. *Management, 11*(3), 203–212.

Paramboukis, O., Skues, J., & Wise, L. (2016). An exploratory study of the relationships between narcissism, self-esteem and Instagram use. *Social Networking, 5*(2), 82–92.

Reid, E., & Novak, P. (1975). Personal space: an unobtrusive measures study. *Bulletin of the Psychonomic Society, 5*(3), 265–266.

Seidman, G. (2013). Self-presentation and belonging on Facebook: how personality influences social media use and motivations. *Personality and Individual Differences, 54*(3), 402–407.

van de Ven, N., Bogaert, A., Serlie, A., Brandt, M. J., & Denissen, J. J. (2017). Personality perception based on LinkedIn profiles. *Journal of Managerial Psychology, 32*(6), 418–429.

Webb, E., Campbell, D., Schwartz, R., & Sechrest, L. (1966). *Unobtrusive measures.* New York: Rand-McNally.

6.3 SITUATIONAL JUDGEMENT TESTS

What are they?
These involve presenting people with a typical, problematic work situation and choosing from a number of possible responses which are scored from best to worst, yielding a total score.

How do they work?
Ideally, high scorers who choose the best responses to typical workplace scenarios have been shown to be better performers on the job.

What of the evidence?
Well-constructed, updated and properly validated, they can work very well, as they are liked by candidates.

Practical problems: cost, ethics, politics
There are a few ethical and political problems, but they tend to be very limited to particular organisations, sectors, cultures and time periods.

Recommendations for use
They can supplement other methods very well.

6.3.1 Introduction

These were first invented around 100 years ago and called *social intelligence tests*. Furthermore, as in the case of many other tests they were used to select people for the Second World War. From then onwards they were mainly used to select supervisor personnel. They saw a revival in the 1990s often called *tacit knowledge tests*. Although they differ widely on many criteria, it is often maintained that have very specific advantages: they have low adverse impact against many groups; they can assess soft skills like social judgements well; they have good acceptance by applicants and they can assess very specific job-related skills not assessed by other methods.

It is important to differentiate between Situational Judgement Tests (SJTs) and work-sample tests, the latter are effectively job tryouts and may last many days. They are also called simulation tests (Gatewood et al., 2015). They do not provide signals, signs or data that may predict job performance but rather samples of actual job behaviour.

SJTs provide people with typical situations that may differentiate the behaviour of very talented workers and provide them with alternatives. They may ask 'What is the best thing to do?' or 'What would you do?' The former task is related to intelligence and the latter to personality (Cook, 2016).

SJTs have been defined as 'any paper-and-pencil test designed to measure judgement in work settings' (McDaniel et al., 2001, p. 730). Effectively they present scenarios/critical incidences where people are given options. This example is given by Whetzel et al. (2020) to measure conscientiousness:

You have been asked to give a presentation to the Board of Trustees at your organisation. You have sufficient time and resources to prepare the presentation. What should you do?

A. Start preparing the presentation one hour in advance since you work best under pressure.

> B. Start preparing the presentation two or three days in advance and practice it a few minutes before the presentation.
> C. Prepare the presentation well in advance, carefully checking it for accuracy and practice just before the presentation.
> D. Prepare the presentation well in advance, carefully checking for accuracy and practice several times so that it feels natural to talk in front of the Board.

SJT can be presented electronically (video) or by written means, the former being more expensive (to develop) but more realistic. They aim to show work situations that are typical and comprehensible. The situations are derived first from job incumbents and supervisors that challenge workers and are crucial for the job. These are reviewed, edited and grouped, and then compared to job analysis data. They form the basis of a survey where workers show how they would, should or might react to that situation. These are then given to known employees so that a scoring process can be derived.

The idea is that the candidate looks at the situations and responds (verbally or on paper) through different possible options: Write down what you are most/least likely to do? Pick the best/worst answer from those provided; rate each response for its effectiveness. The responses may get weighted so that a total score is possible.

Construction of a psychometrically valid test usually involves a number of processes:

1. Identify the job or class of job (i.e. sales, serving, supervision) the SJT is to be used for.
2. Write and sort out into categories critical incidences that differentiate good vs average vs poor performers (issues may include too much work; problematic boss, co-workers, subordinates, customers who are rude, lazy, corrupt).
3. Generate a number (4–6) of typical responses that a good vs poor employee would give. These have to be realistic, subtle and possible.
4. Give these to large groups of workers whose performance is known to see which incidences and items differentiate between workers.

These scores can be weighted in the same way as biodata items (see Chapter 9).

Studies provided additional support for both the predictive and incremental validity of SJTs over and above personality and intelligence when it comes to explaining work outcomes. Chan and Schmitt (2002) assessed data from 160 Singaporean civil service employees and found that overall job performance, as well as three specific performance dimensions (task, motivational or contextual and interpersonal performance), was linked to SJT scores beyond personality and intelligence measures. Even when intelligence and major personality dimensions are taken into account, SJT scores were linked to interpersonal performance (.17), task performance (.24) and especially contextual performance or job dedication (.30). It is noteworthy that they also controlled for previous job experience, though this predictor was not significantly related to any of the criteria when other measures were considered.

There are many papers that describe the development of SJTs such as a recent paper designed to select teachers in Oman (Al Hashmi & Klassen, 2019). These are often done in very specific settings like medicine, for example, Pangallo et al. (2016) described the development of an SJT instrument designed to measure resilience in palliative care workers. In their paper, they provided an example from their test.

Sharif is in extreme pain and is asking for his family. Sharif is a 20-year-old man with a history of drug abuse. He is not responding to pain medication and is in an enormous amount of pain. Sharif pleads with you to contact his family. You do so, but his family inform you that they cannot bring themselves to see him, despite the fact that he is dying. As he reaches the end of his life, he cries out for his mum and dad.

Choose the three most effective actions you would take in this situation:

A. Provide the usual care to Sharif

B. Make excuses for his family not being there

C. Arrange for someone to be with Sharif all the time

D. Explore with Sharif's family any way of getting to his bedside

E. Let Sharif know you are in contact with his family

F. Accept the situation for what it is; there is only so much you can do

G. Tell Sharif his family are on their way

H. Remind yourself that Sharif brought this on himself

Key: 3 points (D); 2 points (C, E); 1 point (A, F); 0 points (G, H, B)

6.3.2   What Do SJTs Actually Measure?

Although SJTs are a method rather than a construct, they measure individual differences and therefore latent psychological constructs. Theoretically it is important to identify the psychological attributes that underlie performance differences in SJTs in order to better understand the determinants of individual differences at work and identify the best ways to assess these differences.

As noted, early SJTs were believed to measure 'keen judgment, and deep human motives' (Moss & Hunt, 1926, p. 26) and fell within the 'social intelligence' or interpersonal competence domain. Since then, a key issue in SJT search has been the distinction between academic and non-academic competencies, where the former fall within the realm of IQ or cognitive ability and the latter hypothesised as independent and largely unrelated. However, research repeatedly found that SJTs are g-saturated (Northrop, 1989; see Section 4.1.2 and earlier), especially in their paper-and-pencil form (Lievens & Sackett, 2006). Despite clear evidence on the associations between traditional ability tests and SJTs, recurrent assumptions have been made on the independence of the constructs assessed by both methods/measures.

McDaniel et al. stated that SJTs measure 'a variety of constructs' (2001, p. 732), though in most cases they are designed to assess 'common sense, experience, and general knowledge, rather than logical reasoning' (2001, p. 731), which are arguably job-related skills or abilities (Weekley & Jones, 1997). There is a long academic dispute in psychology about the extent to which 'common sense' and practical skills – often labelled 'social intelligence' (Peterson & Seligman, 2004), 'practical intelligence' (Sternberg et al., 2000), 'emotional intelligence' (see section 7.19), 'interpersonal' or 'social skills' (Furnham, 1986) or 'tacit knowledge' (Sternberg & Horvath, 1999) – are independent of 'academic' or intellectual abilities. As seen earlier, this was an issue of concern in the validation of SJTs, as their usefulness in personnel selection will largely depend on the extent to which they predict work-related outcomes independently of intelligence and personality measures.

Some examples:

Situation A
Your manager has called you into a meeting to tell you about the proposed changes that will impact the delivery of a report you are currently working on. You had almost completed the task and were about to submit this slightly ahead of the set deadline. The changes your manager wants you to make will result in a significant amount of re-work to one area of the report and this will put the deadline at risk of being missed.

	Most Effective	Least Effective
Revisit your work to carefully and plan what will need to be amended and how long this will take in order to organise your work to meet the deadline.		
Identify the areas of the report that will be affected and work through them one by one with the aim of meeting the deadline.		
Try to understand the reasons why the changes need to be made before agreeing to take the work on.		
Ask your manager for their advice on how to proceed given the impact these changes will have on your work.		

Situation B
You have been given a new project to plan and manage. However, some of the requirements have not been clearly defined. The planned delivery date is currently unknown and the stakeholders of the project will not confirm this until the project is signed off by the head of your department. It is likely that the project will need to begin as soon as the project is signed off.

	Most Effective	Least Effective
Discuss the project with your manager and try to estimate what the deadline might be so you have a date to work towards.		
Organise and lead an initial meeting with the key stakeholders to work out what tasks need further explaining in order to ensure the project can be fully scoped.		
Request further information from the stakeholders before completing any work on the project.		
Pull together a draft plan based on the facts that you know highlighting where information is missing.		

6.3.3   Faking and Social Desirability

SJTs require people to say what they would or should do in reaction to any particular situation.

As any person who has tried to devise an SJT knows, it is difficult to find items/responses which seem sensible and plausible without being obviously the best or worst. Also there remain lots of concerns about fakeability of SJTs. The answer appears to be first, that indeed they are open to problems associated with social desirability (Kaminski et al., 2019) but less so than standard personality tests (Kasten et al., 2018). Moreover, the widespread use of these tests in medical setting has led researchers to ask whether candidates can be coached so that they get better scores (Stemig et al., 2015).

Corstjens et al. (2017) noted that SJTs were less prone to faking and test-re-test effects particularly if they were knowledge based.

6.3.3.1   Examples of Integrity SJTs

A. Jane works as a sales clerk in a store beside the Interstate Highway/Main Motorway. The store's customers are mostly tourists who stop to buy gasoline, snacks, and souvenirs. One day Jane accidentally gives a man change for a $10 bill when he actually had given her a $20 bill. After the man left, Jane saw the $20 bill in the cash drawer with the tens and realised what she had done. At this point Jane might react in several ways. Indicate whether you agree with each of these possibilities.

1. Jane decides to deny that she shortchanged the customer if he returns for his $10. That will save her a lot of embarrassment. Do you agree? Yes/No

2. Jane regrets the incident but decides to make the best of a bad situation. She takes $10 from the cash drawer and tells her supervisor she is sick and wants the rest of the day off. Do you agree? Yes/No

3. Jane will gladly return the $10 to the customer if she sees him again. Meanwhile, she turns the extra money over to the store manager and decides to make up for the mistake by contributing $10 of her own money to a local charity. Do you agree? Yes/No

4 Jane turns the extra money over to the store at the end of her shift because the customer has not returned. She also writes down everything she can remember about how the man looks. If he ever stops at the store again, she will repay him with her own money. Do you agree? Yes/No

B. Your work team is in a meeting discussing how to sell a new product. Everyone seems to agree that the product should be offered to customers within the month. Your boss is all for this, and you know he does not like public disagreements. However, you have concerns because a recent report from the research department points to several potential safety problems with the product. Which of the following do you think you would most likely do?

A. Try to understand why everyone else wants to offer the product to customers this month. Maybe your concerns are misplaced. [−1]

B. Voice your concerns with the product and explain why you believe the safety issues need to be addressed. [1]

C. Go along with what others want to do so that everyone feels good about the team. [−1]

D. Afterwards, talk with several other members of the team to see if they share your concerns. [0]

C. You're a manager doing a performance evaluation for Jerry. Jerry has not performed well this year. He is mad because you gave him a rating of 3 ('met expectations') on quality of work, and he believes that he deserves a 5 ('exceeds expectations'). You believe the rating of 3 is fair and accurate, but Jerry threatens to go to your boss to complain. What would you most likely do?

A. Tell Jerry to go to hell. [−1]

B. Explain to Jerry why you gave him the rating that you did, but refuse to change your rating. [1]

C. Seek a compromise, such as giving Jerry a 4. [−1]

D. Schedule a meeting with your boss so that you and your boss can decide which rating is best. [1]

D. You're a new clerk in a clothing store and are being trained by Angie, a veteran employee. She quietly tells you that because employees are paid minimum wage, most people sometimes take home clothes for themselves. Employees who don't are considered dumb and arrogant. At closing time, Angie hands you a scarf to take home. Which of the following would you most likely do?

A. Take home the scarf and keep your mouth shut. [−1]

B. Take home the scarf, but return it to the shelf later without letting other employees see you. [−1]

C. Politely tell Angie that you don't need any more scarves. [0]

D. Tell Angie that you don't want to take home any clothes, now or ever. [1]

E. A few days ago, one of your customers asked you when a certain shipment of your products would be delivered. You knew it would take at least two weeks until delivery, but to keep the customer from getting mad you told them it would be no more than one week.

A. Let it go this time but resolve not to do this again. Confide in several people you trust about what you did and listen to their advice.

B. Talk to shipping and see if they can get the shipment there in under two weeks. Make clear to them that it must arrive in under 10 days.

C. Call the customer back and tell them that you were mistaken, and that the shipment will not arrive for at least two weeks.

D. Understand that this sort of thing is necessary in business and that almost everyone knows that promises such as this might not be kept.

6.3.4   Evaluation

McDaniel et al. (2001) published a widely cited meta-analytic estimate of the correlation between SJT and work criteria on the one hand, and cognitive ability on the other. They concluded that

SJTs were an assessment measurement method rather than construct and that they assessed a variety of constructs depending on the measure. They also noted that most SJTs were standard paper-and-pencil inventories that were administered in written form, and that they comprised similar types of items – hypothetical work scenarios being the most obvious. Their initial inspection of the studies also led to suggestions that the SJTs were *adequate predictors of work-related criteria*, though they tended to be generally correlated with cognitive ability or intelligence tests (although there is no objective statistical cut-off point for determining how high correlations can be before the two measures are deemed conceptually 'too similar', correlation coefficients $>.6$ are generally considered problematic).

Most of McDaniel et al.'s conclusions have been supported by subsequent evidence and are still valid, except the remark that 'paper-and-pencil' was the typical way to administer SJTs. One study found that with the popularity of the World Wide Web, SJTs are increasingly administered online A more specific inspection of the results also reveals interesting differences in the validity estimates of the SJT according to the specific tests examined.

The *Supervisory Judgement test* was more valid than the Richardson, Bellows & Henry (RBH) and, especially, the *How to Supervise test*. SJTs that took into account the specific characteristics of the job ('based on job analysis') were more valid than those that did not; SJTs that included general questions were slightly more valid than those comprising detailed questions; SJTs that were highly 'g-loaded', that is correlated substantially with tests of cognitive ability or intelligence, were more valid than those with low 'g-loadings' ('uncorrelated with intelligence'). Finally, as is often the case in validity studies, concurrent studies – which assessed SJT and the criterion at the same time – showed higher validities than predictive studies (which assessed SJT at time 1 and the relevant work outcomes at time 2, for example three years later).

McDaniel et al. also examined the empirical link between SJTs and tests of cognitive ability from an applied/personnel selection perspective. This question is important as the validity of any new or different rather than detailed questions were more highly related to the intelligence. The authors noted that their estimates are likely to be conservative and underestimate the population-based correlation between SJTs and intelligence tests as they did not correct for restriction of range. Moreover, they argued that SJTs have incremental validity over and above cognitive ability tests when it comes to explaining work-related outcomes. In fact, they estimated that a composite of SJT and cognitive ability would explain an additional 5–6% of the variance in work-related outcomes than either measure alone.

Thus McDaniel et al.'s conclusion was that:

It is clear that [SJTs] are good predictors of job performance. Our data suggest that general cognitive ability is a construct partly reflected in such measures, although general cognitive ability does not typically account for all the variance ... Future research should repeat our moderator analyses on larger data sets and attempt to identify other possible moderators to allow a more complete understanding of the nomological network within which test situational judgment measures reside.

(p. 738)

There have been two recent, comprehensive reviews of SJTs. Corstjens et al. (2017) stress the contextualisation issue: that is, all SJTs are designed for, and work only in, a particular social and organisational context. They also discuss the all-important psychometric issues. From their assessment they were happy to announce the evidence suggests that they are 'sufficiently reliable'. More importantly, from a criteria-related validity perspective, they concluded that SJTs are comparable to other selection techniques and offer incremental validity over and above personality and intelligence tests. They also confirmed other reactions: there are relatively few subgroup differences (race and sex); candidates like them because they are job related and interactive, particularly if the situations are on video. With regards to future research they make various suggestions: to understand why some SJTs work better than others in predicting various criteria at work, distinguishing between general and job-specific SJTs, and exploring their cross-cultural validity.

Whetzel et al. (2020) note five crucial issues which concern those using SJTs: criterion-related and construct validity, group differences, item presentation methods, faking and coaching.

Although SJTs are a method rather than a construct, they measure individual differences and therefore latent psychological constructs. Theoretically it is important to identify the psychological attributes that underlie performance differences in SJTs in order to better understand the determinants of individual differences at work and identify the best ways to assess these differences.

As noted, early SJTs were believed to measure 'keen judgment, and difficult to assess human motives' (Moss & Hunt, 1926, p. 26) and fell within the 'social intelligence' or interpersonal competence domain. Since then, a key issue in SJT search has been the distinction between academic and non-academic competencies, where the former fall within the realm of IQ or cognitive ability and the latter hypothesised as independent and largely unrelated. However, research repeatedly found that SJTs are g-saturated (Northrop, 1989; see Section 4.1.2 and above), especially in their paper-and-pencil form (Lievens & Sackett, 2006). Despite clear evidence on the associations between traditional ability tests and SJTs, recurrent assumptions have been made on the independence of the constructs assessed by both methods/measures.

6.3.5 Trends and Developments

Over the years there have been some important trends in SJTs. The first is using video or 3D animation to present the situations.

These are maximally realistic using actors in real settings. Also, it is possible to assess more than the candidate's endorsement of one particular response. Thus, they could be filmed and or physically recorded (wired up) when completing a test. Another idea has been to not simply list situations but rather to look at sequences: that is, show the consequences of the candidate's response so that the slightly changed situation is reported. This is clearly related to gamifications.

Another theme is to use SJTs to measure general domain knowledge, that is less context dependent.

Whetzel et al. (2020) provided a very useful 'Review of Best Practice Guidelines' (p. 12):

Scenarios

- Critical incidents enhance realism of scenarios.
- Specific scenarios tend to yield higher levels of validity, because they require fewer assumptions on the part of the examinee.
- Brief scenarios reduce candidate reading load, which may reduce group differences.
- Avoid sensitive topics and balance diversity of characters.
- Avoid overly simplistic scenarios that yield only one plausible response.
- Avoid overly complex scenarios that provide more information than is needed to respond to the question.

Response options

- Ask SMEs for what they would do to ensure viability of response options.
- Create response options that have a range of effectiveness levels for each scenario.
- If developing a construct-based SJT, be careful about transparency of options.
- List only one action in each response option (avoid double-barreled responses).
- Distinguish between active bad (do something wrong) and passive bad (do nothing).
- Check for tone (use of loaded words can give clues as to effectiveness).

Response instructions

- Use knowledge-based ('should do') instructions for high-stakes settings (candidates will respond to this question regardless of instruction).
- Use behavioral tendency ('would do') instructions if assessing non-cognitive constructs (e.g. personality).

Response format

- Use the rating format where examinees rate each option, as this method (a) provides the most information for a given scenario, (b) yields higher reliability and (c) elicits the most favourable candidate reactions.
- Single-response SJTs are easily classified into dimensions and have reliability and validity comparable to other SJTs, but they can have higher reading load given each scenario is associated with a single response.

Scoring

- Empirical and rational keys have similar levels of reliability and validity.
- Rational keys based on SME input are used most often.
- Develop 'overlength' forms (more scenarios and options per scenario than you will need).
- Use 10–12 raters with a diversity of perspective. Outliers may skew results if fewer raters are used.
- Use means and standard deviations to select options (means will provide effectiveness levels; standard deviation will provide level of SME agreement).

Reliability

- Coefficient alpha (internal consistency) is not appropriate for multidimensional SJTs.
- Use split-half, with Spearman–Brown correction, assuming content is balanced.

Validity

- Knowledge and behavioural tendency instructions have similar levels of validity.
- SJTs have small incremental validity over cognitive ability and personality.

- SJTs have been used in military settings for selection and promotion.
- SJTs likely measure a general personality factor.
- SJTs correlate with other constructs, such as cognitive ability and personality.

Group differences

- SJTs have smaller group differences than cognitive ability tests.
- Women perform slightly better than men on SJTs.
- Behavioural tendency instructions have smaller group differences than knowledge instructions.
- Rate format has lower group differences than rank or select best/worst.

Presentation methods

- Avatar- and video-based SJTs have several advantages in terms of higher face and criterion-related validity, but they may have lower reliability.
- Using avatars may be less costly, but developers should consider the uncanny valley effect when using three-dimensional human images.

Faking

- Faking does affect rank ordering of candidates and who is hired.
- Faking is more of a problem with behavioural tendency (would-do) response instructions, especially in high-stakes situations.
- SJTs generally appear less vulnerable to faking than traditional personality measures.

Coaching

- Examinees can be coached on how to maximise SJT responses.
- Scoring adjustments (e.g. key stretching, within-person standardisation) can reduce this effect

6.3.6   Conclusion

It takes a long time to develop good SJTs, which may be limited to a particular job (sales, security), as well as a particular organisation, culture and period of time. This means that they do not travel well, nor are they easy to obtain or purchase 'off the shelf'. If customised and validated, they do make an excellent method for measuring an applicant's ability and personality.

The other standard questions remain (Gatewood et al., 2015): Do they have an inverse impact? Can they be faked? Can people be coached on how to do better? The answer is yes – to some extent. But if these SJTs have been designed to evaluate a single construct (i.e. teamwork, negotiation), candidates rate how good each response is, clear differences emerge from good/average/poor employees and scoring is corrected for various artefacts, they make excellent selection devices.

REFERENCES

Al Hashmi, W., & Klassen, R. M. (2019). Developing a situational judgement test for admission into initial teacher education in Oman: an exploratory study. *International Journal of School & Educational Psychology, 7*(1), 1–12.

Chan, D., & Schmitt, N. (2002). Situational judgment and job performance. *Human Performance, 15*(3), 233–254.

Cook, M. (2016). *Personnel selection: Adding value through people – A changing picture* (6th ed.). Chichester, UK: John Wiley & Sons.

Corstjens, J., Lievens, F., & Krumm, S. (2017). Situational judgement tests for selection. In H. W. Goldstein, , D. E. Pulakos, C. Semedo, & J. Passmore, (Eds.), *The Wiley Blackwell handbook of the psychology of recruitment, selection and employee retention* (pp. 226–246). Chichester, UK: John Wiley & Sons.

Furnham, A. (1986). Social skills training with adolescents and young adults. In C. R. Hollin, & P. Trower (Eds.), *Handbook of social skills training* (pp. 33–57). Oxford, UK: Pergamon Press.

Gatewood, R., Feild, H. S., & Barrick, M. (2015). *Human resource selection* (8th ed.). Boston, MA: Cengage Learning.

Kaminski, K., Felfe, J., Schäpers, P., & Krumm, S. (2019). A closer look at response options: is judgment in situational judgment tests a function of the desirability of response options?. *International Journal of Selection and Assessment, 27*(1), 72–82.

Kasten, N., Freund, P. A., & Staufenbiel, T. (2018). 'Sweet little lies': an in-depth analysis of faking behavior on Situational Judgment Tests compared to personality questionnaires. *European Journal of Psychological Assessment, 36*(1), 136–148.

Lievens, F., & Sackett, P. R. (2006). Video-based versus written situational judgment tests: a comparison in terms of predictive validity. *Journal of Applied Psychology, 91*(5), 1181–1188.

McDaniel, M. A., Morgeson, F. P., Finnegan, E. B., Campion, M. A., & Braverman, E. P. (2001). Use of situational judgment tests to predict job performance: a clarification of the literature. *Journal of Applied Psychology, 86*(4), 730–740.

Moss, F. A., & Hunt, T. (1926). Ability to get along with others. *Industrial Psychology, 1,* 170–178.

Northrop, L. C. (1989). *The psychometric history of selected ability constructs.* Washington, DC: US Office of Personnel Management.

Pangallo, A., Zibarras, L., & Patterson, F. (2016). Measuring resilience in palliative care workers using the situational judgement test methodology. *Medical Education, 50*(11), 1131–1142.

Peterson, C., & Seligman, M. E. P. (2004). Social Intelligence. In *Character strengths and virtues: A handbook and classification* (pp. 337–353). Washington, DC: American Psychological Association.

Stemig, M. S., Sackett, P. R., & Lievens, F. (2015). Effects of organizationally endorsed coaching on performance and validity of situational judgment tests. *International Journal of Selection and Assessment, 23*(2), 174–181.

Sternberg, R. J., & Horvath, J. A. (Eds.). (1999). *Tacit knowledge in professional practice: Researcher and practitioner perspectives.* Mahwah, NJ: Lawrence Erlbaum Associates Inc.

Sternberg, R. J., Forsythe, G. B., Hedlund, J., Wagner, R. K., Horvath, J. A., Williams, W. M., Snook, S. A., & Grigorenko, E. (2000). *Practical intelligence in everyday life.* Cambridge, UK: Cambridge University Press.

Weekley, J. A., & Jones, C. (1997). Video-based situational testing. *Personnel Psychology, 50*(1), 25–49.

Whetzel, D. L., Sullivan, T. S., & McCloy, R. A. (2020). Situational judgment tests: an overview of development practices and psychometric characteristics. *Personnel Assessment and Decisions, 6*(1), 1–16.

6.4 CREATIVITY

What are they?
These are many and various personality-type, self-assessment, thinking-style and ability tests that attempt to measure creativity, defined as the ability to generate novel and useful ideas or products.

How do they work?
Many look like checklists, personality or even intelligence tests, and generate scores that are indicators of an individual general or specific creativity (imaginativeness).

What of the evidence?
Very mixed but there is a serious problem in validating them as there is little agreement about criteria against which to evaluate them.

Practical problems: cost, ethics, politics
There are not many of these problems except the major issue of demonstrating the validity of the tests. A few assessors are interested in measuring creativity, but most are not.

Recommendations for use
Use a battery of tests to attempt to come up with an aggregated score, which gives some indicator of creativity.

6.4.1 Introduction

Some employees are more creative than others. They are more likely to come up with original thoughts and novel solutions and stand out in organisations for their innovative thinking. They seem to prefer innovation to imitation and often enjoy defying the crowd.

Creativity, like nearly all human characteristics, is normally distributed. A few people are very creative: most of us, by definition are 'average'. This is against the assertion of some that 'everyone is creative' or could be taught to be so.

Many organisations say they value creativity because it is the *father of innovation*, which in turn is the *engine of change*. They often spend billions on research and development on a creative process or people which looks to find different, better, cheaper, stronger products and work processes. The importance of creativity, however, depends on the nature of the job.

People like to believe they are all (particularly, especially) creative. Organisations like to believe they need creative ideas which come from creative people. Managers might or might not be wrong depending on the organisation they come from. Others believe that creativity can be relatively easily taught, though the evidence remains weak. Many researchers have been sceptical of the many courses available that supposedly teach creativity.

Do you need to be an expert to appreciate or understand 'real' creativity and can this ability be taught? Is it true, particularly in some areas rather than others? The jury seems to be out on this one (Kaufman et al., 2013).

A great deal of nonsense is talked about creativity. Creativity remains a bit of a scientific backwater. The problem is measurement: there is no simple, agreed, robust and valid measure of creativity. This means it is difficult to test theories and ideas such as where it comes from and whether it can be taught. There are many ideas about creative people and how to make people more creative. Some of these ideas have been tested. Many have not. Some are clearly rather quirky.

Creativity is the exception not the rule. For instance, with respect to classical music, we know 36 composers produced 75%, 16 composers produced 50%; 10 composers produced 40%; 3 composers produced 20% (Mozart, Beethoven, Bach) of *all* greatly acknowledged classical music. To be really creative is really exceptional. However, there is a distinction between great, eminent, productive creativity and small, everyday creativity.

Where do you stand? Read each one and state the extent to which you agree? Or simply note True, Unsure, False.

Creative geniuses are usually left handed.

Creative people 'think outside the box'/are lateral thinkers.

Those who are creative tend to be less intelligent.

Creative people are inspired by and more passionate about learning from new experiences than the general population.

You can spot a creative person in the crowd by their clothes and crazy hair.

Creative people such as dancers and actors tend to be sociable and extraverted.

Creative people such as writers, poets and painters tend to be introverted and prefer their own company.

Creative people are, more often than not, the life and soul of the party.

Only people who are original in their thinking can be creative.

Creative people are enthusiastic and passionate about their work.

Children are just as creative as adults.

Creative geniuses live a life of performing, expressing their internal thoughts/feelings in their work.

Creative people are non-conventional, constantly pushing the boundaries of society.

The more creative the person, the better they are at problem solving.

Creative prodigies are nearly always male.

Creative people are happy people.

Intensiveness is indicative of a creative personality.

Anyone can be creative.

Creative people are always one step ahead.

Creative people are forward thinking and curious when looking for inspiration.

The most creative of people tend not to be recognised until later in life, if not after death.

A creative person can apply one's knowledge and experience in new situations that do not resemble those in which it was gained.

Creative people are too often misunderstood and underappreciated.

One central question in the area is how to measure creativity. Consider the well-known problem which involves connecting dots by drawing just four straight lines, and without lifting the pen from the paper. It has given rise to the expression 'think outside the box' but if we measure how long it takes for someone to find a solution, the question must be what this measure predicts?

Although the topic of creativity has a longstanding history in psychology (dating back to the very beginnings of intelligence testing more than 100 years ago), creativity researchers have repeatedly complained about the fact that insufficient attention is given to the field (Barbot et al., 2019; Furnham, 2018, 2019; Guilford, 1950).

In 1950 Guilford highlighted the importance of increasing creativity research after noting that only 186 of the 121,000 psychological studies in databases had dealt with creativity. The generalised lack of applied research on creativity is in stark contrast with the consensus, particularly in industrialised or developed nations, on the importance of investing in creative employees. Thus, Porter (1990, p. 73) noted that 'national prosperity is created, not inherited' and Amabile (1990) saw individual creativity as the building block for organisational innovation. Indeed, knowledge-based societies have made creativity a common concept in managerial and macro-economic strategies and a key driver of competitiveness.

Rapid advancements in technology lead to shorter product life cycles and generate intense business competition for innovative ideas (Amabile et al., 1996; Andriopoulos, 2003). Furthermore, cultural, aesthetic, and creative aspects of the economies of industrialised nations are growing fast and at unprecedented rates. All this means that selecting employees with creative potential is now not only a priority for many sectors of the economy, but also the cause of higher demand for newcomers and the introduction of diverse working teams (Perretti & Negro, 2007), which inevitably impacts on personnel selection.

There are a number of very interesting personal accounts of the creativity process. Reviewers suggest there is evidence of four stages: *Preparation* (familiarisation with the problem: conscious, effortful, systematic, purposeful but often fruitless work on the problem); *Incubation* (time when no conscious work is done on the problem); *Illumination* ('aha', 'lightbulb', 'key in the lock' experiences and happy thoughts; not complete but points in the right direction; chance configuration, elaboration selection and retention) and finally *Verification* (developing and testing the idea).

As one may expect, neuroscientists are using their theories and methodology to study creativity. Benedek et al. (2019) reviewed those looking at neurological correlates of creative cognitive processes like event-related potentials, shifts in oscillatory potential, blood oxygen levels and fMRI assessments. They pointed out that most studies measured qualitative responses such as oral, written, drawn or musical productions, which enable the neuroscientist to analyse brain activation related to creative performance. The studies usually separate times of creative thought from response production to limit potential confounds with response-related motor activity. It is a promising new direction.

This chapter concerns the measurement of creativity which can focus on creative potential, creative performance or achievement. However, as Barbot et al. (2019) have suggested, the three most common ways to assess creativity is through some sort of divergent thinking assessment, some product-based assessment and through classic self-report (of creative activities, personality).

6.4.2 Creativity in the Arts and Sciences

One important issue is to distinguish between personality correlates of creativity in the arts and sciences. There has long been an interest in the different thinking styles of those in arts from those in science. This debate was structured by C. P. Snow in his 1959 lecture entitled 'The Two Cultures'. He stressed the differences and poor communication between those in the sciences and those in the humanities. This debate has continued for 50 years.

Hudson (1966) stimulated psychological research in this area. He suggested that those with a bias towards convergent thinking moved towards the physical sciences, while those with a divergent thinking bias moved towards the humanities (Hudson, 1973). The book became a citation classic receiving 225 citations up to 1980 (Hudson, 1980) and many hundreds more since then.

The Hudson book and its conclusion attracted criticism (Kinsbourne, 1968), but also replication and extension (Hartley & Beasley, 1969; Hocevar, 1980). Hartley and Greggs (1997) gave four groups of students – pure arts; arts and social science; social science and science; and pure science – some divergent thinking tests. The hypothesis that divergent thinking would decline along the arts–science continuum found support in that arts students as a whole scored significantly higher than science students on the four tests.

Researchers have tested the idea that personality and thinking style differences between arts and science students account for differences in creativity (Haller & Courvoisier, 2010). However, a study of 116 British undergraduates found small learning style differences and no problem-solving differences in arts and science students, leading the author to conclude that modern students have a more balanced educational profile than their more specialised predecessors (Williamson, 2011).

It could be argued that there is a third type of creativity, namely business or commercial creativity, which is concerned with the development and marketing of new, different and successful products and services. It may be a combination of both artistic and scientific creativity.

6.4.3   Definitions and Conceptualisations of Creativity

Creativity is part of everyday vocabulary and laypeople have a fairly good idea of how to define it. Sprecher (1959) investigated lay conceptions of creativity by asking engineers from a large industrial firm to explain the determinants of creativity in highly ranked co-workers (from research groups, service groups and project groups). He found that novelty and worth of ideas were deemed the most relevant factors in creativity, and that independence in problem solving and the achievement of comprehensive answers were also rated highly. Similar results on lay views of creativity have been reported since (Sternberg & O'Hara, 2000), though laypeople often confound creativity and intelligence, seeing them as the same thing. Indeed, Sternberg (1985) found a correlation of $r = .69$ between people's *ratings* of the creativity and intelligence of imaginary targets.

Among experts (both practitioners and researchers), creativity is often defined in terms of *originality*, though this is merely one aspect of creativity. Critics of the conceptualisation of creativity as originality have observed that creativity has finished up by being evaluated simply as an oddity or bizarreness of response relative to the population mean. Creative products should not only be original, but also useful. Amabile defined creativity a the 'production of novel and useful ideas' (1988, p. 126), a definition that has since been endorsed by a large number of researchers (Chamorro-Premuzic, 2007; Kaufman, 2019).

Despite consensus in defining creativity, the term is often used in different contexts: there are more (and less) 'creative' people, ideas, behaviours, works and even jobs (e.g. architect, graphic designer and advertising vs judge, librarian and engineer), though in all jobs some people will be more creative than others. Accordingly, creativity has been *conceptualised as a syndrome or complex, rather than a single phenomenon*, referring to creative people, creative processes, creative products and environmental influence or press on creativity (Rhodes, 1987, Runco, 2004).

Essentially, creativity results from an interaction between: the Individual (occasionally team); the Work Domain/Environment; and the Audience (of peers, judges, consumers).

Creativity has classically been seen as the four Ps: person, process, product and press (environment/situation). As a result, some of the tests used to measure creativity measure either person, process or product (Snyder et al., 2019).

6.4.4   Creative People and Personalities

The person or people approach to creativity focuses on inter-individual differences in creativity and thereby tries to identify and explain the factors that make one person more creative than other. Traditionally, these factors have included cognitive abilities, personality traits and motivation, though in recent years cognitive styles and knowledge have also been emphasised. This multi-determined view of personal creativity has important implications for selection as validated psychometric tests are available for all the individual difference constructs associated with creativity and intelligence. One important assessment and selection consequence is that creativity can efficiently and effectively be measured by personality tests.

But is there a specific combination of scores to highlight the creative potential of a person? Over the past century psychologists have tried to address this question, looking at the various dispositional and ability correlates of creativity.

6.4.4.1 Personality Traits

Barron (1963) provided one of the first comprehensive catalogue of the personality and ability characteristics of more and less creative people. He noted that creative people are 'affected, aggressive, demanding, dependent, dominant, forceful, impatient, initiating, outspoken, sarcastic, strong, and suggestive' if they have lower intellectual abilities, whilst non-creative people with higher intelligence are 'mild, optimistic, pleasant, quiet, unselfish' (p. 22). In at least two ways, Barron's description was ahead of its time as it anticipated a subsequent trend in psychological research to examine the psychopathological aspects of creativity (see Section 5.1.3) as well as the moderating role of cognitive abilities in explaining personality differences in creativity (Peterson & Carson, 2000).

However, most efforts to profile creative people have focused on personality traits. Until the consolidation of the five-factor, or 'Big Five', personality model, psychologists' attempts to identify the key traits that characterise creative people have been somewhat unorganised, such that different labels were often used to refer to the same traits and different levels of generality (from broader trait constructs to primary facets or dimensions of these constructs) were often undermined. Nonetheless, researchers by and large identified the 'bulk' of traits that are currently regarded as core personality markers of creativity.

Torrance (1979, p. 360) pointed out that 'creativity is essentially a personality syndrome that includes openness to experience, adventuresomeness, and self-confidence'. In time, creative people have been described as being risk-takers, self-confident, non-conformist or autonomous, tolerant of ambiguity and driven to accomplish personal and economic goals; that said, studies have also found a negative link between creativity and achievement drive

Work using the Eysenckian three-factor model identified Psychoticism (P) as the major personality determinant of creativity. Eysenck (1994, 1995) produced a model to explain how P and creativity were related. The data suggests the following: persons genetically related to psychotics are usually creative. The trait Psychoticism is related to tested creativity (originality) to creative achievement. Creative persons often suffer psychopathology. Identical cognitive styles are characteristic of psychotics, high P scorers and creative achievers.

He suggested three major variables that interactively relate to creativity as an achievement. Eysenck suggested that it is the process of over-inclusive or allusive thinking that characterises both psychotic and creative thinking.

Provided that there is a link between psychosis and creativity, this need to be explained. If psychoticism taps a unitary dimension underlying susceptibility to psychotic illness, then it is postulated that the important personality factor which acts synergistically with trait creativity (divergent thinking, DT) and which may, under favourable environmental conditions, lead to real-life creative achievement, is psychoticism. The Eysenckian theory, still one of the most inclusive and sophisticated in the area, traces the link from genetics to creativity, which provides many opportunities for exploring and understanding the creativity process at many levels from neuroscience to social psychology.

> Creativity is indexed by certain cognitive styles (over-inclusiveness, allusive thinking, looseness or 'slippage' of ideation), which increase fluency and originality. This type of cognitive style is closely related to psychoticism, and accounts for the many links between psychosis and creativity. Psychosis as such is, of course, likely to *prevent* creative achievement, in spite of being related to the trait of creativity; it constitutes a negative factor in the multiplicative relationship between the factors making for creative achievement. Psychoticism is linked directly with both trait creativity and achievement creativity, the link being over-inclusiveness.
>
> *(Eysenck, 1994, p. 232)*

Most recent research, however, has involved the Big Five (see Chapter 4). Chamorro-Premuzic and Furnham (2005) and Batey and Furnham (2006) reviewed the Big Five correlates of creativity and concluded that Openness was the most important factor to discriminate between creative and non-creative people, though Extraversion and, to a lesser extent, Agreeableness are also useful to explain individual differences in creativity.

The strong link between Openness and creativity is unsurprising as Openness assesses individual differences in aesthetic preferences, values, fantasy, feeling, actions and ideas related to novelty and intellectual experiences and is often interpreted as a self-report of creativity (Chamorro-Premuzic & Furnham, 2005; Matthews & Deary, 1998).

Feist (1998) meta-analysed 83 studies reporting associations between creativity and personality, coding personality traits according to the Big Five taxonomy and comparing scientists vs non-scientists, artists vs non-artists, and creative vs less-creative scientists. Results showed that Openness, Extraversion and Conscientiousness discriminated between scientists and non-scientists. The traits that most strongly differentiated the creative from less-creative scientists were Neuroticism and Openness. Artists, on the other hand, were approximately 1 standard deviation lower on Conscientiousness and .5 standard deviation higher on Openness than non-artists.

Table 6.10 attempts to summarise the literature on personality and creativity using the Big Five model plus Eysenck's Psychoticism. The work on the arts vs science literature suggests Artists are significantly higher on Neuroticism, lower on Extraversion, higher on Openness, lower on Agreeableness, lower on Conscientiousness and higher on Psychoticism than non-artists. On the other hand, scientists are significantly higher on Intelligence than non-scientists, lower on Neuroticism, and higher on Conscientiousness than non-scientists. Also Everyday creatives are significantly higher on Extraversion and Agreeableness than artists or scientists.

Thus, if the person perspective is taken, it seems reasonable to identify creative people as those who, say, score 2 or more standard deviations on a measure of Psychoticism or Openness.

6.4.4.2   Personality Disorders

There is a vast literature on creativity and mental illness, which suggests certain syndromes are associated with high levels of

Table 6.10 *Personality correlates of three types of creativity*

Trait	Artistic creativity	Scientific creativity	Everyday creativity
Intelligence			
Fluid	+	+ + +	+
Crystallised	+ +	+ + +	+
Personality			
N	+ + +	− −	−
E	− −	−	+ +
O	+ + +	+ + +	+ +
A	− −	−	+
C	− −	+ + +	+
P	+ + +	+ +	+

Note. N = neuroticism; E = extraversion; O = openness to experience; A = agreeableness; C = conscientiousness; P = psychoticism. Positive and negative signs indicate the strength and direction between the variables and range from − − − to + + +.

creativity. It seems obvious that the personality disorder (PD) most likely to be associated with creativity is *schizotypal* PD. This disorder, more common in males than females, has been estimated to affect about 3% of the population. In a sense they are 'mild, or subclinical schizophrenics' but do not show the gross disorganisation in thinking and feeling or severe symptoms as the latter.

One possible explanation for these different findings lies in the idea of differentiating positive and negative schizotypy (Kwapil et al., 2012). Positive schizotypy is associated with increased negative affect, thought impairment, suspiciousness, negative beliefs about current activities and feelings of rejection, but not social disinterest or decreased positive affect. Negative schizotypy was associated with decreased positive affect and pleasure in daily life, increased negative affect and decreased social contact and interest. It is possible that the different measures of SPD tap into different aspects of the disorder and that the measure used in this study may have had more positive than negative items.

Schizotypy has been most consistently related to creativity (Batey & Furnham, 2008; O'Reilly et al., 2001). Some have suggested that both *Histrionic* and *Narcissistic* Personality Disorder and *Aggressive* Personality Disorder are implicated in the process of creativity. Furnham et al. (2009) showed Narcissism positively and Obsessive-Compulsiveness negatively related to creativity. Furnham et al. (2013) had similar findings.

There have been a few studies on the relationship between creativity and all the PDs (Furnham & Crump, 2014; Furnham et al., 2009). Using a measure of DT as the dependent variable, Furnham and Crump (2014) found, using a large sample, the personality disorder variables accounted for around 4–9% of the variance. Imaginative/Schizotypal and Colourful/Histrionic were best positive predictors and Diligent (OCD), Dutiful (Dependent) and Sceptical/Paranoid most negative predictors.

There is a very rich and diverse literature on the creativity of people with *bipolar disorder*. Jamison (1993) inspected autobiographical, biographical and, where available, medical records of 36 major British poets born between 1705 and 1805. They were 30 times more likely to have suffered from bipolar disorder, 10–20 times more likely to be cyclothymic, more than 20 times as likely to have been admitted to a mental asylum and at least 5 times as likely to have committed suicide, compared to the general population (Jamison, 1993, pp. 61–72). Jamison interpreted this as persuasive evidence for a relationship between mood disorders and artistic creativity.

Jamison, in *Touched with Fire*, uses a sample of 13 writers, composers and artists born between 1709 (Samuel Johnson) and 1899 (Ernest Hemingway), to draw attention to figures in whom bipolar disorder and creativity are seen and to illustrate the illness's propensity to run in families (Jamison, 1993, pp. 192–237). Jamison is the most renowned figure in the field of bipolar disorder and creativity and her word often appears to be taken as definitive without objective criticism.

There are, and will remain, difficulties in the measurement of madness/insanity/mental illness and creativity of any sort. However, over the past few years there has been a dramatic increase in the quantity and quality of studies linking these two factors.

As noted earlier, academic reviewers have been highly dismissive of the mad genius hypothesis. Consider two: 'There is still no clear, convincing, scientific proof that artists do, in fact, suffer more psychological problems than any other vocational group—and probably little chance of obtaining any' (Schlesinger, 2009, p. 69). 'It is also impossible to build a study's scientific foundation on small, specialized samples, weak and inconsistent methodologies, and a lopsided dependence on subjective and anecdotal sources. The common use of self-selected volunteers is also problematic given that anyone who volunteers for a mood disorders or creativity study may well have personal concerns and experience in that area' (Schlesinger, 2009, p. 70).

All this work would suggest that one way to measure creativity is through measures of very particular syndromes like particular personality disorders.

6.4.4.3 Intelligence

In an early and celebrated study Getzels and Jackson (1962) administered five 'creativity' measures to approximately 500 schoolchildren which were then correlated with IQ test results. The main aim of the studies was to identify two types of students and examine the differences between them. The first group were those children who had high IQ scores and low creativity scores (the High-IQ group). The second group were children who had obtained low scores on the IQ tests, but high scores on the 'creativity' test (the High-C group).

Batey and Furnham (2006) point out five important features of this study. First, the mean IQ of the students tested was 132. Second, the authors wished to compare high IQ with high creativity. This meant that those children who scored high or low on both tests were excluded from the final analysis. Third, the authors did not report many of the inter-correlations between measures. Fourth, the tests were administered in a classroom setting in a manner similar to the administration of IQ tests. Fifth, the 'creativity' tests could not be said to measure creativity per se, but DT.

Torrance (1967), one of the most celebrated creativity researchers, conducted a meta-analysis of 388 correlations between intelligence measures and the Torrance Tests of Creative Thinking. He found a median correlation between the verbal DT tests and IQ on the order of $r = .21$, and a median correlation of $r = .06$ for the figural DT tests. Guilford (1967) reported average correlations of $r = .22$ for verbal DT tests; $r = .40$ for symbolic DT tests; and $r = .37$ for semantic DT tests with measures of IQ.

Batey and Furnham (2006) believe these results are not surprising; Guilford (1967) originally designed the tests of DT as measures of a subset of intelligence. Therefore, correlations between DT and IQ in the order of $r = .20$ to .40 are to be expected, irrespective of either concept used. Batey and Furnham (2006) noted that one of the principal problems with research into the relationship between creativity and intelligence has been the confusion and variability over the choice of a criterion for creativity. The experiments conducted using DT tests as a measure of creativity (Getzels & Jackson, 1962; Guilford, 1967; Torrance, 1967; Wallach & Kogan, 1965) have been criticised (Amabile, 1996; Lubart, 2001). Critics have suggested that DT tests measure aspects of creative intelligence, and as such they cannot also be a measure of creativity. This is especially true if it is argued that creativity involves the production of socially valuable products.

The failure to clearly differentiate between intelligence, creative thinking skills and creative achievement made the vast bulk of the psychometric investigations of creativity problematic. Nevertheless, it does seem that intelligence at say 1 to 2 standard deviations above the norm is a necessary (but not sufficient requirement) for being really creative.

6.4.5 Creative Process

Attempts to describe the creative process have examined the cognitive mechanisms that characterise creative thinking; thus, their goal is to explain the general process of creative thinking in all individuals alike, rather than profiling more and less creative people. In that sense, the process approach to creativity is within-person and more concerned with actual creativity than creative or non-creative people.

A wide range of studies suggested that creative processes are initiated and by particular attentional patterns that have been describe in terms of reduced fostered filtering of stimuli, lower latent inhibition or over-inclusive thinking. Thus, Wallach (1970) argued that defocussed attention is beneficial for creativity as it equips individuals with a wider range of sensory stimuli that serve as raw materials for the production of creative ideas. In line with this, studies have indicated that broader attention occurs more in the absence of pressure (e.g. threat of evaluation), which likely leads individuals to divide attentional resources between task-relevant and task-irrelevant stimuli (Smith et al., 1990).

The idea that lower perceptual or attentional censorship is beneficial for creative processes is also consistent with the lack of ideational or cognitive censorship that characterises the technique of brainstorming, whereby individuals say everything that comes to their mind about a certain topic (without censoring any ideas) in an attempt to postpone judgement in order to increase fluency of responses and originality (Chamorro-Premuzic, 2007).

Other process-centred studies on creativity reported a negative correlation between previous knowledge (which may restrict and eliminate potentially original ideas) and creative performance (Hayes, 1978; Simon & Chase, 1973). In that sense, expertise can have deleterious effects on creative thinking because it reduces flexibility. Indeed, in brainstorming sessions the perceived expertise level of other people the group/session can inhibit individuals' creativity: Collaros and Anderson (1969) found that subjects felt more inhibited if they were told that the other people in the brainstorming group were experts, and that originality and practicality varied according to the degree of perceived inhibition.

There is an extensive literature showing that the creative process is also fostered by intrinsic rather than extrinsic levels of motivation. Thus, creative ideas are more easily generated if one is interested in the task per se rather than the potential rewards or punishments (carrots or sticks!) associated with completing or not completing the task, respectively. This is arguably because intrinsic motivation is a marker of a person's orientation or level of enthusiasm for the activity (Amabile, 1990). As noted by Csikszentmihalyi (1988, p. 337), 'For no matter how original one might be, if one is bored by the domain, it will be difficult to become interested enough in it to make a creative contribution.' Conversely, if people are performing creative tasks simply for a salary, promotion or social recognition, creative thinking is likely to be constrained by others' evaluations (Amabile, 1990).

The most comprehensive model to date for understanding the creative process is Amabile's (1990, 1997) *Componential Model of Organizational Innovation* which identifies three intra-individual variables, namely domain-relevant knowledge, creativity-relevant skills, and motivational orientation, that explain the creative process. Moreover, Amabile's model also conceptualises the environmental characteristics (e.g. of the organisation or company) that facilitate creativity-related processes in an individual, namely organisational motivation to innovate, environmental resources and management practices. Thus, creative processes will not only depend on a combination of intraindividual cognitive processes (from motivation to knowledge), but also adequate environmental stimuli, as discussed in the forthcoming section.

6.4.6 Creative Work Environments: The Press Approach to Creativity

The press approach to creativity looks at the relationship between individuals as creators and their environments. It therefore deals with the contextual or situational determinants of creativity, including the effect of other people or group on an individual's creativity.

Thus, creative environment may predispose an individual to be more creative, accounting for intra- rather than inter-individual differences in creativity. For instance, 'freedom, autonomy, good role models and resource encouragement specifically for originality, [and] freedom from criticism' (Runco, 2004, p. 662) are all contextual factors that can be expected to boost creative production and facilitate creative thinking. Conversely, organisations that frequently downsize increase employee 'perceived job insecurity' which in turn hinders creativity (Probst et al., 2007).

Contextual determinants of creativity include the effect and role of leadership and leadership style on group and individual performance. Studies have shown that groups with participatory leaders tend to be superior at least in the fluency of ideas or quantity of creative output, whereas groups under supervisory leaders tend to produce better-quality creative ideas (Anderson & Fielder, 1964). A more recent study showed that in the presence of creative co-workers, supervision had a detrimental effect on group-member creativity, particularly for employees with less-creative personalities (Zhou, 2003). However, leadership styles that contribute to increasing subordinate self-efficacy tend to raise individual and group creativity (Mumford et al., 1993). It has also been pointed out that individuals prefer organisational values that promote creativity as they tend to encourage uniqueness and originality, especially if people are instructed to be creative (Goncalo & Staw, 2006).

6.4.7 Creative Products

The product approach to creativity studies the characteristics of creative.

Outcomes or products consist of artworks (e.g. paintings, designs and sculptures) and scientific publications (e.g. theories, experiments and discoveries), and indeed creative task performance at work. Accordingly, the approach is largely concerned with productivity and achievement, and focuses on individuals' creations, rather than their personalities or the processes facilitating creative production (Simonton, 2004). This line of research is closely related to the study of creative genius and psychopathology and has often implied that 'there is a thin line between genius and insanity'. Indeed, 'there is a long "Western" tradition from Plato to Freud that has tended to regard creative products as being "divergent, impulsive and messy"' (De Bono, 1992, p. 2).

However, a closer examination of the literature shows a relatively inconsistent pattern of results on the relationship between creativity measures and diverse indicators of abnormal behaviour. Moreover, it is important to distinguish between creativity and psychopathology: whilst a creative product may – at least in a metaphorical sense – be regarded a symptom of creativity, the psychopathological conception of symptoms refer to the expression of unbearable, painful and uncontrollable psychological or physical outcomes Thus, creative individuals may have every intention to produce original associations, whilst psychotic individuals may have little alternative and control over their original, unusual or eccentric ideas. Accordingly, Barron referred to creativity in terms of 'controlled weirdness'. Mental patients on the other hand may not even be aware of the creative nature of their ideas (Merten & Fischer, 1999, p. 941).

6.4.8 Assessing and Measuring Creativity

Despite the potential conceptual usefulness of the above-reviewed approaches for defining and understanding creativity, psychological research in this area can only have applied or practical implications, particularly for personnel election, if it provides robust psychometric information on how to assess and measure creativity. Indeed, psychometric research has explored the question of how to capture individual differences in creativity and some of the salient methods and tests are discussed in this section.

Batey (2012) helpfully created a 3 × 4 table that suggested 12 different ways of assessing creativity (see Table 6.11).

Table 6.11 *Potential objective, self-rated and other-rated measures of individual creativity*

Measurement	Level	Facet	Potential measure
Objective	Individual	Trait	Divergent thinking test scored for fluency
Objective	Individual	Process	Time spent considering the solution to a problem
Objective	Individual	Press	Level of noise in room during creation
Objective	Individual	Product	Number of patents awarded
Self-rated	Individual	Trait	Self-rating of perceived personal creativity
Self-rated	Individual	Process	Self-rating of the extent to which the individual perceives they combine diverse ideas
Self-rated	Individual	Press	Self-rating of perceived threat of evaluation in the environment
Self-rated	Individual	Product	Self-rating the creativity of a product
Other-rated	Individual	Trait	Expert rating of the creativity of an individual
Other-rated	Individual	Process	Expert rating of the amount of time the individual spends problem-solving
Other-rated	Individual	Press	Expert rating of the suitability of an environment for creativity
Other-rated	Individual	Product	Expert rating of the creativity of a product produced by an individual

6.4.8.1   Self-Report Measures

Over the years a number of tests have been developed and evaluated (Silvia et al., 2019).

The **Creative Behaviour Inventory (CBI)** was developed by Hocevar (1979) who generated an item pool by asking college students to list their most creative achievements and behaviours in several domains. Experts then rated each item in the pool, leading to a 90-item scale that measured creative behaviour in fine arts, crafts, literature, math-science, performing arts and music. The original CBI has been used in several past studies. There is also a shortened form developed by Dollinger (2003). Dollinger's short form didn't simply abbreviate the original inventory: the new scale shifted the underlying construct. According to Silvia et al. (2012) the short form should be considered a measure of everyday creativity, whereas the long form covers both everyday creativity and eminent creative achievement.

The **Biographical Inventory of Creative Behaviours** (BICB; Batey, 2007) is a 34-item scale that assesses everyday creativity across a broad range of domains. The BICB uses a forced-choice yes/no response format. The scale's instructions ask people to indicate which activities they have been actively involved in during the past 12 months. The 34 activities are listed, and people simply check the ones that they have been actively involved in. Some examples are: 'Written a short story', 'Drawn a cartoon', 'Made someone a present'.

Smith and colleagues administered the biographical inventory to a group of petroleum research scientists employed in a research lab of Standard SD and reported adequate discriminant validity for the measure (Smith et al., 1961). McDermid (1965) investigated peer- and self-ratings of creativity (of engineers and technicians) and concluded that self-reports and biographical data, especially related to creative interests and achievements, are effective predictors of creative performance in real-life situations. However, Tucker et al. (1967) found low convergence between self- and other-ratings of creativity in pharmaceutical employees. Jones collected self-report data from managers and industrial scientists and found that performance and self-reports correlated up to .67, corrected for bias (Jones, 1964). Likewise, Datta (1964a) reported a correlation of .31 between Remote Associates Test scores and supervisory ratings of creativity in a sample of US engineers.

The **Creative Achievement Questionnaire** (CAQ; Carson et al., 2005) measures creative accomplishments in 10 domains: visual arts, music, dance, architectural design, creative writing, humour, inventions, scientific discovery, theatre and film and culinary arts. It focuses on significant, observable accomplishments and has an innovative and complex scoring approach.

The **Creativity Domain Questionnaire** (CDQ) measures people's beliefs about their level of creativity in different domains and focuses on people's self-concepts. Participants are asked 'How creative would you rate yourself in ... [acting/ computers/ dancing/ leadership/ writing]'. It originated in a work by Kaufman and Baer (2004), which explored the structure and correlates of self-rated creativity. They developed a brief 11-item scale, known as the Creativity Scale for Different Domains (CSDD). Respondents were asked to rate their creativity in different areas – for example, 'How creative are you in bodily/physical movement (for example, dance, sports, etc.)?' – using a five-point scale (1 Not at all, 5 Extremely). Ten items referred to different domains of creativity; the final item asked people to give a global rating of their creativity.

Kaufman's (2012) **Domain-Specific Creativity Scale** (Kaufman, 2012; Kaufman et al., 2019), K-DOCS, is a 50-item self-report measure assessing five domains: (a) everyday, (b) scholarly, (c) performance, (d) science and (e) art. The instructions ask,

Compared to people of approximately your age and life experience, how creative would you rate yourself for each of the following acts? For acts that you have not specifically done, estimate your creative potential based on your performance on similar tasks.

Items were rated on a five-point scale (much less creative to much more creative). Sample items are 'Writing a non-fiction article for a newspaper, newsletter, or magazine' (scholarly) and 'Making a sculpture or piece of pottery' (artistic). Cronbach's alphas (a measure of scale reliability where between 0–1, where 1 suggests all items exactly measure the same thing) were as follows: everyday .81, scholarly .85, performance .92, science .90 and art .89.

Also see Table 6.12.

Table 6.12 *Runco Ideational Behaviour Scale*

The following questions are designed to increase understanding of how you approach ideas and problem-solving. There are no right or wrong answers.

In the past 12 months have you...

1 Written a short story
2 Written a novel
3 Organised an event, show, performance or activity
4 Produced a TV/play script
5 Designed and produced a textile product (e.g. made an item of clothing or household object)
6 Redesigned and redecorated a bedroom, kitchen, personal space, etc.
7 Invented and made a product that can be used

Self-ratings have been shown to be surprisingly valid (Martinsen et al., 2019). As Silvia et al. (2012) commented:

> Creativity research has had many reviews of creativity assessment over the years, and they often end on a grim note ... Many creativity researchers, in our experience, share this glum sense of the field's assessment tools ... Based on past research, our scale-specific analyses, and our analyses of how the scales converge, we think that this group of scales offers good choices for researchers interested in simple self-report measures of creative behavior, achievement, and self-perception.
>
> *(p. 14)*

6.4.8.2 *Divergent Thinking*

Tests of DT represent the most widely employed measures of creativity and have been reported to be good predictors of creative achievement across a variety of settings (Barron & Harrington, 1981; Harrington, 1972), and at all levels of education. Whilst they are very popular and appealing, there still remains controversy as to how the tests are scored (Reiter-Palmon et al., 2019).

Guilford (1967), one of the pioneers in the assessment of creativity, proposed a comprehensive, multidimensional model of intelligence that encompasses more than 120 abilities. One of the core intellectual operations described by Guilford (1967) was DT production, which refers to an individual's production of multiple solutions to problems, rather than the identification of a single, correct response. Unlike convergent thinking, divergent thinking, by definition, cannot be measured by multiple-choice items as objective scoring is not possible unless a predefined correct response is known. However, Guilford (1975) provided four scoring criteria to measure performance differences, namely *flexibility, fluency, originality* and *elaboration*, which would set the foundation for later creativity tests. For example, the alternative or 'unusual uses' test requires individuals to provide 'as many uses as possible' for different objects (paperclip, brick, pen, etc.). Test-takers can be compared on the basis of how many responses they provide (regardless of whether they are original or appropriate fluency), on how different or flexible their response are from each other, how detailed they are (elaboration) and, finally, how unique or original each answer is in comparison to the rest of the sample tested, or population in the case of having normative data.

Divergent thinking is the opposite of convergent thinking. Most popular are the DT tests for Guilford (reviewed in 1967), Wallach and Kogan (1965) and Torrance's Tests of Creative Thinking. There is a figural test by Finke et al. (1992) that could be used. Participants can actually produce something, which is then rated.

There are two major variants – *figural* (produces ideas in picture format) and *verbal* (producing ideas in word form). The verbal test is easiest to administer and score. Furthermore, only the verbal dimension has been found to predict real-life creative achievement (Plucker, 1999).

Typically, the DT tests are administered for approximately 1–3 minutes per item. They may be scored for fluency, originality and sometimes for flexibility and elaboration.

Guilford's (1967) Consequences test is well known. Participants list all the consequences they can think of for an unlikely event occurring: people no longer need to sleep; everybody wakes up to find they are twice as tall; everybody is deaf/blind; everybody is colour blind.

Other include: *Plot Titles* – participants write clever plot titles for a given short story; *Alternate Uses* – participants write as many alternate uses as they can for an everyday object like brick, wooden pencil, paper clip, wire coat-hanger, etc.

Wallach and Kogan's (1965) measures have three verbal measures: *Instances* – participants list as many things as possible that make a noise, move on wheels, etc.; *Alternate uses* – same as for Guilford and *Similarities* – list all the similarities that you can think of between a dog and a cat.

The best-known and most widely validated battery of DT is the Torrance Tests of Creativity and Thinking (TICT; Torrance, 1974), which measure divergent production of semantic units, e.g. 'Name all the things you can think of that are red and edible; Alternative relation, e.g. 'In what different ways are dogs and cats related?' and Production of systems, e.g. 'Write as many sentences as you can using the words "rain", "station" and "summer"'. Torrance reported that intelligence and creativity were only moderately associated, such that 'no matter what measurement of IQ is chosen, we would exclude about 70% of our most creative children if IQ alone were used in identifying giftedness' (Torrance, 1963). These findings are important because they highlight the need to include actual creativity measurement to test creativity (rather than a battery of personality and convergent thinking tests).

The Torrance tests have many variants over the years from 1966 to 2008. These tests are similar to other DT tests, but have more sophisticated (complicated) scoring procedures.

There are figural and verbal tests. Both variants have an A and parallel B form.

Figural: Picture construction – participant uses a basic shape and expands it into a picture; Picture completion – participant finishes simple drawings and provides a title; Lines (form A)/Circle (form B) – participant modifies as many simple stimulus figures of a circle/pair of lines.

Verbal: Asking – participant asks as many questions as possible about the picture; Guessing causes – participants list possible causes for the picture; Guessing consequences – participants list possible consequences for the picture.

The last four tests are self-contained: Product improvement – participants make changes to improve a toy; Unusual uses – same as other variants; Unusual questions – participants ask as many questions as possible about an ordinary item (e.g. cardboard box), much the same as the consequences test.

The scoring and norming of these tests is detailed and time consuming. Extensive norms are available from the test publishers.

Problem-solving/finding scenarios by Chand and Runco (1993) and Runco et al. (2006) can be used. For example: 'It's a great day for sailing, and your friend Kelly, asks you if you want to go sailing. Unfortunately, you have a big project due tomorrow, and it requires a full day to complete. You would rather be sailing. What are you going to do? Think of as many ideas as you can.'

Another widely used measure of creativity is Mednick and Mednick's (1967) **Remote Associate Test**. Like traditional GMA tests, this 30-item psychometric test includes items with correct responses rather than open-ended questions. Mednicks' idea was that remote or unusual association would be indicative of an individual's capacity for generating novel ideas; remote combination are generally more original. For example, participants may be asked to identify a fourth word that is associated with each of the following triad of words:

(a) rat-blue-cottage-???
(b) railroad-girl-class-???
(c) surprise-line-birthday-???
(d) wheel-electric-high-???
(e) out-dog-call-???

Although the answers are less objective than standard IQ test items, Mednick and Andrews (1967) found correlations of $r = .55$ between IQ and a Remote Associate Test.

6.4.8.3   Consensual Assessment Technique (Amabile, 1982, 1996; Hennessey & Amabile, 1988)

The consensual assessment technique (CAT) was developed by Amabile (1982) on the basis of an operational definition of creativity. Assessment relies on a consensus of independent expert judges. Amabile conducted more than 30 investigations using the CAT and showed that the CAT is a reliable method for assessing creativity in children and adults (e.g., Amabile & Gitomer, 1984; Hennessey & Amabile, 1988). The CAT is described here based on Hennessey and Amabile (1988b).

There are three important assumptions made in applying the CAT. First, it is not known what objective features a product will have for the product to be evaluated as creative. If the objective features are already known to us, the product with these features will not be considered as creative, because it is not new. Thus, no criteria are given to expert judges in the CAT: Second, creativity is something that expert judges can recognise and often agree on without being given any definition or criteria. And third, there are varying degrees of creativity; some are more or less creative than others. Hennessey and Amabile (1988b, p. 15) suggest the following procedure to use the CAT.

Participants are asked to complete some task in a specific domain (such as poetry), and then experts in that domain (such as poets) independently rate the creativity of the products. The level of inter-judge agreement is assessed, and if it is acceptable (generally above .70) the results are considered valid.

Several requirements need to be met in applying the CAT, and three of them are important to mention. First, the judges are experts in their relevant domain and have implicit criteria of creativity. Second, the judges assess independently, without any further instructions from the researcher. The integrity of the CAT is described as depending on 'agreement being reached without attempts by the experimenter to impose particular criteria or attempts by the judges to influence each other' (Hennessey & Amabile, 1988b, p. 16). And third, before exercising the CAT, a preliminary assessment regarding technical goodness and aesthetic appeal of a product will provide useful information. While the CAT extracts judges' subjective opinions, the preliminary assessment can be done objectively by judges, or at least less subjectively. Therefore, it is suggested that, if both assessments can be done by judges, they should be compared to see if they are related to or independent from each other.

Several studies by Amabile and others (e.g. Amabile & Gitomer, 1984; Hennessey & Amabile, 1988a) have shown that the CAT could be used reliably in assessing creativity in visual arts (e.g. collages) and writing (e.g. stories).

6.4.8.4   Power/Performance Measures (Measures of Thinking/Output)

There are many tests of this type which are scored in a high-low, correct-incorrect way, which is done in all power tests.

Meanings of Words Each of the 10 words below has more than one meaning. Write down as many meanings for each word as you can.

Bit   Pink
Bolt   Pitch
Duck   Port
Fair   Sack
Fast   Tender

The Barron-Welsh Art Scale (Barron & Welsh, 1952). This scale consists of 86 different black and white pictures arranged and numbered to 8 pictures per page. Participants are instructed to make quick, instinctive, dichotomous judgements about whether they like/dislike each picture. They fill an L for like or a D for dislike for the number corresponding to the picture they are judging on the answer sheet provided. This test requires no language skills, can be used on children and adults, is simple and does not require extensive concentration.

Test for Creative Thinking-Drawing Production (TCT-DP; Urban & Jellen, 1995). It is applicable to a wide variety of age and ability groups. As opposed to traditional DT tests, it encompasses a more convergent conception of creativity (Urban, 2005). It has been acknowledged as culture and gender fair/sensitive (Jellen & Urban, 1988). The evaluation is based on different criteria: continuations; completion; new elements; connections with a line; connections with a theme; boundary braking, fragment-dependent; boundary braking, fragment-independent; perspective; humour and affectivity; four kinds of unconventionality; and speed (Urban, 2005).

There have been some interesting innovations in creativity testing, notably by Sternberg and colleagues. For example, Sternberg's (1982) adaptation of the Goodman (1955) induction riddle requires participants to manipulate imaginary concepts such as 'bleen' (blue until 2004, but green after that year), or 'grue' (green until the year 2004, and blue after that). In a similar fashion, Sternberg and Gastel (1989) designed a test that requires individuals to evaluate logically valid, but factually false, statements, such as 'lions can fly'. Assuming that these items are useful to test individuals' flexibility, Sternberg's tests of induction are measuring an important component of creativity. Indeed, moderate correlations between these measures and fluid ability tests may be indicative of the discriminant validity of Sternberg's tests. Whether these tests measure creativity, flexibility or something else is a matter of interpretation, though.

6.4.9 Summary and Conclusions

Rapid technological advances are creating an increasingly complex world where adaptation to changing environments is crucial. This cultural, as opposed to biological, evolution demands more flexibility from individuals than ever before. Given that creativity contributes to greater flexibility, creative individuals may be more prepared to adapt to the changes in everyday life and remain flexible in their responses to the environment. Thus 'creativity is a useful and effective response to evolutionary changes ... because older adults tend to rely on routines and, unless intentionally creative, become inflexible' (Runco, 2004, p. 658). This may explain why several studies found creativity indicators to be significantly correlated with late-life adaptation and growth.

Yet creativity research remains of much less interest to differential psychologists and test developers compared to personality and intelligence tests.

Snyder et al. (2019, p. 142) made four recommendations for future research in the area: First, use creativity as a contributor variable. Creativity is overwhelmingly measured as an outcome variable. Increasing the measurement of creativity as a contributor or predictor would mean examining its association with psychological and educational outcomes in college students, such as academic achievement and job preparedness. Second, explore self-report measures of creativity. Third, distinguish domain and task diversity in creativity. There is evidence that creativity may be, at least in part, domain specific. Future research should examine domain specificity and type of learning tasks in more detail. Fourth, use multimethod and mixed methods to prevent overreliance on single measures of creativity.

REFERENCES

Amabile, T. A. (1996). Creativity and innovation in organizations. *Harvard Business School Press*, 396–239, 1–15.

Amabile, T. M. (1982). Social psychology of creativity: a consensual assessment technique. *Journal of Personality and Social Psychology*, 43(5), 997–1013.

Amabile, T. M. (1988). From individual creativity to organizational innovation. In K. Grønhaug, & G. Kaufmann (Eds.), *Innovation: A cross-disciplinary perspective* (pp. 139–166). Oslo, Norway: Norwegian University Press.

Amabile, T. M. (1990). Within you, without you: the social psychology of creativity, and beyond. In M. A. Runco, & R. S. Albert (Eds.), *Theories of creativity* (Vol. 115, pp. 61–91). New York City, NY: Sage Publications, Inc.

Amabile, T. M. (1997). Motivating creativity in organizations: on doing what you love and loving what you do. *California Management Review, 40*(1), 39–58.

Amabile, T. M., Conti, R., Coon, H., Lazenby, J., & Herron, M. (1996). Assessing the work environment for creativity. *Academy of Management Journal, 39*(5), 1154–1184.

Amabile, T. M., & Gitomer, J. (1984). Children's artistic creativity: effects of choice in task materials. *Personality and Social Psychology Bulletin, 10*(2), 209–215.

Anderson, L. R., & Fielder, F. E. (1964). The effect of participatory and supervisory leadership on group creativity. *Journal of Applied Psychology, 48*, 227–236.

Andriopoulos, C. (2003). Six paradoxes in managing creativity: an embracing act. *Long Range Planning, 36*(4), 375–388.

Barbot, B., Hass, R. W., & Reiter-Palmon, R. (2019). Creativity assessment in psychological research:(Re) setting the standards. *Psychology of Aesthetics, Creativity, and the Arts, 13*(2), 233.

Barron, F. (1963). The needs for order and disorder as motives in creative action. In C. W. Taylor, & F. Barron (Eds.), *Scientific creativity: Its recognition and development* (pp. 139–152). New York City, NY: John Wiley & Sons.

Barron, F., & Harrington, D. M. (1981). Creativity, intelligence, and personality. *Annual Review of Psychology, 32*(1), 439–476.

Barron, F., & Welsh, G. S. (1952). Artistic perception as a possible factor in personality style: its measurement by a figure preference test. *The Journal of Psychology, 33*(2), 199–203.

Batey, M. (2007). *A psychometric investigation of everyday creativity* (Unpublished doctoral dissertation). University College, London.

Batey, M. (2012). The measurement of creativity: from definitional consensus to the introduction of a new heuristic framework. *Creativity Research Journal, 24*(1), 55–65.

Batey, M., & Furnham, A. (2006). Creativity, intelligence, and personality: a critical review of the scattered literature. *Genetic, Social, and General Psychology Monographs, 132*(4), 355–429.

Batey, M., & Furnham, A. (2008). The relationship between measures of creativity and schizotypy. *Personality and Individual Differences, 45*(8), 816–821.

Benedek, M., Christensen, A. P., Fink, A., & Beaty, R. E. (2019). Creativity assessment in neuroscience research. *Psychology of Aesthetics, Creativity, and the Arts, 13*(2), 218–226.

Carson, S. H., Peterson, J. B., & Higgins, D. M. (2005). Reliability, validity, and factor structure of the creative achievement questionnaire. *Creativity Research Journal, 17*(1), 37–50.

Chamorro-Premuzic, T. (2007). *Personality and individual differences.* Oxford, UK: Blackwell Publishing.

Chamorro-Premuzic, T., & Furnham, A. (2005). *Personality and intellectual competence.* Mahwah, NJ: Erlbaum.

Chand, I., & Runco, M. A. (1993). Problem finding skills as components in the creative process. *Personality and Individual Differences, 14*(1), 155–162.

Collaros, P. A., & Anderson, L. R. (1969). Effect of perceived expertness upon creativity of members of brainstorming groups. *Journal of Applied Psychology, 53*(2), 159–163.

Csikszentmihalyi, M. (1988). Society, culture, and person: a systems view of creativity. In R. J. Sternberg (Ed.), *The nature of creativity: Contemporary psychological perspectives* (pp. 325–339). New York City, NY: Cambridge University Press.

Datta, L. E. (1964a). Remote associates test as a predictor of creativity in engineers. *Journal of Applied Psychology, 48*(3), 183.

De Bono, E. (1992). *Serious creativity: Using the power of lateral thinking to create new ideas.* London, UK: Harper Collins.

Dollinger, S. J. (2003). Need for uniqueness, need for cognition, and creativity. *The Journal of Creative Behavior, 37*(2), 99–116.

Eysenck, H. J. (1994). Creativity and personality: word association, origence, and psychoticism. *Creativity Research Journal, 7*(2), 209–216.

Eysenck, H. J. (1995). *Genius: The natural history of creativity* (Vol. 12). New York City, NY: Cambridge University Press.

Feist, G. J. (1998). A meta-analysis of personality in scientific and artistic creativity. *Personality and Social Psychology Review, 2*(4), 290–309.

Finke, R. A., Ward, T. B., & Smith, S. M. (1992). *Creative cognition: Theory, research, and applications.* Cambridge, MA: The MIT Press.

Furnham, A. (2018). From fascination to research progress and problems in creativity research. In R. J. Sternberg, & J. C. Kaufman (Eds.), *The nature of human creativity* (pp. 77–93). Cambridge, UK: Cambridge University Press.

Furnham, A. (2019). Creativity and psychopathology. In M. A. Runco & R. S. Pritzker (Eds.), *Encyclopedia of creativity* (3rd ed.). New York City, NY: Elsevier.

Furnham, A., Crump, J., Batey, M., & Chamorro-Premuzic, T. (2009). Personality and ability predictors of the 'Consequences' Test of divergent thinking in a large non-student sample. *Personality and Individual Differences, 46*(4), 536–540.

Getzels, J. W., & Jackson, P. W. (1962). *Creativity and intelligence: Explorations with gifted students.* Oxford, England: John Wiley & Sons.

Goncalo, J. A. & Staw, B. M. (2006). Individualism-collectivism and group creativity. *Organizational Behavior and Human Decision Processes, 100*(1), 96–109.

Goodman, N. (1955). *Fact, fiction and forecast* (pp. 72–83). Cambridge, MA: Harvard University Press.

Guilford, J. P. (1950). Creativity. *American Psychologist, 5*, 444–454.

Guilford, J. P. (1967). *The nature of human intelligence.* New York City, NY: McGraw-Hill Publishing.

Guilford, J. P. (1975). Creativity: A quarter century of progress. In I. A. Taylor, & J. W. Getzels (Eds.), *Perspectives in creativity* (pp. 37–59). Chicago, IL: Aldine Publishing Company.

Haller, C. S., & Courvoisier, D. S. (2010). Personality and thinking style in different creative domains. *Psychology of Aesthetics, Creativity, and the Arts, 4*(3), 149.

Harrington, D. M. (1972). *Effects of instructions to 'Be creative' on three tests of divergent thinking abilities* (PhD thesis). University of California Berkeley.

Hartley, J., & Beasley, N. (1969). Contrary imaginations at Keele. *Higher Education Quarterly, 23*(4), 467–471.

Hartley, J., & Greggs, M. A. (1997). Divergent thinking in arts and science students: contrary Imaginations at Keele revisited. *Studies in Higher Education, 22*(1), 93–97.

Hayes, J. R. (1978). *Cognitive psychology.* Homewood, IL: Dorsey Press.

Hennessey, B. A., & Amabile, T. M. (1988). The conditions of creativity. In R. J. Steinberg (Ed.), *The nature of creativity* (pp. 11–38). Cambridge, UK: Cambridge University Press.

Hocevar, D. (1979, April). The development of the Creative Behavior Inventory. Paper presented at the annual meeting of the Rocky Mountain Psychological Association. (ERIC Document Reproduction Service No. ED170350).

Hocevar, D. (1980). Intelligence, divergent thinking, and creativity. *Intelligence, 4*(1), 25–40.

Hudson, L. (1966). *Contrary imaginations: A psychological study of the young student.* New York City, NY: Schocken Books.

Hudson, L. (1973). *Originality.* London, UK: Oxford University Press.

Hudson, L. (1980). This week citation classic. *Social Citation, 43*, 171–172.

Jamison, K. R. (1993). *Touched with fire: Manic depressive illness and the artistic temperament.* New York City, NY: Free Press.

Jellen, H. G., & Urban, K. K. (1988). Test your observational skills and compare your creative potential with children from eleven different countries. *Creative Child and Adult Quarterly, 13*(2), 75–80.

Jones, F. E. (1964). Predictor variables for creativity in industrial science. *Journal of Applied Psychology, 48*(2), 134–136.

Kaufman, J. C. (2012). Counting the muses: development of the Kaufman domains of creativity scale (K-DOCS). *Psychology of Aesthetics, Creativity, and the Arts*, 6(4), 298.

Kaufman, J. C. (2019). Self-assessments of creativity: not ideal, but better than you think. *Psychology of Aesthetics, Creativity, and the Arts*, 13(2), 187–192.

Kaufman, J. C., & Baer, J. (2004). Sure, I'm creative – but not in mathematics!: self-reported creativity in diverse domains. *Empirical Studies of the Arts*, 22(2), 143–155.

Kaufman, J. C., Pumaccahua, T. T., & Holt, R. E. (2013). Personality and creativity in realistic, investigative, artistic, social, and enterprising college majors. *Personality and Individual Differences*, 54(8), 913–917.

Kinsbourne, M. (1968). The contrary imaginations of arts and science students: a critical discussion. *Developmental Medicine & Child Neurology*, 10(4), 461–464.

Kwapil, T. R., Brown, L. H., Silvia, P. J., Myin-Germeys, I., & Barrantes-Vidal, N. (2012). The expression of positive and negative schizotypy in daily life: an experience sampling study. *Psychological Medicine*, 42(12), 2555–2566.

Lubart, T. I. (2001). Models of the creative process: past, present and future. *Creativity Research Journal*, 13(4), 295–308.

Martinsen, Ø. L., Arnulf, J. K., Furnham, A., & Lang-Ree, O. C. (2019). Narcissism and creativity. *Personality and Individual Differences*, 142, 166–171.

Matthews, G. & Deary, I. J. (1998). *Personality traits*. Cambridge, UK: Cambridge University Press.

McDermid, C. D. (1965). Some correlates of creativity in engineering personnel. *Journal of Applied Psychology*, 49(1), 14–19.

Mednick, M. T., & Andrews, F. M. (1967). Creative thinking and level of intelligence. *Journal of Creative Behavior*, 1, 428–431.

Mednick, S. A., & Mednick, M. T. S. (1967). *Examiner's manual: Remote associates test*. Boston, MA: Houghton Mifflin Harcourt.

Merten, T. & Fischer, I. (1999). Creativity, personality and word association responses: associative behavior in 40 supposedly creative persons. *Personality and Individual Differences*, 27, 933–942.

Mumford, M. D., Gessner, T. L., Connelly, M. S., O'Connor, J. A., & Clifton, T. C. (1993). Leadership and destructive acts: individual and situational influences. *The Leadership Quarterly*, 4(2), 115–147.

O'Reilly, T., Dunbar, R., & Bentall, R. (2001). Schizotypy and creativity: an evolutionary connection?. *Personality and Individual Differences*, 31(7), 1067–1078.

Peretti, F., & Negro, G. (2007). Mixing genres and matching people: a study in innovation and team composition in Hollywood. *Journal of Organizational Behaviour, special issue: Paradoxes of Creativity: Managerial and Organizational Challenges in the Cultural Economy, 28*(5), 563–586.

Peterson, J. B., & Carson, S. (2000). Latent inhibition and openness to experience in a high-achieving student population. *Personality and Individual Differences, 28*(2), 323–332.

Plucker, J. A. (1999). Is the proof in the pudding? Reanalyses of Torrance's (1958 to present) longitudinal data. *Creativity Research Journal, 12*(2), 103–114.

Plucker, J. A., Runco, M. A., & Lim, W. (2006). Predicting ideational behavior from divergent thinking and discretionary time on task. *Creativity Research Journal, 18*(1), 55–63.

Porter, M. E. (1990). The competitive advantage of nations. *Harvard Business Review, 68*(2), 73–93.

Probst, T. M., Stewart, S. M., Gruys, M. L., & Tierney, B. W. (2007). Productivity, counterproductivity and creativity: the ups and downs of job in security. *Journal of Occupational and Organizational Psychology, 80*(3), 479–497.

Reiter-Palmon, R., Forthmann, B., & Barbot, B. (2019). Scoring divergent thinking tests: a review and systematic framework. *Psychology of Aesthetics, Creativity, and the Arts, 13*(2), 144–152.

Rhodes, M. (1987). An analysis of creativity. In S. G. Isaksen (Ed.), *Frontiers of creativity research: Beyond the basics* (pp. 216–222). Buffalo, NY: Bearly.

Runco, M. A. (2004). Creativity. *Annual Review of Psychology, 55*, 657–687.

Schlesinger, J. (2009). Creative mythconceptions: a closer look at the evidence for the 'mad genius' hypothesis. *Psychology of Aesthetics, Creativity, and the Arts, 3*(2), 62–72.

Silvia, P. J., Wigert, B., Reiter-Palmon, R., & Kaufman, J. C. (2012). Assessing creativity with self-report scales: a review and empirical evaluation. *Psychology of Aesthetics, Creativity, and the Arts, 6*(1), 19–34.

Simon, H. A., & Chase, W. G.(1973). Skill in chess. *American Scientist, 61*(4), 394–403.

Simonton, D. K. (2004). *Creativity in science: Chance, logic, genius, and zeitgeist.* New York City, NY: Cambridge University Press.

Smith, K. L., Michael, W. B., & Hocevar, D. (1990). Performance on creativity measures with examination-taking instructions intended to induce high or low levels of test anxiety. *Creativity Research Journal, 3*(4), 265–280.

Smith, W. J., Albright, L. E., & Glennon, J. R. (1961). The prediction of research competence and creativity from personal history. *Journal of Applied Psychology, 45*(1), 59–62.

Snyder, H. T., Hammond, J. A., Grohman, M. G., & Katz-Buonincontro, J. (2019). Creativity measurement in undergraduate students from 1984–2013: a systematic review. *Psychology of Aesthetics, Creativity, and the Arts*, 13(2), 133–143.

Sprecher, T. B. (1959). A study of engineers' criteria for creativity. *Journal of Applied Psychology*, 43(2), 141–148.

Sternberg, R. J. (1982). Nonentrenchment in the assessment of intellectual giftedness. *Gifted Child Quarterly*, 26(2), 63–67.

Sternberg, R. J. (1985). Natural, unnatural, and supernatural concepts. *Cognitive Psychology*, 14(4), 451–488.

Sternberg, R. J., & Gastel, J. (1989). Coping with novelty in human intelligence: an empirical investigation. *Intelligence*, 13(2), 187–197.

Sternberg, R. J., & O'Hara, L. A. (2000). Intelligence and creativity. In R. J. Sternberg (Ed.), *Handbook of Intelligence* (pp. 611–630). New York City, NY: Cambridge University Press.

Torrance, E. P. (1963). Creativity. In F. W. Hubbard (Ed.), *What research says to the teacher*. Washington, DC: Department of Classroom Teachers American Educational Research Association of the National Education Association.

Torrance, E. P. (1967). The Minnesota studies of creative behavior: national and international extensions. *The Journal of Creative Behavior*, 1(2), 137–154.

Torrance, E. P. (1974). *Norms-technical manual: Torrance tests of creative thinking*. Lexington, MA: Ginn & Company Publishers.

Torrance, E. P. (1979). *The search for satori and creativity*. Buffalo, NY: Bearly.

Tucker, M. F., Cline, V. B., & Schmitt, J. R. (1967). Prediction of creativity and other performance measures from biographical information among pharmaceutical scientists. *Journal of Applied Psychology*, 51(2), 131–138.

Urban, K. K. (2005). Assessing creativity: The Test for Creative Thinking-Drawing Production (TCT-DP). *International Education Journal*, 6(2), 272–280.

Urban, K. K., & Jellen, H. G. (1995). *Test for Creative Thinking-Drawing (TSD-Z)*. Frankfurt, Germany: Swets Test Services.

Wallach, M. A. (1970). Creativity. In P. Mussen (Ed.), *Carmichael's Handbook of Child Psychology* (pp. 1211–1272). New York City, NY: John Wiley & Sons.

Wallach, M. A., & Kogan, N. (1965). A new look at the creativity-intelligence distinction. *Journal of Personality*, 33(3), 348–369.

Williamson, P. K. (2011). The creative problem solving skills of arts and science students – the two cultures debate revisited. *Thinking Skills and Creativity*, 6(1), 31–43.

Zhou, J. (2003). When the presence of creative coworkers is related to creativity: role of supervisor close monitoring, developmental feedback, and creative personality. *Journal of Applied Psychology*, 88(3), 413–422.

6.5 GAMIFICATION

What is it?

This is the use of 'games', usually but not exclusively video games, to assess people on speed, accuracy, test score and style of play.

How does it work?

Rather than use traditional methods (application form, interview, references) applicants are invited to 'play games' that supposedly provide efficient, reliable and valid data on a candidate's ability, motivation and personality. They are seen to (possibly) get a more accurate measure of actual behaviour with the candidate 'having fun' doing so.

What of the evidence?

There is more absence of evidence (of psychometric properties) than evidence of absence. It may well be that tests do yield valid data in measuring particular issues, but the predictive validity of those scores for other behaviours has not yet been established (or much tested).

Practical problems: cost, ethics, politics

At this stage, it can be very costly to purchase, or commission, assessment gamification tools. There are also ethical issues about whom you might be discriminating against (older people, those from third world countries).

Recommendations for use

Wait until more research is done to prove their validity and, as ever, beware of commercial claims. They may be, initially, more engaging and motivating for gamers, but this may quickly wear off.

6.5.1 Introduction

We know technology is a major driver in the change and development of assessment methods. For many years people have been interested to explore the idea that the way people play electronic games may provide evidence about their motives, ability and personality. We also know that certain people are addicted to gaming, sometimes called internet gaming disorder (Kircaburun et al., 2020).

Some selectors believe that the choice of a sport (team vs solo), the position in a team (attack vs defence), election to team leadership roles (captain), etc. yield useful information about an individual. That is, those who play tennis are psychologically different from those who swim, or cycle or play hockey, rugby or cricket. This may equally be true about a person's choice of other games like bridge or chess or poker, as well as electronic games.

Some games are highly intellectual; others rely more on fitness or reaction times. The question is: if we know what games you like to play and how you play them, can we get some useful information about your ability, personality and motivation?

The issues around selection in gamification are nearly always electronic or computer based. It has been argued that gamification can increase intentions to accept job offers due to increased organisational attractiveness (Collmus et al., 2016). Organisations that use gamification during their recruitment process stress their image: that they are technology focused, forward-thinking and have a good organisational culture. Gamification also helps enhance the selection process for firms by providing new tools to establish job-performance predictors such as cognitive ability, personality and person-organisation fit.

There has been growing interest in the prospective functions of games aside from entertainment, such as their instructional value (Garris et al., 2002), clinical applications (Griffiths, 1997) and how they can contribute to the understanding of cognitive capacity, plasticity and other processes (Boot, 2015).

Gamification can be defined as the use of game design elements (e.g. adaptation, assessment, conflict, challenge, immersion, rules/ goals, feedback) in non-game contexts (Deterding et al., 2011). Gamified elements in the workplace has exploded as a result of more adults playing games in their personal time. For example, in 2014 consumers in the USA spent $22.4 billion dollars on video games (Entertainment Software Association, 2015). That number may have doubled or indeed tripled. Most people know about the features of games like avatars, quests and challenges, badges, points and levels.

Games are thought of as fun and dynamic and are therefore the 'perfect tool' for motivating employees in various situations in the workplace, such as employee training (Alsawaier, 2018; Collmus et al., 2016). Gamification can also be employed during recruitment and selection of new job candidates and personality tests, making them more enjoyable to complete. The central dilemma for researchers is whether this affects test validity, while for developers and test users it is whether it is worth the development costs.

Gamified selection tests for organisations are arguably more beneficial than traditional methods of assessment due to their potential for improved criterion-related validity. Some researchers have suggested that gamified assessments such as PwC's situational judgment test are more predictive of future behaviour than simple selection questionnaires highlighting the usefulness of gamified tests (Lievens & Patterson, 2011).

Another example of how gamification potentially makes assessments more valid is that it is harder to fake or cheat (Armstrong et al., 2015). A number of researchers have shown that scores on standard, but complex, computer games are good measures of cognitive ability as measured on standardised IQ tests (Sin & Furnham, 2018). The question is: are they better than standard tests in terms of their construct and predictive validity?

During traditional assessments, individuals are often susceptible to social desirability bias and may change their responses to what they believe their employers are looking for, which does not reflect their true traits. However, in tests that are gamified and well designed, it is often difficult to identify the behaviours or traits that are being assessed, thus reducing this bias.

The advent of computer games over the past 20–30 years appears to have provided a wonderful and unique opportunity to measure all sorts of behaviour. These games have become 'very realistic' with amazing opportunities to get people immersed in all sorts of scenarios. The question is: can a person's behaviour in a game yield useful information about them in a selection or assessment situation?

There is rapidly growing trend is the use of gamification in the workplace as well as in the education sector (Attali & Arieli-Attali, 2015; Dichev & Dicheva, 2017; Fetzer et al., 2017; Kim & Shute, 2015; Landers, 2014; Mavridis & Tsiatsos, 2017; Nacke & Deterding, 2017; Rabah et al., 2018; Seaborn & Fels, 2015). Apart from cost-saving, gamification is seen to be more engaging for students and more motivational. Thus, it may be that games are more useful in teaching skills than assessing them. Yet there is insufficient evidence that, in educational settings, they have any long-term advantages over more traditional methods.

6.5.2   Evidence

There is very mixed evidence about gamification. Fiore (2016) found no support that gamification could predict individual differences, and also that candidates thought it less valid than standard techniques though there was some evidence that scores were less easy to fake.

One argument in favour of gamification is that games are very good at eliciting positive and negative emotions because they can be very engaging (Mullins & Sabherwal, 2018). We know from cognitive-emotional science that the latter can profoundly influence the former in terms of attention, memory, reasoning and thus provide a unique opportunity to assess an individual.

Whilst there is little academic research in this area, organisations have demonstrated the impact of gamification. PwC in Hungary, for example, developed Multipoly, which allows potential job candidates to virtually test their readiness for working at the firm by working in teams to solve real-world business problems (PwC, 2015). Since launching this program, the firm has reported a 190% growth in job candidates with 78% of users reporting they are interested to learn more about working at PwC, showcasing the influence of organisational attractiveness from gamification. As well as this, the successful hires with Multipoly experience also found onboarding at PwC easier, as they had already experienced firm culture through the game.

Another gamification example has been identified by Mekler et al. (2013), who have highlighted the use of points and leader boards as a popular gamified element. This has been exemplified by LinkedIn, a website that allows people to upload their online resumes. Users can endorse others on their skills, thus increasing their rating in a particular area such as leadership ability. This tool can be likened to the game-like element of score points, where the higher the score, the better.

6.5.3   Measuring Ability

Because games can yield data on information processing speed and accuracy, they have been thought of as an excellent way to measure intelligence. It has been suggested for 40 years that 'strategic games are an invariant expression of certain universal intellectual traits' (Spitz, 1978).

Ideally, these measures should be simple, robust and culturally valid. For instance, a test of proof reading has been found to be a good measure for intelligence (Furnham, 2010). Some researchers have suggested that many computer games that exist and were designed primarily as entertainments could serve as an excellent proxy for intelligence tests as they often measure the efficiency of information processing (Foroughi et al., 2016; Gnambs & Appel, 2017). People seem to respond differently when asked to play a game or take a test: there is less test anxiety, less boredom and less resistance. It is also possible that if a task is described as a game the participant may not fully engage their abilities, thus not showing their full abilities. The issue is the effect on motivation and performance when a cognitive ability task is described as a game or a test.

In a systematic attempt to understand cognition using games, researchers from the Learning Strategies Programme developed a video game that has been used as a research tool, designed to involve skills such as attention, memory and multi-tasking (Mané & Donchin, 1989). Another recent study by Sajjadi et al. (2017) provides evidence for the mapping between dimensions of Gardner's Multiple Intelligences and game mechanics, suggesting that games can be designed using empirical data to suit players with certain abilities and inclinations.

Furthermore, games have the advantage of eliciting greater engagement and intrinsic motivation to perform. Hoffman and Nadelson (2010) found that greater motivational engagement in gaming was partly influenced by more positive responses to failure, particularly in multiple-level games that become increasingly complex and challenging as the player progresses.

Quiroga et al. (2015) required participants played a Wii console game in the laboratory and completed a series of tests measuring fluid and crystallised intelligence. They reported extremely high correlations between latent factors from video games and intelligence on a range of different tests. The game used in this study was of a format largely similar to that of a test, with participants selecting the correct option on the screen in several different question categories such as 'Memorise', 'Visualise', and 'Compute'.

Foroughi et al. (2016) reported high correlation between a video game and the Ravens Progressive matrices, and between the video game and latent variable measuring fluid intelligence. They concluded that it is feasible to create measures of fluid intelligence using their test (Puzzle Creator).

To give two examples, Sin and Furnham (2018) tested over 100 military recruits. The games used in this study were (a) Taboo, a verbal reasoning game and (b) Portal, a spatial reasoning game (see Section 6.5.4). Previous empirical research using Taboo has found that working memory predicts performance in the task as it requires high mental control (Hansen & Goldinger, 2009). Taboo also tests the participants' ability to adapt to constraints and communicate effectively which is expected to be partly determined by intelligence. Portal requires the use of problem-solving, visualisation and perspective-taking skills, as mentioned in one prior study using the game. They found overall, both Portal and Taboo, performance to be significantly correlated with a measure of standardised intelligence.

Adams and Mayer (2014) found that playing Portal did not improve students' ability to learn physics content but did facilitate the development of spatial cognitive skills. While their methodology used Portal as a manipulation, the present study is concerned with performance on Portal as an outcome measure.

These are still early days. We do not know which games yield best results and the processes involved.

6.5.4 Three Examples

1. *Verbal Game – Taboo (by Hasbro)*

Taboo is an interactive verbal reasoning game, in which speakers produce clues to get their teammates to identify a target word, while refraining from using any 'taboo' words. These words are usually salient associates, creating a challenge for the speaker to circumvent the restrictions, while cueing the guesser to the right word. As performance on this game is also largely dependent on verbal ability, including vocabulary and language skills, participants in this study were limited to those with English as a first language.

To overcome the limitation of team effects, the study employed systematic rotation of teams within groups of four players. Participants were randomly assigned to groups based on the order that they were recruited, depending on the time that their medical check-up was completed. The experiment was conducted with two members in each team to eliminate competition effects between guessers. Each player described as many words as possible to their partner within one minute and cards were voided if any Taboo words were used. After all players had a turn as the speaker, the players then rotated teams such that each player had the chance to partner with every other player in the group, to minimise the effect of one partner's ability on an individual's performance. At the end of all three rounds, the scores of each player were then averaged separately for describing and guessing.

2. *Spatial Game – Portal (by Valve)*

Portal is a first-person perspective puzzle game in which players must navigate through a testing chamber to reach the exit using portals to

link locations within each test chamber. Portal requires careful observation, problem-solving and perspective-taking skills. Players user a
portal gun which links two surfaces to complete challenges and progress. Portals allow players to access areas otherwise unavailable and
the puzzles force players to think outside the box (or with one,
depending on the level). Participants completed four consecutive
stages of increasing difficulty without guidance and were instructed
to clear each stage as quickly as possible. The time taken for all four
stages was recorded at the end of stage four. For ease of analysis, the
time taken was then converted into seconds.

3. *Balloon Analogue Risk Task (BART)*

This was developed by Lejuez et al. (2002). The BART is a computer
simulation that shows participants a balloon on screen that can be
pumped up. Alongside the balloon are two buttons labelled 'Pump the
balloon' and 'Collect $$$' and two figures 'Winnings from last round'
and 'Total balance'. The 'Pump the balloon' button inflates the bal-
loon and earns the participant 1 dollar per pump. The 'Collect $$$'
button banks the cash earned in the current round and resets
the balloon.

The following instructions are typically presented to participants before they see the first balloon.

> On the next page you will see 16 balloons, one after another, on the screen.
> Each balloon can be pumped up and eventually it will burst. The balloon
> burst points are randomised. Some balloons might pop after just one pump,
> but others might not pop until they fill the whole screen. You get money for
> every pump. Each pump earns you 1 dollar. HOWEVER, if a balloon pops
> before you bank your earnings (by clicking Collect $$$) you lose the money
> earned on that balloon. After pressing 'Collect $$$' or when a balloon
> explodes you will be asked to start a new round, and a fresh balloon will
> appear. Your total money collected at the end of the game will determine
> your chances of winning a £25 Amazon voucher – if you win 100 dollars
> you will be allocated 100 tickets for the random prize draw, and the more
> tickets you have the higher your chance of winning the £25 prize. (You will

be asked to provide your email address in order to contact you if you win – please note your email address will not be associated with your responses and will be kept confidential.) Press the button below to continue.

The balloons in the BART are randomly set to explode between 1 and 128 pumps. If a balloon explodes, an animation will be shown on screen with an explosion sound effect and any money earned that round will be lost. Following this, a new balloon will appear on screen. No detailed information was given about the probability of a balloon exploding. Dollars were used instead of Sterling denominations (£) to remind participants that they would not be receiving the cash amount at the end of the game. The objective was for participants to collect the greatest amount of money possible as this would give them more raffle tickets and thereby increase their chances of winning the £25 voucher.

Each participant sees 16 balloons (but this can range from any number – studies have used 10 balloons, but the original study suggests 30 balloons) and they were set to explode on a variable ratio of 64 pumps. This level is the break-even point for the task so additional pumps up to 64 pumps provided greater reward than risk but any additional pumps after 64 pumps had greater risk than reward. The aim of this task is to model real-world risk-taking situations in which excessive risk (over 64 pumps) produces diminishing returns (i.e. more chance of an explosion and losing your money). For example, after the first pump the temporary bank has $1 and the second pump would result in a 100% increase in the temporary bank or a loss of $1. However, after the 62nd pump the temporary bank would hold $62 so the 63rd pump would result in a 1.6% increase in the temporary bank but would risk the $62 already accrued.

The following information is recorded for each participant: the total banked amount, the number of pumps for each round of balloon and whether the balloon exploded on that round. From this data the adjusted risk-taking score can be calculated, which is the average number of pumps for the balloons that did not explode. The adjusted risk-taking score is preferred because the rounds in which the balloon exploded create a ceiling for the number of pumps for that round. Additionally, the number of balloon explosions can be used as a variable to indicate more excessive risk-taking behaviour.

A number of studies have utilised the BART; it has been found to have adequate test-retest reliability (White et al., 2008) and is predictive of real-world risk-taking behaviour, such as smoking (Lejuez et al., 2003) and drug use (Hopko et al., 2006). Perhaps the greatest issue with the BART is that it does not correlate very highly with a person's personal responses about their risk taking or that of those that know them.

6.5.5 Conclusion

This is a rapidly developing area of research (Ángeles Quiroga et al., 2015; Attali & Arieli-Attali, 2015; Dichev & Dicheva, 2017; Fetzer et al., 2017; Fiore, 2016; Foroughi et al., 2016; Furnham, 2010; Gnambs & Appel, 2017; Hoffman & Nadelson, 2010; Kim & Shute, 2015; Landers, 2014; Mané & Donchin, 1989; Mavridis & Tsiatsos, 2017; Mekler et al., 2013; Mullins & Sabherwal, 2018; Nacke & Deterding, 2017; PricewaterhouseCoopers, 2015; Rabah et al., 2018; Sajjadi et al., 2017; Seaborn & Fels, 2015).

We have seen before that technology often drives assessment. Over the past 20 years in particular, there has been an explosion in the development and marketing of electronic games for pleasure and enjoyment. The assessment industry has noticed, however, that they can be used, and indeed designed, to assess individual differences. There is therefore a gamification industry designed to assess using games. The research literature lags behind however, and it remains unclear whether the data they generate for investment are as psychometrically robust as is claimed.

REFERENCES

Adams, D. M., & Mayer, R. E. (2014). Cognitive consequences approach: what is learned from playing a game? In R. E. Mayer (Ed.), *Computer games for learning: An evidence-based approach* (pp. 171–224). Cambridge, MA: MIT Press.

Alsawaier, R. S. (2018). The Effect of Gamification on Motivation and Engagement. *International Journal of Information and Learning Technology, 35*(1), 56–79.

Ángeles Quiroga, M., Escorial, S., Román, F. J., Morillo, D., Jarabo, A., Privado, J., Hernández, M., Gallego, B., & Colom, R. (2015). Can we reliably measure the general factor of intelligence (g) through commercial video games? Yes, we can! *Intelligence, 53*, 1–7.

Armstrong, M. B., Landers, R. N., & Collmus, A. B. (2015). Gamifying recruitment, selection, training, and performance management: Game-thinking in human resource management. In D. Davis, & H. Gangadharbatla (Eds.), *Emerging research and trends in gamification* (pp. 140–165). Hershey, PA: IGI Global.

Attali, Y., & Arieli-Attali, M. (2015). Gamification in assessment: do points affect test performance?. *Computers & Education, 83*, 57–63.

Boot, W. R. (2015). Video games as tools to achieve insight into cognitive processes. *Frontiers in Psychology, 6*(3), 1–3.

Collmus, A. B., Armstrong, M. B., & Landers, R. N. (2016). Game-thinking within social media to recruit and select job candidates. In R. N. Landers, & G. B. Schmidt (Eds.), *Social media in employee selection and recruitment: Theory, practice, and current challenges* (pp. 103–124). Basel, Switzerland: Springer International Publishing.

Deterding, S., Dixon, D., Khaled, R., & Nacke, L. (2011, September). From game design elements to gamefulness: defining 'gamification'. In *Proceedings of the 15th International Academic Mindtrek Conference: Envisioning Future Media Environments* (pp. 9–15), Tampere, Finland.

Dichev, C., & Dicheva, D. (2017). Gamifying education: what is known, what is believed and what remains uncertain: a critical review. *International Journal of Educational Technology in Higher Education, 14*(9), 1–36.

Entertainment Software Association. (2015). *Essential facts about the computer and video game industry*. Washington, DC: Entertainment Software Association.

Fetzer, M., McNamara, J., Geimer, J. L., Goldstein, H. W., Pulakos, E. D., Passmore, J., & Semedo, C. (2017). Gamification, serious games and personnel selection. In H. W. Goldstein, E. D. Pulakos, , C. Semedo, & J. Passmore (Eds.), *The Wiley Blackwell handbook of the psychology of recruitment, selection and employee retention* (pp. 293–309). Chichester, UK: John Wiley & Sons.

Fiore, C. A. (2016). Gamification of individual differences. *Culminating Projects in Psychology*. Paper 4. London: UCL.

Foroughi, C. K., Serraino, C., Parasuraman, R., & Boehm-Davis, D. A. (2016). Can we create a measure of fluid intelligence using Puzzle Creator within Portal 2?. *Intelligence, 56*, 58–64.

Furnham, A. (2010). Proofreading as an index of crystallised intelligence. *Educational Psychology, 30*(6), 735–754.

Garris, R., Ahlers, R., & Driskell, J. E. (2002). Games, motivation, and learning: a research and practice model. *Simulation & Gaming, 33*(4), 441–467.

Gnambs, T., & Appel, M. (2017). Is computer gaming associated with cognitive abilities? A population study among German adolescents. *Intelligence, 61*, 19–28.

Griffiths, M. (1997). Computer game playing in early adolescence. *Youth & Society, 29*(2), 223–237.

Hansen, W. A., & Goldinger, S. D. (2009). Taboo: working memory and mental control in an interactive task. *The American Journal of Psychology, 122*(3), 283–291.

Hoffman, B., & Nadelson, L. (2010). Motivational engagement and video gaming: a mixed methods study. *Educational Technology Research and Development, 58* (3), 245–270.

Hopko, D. R., Lejuez, C. W., Daughters, S. B., Aklin, W. M., Osborne, A., Simmons, B. L., & Strong, D. R. (2006). Construct validity of the balloon analogue risk task (BART): relationship with MDMA use by inner-city drug users in residential treatment. *Journal of Psychopathology and Behavioral Assessment, 28*(2), 95–101.

Kim, Y. J., & Shute, V. J. (2015). The interplay of game elements with psychometric qualities, learning, and enjoyment in game-based assessment. *Computers & Education, 87*, 340–356.

Kircaburun, K., Pontes, H. M., Stavropoulos, V., & Griffiths, M. D. (2020). A brief psychological overview of disordered gaming. *Current Opinion in Psychology, 36*, 38–43.

Landers, R. N. (2014). Developing a theory of gamified learning: linking serious games and gamification of learning. *Simulation & Gaming, 45*(6), 752–768.

Lejuez, C. W., Aklin, W. M., Jones, H. A., Richards, J. B., Strong, D. R., Kahler, C. W., & Read, J. P. (2003). The balloon analogue risk task (BART) differentiates smokers and nonsmokers. *Experimental and Clinical Psychopharmacology, 11*(1), 26–33.

Lejuez, C. W., Read, J. P., Kahler, C. W., Richards, J. B., Ramsey, S. E., Stuart, G. L., Strong, D. R., & Brown, R. A. (2002). Evaluation of a behavioral measure of risk taking: the Balloon Analogue Risk Task (BART). *Journal of Experimental Psychology: Applied, 8*(2), 75–84.

Lievens, F., & Patterson, F. (2011). The validity and incremental validity of knowledge tests, low-fidelity simulations, and high-fidelity simulations for predicting job performance in advanced-level high-stakes selection. *Journal of Applied Psychology, 96*(5), 927–940.

Mané, A., & Donchin, E. (1989). The Space Fortress game. *Acta Psychologica, 71*(1–3), 17–22.

Mavridis, A., & Tsiatsos, T. (2017). Game-based assessment: investigating the impact on test anxiety and exam performance. *Journal of Computer Assisted Learning, 33*(2), 137–150.

Mekler, E. D., Bruhlmann, F., Opwis, K., & Tuch, A. N. (2013). Disassembling gamification: the effects of points and meaning on user motivation and performance. W. E. Mackay (Conference Chair), P. Baudisch, & M. Beaudouin-Lafon (Technical Program Chairs), *Proceedings of CHI'13 extended abstracts on human factors in computing systems* (pp. 1137–1142). New York: Association for Computing Machinery.

Mullins, J. K., & Sabherwal, R. (2018, January). *Beyond enjoyment: A cognitive-emotional perspective of gamification*. Paper presented at the 51st Hawaii International Conference on System Sciences, Honolulu, Hawaii.

Nacke, L. E., & Deterding, S. (2017). The maturing of gamification research [Editorial]. *Computers in Human Behavior, 71*, 450–454.

PricewaterhouseCoopers. (2015). *Multipoly: A selection game*. Budapest, Hungary: Author.

Rabah, J., Cassidy, R., & Beauchemin, R. (2018). *Gamification in education: Real benefits or edutainment?* Paper presented at the 17th European Conference on e-Learning, Athens, Greece.

Sajjadi, P., Vlieghe, J., & De Troyer, O. (2017). Exploring the relation between the theory of multiple intelligences and games for the purpose of player-centred game design. *Electronic Journal of e-Learning, 15*(4), 320–334.

Seaborn, K., & Fels, D. I. (2015). Gamification in theory and action: a survey. *International Journal of Human-Computer Studies, 74*, 14–31.

Sin, J., & Furnham, A. (2018). Do commercial games tap into cognitive ability? *Computer Games Journal, 7*, 27–37.

White, T. L., Lejuez, C. W., & de Wit, H. (2008). Test-retest characteristics of the Balloon Analogue Risk Task (BART). *Experimental and Clinical Psychopharmacology, 16*(6), 565–570.

7 Physiology

What are they?

EEG stands for *electroencephalogram*, which measures brain states when electrodes are placed on the skull; and fMRI stands for *functional magnetic resonance imaging*, which is done in a large scanner, where participants lie inside and are exposed to a strong magnetic field.

How do they work?

EEG measures oscillating brain rhythm frequencies. Magnetic fields created by the MRI machine measure differences in blood oxygen levels. Larger changes in oxygen levels are used to infer brain activity as more brain activity requires more oxygen to generate energy from neurons and glial cells (cell support system, like scaffolding for the neurons) during respiration.

What of the evidence?

Evidence is extremely objective (in comparison to other methods) but lacks ecological validity. It is often hard to distinguish exactly what increased activity in certain regions of the brain means for the participant and our brain activity as a whole. Evidence of the diagnostic power of these techniques to measure ability and personality is in its infancy.

Practical problems: cost, ethics, politics

Objective but very expensive to collect data, and possibly highly inappropriate for selection. As a result, it not used in personnel selection, but if it was, large ethical concerns will arise as recruiters could spot and select based on mental and physical health and personality disorders. Furthermore, just because one brain region is activated, the message does not directly translate into a specific, prescribed behaviour. Individuals may have learnt to deal with negative emotion/impulses and use their environment to control their behaviour, none of which is easily measurable in laboratory conditions.

Recommendations for use
Only use for medical diagnosis, and potentially forensic investigation (to verify personality disorders), not for personnel selection.

7.1.1   Introduction

In medicine, there is the *BioPsychoSocial* model which suggests that health and illness is dependent on *three* interacting factors that are essentially *biological, psychological and social*. Experts in any illness acknowledge this fact though they tend to place greater emphasis on one factor rather than another. The factor that, for many, holds most promise and is most 'scientific' is the biological/physiological model. This is the basis for the famous medical model: health and illness are defined primarily in terms of physiological phenomena. Others argued that social factors are just as much both the cause and the cure for many mental illnesses.

As noted in Chapters 1 and 2 those interested in assessment have always exploited the technology of the day to get a better insight into people. Furthermore, there has always been a hope that we can get an accurate, subtle and reliable measure of an individual that is not 'contaminated' by impression management, observer foibles and systematic biases. Hence the great interest in neuropsychology or indeed neuroscience, which, for many, holds out exactly that hope.

Atabaki and Sperling (2014) have argued that the thirst for studying brain functions was fuelled by the advances in the field of cognitive neurosciences. The field has united scientists with different backgrounds from informatics, physics, engineering, biology, and psychology to medicine around a common mission. The most prominent driver has been the use of modern brain imaging techniques like fMRI.

Starting from the 1980s the number of scientific publications using fMRI has grown exponentially, with 28,600 peer-reviewed publications in 2013, compared to only 200 in 1983. These expensive imaging devices are available in clinical and medical settings (and now psychology laboratories) and allow researchers to indirectly measure a proxy for brain activity. They note that as insightful and valuable these new data have been, the dissemination and often laymen interpretation have led to many misconceptions of how the human brain works. These misconceptions also found their way into the corporate world, with consultants talking of the design and application of neuropsychology training, and shaping how executives think about their brain functions.

Some psychologists have been concerned with the myths and misconceptions in the area. One book entitled *Great Myths of the Brain* by Jarrett (2014) listed 41 myths under various headings like defunct myths, immortal myths and myths about the physical structure of the brain. Furnham (2018) tested these myths and found that more than 40% of the respondents said that the following items were Definitely True: the brain is very well designed (57%); after head injury, people can forget who they are and not recognise others, but be normal in every other way (51%); the Brain receives information from the five separate senses (43%); and brain cells join together forming a huge net of nerves (41%).

He also found on various items a quarter or more of the respondents said that they Don't Know: Glial cells are little more than brain 'glue' (54%), mirror neurons make us human (52%), epilepsy is caused by abnormalities in blood flow in the brain (34%), and the female brain is more balanced than the male brain (25.9%). The results show that laypeople remain very ignorant in this whole area, which makes them vulnerable to be sold products and processes that have little proven psychiatric validity.

In this chapter two of these technologies are briefly reviewed. The first has been researched by psychologist for nearly 50 years, while the second is relatively new and still developing. This book attempts to answer the question: *is there evidence that this method is able to give an accurate (as well as ethical and cost-effective) picture of an individual's ability, personality and motivation* (see Chapter 1)?

7.1.2 Electroencephalogram (EEG)

EEG can be used to study the relationship between brain arousal and personality dimensions. Much of the early work was stimulated by Eysenck's biological model of personality, which described cortical arousal, and the ascending reticular activating system. The EEG is measured by putting electrodes on the scalp, which measure oscillation frequencies or brain rhythms as function of the synchronisation of neurons.

The theory essentially assumes that the features of the intrinsic oscillatory phenomena are related to the structures and functions of the brain. That is, different features in EEG bands may predict individual differences in brain function and structures. So, *if* personality and intelligence is manifest in brain structures (see Phrenology, Section 3.4), a measure such as the EEG may be useful as a predictor.

Some of the early work was done by Gale (1983), who tested Eysenck's theory and argued that the kind of social environment mediates physical arousal. He predicted a relationship between brain alpha characteristics and *Extraversion*, which occurred only in those specific settings that provided a moderate level of arousal. He used resting conditions with eyes closed to be the situation of low arousal, conditions with repeated opening and closing of the eyes to be of moderate arousal and various kinds of task performance to be of high arousal. Thus, according to the theory, Extraverts and Introverts would differ in their EEG measurable responses to these differently arousing situations. He found mixed evidence to support this theory.

Twenty years ago Robinson (1999, 2000, 2001) claimed that delta, theta and alpha waves are associated with the activity of the brainstem, limbic system and the thalamo-cortical arousal system, respectively, all of which are related to personality. The main evidence supporting this view is that direct stimulation of the brainstem and thalamic arousal systems produce corresponding characteristic frequencies of around 4 and 10 Hz in scalp EEG recordings, respectively while stimulation of the limbic system produces hippocampal waves of about 7 Hz (Gray, 1991).

Robinson (2001) asserted that EEG activity's spontaneous alpha frequency is the natural frequency of thalamo-cortical free oscillation, and that the thalamo-cortical alpha system exerts an inhibitory effect over the brainstem delta system. This is based on both the fact that the diffuse thalamic projection system exerts an inhibitory effect on the ARAS in a general way (Samuels, 1959) and on the results from averaged evoked potential (AEP) analyses by Robinson himself. Knyazev et al. (2003) supported this inhibition theory with the results of absolute spectral power measurements.

Anokhin (2016) recently reported a number of studies correlating neuroelectric signals with personality traits and psychopathology symptoms. They tend to focus on frontal EEG asymmetry – difference in 'alpha-band power' between left and right anterior scalp regions (read: electrical differences from the back of the head). Lots of alpha-band oscillations (8–13 Hz) reflect cortical deactivation, whereas minimal oscillations are linked to activation.

There is good evidence of test reliability, moderate heritability; however, mixed evidence relating measures to personality. The EEG is still considered by many researchers as an indicator of *affective style* and *risk for internalising psychopathology*. Also, developmental studies suggest that relatively greater right frontal activation is associated with anxious and withdrawn temperaments in infants and children; it is also believed that greater left frontal alpha-band power indicates *lower* left than right level of prefrontal activation, which is associated with stronger withdrawal motivation (avoidance) and increased vulnerability to depression, while the opposite pattern of asymmetry is associated with stronger approach motivation and low risk for depression.

Yet there still emerge studies under the 'Neuro-Assessment' banner than makes claims for its validity and more importantly usefulness in selection and development Thus, Fingelkurts et al. (2019) used quantitative electroencephalogram (qEEG) screening to build the individual profiles of eleven middle-aged people wanting business coaching. They used the EEG to assess various baseline traits like 'sociability' and 'anxiety tendency' so as to 'develop the coaching interventions to enhance effective and minimise ineffective behaviour'. Based on these target profiles considered a four-month coaching programme was undertaken.

> Results indicated that participation in a qEEG-informed and individually designed coaching program was associated with (i) significant optimization of vigilance level, speed of cognitive and memory performance, emotional-motivational tendency, sociability, anxiety tendency, (ii) improvement in stress-resistance and recovery (resilience), overall brain resources and (iii) minimized deviation from the optimal brain state as indicated by the metrics in the qEEG-profile. This optimization is related to traits which characterize successful transformational leadership. For example, successful transformational leaders have a tendency to keep anxiety levels low, and able to control their emotions, keeping some level of positivity even in difficult and stressful situations.
>
> *(p. 21)*

There are many problems associated with studies, including many acknowledged by the authors including a very small number of volunteer participants. Most important was the lack of a control group who should not have been given any sort of specialised coaching but given a placebo activity.

EEG research continues but early hopes that it would give subtle and reliable readings of personality, intelligence and mental illness have not materialised.

Certainly, it seems as if it has never been used in a job selection assessment setting. Furthermore, it has largely been taken over by newer technologies (see next).

7.1.3 *Functional Magnetic Resonance Imaging*

Functional magnetic resonance imaging (fMRI) measures small changes in blood flow that occur with brain activity. It is most used to examine the brain's functional anatomy, as it may detect abnormalities within the brain that cannot be found with other imaging techniques.

In technical terms: 'Blood Oxygen Level Dependent (BOLD) functional magnetic resonance imaging (fMRI) depicts changes in deoxyhaemoglobin concentration consequent to task-induced or spontaneous modulation of neural metabolism. Since its inception in 1990, this method has been widely employed in thousands of studies of cognition for clinical applications such as surgical planning, for monitoring treatment outcomes, and as a biomarker in pharmacologic and training programs' (Glover, 2011, p. 133).

There have been and continue to be rapid technical developments and it has become commonplace for clinical uses such as presurgical planning, fundamental cognitive neuroscience investigations, behaviour modification and training.

For the psychologist this offers a wonderful opportunity to study brain anatomy and functioning with respect to all sorts of behaviour. Thus, people are able to determine where in the brain certain centres are located that relate to different kinds of behaviours and how they function under specific conditions.

It is no surprise then that differential psychologists interested in personality and intelligence have used this technique to study traits and intellectual functioning. As a result, there are a number of studies of interest to the differential psychologist looking at personality and ability correlates of 'brain activity'.

Table 7.1 summarises the (statistically) significant findings of some of these studies. to the left and right hemispheres of the brain.

Consider some studies done over the last decade. Gao et al. (2013) found trait Extraversion positively correlated with clustering – measure of interconnectedness of the nodes. The authors suggested that this suggested Extraverted people have either a higher arousal threshold, in that more activity is needed to engage the nodes; extraverted people have a higher level of arousal tolerance, therefore less stimulating things won't be 'flagged' as interesting or exciting by the brain.

Table 7.1 *Summary of some fMRI studies*

Sample size	Ages	Personality assessment	Key findings
265	20–85	Big Five traits	Neuroticism (N) → less total brain volume … Extraversion (E) → less inferior frontal gyrus thickness Conscientiousness (C) → less localisation of the temporoparietal junction
65	21–56	"	E → Total grey matter volume; larger right orbitofrontal cortex
62	20–40	"	Agreeableness (A) → Smaller regional cerebellar volume Openness (O) → larger left superior orbitofrontal cortex
87	64–80	"	N → larger ventral vision-related areas E → larger dorsolateral prefrontal cortex and temporal regions O → smaller right medial prefrontal cortex and left insula A → smaller dorsomedial prefrontal cortex C → larger areas related to motor (movement) planning
116	18–40	"	N → differences in a wide array of brain regions E → larger medial orbitofrontal cortex A → larger fusiform gyrus, smaller superior temporal sulcus C → smaller left middle frontal gyrus and posterior fusiform gyrus
113	23–50	"	N → linked to smaller hippocampi in methionine allele carriers of the brain-derived neurotrophic factor

Table 7.1 (*cont.*)

Sample size	Ages	Personality assessment	Key findings
			Val66Met polymorphism (specific gene mutation associated with geriatric depression; Hwang et al., 2006)
186	21–40	Temperament	Harm avoidance (HA) → smaller right side of hippocampus in both sexes, smaller left anterior prefrontal cortex in women only
56	22–40	"	HA → larger left side of amygdala in women
			Novelty Seeking (NS) → larger left medial prefrontal gyrus
			Reward dependence → larger right caudate (tail)
100	20–40	"	HA → larger right anterior cingulated gyrus
			NS → larger lift posterior cingulate region
114	18–53	Behavioural activation/ inhibition	Behavioural inhibition → smaller right and medial orbitofrontal cortex and precuneus

Source: Adapted from Anokhin (2016).

Anokhin (2016) was interested in personality traits linked to reward seeking; for both the expectation and enjoyment of the reward there were links to specific regions of the brain: 'positive correlations with the activation of the ventral and dorsal striatum and orbitofrontal cortex, subgenual and ventral ACC' (p. 81). Withdraw-avoidance personality traits were related to amygdala activation in response to negative things (amygdala for fear, 'animal emotion'; in the brain stem) as well as decreased connectivity of the amygdala with the prefrontal cortex, accumbens and hippocampus – the reward circuitry.

He concluded: 'Neuroticism was associated with decreased activation in the ACC, thalamus, hippocampus/parahippocampus, striatum, and several temporal, parietal, and occipital brain areas, as well as increased activation in the hippocampus/parahippocampus and frontal and cingulate regions. Interestingly, different types of studies tended to contribute to negative versus positive correlations between neuroticism and negative > neutral activation.' (p. 81)

Dubois et al. (2018) related the Big Five personality traits to brain alpha waves. They found Openness was the only reliability-predicted personality factor by *resting-state* functional brain connectivity across their three statistical methods. They also looked at higher-level personality types (alpha/beta) and found that resting-state connectivity also predicted beta, personal growth and plasticity.

The fMRI has been used to try to diagnose the *personality disorders*. Tang et al.'s (2013) study, 'Identifying Individuals with Antisocial Personality Disorder Using Resting-Sate fMRI' had 32 ASPD participants and 35 controls; fMRI was able to identify the differences with 86.57% accuracy.

Soloff et al. (2017) were interested in how impulsivity and aggression mediate regional brain responses in borderline personality disorder (BPD) participants using an fMRI study. They used 31 BPD cases, 25 controls; all participants were women due to the higher incidence of BPD in women than men. Results suggested differences in the effect of impulsivity between BPD and controls. They reported 'In BPD, trait impulsivity was positively correlated with activation in the dorsal anterior cingulate cortex, orbital frontal cortex (OFC), basal ganglia (BG), and dorsolateral prefrontal cortex, with no areas of negative correlation. In contrast, aggression was negatively correlated with activation in OFC, hippocampus, and BG, with no areas of positive correlation. Depressed mood had a generally dampening effect on activations' (p. 390).

van Schie et al. (2020) used 26 people with BPD, 32 healthy controls and 22 controls with low self-esteem. All performed a social feedback task (positive and negative messages) while in a fMRI scanner. It has been shown that that anterior cingulate cortex (ACC), insula, precuneus, PCC, and temporoparietal junction (TPJ) areas are involved in the processing of positive and negative feedback. The authors were interested in the TPJ, which is between the parietal and temporal brain regions, and involved in information processing and integration as well as self–other distinctions. They found healthy controls had higher precuneus activation to negative feedback than positive. BPD was low in both positive and negative feedback. Healthy control had increased TPJ activation to positive feedback than negative, while BPD showed more TPJ activation to negative feedback. They concluded: 'The negative self-views that BPD have, may obstruct critically examining negative feedback, resulting in lower mood. Moreover, where HC [healthy controls] focus on the positive feedback (based on TPJ activation), BPD seem to focus more on negative feedback, potentially maintaining negative self-views. Better balanced self-views may make BPD better equipped to deal with potential negative feedback and more open to positive interactions' (p. 1)

There are many intriguing studies in this area. Mameli et al. (2016), in an interesting study, suggested that lying requires more brain activation to increase cognitive control. In contrast to truth telling, the act of lying involves intense activity in prefrontal brain regions. They noted that children without a fully developed relevant brain area have even less ability to deceive than people with frontal cortex developmental conditions.

The main theories of empathy suggest that seeing an emotion in others activates the same regions in our brains that would be activated if we were experiencing the same events ourselves. However, vicarious pain does not show the same patterns of brain activity. There is a gradient in the insula's brain activity for one's own pain, that isn't there when one sees the pain of someone else. Typical ways of measuring interpersonal differences between people is by seeing how levels of brain activity differ for people that scale differently on psychometric measures of empathy or emotional intelligence. This has shown increased activity in the brain's 'empathy network', made of the insula, nucleus accumbens and sensorimotor cortices, as well as may others.

Can we measure intelligence by using brain waves? Some studies reported that the Ravens measure of fluid intelligence could be predicted from resting-state fMRI in the healthy participant data set (Finn et al., 2015; Noble et al., 2017).

7.1.4 Conclusion

It is no surprise that so many psychologists now prefer to call themselves neuroscientists as they see revolutionary developments in our understanding of the structure and function of the brain through the use of new technology. To the sceptic it looks like magneto-phrenology seeking to establish where in the brain certain structures and processes occur that determine patterns of behaviour.

Inevitably the cost of this equipment is coming down and the sophistication is increasing. But will there be a day when, prior to selection, interview candidates agree to, or are required to, go through an fMRI (or equivalent) examination to understand their ability, motivation and potential? Furthermore, what are the ethical implications of such an examination? Time will tell.

REFERENCES

Atabaki, A., & Sperling, J. (2014). *Learning – Neuromyths and Reality*. McKinsey Consulting.

Anokhin, A. P. (2016). Genetics, brain, and personality: searching for immediate pheontypes. In J. R. Abscher, & J. Cloutlier (Eds.), *Neuroimaging Personality, Social Cognition, and Character* (pp. 71–90). Academic Press.

Dubois, J., Galdi, P., Han, Y., Paul, L. K., & Adolphs, R. (2018). Resting-state functional brain connectivity best predicts personality dimension of openness to experience. *Personality Neuroscience*, 5;1:e6

Fingelkurts, A., Fingelkurts, A., & Neves, C. (2020). Neuro-assessment of leadership training. *Coaching*, 13, 107-145.

Furnham, A. (2018). Myths and misconceptions in developmental and neuro-psychology. *Psychology*, 9, 249–259.

Gale, A. (1983). Electroencephalographic studies of extraversion–introversion: a case study in the psychophysiology of individual differences. *Personality and Individual Differences, 4*, 371–380.

Gao, Q., Qiang, X., Duan, X., Liao, W., Ding, J., Zhang, Z., Li, Y., Lu, G., & Chen, H. (2013). Extraversion and neuroticism relate to topological properties of resting-state brain networks. *Frontiers in Human Neuroscience, 7*, 257.

Glover, G. H. (2011). Overview of functional magnetic resonance imaging. *Neurosurgical Clinics of North America, 22*, 133–139.

Gray, J. A. (1991). Neural systems, emotion and personality. In J. Madden IV (Ed.), *Neurobiology of learning, emotion and affect* (pp. 273–306.). New York: Raven Press.

Hwang, J.-P., Tsai, S.-T., Hong, C.-H., Yang, C.-H., Lirng, J.-F., & Yang, Y.-M. (2006). The Val66Met polymorphism of the brain-derived neurotrophic-factor gene is associated with geriatric depression. *Neurobiology of Aging, 27*(12), 1834–1837.

Jarrett, C. (2014). *Great myths of the brain.* New York: Wiley-Blackwell.

Mameli, F., Sartori, G., Scarpazza, C., Zangrossi, A., Pietrini, P., Fumagalli, M., & Priori, A. (2016). Honesty. In J. R. Abscher, & J. Cloutlier (Eds.), *Neuroimaging personality, social cognition, and character* (pp. 305–322). London, UK: Academic Press.

Robinson, D. L. (1999). The technical, neurological, and psychological significance of 'alpha', 'theta', and 'delta' waves confounded in EEG evoked potentials: 1. A study of peak latencies. *Electroencephalography and Clinical Neurophysiology, 110*, 1427–1434.

Robinson, D. L. (2000). The technical, neurological, and psychological significance of 'alpha', 'delta' and 'theta' waves confounded in EEG evoked potentials: a study of peak amplitudes. *Personality and Individual Differences, 28*, 673–693.

Robinson, D. L. (2001). How brain arousal systems determine different temperament types and the major dimensions of personality *Personality and Individual Differences, 31*, 1233–1259.

Samuels, I. (1959). Reticular mechanisms and behaviour. *Psychological Bulletin, 56*, 1–22.

Soloff, P. H., Abraham, K., Burgess, A., Ramaseshan, K., Chowdury, A., & Diwadkar, V. A. (2017). Impulsivity and aggression mediate regional brain responses in Borderline Personality Disorder: an fMRI study. *Psychiatry Research: Neuroimaging, 268*, 76–85.

Tang, Y., Jian, W., Liao, J., Wang, W., & Luo, A. (2013). Identifying individuals with antisocial personality disorder using resting-sate fMRI. *PLoS ONE, 8*(4), e60652.

van Schie, C. C., Chiu, C.-D., Rombouts, S. A. R. B., Heiser, W. J., & Elzinga, B. M. (2020). Stuck in a negative me: fMRI study on the role of disturbed self-views in social feedback processing in borderline personality disorder. *Psychological Medicine, 50*(4), 625–635.

7.2 THE LIE DETECTOR (POLYGRAPH)

> **What is it?**
> It is a device that measures physiological changes in body functioning like heartbeat, skin conductance, etc. People are 'wired up' to the device and then interviewed. Investigators look at the reactions to different questions.
>
> **How do they work?**
> They are based on the assumption that when uncomfortable or anxious when lying and/or when caught lying, people manifest physiological reactions which do not occur when they are telling the truth. Thus, by examining the responses to a range of very specific and pre-planned questions, it is possible to detect physical changes associated with anxiety and stress which *may be* an index of lying.
>
> **What of the evidence?**
> There is a mountain of evidence often sponsored by academic bodies and government agencies which suggests the test is too unreliable to use: that is, it misidentifies truth as lies and vice versa far too often to be used in any serious decision-making about an individual's fate.
>
> **Practical problems: cost, ethics, politics**
> Whilst it is possible to purchase a crude lie detector, the better examples are very expensive and technologically sophisticated and demand some skill in use and interpretation. Hence, getting lie detector data may be very expensive. Furthermore, candidates in classic interview situations are often offended by its use. More importantly, it is likely that the test results would not stand up to scrutiny in a court of law.
>
> **Recommendations for use**
> There are almost no circumstances in which it should be used in assessment and selection; if it is, the data should be substantiated by other methods.

7.2.1 *Introduction*

You are invited for an interview for a government agency which deals in sensitive data. They warn you that you may have to be interviewed with a lie detector at selection, but also whilst in the job. Would you be happy to agree?

You are a selector and you really need to get honest answers from a candidate about some very specific issues. Would you use a lie detector? If not, how can you ensure that you would get accurate and honest answers to your questions?

The idea of having a reliable, physiologically based way of catching liars has always appealed to people. The appeal of physiology is that it is *assumed* that you cannot lie your way out of these tests: *the body does not lie*. It is supposed that people cannot suppress physiological changes that occur when they feel the guilt of lying; that we can easily and reliably record these changes which are a probable index of lying.

7.2.2 *Background and History*

The polygraph (or lie detector) has been passionately discussed and debated for most of the last century, and yet scientists remain divided on the issue (Iacono & Ben-Shakhar, 2019; Iacono & Lykken, 1997). The earliest records of quasi lie detectors can be found in the ancient Hindu culture and the medieval church who devised methods of *finding the truth*. Suspects were asked to chew various substances and then spit them out. The ease of spitting and glutinousness of the spittle, they argued, reflected guilt. What these people had observed was that fear leads to saliva diminishing in volume and becoming viscid in consistency. Today, we would say that 'anxiety influences the activity of the autonomic nervous system that controls salivation'. Note that it does not tell us about what caused the anxiety.

In the nineteenth century, scientists tried measuring other supposed physical concomitants of fear. These include the plethysmograph (which records pulse and blood pressure in a limb), finger trembling, reaction time, word association and so on, all done while investigating suspects.

A famous researcher, reviewer and sceptic Lykken (1998) reviewed the uses and abuses of the lie detector. He noted that

William Marston wrote a book, *The Lie Detector Test* published in 1938, but this was nearly 20 years after he first used the term and tried to publicise the machine. Marston was a publicist, not a scientist, like many who have wandered into this area.

It was a Californian police officer, John A. Larson – later a forensic psychiatrist – who started scientific work observing continuous measures of blood pressure and respiratory changes during interrogation. Larson wrote a book in 1932 which was, in essence, the first scholarly book on lying and lie detection. He was, unlike many others, a sceptic to the end.

Two of his associates – Lee and Keeler, from the Berkley police force – continued his work. Lee developed a portable 'field' polygraph and even a manual for polygraph users. Keeler developed his own portable machine, named after himself. Keeler moved to Chicago where he met others who were to proselytise this cause, including John Reid, who also developed his own pseudonymous machine. Reid was a lawyer, who developed a *College of Detection of Deception* and new ideas regarding polygraphic interrogation.

Up until the Second World War, the favoured technique was the *R/I* (relevant/irrelevant questions) approach. This involves alternating between a mix of irrelevant and relevant questions; for example, 'What day of the week is it?' 'Who is Prime Minister?' and 'Where were you on the night in question?' 'Did you know the victim?' The idea was the relevant questions (only) could, and did, generate stress in the innocent.

Reid developed the now famous *Control Question Test*, where those interrogated were asked questions like 'Have you even stolen anything?' 'Have you ever been late for an appointment?' 'Have you ever taken credit for something you did not do?' If the questions were answered 'No', it was highly likely that the subject was lying. Hence, one had a 'base rate' measure or standard against which the really interesting questions could be asked. This is an important concept as we know people react very differently in these situations: compare the reactions of a neurotic and a psychopath, the latter's guiltlessness, having a major effect on their responses.

Reid also used what were called 'guilt complex questions' to see how the subject behaved when questioned about a similar, utterly fictitious but related crime. This was a good control question. Reid also, very controversially, listed the typical behavioural symptoms of truthful vs lying subjects, which seems today very arbitrary.

People are asked *neutral questions, relevant questions* and *control questions*: the latter related to the crime but not referring to it. The main problem with the technique is that it is very different to devise plausible questions that would ensure the eliciting of stronger reactions in an innocent person than would be relevant to a question relating to the crime of which they had been accused.

Later, Cleve Backster, introduced two important ideas. The first was the *zone of comparison* format, where only the totally adjacent relevant and control questions were compared to look for the person's reactivity over the course of the test. He also developed a scoring technique to score a person's relevant response over all channels and all repetitions of the same question to get a total score. The overall verdict is based entirely on the polygraphic record – not using case facts, behaviour symptoms and so on – and inevitably the polygraph examines preconceived ideas.

It was not until the 1960s that the lie detector emerged from the police forensic laboratory into the marketplace. Operators approached many companies, especially banks and rental stores, saying their machines could screen *job applicants* to determine whether their application forms were truthful and whether they had stolen from previous employers, ever used illegal drugs, had any outstanding debts or had any undisclosed criminal records.

They also said that job incumbents could be effectively and efficiently screened for embezzlement, misappropriation of funds and theft. This looked like incredibly useful 'cutting-edge' science that provided crucial information no other technique could equal.

Soon, more than two million Americans were being tested every year. It was a multi-million-dollar business. Furthermore, some serious university-based researchers seemed to endorse the technique.

Indeed, the same today could be seen with other techniques discussed in this book (e.g. gamification).

But, from the mid-1970s, various psychologists started serious investigations into the lie detector, and all condemned it. In 1988, the *Polygraph Protection Act* prohibited American employers from requiring or requesting that employees be polygraphed. 'Hundreds of journeymen polygraphers had to seek other employment and millions of citizens no longer had to face the humiliation of having their character vetted in an hour's time by some graduate of a six-week course in polygraphy' (Lykken, 1998, p. 37). Polygraphs are still used throughout the world – Canada to Thailand, Israel to Taiwan – though their use is limited. The test is also seen to be used on popular television programmes usually to check the veracity of what couples say about each other.

Twenty years ago, Ekman (2001), the leading researcher on lying, noted over a million polygraph tests are still given every year in the USA. Private employers, criminal investigators, the federal government and the Department of Defense are the major users.

Oswald (2020) concluded:

> There was no one inventor of the lie detector, despite the use of this construct in contemporary reporting . . . Furthermore, the term 'lie detector' was 'a form of linguistic "black boxing": the simplification of scientific complexity and human agency.' Fundamentally though, all recognised polygraph methodologies share the same premise: that 'certain psychological processes result in physiological cues that can be measured and interpreted with the polygraph for the purpose of aiding in the detection of deception' with such measurements remaining largely unchanged from Keeler's original models.
>
> *(p. 218)*

7.2.3 *How Polygraphs Work*

The polygraph attempts to measure autonomic nervous system activity by sensors attached to different parts of the body: chest, stomach, fingers. These sensors measure changes in breathing (depth and rate), cardiac activity (blood pressure) and perspiration. It is also possible to measure brain electrical activity (event-related potentials). Indeed, it is in this area that most developments have taken place.

The indicators only show physiological changes usually induced by emotion. The machine amplifies signals picked up from sensors put on specific parts of the body. It does not detect lies but, rather, physical changes that are results of specific emotions (fear, anger, guilt) but which are not clear. People are asked 'hot' or relevant questions as well as 'cool' or control questions. The assumption is that, for the innocent person, there is no physical difference in the way he/she responds to relevant and control questions.

Problems of individual differences arise. Some people are more reactive than others. Drugs can be used to suppress autonomic nervous system activity and make any physiological recording inconclusive. More worryingly, people can be trained to defeat the test with a range of techniques.

Tests would therefore not only be highly unreliable, but also counter-productive: alienating and misclassifying the innocent and letting the guilty get away scot-free. In psychometric terminology they are neither reliable nor valid.

The lie detector is still in use in three separate contexts: criminal investigation, security vetting and personnel selection. Some have argued the polygraph is worthless in selection because it can only speak to the past, not the future. Others argue that the past, indeed, predicts the future. If you have lied in the past you are more likely to do so in the future. Some people are 'habitual liars'!

There is much less research on pre-employment screening. Some argue the base rate of liars is too low to ever be accurate. Others suggest that the test causes a poor impression. However, some argue that taking the test, or being threatened they will have to take it, leads people to admitting important things they otherwise would not admit. Thus, a test can have utility even without accuracy.

Ekman (2001) contends that there are many important issues associated with the polygraph like: how the polygraph may be useful even if it is not accurate. The threat of lie detection acts as a deterrent and can inhibit lying even if the procedure is faulty.

In every generation lie detectors look more 'scientific and sophisticated' but essentially, they are attempting to do the same thing albeit with more sensitive technology.

7.2.4 *The Validity of the Lie Detector*

What is remarkable, given the large body of relevant research, is that claims about the accuracy of the polygraph made today parallel those made throughout the history of the polygraph: practitioners have always claimed extremely high levels of accuracy, and these claims have rarely been reflected in empirical research.

National Research Council of the National Academy of Sciences (2003, p. 107)

To be acceptable as a test, a lie detector (like any other devise) must minimally fulfil a number of criteria:

First, there must be a standardised method of administration that is fully described, clear and repeatable.

Second, there must be objective scoring; not subjective, based on personal experience scoring.

Third, there must be external valid criteria – it must be shown to differentiate between truth and lie.

Critics have noted the lie detector is not a test but an interrogation device because methods are semi-standardised, it requires clinical observation and validity data is poor. Data on the lie detector comes from two sources: *clinical case studies and experimental evidence.*

It must be pointed out that, in 'real life' cases, it is often very difficult to establish validity because many crimes are never solved and confession (often false) is the only real feedback. It is possible, however, to use laboratory studies using students. But, as Lykken (1998, pp. 84–85) observed, these also have problems.

Laboratory studies have serious disadvantages for predicting lie detector accuracy in real-life criminal investigations.

1. The volunteer subjects are unlikely to be representative of criminal suspects in real life.
2. The volunteers may not feel a lifelike concern about mock crimes that they have been instructed to commit and about telling lies they are instructed to tell.
3. Compared to criminal suspects, who know they may be in real trouble should they fail the lie test, volunteers are unlikely to be as apprehensive about being tested, with respect to mock crimes for which they will not be punished, irrespective of the test's outcome.
4. The administration of the polygraph tests tends not to resemble the procedures followed in real life. For example, unlike real-life tests, which are most often conducted well after the crime took place, laboratory subjects are typically tested immediately after they commit the mock crime. Moreover, in laboratory research, to make the study scientifically acceptable, there is an attempt to standardize the procedure (e.g. all subjects are asked identical questions), a factor that distinguishes these from real-life tests.

Most of the researchers in the field have tried to evaluate the more widely known methods of lie detection. The *Control Question Technique* must emotionally arouse the innocent person with the control as much as the crime-related questions, otherwise it makes an error.

There is, rightly, a tremendous concern with the innocent person being mislabelled or judged guilty. This may easily occur in the nervous, anxious, person – particularly if he/she believes polygraphs are fallible (which, of course, they are) and when they can (often, relatively easily) detect the difference between relevant and control questions. Innocent people might believe the police/polygraph operators are fallible as are their machines, or that they are unfair. Fearful, guilty, hostile, impulsive, volatile people react badly to authority figures wiring them up. Their reactions may unfairly condemn them. Furthermore, an innocent person may be so unhappy or disturbed by a crime they did not do – but having found the body or knowing the victim – that they react physiologically dramatically, seeming to show guilt.

Vrij (2000) noted many criticisms of the Control Question Test. The first is the possibility that innocent victims give larger physiological responses to control, rather than relevant, questions. The next is that guilty suspects are not less concerned with control, rather than relevant, questions. Furthermore, examiners have to be experienced and subtle in the choice and phrasing of the questions. It is easy to frighten, embarrass and intimidate others, as well as to 'leak' their own beliefs and suspicions non-verbally. Next, there is the judgement problem: how to interpret the difference in responses to repress to control vs relevant questions. It depends not only on the size of the difference in response, but also the base-rate: every individual that is a low-reactive person might show the same absolute physical differences as a highly reactive person but, in effect, the former is much more dramatic than the latter. A related issue is that scoring polygraph charts is still a 'subjective art', rather than a 'precise science'. Finally, there are ethical and legal problems in deceiving people in some of the control questions.

The *Guilty Knowledge Test*, on the other hand, works on the assumption that the lie detector operator has information about the crime exclusive to the guilty person (i.e. precisely how much was stolen; the denomination of the notes). The idea is that, when questioned in detail, the guilty person recognises descriptions of events, objects, people linked to the crime, and this rouses him/her, showing up on the polygraph recordings.

In a review, Miner and Capps (1996) found for liars correctly identified in field studies, 71–99%; in analog studies using the control question technique, 35–100%; in analog studies using the guilty knowledge test, 61–95%. For truthful persons correctly identified: in field studies, 13–94%; in analog studies using the control question technique, 32–91%; in analog studies using the guilty knowledge test, 80–100%. For a truthful person incorrectly identified: in field studies,

0–75%; in analog studies using the control question technique, 2–51%; in analog studies using the guilty knowledge test, 0–12%. For liars correctly identified: in field studies, 0–29%; in analog studies using the control question technique, 0–29%; in analog studies using the guilty knowledge test, 5–39%.

Also, it is not always easy to find appropriate questions and keep all details secret. Sometimes the criminal may not have noticed certain details that an innocent person at the scene of the crime might have. Problems arise in the questions, and a person may have guilty knowledge without being guilty. However, it is clear that experts in the area are much more likely to endorse the credibility of the Guilty Knowledge Test over the Controlled Question Test.

As noted, studies on the accuracy/validity of the polygraph can be categorised into two types: field studies of actual, real-life incidents and analogue/experimental studies. Both have distinct advantages and disadvantages. There is actually a rarer type called 'hybrid studies', where the researcher arranges for a crime to occur.

Ekman (2001) reviewed 30 studies: 10 field, 14 analogue, 6 hybrid. He concluded that accuracy was better in the field studies because there was more emotional arousal, less-educated people and less certainty about the ground truth. 'Disbelieving-the-truth' mistakes and 'believing-a-lie' mistakes are highest in the Guilty Knowledge Test.

Ekman (2001) notes that some critics believe the figures under-estimate accuracy, while some stress the precise opposite. He also believes more weight should be given to a test that shows innocence as an outcome, rather than lying. Furthermore, even when a test suggests lying, this should only be used to pursue an investigation, rather than being enough evidence to proceed with a prosecution or a conviction. He argued that one cannot properly evaluate the polygraph without understanding some fundamental concepts. Four are essential:

1. The difference between accuracy and utility – how the polygraph might be useful even if it isn't accurate
2. The quest for ground truth – how hard it is to determine the accuracy of the polygraph without being absolutely certain who the liars are

3. The base rate of lying – how a very accurate test can produce many mistakes when the group of suspects includes very few liars
4. Deterring lying – how the threat of being examined might inhibit some from lying, even if the examination procedure is faulty

Vrij (2000) also reviewed various studies. Looking at laboratory studies of the Control Question Test, he found that 73% of guilty people and 66% of innocent people were correctly classified. Also, 9% of the guilty were judged innocent and 13% of the innocent falsely accused. Laboratory studies of the Guilty Knowledge Test were better: 96% of the innocent were correctly identified and only 4% falsely accused. Similarly, 82% of the guilty were correctly classified but 18% judged innocent.

A British evaluation

The British Psychological Society published a long, edited book (Gale, 1988) called *The Polygraph Test: Lies, Truth and Science*. It may be some 30 years ago but the issues have not changed.

The conclusion, stated at the beginning of the book, is a good example of British scientific diffidence and caution. The editor writes:

> The truth is that we do not know the full truth about polygraphic lie-detection. (p. 2)
>
> Advances in science and technology are unlikely to leave our lives untouched, and the polygraph is no exception. The polygraph is a scientific instrument used for research into bodily responses and their relationships with psychological processes. As an instrument, it is reliable in producing a record of bodily events. However, this does not imply that the uses to which the polygraph might be put are also reliable. Some members of the British Psychological Society have expressed concern that the use of the polygraph for lie detection might reflect badly on its use in basic research. Criticism has also been made of the term 'the polygraph test', a misnomer which is said to give lie detection procedures some respectability by their association with a scientific instrument.
>
> *(p. 9)*

The issue considered is the vexed question of various procedures, their accuracy and validity; what we mean by truth and honesty, and whether, indeed, the test measures it; what the test measures; whether the use of the test will actually be useful and cost-effective in national security vetting; and the many legal and civil rights issues surrounding such tests.

Bull (1988) notes that the data are clear concerning the detection of lying just by observation. It is difficult, highly unreliable and not easily trained. One can, as Ekman (2001) has shown, never come to a final conclusion on whether a person is lying or telling the truth. Bull (1988), like all reviewers, was worried about misclassification – particularly the innocent being judged guilty. All sorts of issues come into play: is the person aware that they are lying; how valid do they believe the polygraph to be; how good is the polygrapher. He concludes: 'Until it is made absolutely clear on which forms of the testee's behaviours and responses decisions about deceptions are based, there can be no proper scientific study of the validity of the polygrapher's procedures' (Bull, 1988, pp. 17–18).

Carroll (1988) did an early review on the accuracy of the polygraph based on reliability (agreement between examiners; subject consistency across time) and accuracy. He found both the reliability and validity data unconvincing, and concluded thus:

> If proponents wish to convince the scientific community of the merits of polygraph lie detection, I submit that they will have to develop a more convincing case than the one currently on offer. Their case must be founded on studies which include the necessary controls for non-polygraphic sources of information, that is, studies which compare the accuracy of assessments derived from case-file material and the subject's demeanour during questioning with that based on these sources plus the polygraph record. I strongly suspect that such studies would confirm what the available data suggest: that polygraph lie detection adds nothing positive to conventional approaches to interrogation and assessment.
>
> *(Carroll, 1988, p. 28)*

In a very British, BBC and balanced way, the report allows the two famous American adversaries to describe and defend their position. In the pro-corner, Raskin (1988) – who addressed his essay thus, 'Does science support polygraph testing?' – set about marshalling the pro-evidence. He concludes:

> Careful consideration of the available evidence seems to indicate that there is scientific support for certain applications of polygraph techniques. Appropriate use of those techniques by qualified professionals in criminal investigation and forensic applications can achieve rates of accuracy that compare favourably with other forms of evidence, such as criminalistics, and are higher than common forms of evidence, such as eyewitness identification.
>
> Polygraph testing can have serious problems of inaccuracy in the most common application, commercial pre-employment screening. That application most likely produces such high rates of error that tremendous social and personal damage results from its widespread use. There seems to be little scientific support for such uses of polygraphs.
>
> Polygraph examinations in the context of national security programs raise the most complex issues. Assessments of lifestyle and prior history produce problems similar to those that arise in commercial employment screening. The problems associated with low base rates of espionage in counter-intelligence contexts must be balanced against the need to identify spies because of the great security and monetary costs of failing to do so. Often, national security needs are pitted against the social and ethical needs of protecting individuals. Only the most careful programmes and techniques, coupled with research and development to minimize the errors, can help to reduce those problems. Ultimately, the future of government uses of polygraph methods will be determined by political and social considerations, hopefully enlightened by objective and thorough scientific evaluations.
>
> *(Raskin, 1988, pp. 109–110)*

In the anti-corner, Lykken (1998) – a long-time opponent of the polygraph – presented, in equal measure, his analysis of the issue. Note how different his conclusion is:

Unlike the fictional Pinocchio, we are not equipped with a distinctive physiological response that we emit involuntarily when, and only when, we lie. There are many reasons other than deception why a truthful person might show physiological disturbance in response to an accusatory question. Polygraphers cannot delude each innocent suspect into the belief that he or she has nothing to fear from the relevant questions but something important to fear from the 'controls'. The fact that one of several accusatory questions causes my heart to beat harder, my palms to sweat more, than the other questions does not necessarily mean that I am guilty of that accusation. The assumptions on which the various forms of lie-detector test are based have only to be articulated to be seen to be implausible.

Many poorly designed badly controlled studies are to be found in the polygraph literature. The few relatively competent studies agree with each other and with what one might expect from the theory: polygraphic lie detection is wrong about one third of the time overall; it is seriously biased against the truthful subject; deceptive subjects with minimal coaching can deliberately produce augmented responses, undetected by the examiner, which will allow them to defeat at least one common type of lie test.

It seems to me that we must now acknowledge that this application of psychophysiology has been a failure; that polygraph lie detection does not and, in the foreseeable future, probably cannot work well enough to justify its continued use in the field. Polygraphic detection of guilty knowledge, based on entirely different and more plausible assumptions, has proved itself in the laboratory and deserves controlled study in the field of criminal investigation.

(Lykken, 1998, pp. 124–125)

7.2.5 Beating the Lie Detector

Can you beat the lie detector? Essentially, there are two ways of doing this: *physical* and *mental*. Physical measures may involve self-inflicted pain (biting the tongue, kicking a drawing pin hidden in shoes, tensing and releasing muscles). Mental methods may include counting backwards and fantasising. Physical measures are meant to give real, dramatic but misleading physiological responses picked up on the polygraph. The latter is meant to screen-out the questions, so making them indistinct. Studies have shown them equally effective, and there seems to be some evidence that people in security jobs are taught to use them effectively. But there are limitations. First, the person has to conceal carefully precisely what they are doing. Second, it is harder to fake in the Guilty Knowledge Test than in the Control Question Test.

Gudjonsson (1988) addressed the problem of how (best) to defeat the polygraph. This was his conclusion:

The use of different classes of countermeasures has been reported in the literature. The available evidence shows that mental countermeasures and the use of pharmacological substances (such as tranquilisers) are only moderately effective at best, whereas physical countermeasures can be highly effective under certain conditions. Two conditions appear important to the effective use of physical countermeasures. First, employing multiple countermeasures simultaneously improves the person's chances of defeating a polygraph test, at least as far as the control question technique is concerned. Second, physical countermeasures appear relatively ineffective unless people are given special training in their use. It is generally not sufficient merely to provide people with instructions about polygraph techniques and countermeasures.

Although there are clear individual differences in the ability to apply countermeasures effectively, training by experts in the use of physical countermeasures poses a potentially serious threat to the validity of polygraph techniques. For this reason, it becomes very important that the use of countermeasures is readily identified by polygraph examiners. Unfortunately, subtle and effective physical countermeasures are not readily observable without special expertise and equipment which are not generally available to field examiners.

(Gudjonsson, 1988, pp. 135–136)

It would, indeed, be naïve to believe there is a simple foolproof physiological method to detect deceit. Clearly, under certain circumstances the lie detector can be an extremely useful and impressive diagnostic. The worry, however, is the cost of misclassification – the innocent judged guilty and the guilty innocent. A reasonable question is that which asks for an alternative. In serious situations, where other material can be brought to bear in the decision, it seems reasonable at least to consider using the polygraph.

Increase in, or at least concern about, certain types of crime like sexual offences has led researchers to go back to the polygraph. Gannon et al. (2008) have looked again at what they call 'polygraph-assisted risk assessment'. They note that for *post-conviction*, polygraph testing can be seen as an excellent truth *facilitator*. That is, convicted offenders may say much more if polygraphed after being convicted, which may really help their treatment regimen. This allows for better risk assessment, which is particularly important in certain cases.

7.2.6   *Recent Reviews and Developments*

Iacono and Ben-Shakhar (2019) updated a review and concluded:

> Lie detection tests have profound life-altering consequences ranging from public perceptions of an examinee's credibility and integrity to effects on job security and possible incarceration. In 2003, the National Academy of Sciences concluded that polygraph testing had a weak scientific basis and unknown error rate. Analysis of research conducted over the last 15 years indicates that these conclusions remain valid. As polygraph tests are routinely used by law enforcement agencies in North America and other countries, it is vital that the public be aware of their shortcomings.
>
> *(p. 86)*

Can robots catch you lying? This was the question asked by Gonzalez-Billandon et al. (2019), who showed people short movies of robberies and then interrogated by a human and by a humanoid robot 'detective'. Participants provided honest/veridical responses to half of the questions and false/untrue replies to the other half. They measured eye movements, time to respond and eloquence and they found the participant's behavior showed strong similarities during the interaction with the human and the robot. These behavioral features were used to train and test a lie-detection algorithm. They noted that the selected behavioral variables are valid markers of deception both in human–human and in human–robot interactions and could be exploited to effectively enable robots to detect lies. Again, is this the 'science fiction' of our day?

Meijer et al. (2016), in a review, noted that the main challenge of future research is to find paradigms that can isolate cognitive factors associated with deception, rather than the discovery of a unique (brain) correlate of lying. They argued that the Comparison Question Test currently applied in many countries has weak scientific validity, which cannot be remedied by using neuroimaging measures. Other paradigms are promising, but the absence of data from ecologically valid studies poses a challenge for legal admissibility of their outcomes.

The conclusions are always the same. New sophisticated methods from neuropsychology promise much but there remains little proof. Furthermore, the ethical issues will not go away. Toscano (2019), in an America-focused review, concluded that polygraph examinations should not be admissible in federal court. Examiners may not pass the threshold requirements of the Federal Rules of Evidence due to issues relating to certification requirements. The test itself and the way it is administered have been questioned by numerous studies and courts, and currently may *not be reliable enough* to be presented to a jury. Also, the results of a polygraph examination and an examiner's testimony regarding the results are exceedingly prejudicial in nature. Therefore, they argue federal courts should continue the rule that polygraph examiners cannot give opinion testimony due to the many issues arising from the current status of polygraph examinations and examiners.

7.2.7   *Voice Stress Analysis*

Voice contains a lot of data: the way words are pronounced, the tone of the voice, etc. Most people have been surprised when they see a 'favourite radio personality' because he/she did not look like the person they imagined. It is not always possible even to determine the sex and age of a person from their voice alone. Yet we know some voices are judged to be more sincere or sexier than others. Thus people try to change their voice for affect: Baroness Thatcher was famously encouraged to speak more slowly and more deeply to sound more authoritative though many recall the 'shrill', high-pitched speech in the House of Commons when she was angry or excited (Beattie et al., 1982).

There are obvious and interesting 'between people' voice analysis but also a 'within person' voice analysis. If you know somebody well you can 'hear' if they are tired, or stressed or intoxicated. There are various acoustic clues people use. One central question is, can we detect accurately how stressed a person is by their voice?

There has long been evidence that we can detect 'stress' in the voice (Cestaro, 1996; Fuller, 1984; Laukka et al., 2008; Smith, 1977). The next issue is, can we build devices that accurately and sensitively measure stress in the voice? If yes, the issue is what does this tell one (Kleinberg et al., 2018)? Just as in polygraph, the reasoning goes: for most people lying and deception causes anxiety and stress, partly because of the effort in doing so and the guilt involved, but also the fear of being caught. Thus, if we can measure a change in voice and see indicators of stress, it may be (or probably is) because they are lying.

Over the years linguists and computer experts have developed Voice Stress Analysis (VSA), which, a bit like a classic lie detector, measures acoustic changes in the voice, usually as a function of stress. The idea has immediate commercial appeal. Thus an insurance company might use a VSA to study reports and claims over the telephone. Similarly, police departments would be attracted to the technology in interrogating subjects to determine their guilt.

VSA software programs measure changes in voice patterns caused by the stress, or the physical effort, of possibly trying to hide deceptive responses. VSA programs interpret changes in vocal patterns and indicate on a graph very similar to polygraph testing, measuring changes in respiration, heart rate and galvanic skin response. The polygraph does not test audio or video recordings, or statements made either over a telephone or in a remote setting such as a police station or shop: hence the attraction of VSA.

There is also a cost-benefit analysis of using this technology. Damphousse (2008) notes:

> It is important to look at both "hard" and "hidden" costs when deciding whether to purchase or maintain a VSA program. The monetary costs are substantial: it can cost up to $20,000 to purchase LVA. The average cost of CVSA® training and equipment is $11,500. Calculating the current investment nationwide – more than 1,400 police departments currently use CVSA®, according to the manufacturer – the total cost is more than $16 million not including the manpower expense to use it. The hidden costs are, of course, more difficult to quantify. As VSA programs come under greater scrutiny – due, in part, to reports of false confessions during investigations that used VSA – the overall value of the technology continues to be questioned.

In an important review, Damphousse (2008), quoting his long report (Damphousse et al., 2007), asked and answered the question: 'Does VSA actually work?' He noted that 1,400 law enforcement agencies in America at the time used a VSA device and that the National Institute of Justice funded the analysis of two popular devices at the time (NAC, 2003). In a study in which his research team used VSA programs while questioning more than 300 arrestees about their recent drug use, he attempted to answer the fundamental question. The results of the VSA output were then compared to their urine drug test results. They found 15% who said they had not used drugs – but who, according to their urine tests, had – were *correctly* identified by the VSA programs as being deceptive. Also, 8.5% who were telling the truth – that is, their urine tests were consistent with their statements that they had or had not used drugs – were *incorrectly* classified by the VSA programs as being deceptive.

They also found that arrestees who were questioned using the VSA instruments were less likely to lie about illicit drug use compared to arrestees whose responses were recorded by the interviewer with pen and paper. They concluded that the ability of the VSA to accurately detect deception about recent drug use was about 50%, which is quite unacceptable.

Damphousse and his team interviewed a random sample of 319 recent arrestees using two different data analysis packages. The arrestees were asked questions about marijuana use during the previous 30 days, and cocaine, heroin, methamphetamine and PCP use within the previous 72 hours. Thereafter, the arrestee provided a urine sample that was later tested for the presence of the five drugs. These results were compared with the VSA output results to see whether the VSA gave the same result of truthfulness or deceptiveness. They calculated two scores: *Sensitivity rate* (the percentage of deceptive arrestees correctly identified by the VSA devices as deceptive) and *Specificity rate* (the percentage of nondeceptive arrestees correctly classified by the VSA as nondeceptive).

They found an average of 15% (21% for one test; 8% for the other) of the responses by arrestees who lied (based on the urine test) about recent drug use for all five drugs. The specificity rates showed an average of 91.5% accuracy for the five drugs. They then compared the sensitivity and specificity rates to calculate each VSA program's overall 'accuracy rate' in detecting deception and they found that the average accuracy rate for all five drugs was approximately 50%.

They were also interested in the question: does the use of a VSA during an interrogation encourage a person to be more truthful? They note the idea that people will answer more honestly if they believe that their responses can be tested for accuracy is called the 'bogus pipeline' effect. They compared the percentage of deceptive answers to data conducted by the same VSA researchers in the same jail using the same protocols. In both studies, arrestees were told that they would be asked to submit a urine sample after answering questions about their recent drug use. In the VSA study, arrestees were told that a computer program was being used that would detect deceptive responses. They found 14% of the VSA study arrestees were deceptive about recent drug use compared to 40% of the other arrestees.

Other studies essentially found the same results (Harnsberger et al., 2009; Hopkins et al., 2005).

For instance, Horvath et al. (2013) concluded:

> The findings in this field assessment of the LVA's value in detecting deception do not provide any reason for optimism. Here, the LVA operators produced correct calls of deception, on average, only 25% of the time when deception was verified by the polygraph examination result; when deception was not present, when persons were truthful according to the polygraph examination outcome, the LVA operators were correct only 49% of the time. When the 'guilty' persons had confessed their involvement in the matter under investigation and thus had acknowledged their deception, the accuracy of LVA analysis averaged only 48%. There was no instance in which the LVA produced correct decisions beyond chance.
>
> *(p. 6)*

Thus the results of voice analysis are very much like that of the polygraph in the attempted detection of lying. There are too many false positives and false negatives. However, the technology may be of use to deter liars: that is when told they would have to take a voice stress test in an interview, fewer people appear to lie. This is however an expensive and highly dubious way of encouraging people to be more honest in interviews.

7.2.8 Conclusion

All people interested in selecting those whose integrity is fundamental to the job would like a simple, cheap, valid test that helped them *select in* those with integrity but *select out* those more likely to be compromised. They have an impressive choice ranging from simple questionnaires to new voice stress analysers, which may be used to analyse telephone calls.

The central issue for the researchers and the selector is reliability and thence validity. Any test that 'labels' the guilty innocent, the psychopath full of integrity or the deceiving employee a model worker has clearly failed in its primary duty. More serious from both a morality and a libel point of view is a test that erroneously judges the innocent guilty or those who do have integrity as not having it. Some argue that around 10–20% of people are misclassified: the guilty innocent and the innocent guilty, which is quite unacceptable.

There are good tests and bad tests: those which have been properly devised and tested and those which are 'quick and dirty' attempts to make publishers a great deal of money. Certainly, there are those implacably against tests and those who think they are useful. Looking at pen-and-paper tests, it seems the reviewers conclude they can be useful. The test results can usefully *aid* decision-making. That is, with test results and *other corroborative evidence* of guilt or innocence, it is possible to achieve significant improvement in the probability of detecting those who have committed, or will commit, counterproductive work behaviours.

Tests improve the *probability* of detection. Tests alone should never be relied upon to do this. This situation is even more the case with the polygraph, which has been very extensively tested. For some people, the idea of psychological – as opposed to self-report – responses is very attractive. It seems much harder to 'beat the lie detector' then come up as convincing on a questionnaire.

Yet, reviews have showed that, whatever technique is used, there are errors of classification. The optimist points to the overwhelming number of correct classifications, the pessimist to the errors.

As Oswald (2020) noted:

> The polygraph machine cannot 'detect lies'; it merely records bodily changes, and human interpretation of its results is required for any diagnosis of deception. Neither can a machine learning tool independently 'predict' risk or a person's future; rather real-world

experience is reduced to variables and an algorithm trained to detect patterns or similarities based on probabilities. The interpretation of the output as a prediction or contribution to a 'risk' assessment should be a human one ...

The lie detector experience shows us that, despite a ban on its use in some contexts, it will continue to be deployed in others due to a belief in its utility, whether or not it 'works'. If we are not to find ourselves in a similar position with respect to machine learning, we must develop an oversight framework based upon a combination of scientific validity and relevance standards, fairness principles and the role of the legitimate human decision-maker. Father Brown wisely said that 'no machine can lie ... nor can it tell the truth;' if we remember that machines are just that – machines – and cannot make the decisions which in our legal systems should be reserved for human judgement and discretion, then we will be half way there.

(p. 222)

REFERENCES

Beattie, G. W., Cutler, A., and Pearson, M. (1982). Why is Mrs Thatcher interrupted so often. *Nature, 300*(5894), 744–747.

Bull, R. (1988). What is the lie-detection test? In A. Gale (Ed.), *The polygraph test: Lies, truth and science* (pp. 10–19). London, UK: Sage Publications, Inc; British Psychological Society.

Carroll, D. (1988). How accurate is polygraph lie detection? In A. Gale (Ed.), *The polygraph test: Lies, truth and science* (pp. 19–28). London, UK: Sage Publications, Inc; British Psychological Society.

Cestaro, V. L.(1996). A comparison between decision accuracy rates obtained using the polygraph instrument and the Computer Voice Stress Analyzer (CVSA) in the absence of jeopardy. *Polygraph, 25*, 117–127.

Damphousse, K. (2008). Voice stress analysis. National Institute of Justice. July.

Damphousse, K., Pointon, L., Upchurch, D., & Moore, R. K. (2007). Assessing the Validity of Voice Stress Analysis Tools in a Jail Setting. Department of Justice.

Ekman, P. (2001) *Telling lies: Clues to deceit in the marketplace, politics and marriage.* New York City, NY: W. W. Norton.

Fuller, B. F. (1984). Reliability and validity of an interval measure of vocal stress. *Psychological Medicine, 1984*, 159–166.

Gale, A. (Ed.). (1988). *The polygraph test: Lies, truth and science.* London, UK: Sage Publications, Inc; British Psychological Society.

Gannon, T. A., Beech, A. R., & Ward, T. (2008). Does the polygraph lead to better risk prediction for sexual offenders? *Aggression and Violent Behavior, 13*(1), 29–44.

Gonzalez-Billandon, J., Aroyo, A., Pasquali, D., Tonelli, A., Gori, M., Sciutti, A., Sandini, G., & Rea, F. (2019). Can a robot catch you lying? A machine learning system to detect lies during interactions. *Frontiers in Robotics and AI, 6*(64), 1–12.

Gudjonsson, G. H. (1988). Compliance in an interrogative setting: a new scale. *Personality and Individual Differences, 10,* 535–540.

Harnsberger, J. D., Hollien, H., Martin, C. A.,& Hollien, K. A. (2009). Stress and deception in speech: evaluating layered voice analysis. *Journal of Forensic Science,54*(3), 642–650.

Hopkins, C. S., Ratley, R., Benincasa, D., & Grieco, J. (2005). Evaluation of Voice Stress Analysis Technology. Proceedings of the 38th Annual Hawaii International Conference on System Sciences. Honalulu, HI.

Horvath, F., McCloughan, J., Weatherman, D., & Slowik, S. (2013). The accuracy of auditors' and Layered Voice Analysis (LVA) operators' judgments of truth and deception during police questioning. *Journal of Forensic Sciences, 58*(2), 385–392.

Iacono, W. G., & Ben-Shakhar, G. (2019). Current status of forensic lie detection with the comparison question technique: an update of the 2003 National Academy of Sciences report on polygraph testing. *Law and Human Behavior, 43*(1), 86–98.

Iacono, W. G., & Lykken, D. T. (1997). The validity of the lie detector: two surveys of scientific opinion. *Journal of Applied Psychology, 82*(3), 426–433.

Kleinberg, B., van der Toolen, Y., Arntz, A., & Verschuere, B. (2018). Detecting concealed information on a large scale: possibilities and problems. In J. P. Rosenfeld (Ed.), *Detecting concealed information and deception: Recent developments* (pp. 377–403). New York: Elsevier Academic Press.

Larson, J. (1932). *Lying and its detection: A study of deception and deception tests.* Chicago, IL: University of Chicago Press.

Laukka, P., Linnman, C., Åhs, F., Pissiota, A., Frans, Ö., Faria, V., Michelgård, Å., Appel, L., Fredrikson, M., & Furmark, T. (2008). In a nervous voice: acoustic analysis and perception of anxiety in social phobics' speech. *Journal of Nonverbal Behavior, 32*(4), 195–214.

Lykken, D. (1998). *A tremor in the blood: Use and abuse of the lie detector.* New York City, NY: Plenum Publishing Corporation.

Meijer, E. H., Verschuere, B., Gamer, M., Merckelbach, H., & Ben-Shakhar, G. (2016). Deception detection with behavioral, autonomic, and neural measures:

conceptual and methodological considerations that warrant modesty. *Psychophysiology*, 53(5), 593–604.

Miner, J. B., & Capps, M. H. (1996). *How honesty testing works*. Westport, CT: Greenwood Publishing Group.

National Research Council. (2003). *The polygraph and lie detection*. Washington, DC: National Academies Press.

Oswald, M. (2020). Technologies in the twilight zone: early lie detectors, machine learning and reformist legal realism. *International Review of Law, Computers & Technology*, 34(2), 214–231.

Raskin, D.C. (1988). Does science support polygraph testing? In A. Gale (Ed.), *The polygraph test: Lies, truth and science* (pp. 96–110). London, UK: Sage Publications, Inc; British Psychological Society.

Toscano, Matthew J. (2019). *Polygraph examiners: history, modem status, and admissibility in court*. Law School Student Scholarship. 1020. https://scholarship.shu.edu/student_scholarship/1020

Vrij, A. (2000). *Detecting lies and deceit: The psychology of lying and implications for professional practice*. Chichester, UK: John Wiley & Sons.

8   Biography

What is it?
It is belief that the best indicator of the future is the past: that features of a person's biography are subtle, powerful and valid predictors of their future behaviour.

How does it work?
A wide range of empirically validated facts about an individual's life history are correlated with measures of the job success to provide the basis of an algorithm to use to score a CV or biography or autobiography.

What of the evidence?
There is a lot of evidence, some equivocal, but given particular constraints, like type of job, the method has been shown to be valid: personal history predicts future behaviour.

Practical problems: cost, ethics, politics
The process is costly to validate over periods of time and there are often considerable ethical problems associated with both unintended discrimination and privacy issues.

Recommendations for use
Much depends on the nature of the job and the type of individual applying, but it has proven for more than 100 years to be an effective selection tool if treated cautiously.

8.1.1   Introduction

We are not victims but products of our past: when and where we grew up, our parents' social class values and parenting style, our education, etc. There have been, over the years, many attempts to profile individuals on the basis of their personal history. It is the link between individuals' life history and their educational, work and social history. It is based on the simple assumption that the best predictor of the future is the past.

It is also known as profiling. One of the best known is *Offender or Criminal profiling*. This can take many forms (a clinical, geographic, typological approach), but the primary aim in most cases is to identify (and then detain) a criminal or criminal gang. There is also *Psychobiography*, which is more than biography as it attempts to use psychological theories to interpret and explain, as well as describe, a (living or dead) person's behaviour. It tends to focus on motives and on how particular events shaped people. This technique dates back to Freud, and there are many books written by psychologists and others on the psychological makeup of various famous people.

People profiling involves collecting a great deal of information, verifying it and putting it together in some meaningful way.

There are essentially three ways of doing this:

1. *The typological approach*: This usually involves having a set of pre-existing types or categories and trying to see which one the target person best fits. It is attractively simple but tends to overlook significant data and to simplify rather than clarify. People are too easily 'fitted' into pre-ordained boxes that may not capture sufficiently the complexities and inconsistencies of human behaviour that is so important.

2. *The algorithm approach*: This method is derived from multivariate statisticians who collect specific data that they 'feed' into a mathematical model which weights, processes and combines the data in a particular way. There is a pre-ordained formula: the sort of thing that actuaries use when making their calculations. It appears to be very scientific but can be misleading given the nature of what is 'fed in' and the evidence for the particular algorithm. Everything depends on the accuracy of a formula that may not easily be able to cope with the sort of data we have about elements such as a person's motivation.

3. *The thematic approach*: This involves making a semi-clinical and experiential judgement based on a weighting of factors. It differs from the algorithmic approach in that the gestalt judgement has to be based on

clinical judgement. Inevitably, this requires considerable training in the field to ensure conclusions are both reliable and insightful.

In this chapter we will consider a number of different but related techniques that are based on the simple assumption that understanding what an individual has done is the best way to predict what he or she will do.

8.1.2 Biodata

Biographical data – simply known as *biodata* – is information about a person's background and life history, such as years of higher education, the date of first job and time in last job. The idea is to find those biographical factors that are related to some important outcome like academic or job performance and employment turnover, so that assessors can make better decisions (Song et al., 2019). For the most part it is totally, or as Cook (2016) notes, 'mindlessly empirical'.

Biodata are typically obtained through *application forms*, which are used extensively in most Western countries. In biodata terms they become *weighted application blanks (WABs)*. The aim is to design an application form which collects only *data known and shown to demonstrably predict specific work-related performance*. The form collects biographical information that has previously been correlated with desirable work criteria (notably job performance). Furthermore, it incorporates 'weighted scoring' by which questions are coded and treated as individual predictors of relevant work criteria. They are weighted because some features are more important/predictive than others.

Thus, if it has been shown that education does not predict job success, no information is collected on the type and amount of education an individual has received (from primary school to postgraduate training). Equally, if family size (number of siblings) or sporting success has been shown to be predictors, then detailed information is collected on those variables.

For example, Sulastri et al. (2015) were interested in biodata markers of young people finding a job. Predictably, exam success (Grade Point Average) showed significant relationship with success in finding psychology-based jobs. Work experiences predicted the success in finding a job in general while extracurricular activities, foreign language skill and participation in general enrichment programmes showed significant relationships with success in finding psychology-based jobs. However, computer skills did not emerge as a determinant of getting a job.

Gatewood et al. (2015) gave examples of the sort of information that application forms usually ask: name, age, gender, marital status, children, education, ethnicity; physical characteristics (height and weight), religion, health status (physical and mental), citizenship (past and present), military service, arrest/conviction record; hobbies/clubs; credit rating, drivers licence, emergency contact details. They also noted acceptable vs unacceptable ways of getting this data. Thus, if it is not advised to ask date of birth, you ask 'are you over 18 years'; and for religion you say, 'The employer may state the days, hours and shifts to be worked'.

Often whether it is done formally and explicitly the information collected in application forms is often used to assess abilities (particularly leadership, language, maths, physical), interpersonal skills and particularly motivation (Gatewood et al., 2015).

8.1.3 Typical Questions

The following are typical biodata items:

As you grew up, how did you feel about school?

1. Liked it very much
2. Liked it most of the time
3. Just accepted it as necessary
4. Was often a little unhappy with it
5. Cordially disliked it and was glad to finish

How many times did you change schools before you were 16 years of age other than by graduation?

1. Never
2. One or two times

3. Three to five times
4. Six or more times
5. I can't remember

About how many new friends have you made in the past year?

1. No need to make new friends
2. One or two
3. Three or four
4. Six or more
5. Can't remember exactly

Before you were 18 years of age, how many times did your family move from one house to another?

1. Never
2. Once
3. Two or three times
4. Four or five times
5. Move every year or so

In what section of town did your family live longest while you were growing up?

1. Lived in one of the most exclusive sections of town
2. Lived in a good but not the best section
3. Lived in an average section of town
4. Lived in one of the poorer sections of town
5. Lived in a rural area

While in school, how often did your father or guardian appear to take an interest in how you were doing in your classes?

1. Never
2. Once in a great while
3. Frequently
4. Always

While in high school, about how many evenings a week did you go out?

1. Less than one
2. One
3. Two
4. Three
5. Four or more

How to construct good biodata items? There are a number of criteria that are recommended: brevity; options should be expressed in numbers and contain all alternatives; items should convey a neutral or pleasant connotation; an item should not try to retrieve information beyond the memory of the respondent; extremes on the continuum of choices may be more consistent than those in the middle position; statements should be positively worded; a response continuum should not be defined in qualitative terms, for instance 'seldom', 'occasionally', and 'frequently'.

Some biodata is easy to score like demographics, but much of what selectors are interested in is more difficult like the quality and quantity of training an applicant has had, as well as his/her salient job experience.

8.1.3.1 Crucial Dimensions for Valid Data

Not all questions about an individual's biography make up valid items. Indeed, there are nine features that differentiate a valid biographical question diversity of constructs assessed (explicitly or implicitly) by biodata is such that there is no common definition for biodata.

1. Verifiable vs unverifiable: All responses can be verified by different sources.
2. Historical vs futuristic: It concerns the past, not the future.
3. Actual vs hypothetical behaviour: All data concerns actual behaviour that has occurred.
4. Memory vs conjecture: It can be verified by the memory of many involved.
5. Factual vs interpretive: All data is factual and not interpretative.

6. Specific vs general: Everything is about actual specific behaviours.
7. Response vs response tendency: Questions concern actual responses to situations.
8. External events vs internal events: They are about actual behaviours that could be observed.
9. Strictly biographical vs attitudes: This is about behaviours rather than beliefs and attitudes.

Gatewood et al. (2015) gives examples of these (Table 8.1).

Indeed, 'biodata scales have been shown to measure numerous constructs, such as temperament, assessment of work conditions, values, skills, aptitudes, and abilities' (Mount et al., 2000, p. 300). Some have argued that biodata represent a more valid predictor of occupational success than traditional personality tests (Mumford et al., 1996), as well as reducing aversive impact in comparison to cognitive ability/intelligence tests (Stokes et al., 1994).

8.1.3.2 Structure of Biodata

The following are typical groups or clusters of data points collected by biodata researchers: habits and attitude; health; human relations; money; parental, home, childhood and teen experiences; personal attributes; present home, spouse and children; recreation, hobbies, and interests; school and education; self-impressions; values, opinions, and preferences; and work experience.

Mumford et al.'s *ecology model* (Mumford et al., 1990) postulated that biodata can be organised in terms of core knowledge, skill, ability, value and expectancy variables that explain how people develop their characteristic patterns of adaptation at work and beyond. These constructs 'facilitate the attainment of desired outcomes while conditioning future situational choice by increasing the likelihood of reward in certain kinds of situations' (Mumford & Stokes, 1992, p. 81).

Dean and Russell's (2005) results provide a robust source of evidence in support of the validity of coherently constructed and scored biodata scales, not least because they organised their items

Table 8.1 *The eight criteria of good biodata items*

1. Verifiable:	**Unverifiable:**
Did you graduate from college?	How much did you enjoy high school?
2. Historical:	**Futuristic:**
How many jobs have you held in the past 5 years?	What job would you like to hold 5 years from now?
3. Actual behaviour:	**Hypothetical behaviour:**
Have you ever repaired a broken radio?	If you had your choice, what job would you like to hold now?
4. Memory:	**Conjecture:**
How would you describe your life at home while growing up?	If you were to go through college again, what would you choose as a major?
5. Factual:	**Interpretive:**
How many hours do you spend at work in a typical week?	If you could choose your supervisor, what characteristic would you want him or her to have?
6. Specific:	**General:**
While growing up, did you collect coins?	While growing up, what activities did you enjoy most?
7. Response:	**Response Tendency:**
Which of the following hobbies do you enjoy?	When you have a problem at work to whom do you turn for assistance?
8. External Event:	**Internal Event:**
When you were a teenage, how much time did your father spend with you?	Which best describes the feelings you had when you last worked with a computer?

according to established constructs (interpersonal skills, personality, and values). Among the different scales or aspects of biodata, intellectual resources predicted job performance best, followed by choice processes and social and personality resources; filter processes were only weakly related to job performance.

Studies have also shown that purpose-built biodata that include a defined structure (different scales) can be used successfully to predict performance in college, even when entry exam scores (SAT) and personality factors are taken into account (Oswald et al., 2004).

Oswald et al. (2004) looked at biodata (115 items) in a sample of 654 college students and identified 12 major dimensions which they used to predict final academic grades, such as:

> *Knowledge* ('Think about the last several times you have had to learn new facts or concepts about something. How much did you tend to learn?')
>
> *Citizenship* ('How often have you signed a petition for something you believe in?)
>
> *Leadership* ('How many times in the past year have you tried to get someone to join an activity in which you were involved or leading?')
>
> *Ethics* ('If you were leaving a concert and noticed that someone left their purse behind with no identification, what would you do?)

They also tested the extent to which their 12 biodata factors predicted GPA, absenteeism and peer ratings while controlling for SAT and personality scores. Their results showed that six facets were still significantly linked to these outcomes even when previous academic performance and psychometrically derived trait scores were included in the regression model. As seen, leadership and health were linked to GPA, citizenship, interpersonal and learning-predicted peer ratings, and absenteeism was predicted by health and ethics.

8.1.3.3   Scoring of Biodata

It is the very scoring of biodata that sets it apart from the more informal use of application forms, references or CV (where employers may simply eliminate candidates on the basis of eye-balling these documents). There are three different but related ways of scoring data. These different methods have been compared (Cucina et al., 2012).

One rigorous and effective approach for scoring biodata is the so-called *empirical keying*, which codes each item or question into yes = 1 or no = 0 and weights them according to their correlations with the criterion (as derived from previous samples or a subset of the current sample). Item scores are all added up for each candidate.

It has been reported that empirical keying shows incremental validity in the prediction of occupational success over and above personality scales and cognitive ability measures (Mount et al., 2000). Empirical keying makes biodata markedly different from standard personality inventories, which are scored in terms of reliability or internal consistencies but not on the basis of their association with the criteria they are used to predict. In that sense, personality measures are internally constructed whereas biodata items are externally constructed.

Biodata can also be scored via *factorial/internal keying*, which identifies higher-order domains or common themes underlying groups of items, just like personality scales group questions on the basis of specific traits. Mumford and Owens identified the factors of adjustment, academic performance, extraversion and leadership in over 20 studies (Mumford & Owens, 1987). Others have scored biodata items in terms of family and social orientation (Carlson et al., 1999) and money management (Stokes & Searcy, 1999).

Other than that, factorial-keyed biodata are 'indistinguishable from personality items in content, response format, and scoring. Personality tests typically contain items regarding values and attitudes and biodata items generally focus on past achievements of behaviours, but even this distinction is not obvious in many biodata applications today' (Schmitt & Kunce, 2002, p. 570).

Third, *rational keying* is used to design biodata inventories that are based on the specific job requirements or characteristics. Fine and Cronshaw (1994) proposed that a thorough job analysis informs the selection of biodata items. Rational keying refers to the construction rather than analysis or scoring phase of biodata and there is no reason why it cannot be combined with factorial keying. Drakeley found rational keying to be more valid than empirical keying (Drakeley et al., 1988), though more recent and robust investigations estimated both methods to have comparable validities (Stokes & Searcy, 1999).

Each method has its advantages and disadvantages: empirical keying is advantageous in that it makes biodata 'invisible' and hard to fake for the respondents, as many predictors of occupational success are bound to be counter-intuitive and identified purely on an empirical basis. Additional problems with empirical keying are that it does not generalise well to other samples and it does not advance our theoretical understanding of the reasons for which items predict occupational success (Mount et al., 2000).

Rational keying may be easy to justify from a theoretical point of view and provides an opportunity for excluding items with adverse impact (Hough & Paullin, 1994; Schmitt et al., 1999). However, the advantages of rational keying may come at the expense of making 'correct responses' too obvious for respondents and increasing the likelihood of faking (Lautenschlager, 1994).

Factorial keying makes biodata identical to personality inventories, especially if attitudinal or subjective items are also included. It has been argued that even experts would fail to distinguish between personality scales and factorial-keyed biodata (Robertson & Smith, 2001). Moreover, personality scales have some advantages over biodata, such as being more 'theory-driven', assessing higher-order and more stable dispositions, and generalising quite easily across settings and criteria.

However, there are other methods, such as coding their free responses to specific questions. This has been shown to lower faking and measure verbal ability rather well (Levashina et al., 2012). Indeed, great sophistication in web technology has meant that organisations are analysing individuals' Facebook pages to get many ideas about their values and lifestyle.

There have been many developments in this area, which means that it will probably become more popular (Speer et al., 2020)

8.1.3.4   Verifiability of Biodata and Faking

A main difference between personality and biodata inventories is that the latter include a larger number of verifiable or 'harder' items, such as basic demographic or background information. These items are uncontrollable (what can one do about one's place of birth or ethnicity?) and intrusive compared to the 'softer', more controllable unverifiable items assessing attitudes and behaviours: e.g. What are your views on recycling? How often do you go to the gym? Do you think people should drink less? Do you like country music?

It has, however, been suggested that unverifiable items increase the probability of faking (Becker & Colquitt, 1992). Indeed, although some degree of inflation does exist for verifiable items, early studies reported inter-correlations in the region of .95 between responses given to different employers (Keating et al., 1950), showing that verifiable items yield very consistent responses even across different jobs. Yet, a review of the literature concluded that faking affects both verifiable and non-verifiable items and that attempts to control it have been largely unsuccessful, though empirical keying prevents faking more than other keying types (Lautenschlager, 1994).

Biodata can be collected from an application form. Some are more complicated than others and collect considerable amounts of information. Often a problem with these is that people lie, particularly because it is so difficult and expensive to check all details. Hence, there are now companies who offer this service. Consider what is the below:

Confirming Employment History Checks

When recruiting it's likely that you're looking for a candidate with relevant experience and an applicable employment history. You need to be sure that your successful applicant hasn't elaborated on their previous roles or, even worse, falsified them entirely.

But tracking someone's employment history can be time consuming, difficult and prone to mistakes. So when it comes to employment verification, trust the experts.

Using a contacts database created by our skilled researchers, HireRight will provide an accurate overview of a candidate's employment history. By contacting former employers or authorised agents, we'll provide you with the important information you need to ensure that you hire the right person.

> By thoroughly checking and verifying someone's employment history, we'll show you whether or not your applicant has the correct skills and experience for the role on offer, allowing you to make a sensible, informed decision.

One study compared the validity of verifiable and non-verifiable biodata items in call centre employees and applicants (Harold et al., 2006). Results showed that although applicants did not score significantly higher on overall biodata items than their incumbent counterparts, non-verifiable items had lower validities in the applicant sample. Harold et al. (2006) concluded that 'the good news is that a biodata inventory comprised of all verifiable items was equally valid across incumbent and applicant samples regardless of the criterion examined', but '[T]he bad news, however, is that the validity of non-verifiable items shrank in the applicant sample' (p. 343).

Regardless of these results, modern jobs, which require customer/client services and teamwork, call for attitudinal and inter-personal constructs to be assessed in order to predict occupational success. Thus, non-verifiable, soft, subjective items will inevitably be incorporated in contemporary biodata scales. Schmitt and colleagues proposed that in order to reduce faking and social desirability respondents should *elaborate* on their answers – a method previously used in 'accomplishment records', e.g. 'give three examples of situations where you showed to work well under pressure' or 'can you recall past experiences where you showed strength and leadership?' (Hough, 1984).

Results indicated that respondents tended to score lower (be more modest) on items that required elaboration (Schmitt & Kunce, 2002); indeed scores on elaborative items were .6 SD lower, which is roughly the difference found between participants instructed to respond honestly and those asked to 'fake good' in laboratory studies (Ellingson et al., 1999; Ones et al., 1996). Furthermore, a subsequent study showed that the validities of elaborative items were in line with standard biodata items and in some cases even higher (Schmitt et al., 2003). The validities (predicting self-ratings, self-deception, impression management, GPA and attendance) were unaffected by elaboration instructions even though lower means were found for the elaborative items.

Other methods for reducing the likelihood of faking in respondents have included *warnings* (Schrader & Osburn, 1977), such as 'Any inaccuracies or fake information provided will be checked and result in your no longer being considered for this job', to the more creative use of 'bogus' (fake) items that may trick respondents into faking good (Paunonen, 1984): for example, 'How many years have you been using the HYU-P2 software for?' However, including bogus items is widely deemed unethical.

Cook (2016) noted that the fakeability of biodata has still attracted attention and that all sorts of methods are used to attempt to reduce it like, including bogus items, and warning that the measure has lie-detection questions.

There is also one other important issue rarely discussed: fairness and discrimination. There can be all sorts of subtle issues that do this. Imagine one found a sport (rugby/soccer) was a predictor but is played much more by one gender rather than another, or that family size or type of schooling were strong predictors which are related to social status.

8.1.3.5 Validity of Biodata

This is, as always, the crucial question. Early empirical evidence on the validity of biodata was provided by England (1961), who reported an average correlation of .40 between weighted application blanks and turnover. Another investigation by Wernimont (1962) identified three main variables that predicted length of service in female officers from 1954 to 1959 with similar accuracy: namely high proficiency at shorthand, whether they left their previous jobs because of pregnancy, marriage, sickness or domestic problems, and whether they were willing to start with their news job within the next week.

Meta-analyses are particularly important in biodata research because of the heterogeneity of different biodata studies and the importance of testing whether validities generalise from one sample to another. Validities for biodata have varied significantly, e.g. from the low-to-mid .20's (Hunter & Hunter, 1984; Schmitt et al., 1984) up to the .50's (Reilly & Chao, 1982). Although even the lower-bound validity estimates are higher than the validities reported for most personality scales (see Section 4.2), and Schmidt and Hunter's seminal meta-analysis of 85 years of validity studies estimated a validity of .35 for biodata (Schmidt & Hunter, 1998), it is important to provide an accurate estimate of the validity of biodata, which requires identification of the factors that moderate the impact of biodata predictors on occupational criteria.

Bliesener (1996) meta-analysed previously reported meta-analyses, paying careful attention to methodological differences among different validity studies. Over one hundred samples including 106,302 participants were examined, yielding an estimated (uncorrected) validity of .38 (SD = .19). However, when correcting for methodological artefacts and statistical errors, the overall validity for biodata inventories dropped to .22 (usually, corrected estimates tend to yield higher rather than lower validities), which still meets the criteria for utility and incremental validity (Barthel & Schuler, 1989). Bliesener's results showed that biodata was a more valid predictor of occupational success for women (.51) than for men (.27). Larger-than-average validities were found for studies that concurrently administered all measures (.35). He concluded that 'Biographical data are a valid predictor of an applicant's suitability. This, combined with their high economy, their universal applicability, and the ease of combining them with other predictive procedures, makes them a valuable instrument in personnel selection' (Bliesener, 1996, p. 118).

Regarding the generalisability of biodata, Carlson and colleagues (1999) constructed a 5-factor biodata inventory, which they found to correlate at .52 with occupational success in one organisation. They then administered the same inventory to 24 organisations (including 7,334 employees) and found an overall validity of .48, indicating that biodata scales do indeed generalise to different organisations. That said, validities for biodata scales have been found to vary depending on job type. As shown, biodata have been found to be consistently more valid for clerical jobs, followed by managerial jobs. Sales jobs have yielded more heterogeneous results, and military jobs have produced consistently lower validities.

Another study found that people's capacity to cope with change, self-efficacy for change and past experiences, as assessed via biodata items, predicted occupational success over and above cognitive ability (though cognitive ability was a more powerful predictor; Allworth & Hesketh, 2000). In regards to personality, studies have shown biodata scales to predict performance outcomes incrementally in US cadets (q); for a replication see McManus and Kelly (1999). Moreover, Mount et al.'s study simultaneously controlled for the Big Five personality traits (see Section 4.3.3) and general cognitive ability (see Section 4.2.2) and found that biodata still explained unique variance in four occupational criteria (Mount et al., 2000). Biodata explained 2% of unique variance in problem-solving performance (even this incremental validity was significant, albeit marginally), 5% of unique variance in quantity and quality of work, 7% of additional variance in interpersonal relationships, and 17% of extra variance in retention probability.

Gatewood et al. (2015) reviewed various studies which looked at biodata markers of various criteria with large samples (nearly all more than 3,000). The average validity coefficient ranged from .21 to .37. Cook (2016), who examined different types of validity (construct, incremental, transport), did point out that validity does differ between types of jobs (clerical, sales, managerial) but that they tend to range from .30 to .40, which is very acceptable.

Studies have also provided evidence for the *incremental validity* of biodata over established personality and cognitive ability measures. These studies are important because of the known overlap between these measures and biodata and show that even if personality and intelligence are measured and taken into account biodata scales provide *additional useful information* about the predicted outcome. Incremental validity of biodata over cognitive ability tests has been demonstrated in samples of army recruits (Mael & Ashforth, 1995) and air traffic controllers (Dean et al., 1999; see also Karas & West (1999)).

8.1.3.6 An Evaluation of Biodata

The latest developments in this area include internet-based resume screening using keywords. There are various arguments in favour of biodata: it is empirical not theoretical; candidates like it; it can appraise non-cognitive aspects of people; people can be compared; people are unlikely to lie; biodata are objective and consistent; minorities can be identified and treated fairly. Yet others claim it leads to organisational homogeneity vs heterogeneity. There is a cloning of the past. Critics claim it is atheoretical, time consuming and prone to faking. Other objections are that biodata doesn't travel well, validity shrinks over time and fairness in the law cannot be guaranteed.

Although biodata vary widely in their structure, form and how they are collected and scored, they include both objective (hard and verifiable) and subjective (soft and unverifiable) items. The latter are more easily faked – and influenced by socially desirable responding and impression management – than the former, though faking can potentially affect any form of biodata. One way of reducing faking appears to be to request respondents to elaborate further on their answers to biodata items.

The most important conclusion is that biodata no doubt represent a valid approach for predicting occupational success (in its various forms). Indeed, meta-analytic estimates provided validities for biodata in the region of .25, and this is probably a conservative estimate. In any case, this means that biodata are as valid predictors as the best personality scales, though the fact that biodata scales overlap with both personality and cognitive ability measures limits the appeal of biodata. Incremental validity studies have shown that even when established personality and intelligence measures are taken into account, biodata still predict job performance. To some biodata research is a quaint research backwater for selection researchers, yet it refuses to be dismissed and seems to be attracting more and better research.

In summary, the *Advantages* are argued to be:

Objectivity: The same questions are asked of everyone who completes the form, and the answers given are assessed in a consistent way. It is also possible to monitor candidates' responses to individual questions and eliminate items that show evidence of discrimination against some social groups.

Cost: Although there may be fairly extensive R&D costs, once criteria are known, biodata are very cheap. Biodata forms can be developed in multiple-choice formats which are amenable to machine scoring or direct entry to a computer terminal. Thus, processing large numbers of applicants can become a routine clerical activity, freeing valuable personnel professionals' or line-managers' time.

Checkability: It is possible, in theory at any rate, to check up on the answers of the respondents. This fact may reduce faking.

Validity: Nearly all the studies have shown that biodata are a valid and reliable way of selecting individuals. Certainly, the results look as if biodata are better than interviews and personality questionnaires, and as good as ability tests.

Similarly, the *Disadvantages* are seen to be:

Homogeneity versus heterogeneity: If many biographical items are used in selection, the organisation inevitably becomes more homogeneous, which has both advantages and disadvantages. Heterogeneity may occur across divisions (with different criteria) but not within them.

Cloning the past: Biodata work on the idea that past behaviour predicts current performance, but if current criteria are very unstable (say in a rapidly changing market) one is perpetually out of date. Biodata may be best in stable organisations and environments.

Faking: Biodata has been shown to be fakeable. Goldstein (1971) checked information given by applicants for a nursing aide post with what previous employers said. Half the sample overestimated how long they had worked for their previous employer. Overstating previous salary and describing part-time work as full time were also common. More seriously, a quarter gave reasons for leaving their previous job with which the employer did not agree, and no fewer than 17% gave as their previous employer someone who had never heard of them.

Fairness in the law: If biodata items show major biographical correlates such as sex, race, religion and age, one may want to select or reject particular individuals, which is illegal. Items such as age, sex and marital status may in fact be challenged by the courts if such items are included in inventories for the purpose of personnel selection. In that event, whatever gains in predictive power are to be derived through the inclusion of these items must be weighed against the possible expenses of legal defence.

Discovering the selection criteria can be useful in itself: Many organisations have never really examined their selection in detail. The criteria have just gone up over time or reflect the personal preferences of recruiters. The process of diagnosing clear selection criteria in advance of setting up a biodata system will have considerable benefits for the whole selection process.

8.1.4 Psychobiography

There are whole sections of bookshops dedicated to biographies of heroes and villains, politicians and film and sport stars. There are also revealing autobiographies where people tell their life story. Cynics and sceptics often treat autobiographies with scorn because of the motives of the writers: what is left out, what is exaggerated, what is simply changed.

But what can an accurate personal history or biography tell us about an individual? Does the past really predict the future? But what information is relevant and predictive?

Data can include (a) autobiographies; (b) diaries; (c) letters; (d) unstandardised, open questionnaires; (e) oral reports like interviews; and (f) certain literary products. Allport calls these first-person documents, but besides these we can use reports obtained from a third person, just as (g) case studies, (h) life stories and (i) biographies (Kőváry, 2011).

There is an area of research called psychobiography. It seeks to understand an individual by looking at their life and the factors that marked it. There have been a number of biographies written by psychologists, noticeably Freud, who wrote a highly contested life of Leonardo da Vinci. They differ in many ways from conventional biographies for trying to understand the consequences of particular events. Hence, it is possible to find and test particular hypotheses:

Firstborns: Firstborns are groomed for a life of perfectionism, leadership, and drive, and have the responsibility of wearing the family mantle of leadership.

Frequency of travel/transiency: Instils self-sufficiency, independence, perseverance, temerity and ability to cope with the unknown. Children learn how to effectively deal with ambiguity.

Little formal education: Instils the need to overachieve. Insecurity makes children try harder. Boarding schools instil autonomy, independence and self-confidence.

Fantasy hero mentors: Imprint children with an unconscious feeling of omnipotence and removes all limits for potential achievement. Great role models for achievement.

Early traumas: Early crises indelibly imprint children with unusual resolve and endow them with higher-than-normal risk-taking propensity and drive.

Positive role mentors: Independent and self-employed fathers instil autonomous spirit and demonstrate ability to make it in a world outside a corporate womb.

Permissive families: Instil temerity and independence. Freedom to risk and err without remorse builds coping skills and positive/optimistic views of the unknown.

The above are interesting and reasonable hypotheses but nothing more. Indeed, they have been condemned by many biographers as being simple-minded, over-generalisations that downplay other important and complex life-history factors that have many consequences. It is also an area where many psychologists are hesitant, though there are recognised experts such as Runyan. For instance, in a celebrated paper, Runyan (1981) looked at 13 different explanations as to why van Gogh cut off his ear. His conclusion to an evaluation of this sort was

> It is sometimes suggested that interpretation of single cases is little more than an arbitrary application of one's theoretical preferences. No doubt this happens at times, but any method can be poorly used. Effective use of the case study method requires not only the formulation of explanations consistent with some of the evidence but also that preferred explanations be critically examined in light of all available evidence, and that they be compared in plausibility with alternative explanations. After the implausible alternatives have been eliminated, more than one explanation consistent with the available evidence may remain, but this is far different from saying that the facts can be adequately explained in terms of any theoretical conjecture ...
>
> In spite of these difficulties, the problem of developing explanations of events in individual lives deserves our critical attention as it is inevitably encountered in everyday life and is a crucial task within personology, psychobiography, and the clinical professions. Further work is needed both on the intriguing epistemological question of what degrees of certainty can and cannot be attained in the explanation of events in individual lives and on the methodological problem of how best to develop such explanations.
>
> *(p. 1076)*

So, what sort of questions would psychobiographers use in trying to assess, evaluate or understand an individual? Taylor et al. (2014), in a book called *Revealed*, suggested that the following questions yielded interesting and important information that might help fully understand an individual as well as predict their future.

8.1.4.1   *Research Questions*

Family and early years:

Basic biographical details:

What was the person's date and place of birth?
What was the socio-political status of that place?
Did they have any major geographic moves before the age of 15?

Parents:

Were the person's parents close/separated/divorced?
What was their parenting style – tough, loving, absent?
Did someone else assume the role of carer?

Social status:

Does the subject come from a wealthy or poor background?
Were or could they be considered as being from a minority? If so,
   which?

Parental approach to learning:

Are the subject's parents intellectually strong and did they provide an
   intellectually stimulating environment during childhood?

Siblings:

How old and what gender are the subject's siblings?
What is their relationship with them like?

Misfortunes:

Did the subject suffer any major misfortunes or traumas in early
   childhood (up to the age of say 15), e.g. parental loss, messy
   divorce, witnessing a horrid death in war or closer to home, sexual
   abuse?

Emotional and practical support:

Did the subject have supportive friends and family or others
   around them?
Who were the most significant/influential people in their early lives?
Did they feel in any other way deprived?

Education:

What kind of school did the person attend?
Were their teachers competent and supportive?
Were they successful in their studies? Were they elected to positions
of leadership?

Social:

Was the subject brought up in a rich social environment with many
friends from culturally or socially different backgrounds?
Did they travel a lot?

Later life:
Education:

What topics and disciplines did the person study at higher level
and where?
Did they do post-graduate studies? What was their grades?
Have they undertaken any other personal development activities?

Work:

What were the person's first jobs?
Did they work in a family firm or for other known individuals?
Have they changed job frequently?
How were they rated? How quickly were they promoted?

Experiences:

Has the person undergone any major trauma or unusual or difficult
experience (seriously ill, abused, neglected) and, if so, how did
they cope?
Have they lived or worked abroad and, if so, on a short or long-term
basis? And how well did they settle?

Own family:

Is the person single/married/have a partner?
Are they divorced?
Do they have children?
What is their parenting style?

Interests:

How does the person spend their leisure time/holidays?
Are they members of clubs/associations?
Do they read a lot? Are their pass-times social or not?

Their question was what biographical information gives us clues? Growing up in rural poverty as opposed to suburban wealth will impact on any individual. Important indicators are health and nutrition, the home environment, parental interaction with the child, the parents' mental health and neighbourhood conditions. What are the long-term consequences of a poor diet, limited access to educational and other resources, cramped living conditions in high crime areas, stressed parents who worked long hours?

Taylor et al. (2014) suggest a number of factors:

1. *Parental influence*: These could be in terms of parental endowments and investments. Parents influence children through their own behaviour. They present situations that elicit certain behaviour in children, for example frustration leads to aggression They serve as role models for identification and they selectively reward behaviours. Parenting style has been shown to have a considerable effect on an individual's later life motivation and values.

2. *Serious misfortunes*: These can take many forms. Death is the most studied of the misfortunes, but include absence, physical infirmity, deprivations and the horrors of war or a terrorist act, lack of parental love, divorce, sickness, alcoholism or drug addiction. The following are typical factors:

   Insecurity/inferiority [identity confusion]
   Relationship problems [isolation/loneliness/authority]
   Emotional problems [anxiety, depression, resentment, jealousy]
   Family problems [parental incompetence, sibling rivalry, rejection]
   Health problems [disability, clumsiness]
   Social problems [discrimination – anti-Semitism, Catholicism, gender]
   Death experiences [parents, siblings]

   Therivel (1993) combined the incidence of misfortunes with the level of support available to the child at the time and the intellectual and genetic endowment of the child. His GAM (*Genetic, Assistances and Misfortune*) theory provides a fascinating study of a number of individuals blessed with great skills or qualities. In his book on the subject, Therivel provides convincing theories to explain why Mozart was a better composer than Salieri, despite their very similar historic, social and intellectual backgrounds. His case studies include Dostoyevsky, Balzac, Goethe, Tolstoy and many others.

In Therivel's descriptions, those who fall into the low misfortune sectors are conventional types; this is where most people sit. He is interested in those who are challenged and who have a good genetic endowment. According to him, this is where talent and serious creativity can be found.

3. *Birth order*: Interest in this topic goes back over a century. Recent research has been dominated by Sulloway (1996), who demonstrated how firstborn children behave differently from their younger siblings. His thesis is that children compete for parental attention by creating distinctive niches. Firstborn children tend to be responsible, competitive and conventional. Children born later are more playful, cooperative and rebellious.

Firstborn child: highest academic success, highly motivated, most likely to be a leader, most likely to become a politician, most affiliative, most influenced by authority, mature behaviour, self-disciplined, least emotionality

Middle-born child: feelings of not belonging, sociable, fewest 'acting out' problems, success in team sports, relates well to older and younger people, competes in different areas than oldest, more faithful in monogamous relationships

Last-born child: higher social interest, agreeableness, more rebellious, more empathetic, overrepresentation of psychiatric disorders, more artistic and less scientific, highest self-esteem, lowest IQ

Only child: high achievements/intelligence, most need for achievement, most likely to go to college/university, most behaviour problems, lowest need for affiliation, selfish, need for affiliation under stress

4. *Social class and caste*: All cultures make distinctions based on class and caste that are linked to historical and religious developments. Membership of any one can, much as knowing that one is of a particular nationality, allow us to make certain broad assumptions regarding the influences to which a subject has been exposed and the behaviours and attitudes that would tend to predominate amongst individuals of that group. Belonging to a particular class or caste would tend to mean that you marry or socialise within the same

group, hold similar political views, aesthetic preferences and take up similar status occupations. In religions such as Hinduism and Islam, distinctions are often fairly apparent and constant, whereas class membership can be much more difficult to determine and more subject to change.

5. *Work experiences*: This may be a part-time job at school, a relatively unskilled summer holiday job at university or one of the first jobs they ever had. For some it was the unadulterated tedium or monotony that powerfully motivated to avoid similar jobs in the future. For others it was a particular work style or process that they have retained all their lives. This is something that can be identified and selected for.

> *Hardships of various kinds.* It is about attempting to cope in a crisis that may be professional or personal. It teaches the real value of things: technology, loyal staff, supportive head offices. The experiences are those of battle-hardened soldiers or the 'been there, done that' brigade. Hardship teaches many lessons: how resourceful and robust some people can be and how others panic and cave in. It teaches some to admire a fit and happy organisation when they see it. It teaches them to distinguish between needs and wants. It teaches about stress management and the virtues of stoicism, hardiness and a tough mental attitude.

6. *Illness (mental and psychological)*: At some stage of their lives most people experience physical illness. There are many stories of how 'sickly' children used their experience to learn some skills. Similarly, near-death experiences, the loss of a limb or other body part or an illness that leaves internal scars can profoundly influence people. Clearly, illness can have a major impact on a person's outlook and needs to be taken into account to understand their motives, decision-making and general behaviour.

Let's look at an example. Using their particular framework, Taylor et al. (2014) sought to understand a number of historical figures. This is their analysis of Britain's first woman prime minister.

8.1.5   The Example of Baroness Margaret Hilda Thatcher

8.1.5.1   Brief

To what aspects of her character and past can we attribute Thatcher's success and failures as a politician?

8.1.5.2 Culture

A strong sense of patriotism, belief in hard work and personal responsibility coupled with a willingness to challenge the status quo and established ways of operating.

'We shall have to learn again to be one nation, or one day we shall be no nation.'

As a child and young adult, Thatcher witnessed the struggles of ordinary people in the inter-war period and WWII and the community's tremendous resilience and resourcefulness in the and politics and she would have been exposed from an early age to jingoistic debate and key British values leaving lasting impacts on her outlook and behaviours.

Power distance (the British rank as low in this dimension). She had a fundamental belief in equality, contributing to her resolve to break into political circles, at the time predominantly the domain of men and the upper classes. Being accepted at Oxford and subsequently rising up the political ranks, she considered herself living proof that, despite a relatively humble upbringing, given opportunity and hard work, advancement was something everyone could achieve.

She was candid about the benefits of a privileged background, but she was not in awe of it. She judged colleagues and others primarily according to how well they fulfilled their role or how useful they were to her ambitions. This could cause a mixture of upset and dislike amongst those who perhaps felt that their background and position were worthy of more acknowledgment, but also admiration. Even as prime minister she did not baulk from menial tasks, such as darning socks or cooking a simple supper rather than ask junior staff, with whom she was known to be highly courteous and thoughtful, earning her huge respect and loyalty.

Masculinity (the British rank as high in this dimension): Her personal drive and desire to succeed is legendary. At school she worked hard, enjoying debate and putting herself forward for positions of authority, and demonstrated huge persistence in her studies and as a junior MP. She had a highly developed sense of competition from an early age. Some even suggest her marriage to Dennis was largely strategic in that it gave her an easier route into the circles that would enable her to rise up the political ladder.

Her focus was always work rather than family and leisure. She trained and qualified as a barrister while pregnant and a new mother of twins, only later in life admitting to some regret for spending less time with her family. In what many might consider an un-British fashion, rather than adopt a more self-effacing and understated approach she reinforced the belief in equality, particularly prevalent amongst the British educated classes, by making no secret of her self-belief and achievements. She was often criticised for not doing more for women in politics and business but to do so would arguably have weakened her position. As it was, in the male-dominated polite upper-class circles she was intimidating and difficult to oppose. This may have contributed to her latterly developing a greater sense of superiority and infallibility than warranted.

Individualism (Britain ranks amongst the highest on this dimension): Thatcher wholeheartedly applauded individual initiative, the idea that personal fulfilment is happiness and that it is down to each of us to make our way and contribute to society. Her father was particularly influential in this respect in that he was actively involved in politics, the church and community. He taught her by example to stand up for what she believed in and that it is only through action that change can happen. In addition, the war years were a time when society exhorted everyone to do their bit and develop independence. Choosing Granville, the town of her birth, for her peerage is indicative of the extreme importance of the role her early years there played in building the character and beliefs that led to her success.

Uncertainty avoidance (low): A low ranking on this dimension indicates that a society has a clear vision of where it wants to go but shows a degree of pragmatism and creativity in how it gets there – the process does not have to be set in stone.

Thatcher urged respect for history and tradition but was unafraid to challenge the current way of doing things. She was impatient with those who were too lazy or reluctant to go back to fundamental principles and chose instead to rely on tried and tested formula. She had a passion for detail, but she did not let herself be hidebound by it. Her approach was rather to analyse situations in the light of the best and widest current information and only then decide what action to take.

Her willingness to take a principled stance on issues of import-ance, in the face of often great uncertainty and lack of precedent, is one of the aspects of her leadership which has attracted most admir-ation in her and other British figures such as Winston Churchill, by whom she was deeply influenced.

Indulgence (middle-high): Britain ranks relatively high in terms of indulgence, though this is something not associated with Thatcher, perhaps due to the over-riding influence of her early years. She did not seek gratification in terms of luxury and leisure. She could be extremely frugal and where she was indulgent, for example, in her dress and appearance – something perhaps bol-stered by her mother who was a seamstress – it also had a degree of functionality – to create the right impression. Her idea of relax-ation was polishing shoes, mending clothes or tidying, and just occasionally listening to opera or a musical and watching a film or thriller on TV. She rarely took time off and was most energised when employed in some task.

In some ways Thatcher came to symbolise a more austere and careworn era from which by the 1990s the younger generation in particular were keen to move on. This was undoubtedly a factor in the fall in her personal popularity and her move towards more lenient and forgiving policies.

8.1.5.3 Biography
A family that imbued her with a strong sense of moral duty and a heightened sense of ambition and self-worth. Practical experience of hardship in the form of war and poverty and overcoming barriers to senior political circles

I owe almost everything to my father. He taught me that you first sort out what you believe in and then apply it. You don't compromise on things that matter.

Life was not to enjoy ourselves. Life was to work and do things.

When Thatcher came to power, Britain's image was tarnished by labour disputes and economic woes. She spoke to a generation with memories of a more unified, respected and dynamic Britain with passion and conviction, successfully instilling the belief that those days could be recreated through personal initiative and responsibility. Abroad she also sought to resurrect perceptions of Britain in earlier times, revelling in her image as 'The Iron Lady', which she felt reflected accurately not only her own resolve but that of the people of Britain when facing adversity.

Margaret Thatcher (née Roberts) was born in 1925 to a strict close-knit Methodist family in the market town of Grantham, Lincolnshire. Her father, a shopkeeper, preacher and alderman influenced her heavily, involving her in his political and community activities from an early age. Thatcher's keen interest in clothes, thriftiness and family duty – she cooked Dennis' breakfast every day – is thought to have come from her mother, a quiet figure. She had an elder sister with whom she corresponded regularly, especially in her late teens and early twenties, who married one of Thatcher's first beaux, at Margaret's instigation.

Thatcher married Dennis, a successful businessman twelve years her senior, in 1951. It was a good match, him being content for her to follow her heart and ambitions. 'What a husband. What a friend.' She was a dutiful if not particularly loving parent, assiduous in attending school meetings and events but only late in life developing a close relationship with her grandchildren.

She was one of the few women at the time to get a scholarship at Somerville College, Oxford, where she said she wished she had been able to say she'd studied at Cheltenham Ladies College. She worked hard to suppress her Lincolnshire accent, some criticising her for trying to hide her background while it was likely a practical response to her perceived need to be more readily accepted. She was President of the Oxford University Conservative Association in 1946, the beginning of a long career in politics, an early and perhaps defining influence being Friedrich van Hayek, who condemned economic intervention by government. Additional influences were in all probability her interest in Israel due to the family taking in a Jewish refugee when she was a child and in 1967 a six-week International Visitor Leadership Programme to US when she met various politicians and institutions such as the IMF. She first became an MP in 1959 and went on to be Cabinet Minister in 1970 and Prime Minister in 1979.

8.1.5.4 Intelligence

Clever but not brilliant, analytical brain with strong desire to learn. Overdependence on those with similar thinking styles or able to present arguments in a format which resonated with her, making her at times unreceptive to criticism or other points of view

A second-rate brain.

Do your best and never follow the crowd.

Condemned by one of her Oxford professors as having a 'second-rate brain', in reality Thatcher demonstrated a keen analytical mind powered by a strong need for personal advancement and ambition. Encouraged by her father she did well at school, demonstrating enormous academic discipline and interest in learning from a very early age.

Expressed in executive intelligence terms, her greatest strength was in getting a solid, meticulous grasp of situations and using this knowledge to shape policy and strategy – meeting the challenge of a task. As a politician she always prepared meticulously, with a huge capacity for detail that she used to great effect in political argument. This meant that often she came to meetings seemingly with her mind made up, while in reality she enjoyed debate and could be persuaded if a case was argued well or she had developed trust in her interlocutors.

When dealing with people, this same analytical brain trained her into always seeking the weaknesses in other people's arguments. She was genuinely open to discourse and debate, and willing to adopt new ideas and approaches, but looked for equals in argument. Few had her work ethic or thoroughness and she was often disappointed. Many found her impatient, dismissive and humourless. She deployed acerbic wit, reportedly the only humour in which she actively engaged, with those she felt were on an equal footing to her. This could cause offence and discomfort, particularly amongst men unused to public humiliation, and lead to many distancing themselves or being intimidated into silence.

This had a deleterious effect on her ability to regulate self. As the years went by, she was forced to rely on fewer and fewer trusted advisors – mostly those who spoke or presented in her language and shared her beliefs – contributing to reduced access to and acceptance of other points of view and so her greater sense of her infallibility.

8.1.5.5   Personality

Savvy and charming when managing people and situations to meet her aims but with a single-mindedness and extreme conscientiousness that could make her appear unfeeling and unsympathetic to others. In reality her actions were unselfish and underpinned by integrity, compassion and understanding of others.

> Defeat – I do not recognise the meaning of the word.
>
> You know if you set out to be liked, you would be prepared to compromise on anything, wouldn't you, at any time, and you would achieve nothing.

This quote might suggest that Thatcher was unconcerned by others' opinion of her, which in a sense she was. In her private life she tended to rely on a few close friends and colleagues and by nature she was somewhat of an introvert, often appearing aloof, serious and intense in company. Nonetheless, she was adept at charming and mixing with people and cutting a figure – clearly understanding the importance and political expediency of mixing in the right circles and engaging in debate. 'Personal' did not really come into it, as in her actions and mind she did not separate herself from what she stood for and was prepared to sacrifice popularity to achieve her political aims. Everything else was of secondary importance.

Whether Thatcher did or did not only sleep five hours a night, her reputation as being a tough workaholic, who worked relentlessly and with passion and determination, is perhaps what defines her most clearly in people's minds. She worked on countless redrafts of speeches, was utterly thorough, ordered and disciplined in her approach to everything she did. She set high standards for herself – whether in dress, speeches or being a dutiful wife and mother – and was prepared to be judged on her performance. She sought out others with similar integrity who were selfless and prepared to stand up for what they believed in. She was extremely intolerant of others she considered responsible and yet who failed in their task through lack of dedication or hard work.

Given her tough public persona, her capacity for compassion, loyalty and consideration may come as a surprise to many. She wrote personally to all those who lost relatives in the Falklands War, always showed an interest in the welfare of her Downing Street staff, remembering birthdays and family members and unfailingly supported them if she felt they were in danger of being unfairly treated. Having built and achieved so much based on the image of the Iron Lady, she underestimated the importance of highlighting her softer, more 'feminine' side.

8.1.5.6   Dark Side Traits

Extremely diligent and conscientious which led her to be demanding of others if she felt that they failed, without reason, to live up to her high standards. In later years developed an unassailable belief in her own views and abilities:

> You turn if you want to. This lady's not for turning.
> Eyes of Stalin/Caligula and voice of Marilyn Monroe.

Thatcher, for many, at home and abroad, was the epitome of a strong, decisive leader. These quotes might suggest that with that power she could be utterly ruthless and focused on a task at the expense of all moral considerations, Machiavellian perhaps. In reality, she did not have the win-at-all-costs amoral approach that this term implies. True, she was not adverse to using her womanly charms if beneficial and embraced the image of Battling Maggie – the Iron Lady – when she thought it gave her the profile she needed to get things done, but she was always guided by a strict sense of duty, honesty and service. She had extraordinary self-belief but also belief in the need to act in accordance with what is morally and intellectually defensible.

Far more notable in terms of dark side traits was her extreme conscientiousness and diligence. As highlighted above, ultimately this resulted in her increasing isolation, arrogance and heightened sense of superiority and self-confidence.

Towards the end of her tenure as Prime Minister and beyond she displayed symptoms of the Hubris Syndrome identified by Dr David Owen. The strength of character, conviction and leadership so valued in her early years when Britain was suffering an economic crisis and during the Falklands War, led to increasing isolation and contempt for others. Her error came in increasingly thinking that her approach was more informed and sound than alternatives proposed by those around her. Her frequent use of the word 'we' signalled her inability to distinguish between herself and some higher cause. Indeed, towards the end, she branded those who disagreed with her as disloyal both to her and so, in her mind, to the betterment of Britain. Ultimately her tendency to self-refer in the first instance, immunity to criticism and reluctance to acknowledge mistakes and other points of view were her downfall.

8.1.5.7   Motivation
Highly motivated by achievement orientated towards upholding the beliefs and values instilled in her when growing up, power and influence were a means to an end rather than motivation in themselves.

These beliefs or values were something that you need to act upon. It's not what you've done that counts. It's what you do next.

While highly ambitious from an early age, Thatcher is said to have had an intrinsic disregard for the trappings of power or office. She was frugal in her home life, unconcerned with material possessions or pleasure pursuits, was prepared to take risks and cared very little for what others thought of her, except if it could help her or, conversely, threatened to get in her way.

Her interest was above all action and action orientated not towards personal gratification but towards the fundamental community values and beliefs instilled in her as a child. She was in every sense a conviction politician with power, influence and recognition only important to the extent that they allowed her to get things done, to achieve something worthwhile.

In the end, however, her conviction about how Britain could realise her vision of greatness was not shared by the populace, and nor was her conviction in her unique ability to help the country chart its course towards success. Times had moved on, and her formula of strong leadership and government was rejected in favour of individual effort and achievement, ironically the very values she had sought to promote.

8.1.5.8 In Sum

Thatcher's early influences set her on a course which, coupled with her unassailable self-belief, conscientiousness and sense of duty to the British people, led her to overcome many of the obstacles she faced in politics – primarily male dominance and a perception that the state and organisations should somehow compensate for a lack of individual effort and responsibility. Her vision of a united and strong Britain, built on the values and beliefs with which she was brought up, was compelling at a time of economic crisis and political disarray. However, in a period of greater prosperity built on the values of personal freedom and initiative that she espoused, the iron resolve for which she was known, and which she exhibited to the exclusion of consensus and debate, ultimately undermined her position.

8.1.6 Conclusion

The basic premise of biodata and biographical research is that the past predicts the future. People tend to be stable over time and show strong and consistent preferences. Most people accept this though it disputed by some. The argument is that we are marked and shaped by (particularly early) life experiences which (and partly) determine the choices we make: who we marry, where we work, what risks we take.

The major problem with this approach pertains to legal and moral objections. These suggest that past behaviour (i.e. criminal acts) should, indeed must, not be used as an indicator that a person might offend again. Next, it is difficult to think of many biographical factors that are correlates of other factors (sex, social class, health) that it is illegal to discriminate against.

REFERENCES

Allworth, E., & Hesketh, B. (2000). Job requirements biodata as a predictor of performance in customer service roles. *International Journal of Selection and Assessment, 8*(3), 137–147.

Barthel, E., & Schuler, H. (1989). Utility calculation of personnel selection methods using the example of a biographical questionnaire. *Zeitschrift für Arbeits- und Organisationspsychologie, 33*(2), 73–83.

Becker, T. E., & Colquitt, A. L. (1992). Potential versus actual faking of a biodata form: an analysis along several dimensions of item type. *Personnel Psychology, 45*(2), 389–406.

Bliesener, T. (1996). Methodological moderators in validating biographical data in personnel selection. *Journal of Occupational and Organizational Psychology, 69*(1), 107–120.

Carlson, K. D., Scullen, S. E., Schmidt, F. L., Rothstein, H., & Erwin, F. (1999). Generalizable biographical data validity can be achieved without multi-organizational development and keying. *Personnel Psychology, 52*(3), 731–755.

Cook, M. (2016). *Personnel selection: Adding value through people – A changing picture* (6th ed.). Chichester, UK: John Wiley & Sons.

Cucina, J. M., Caputo, P. M., Thibodeaux, H. F., & Maclane, C. N. (2012). Unlocking the key to biodata scoring: a comparison of empirical, rational, and hybrid approaches at different sample sizes. *Personnel Psychology, 65*(2), 385–428.

Dean, M. A., & Russell, C. J. (2005). An examination of biodata theory-based constructs in a field context. *International Journal of Selection and Assessment, 13*(2), 139–149.

Dean, M. A., Russell, C. J., & Muchinsky, P. M. (1999). Life experiences and performance prediction: toward a theory of biodata. In G. Ferris (Ed.), *Research in personnel/human resources* (pp. 245–281). Westport, CT: JAI Press.

Drakeley, R. J., Herriot, P., & Jones, A. (1988). Biographical data, training success and turnover. *Journal of Occupational Psychology, 61*(2), 145–152.

Ellingson, J. E., Sackett, P. R., & Hough, L. M. (1999). Social desirability corrections in personality measurement: issues of applicant comparison and construct validity. *Journal of Applied Psychology, 84*(2), 155–166.

England, G. W. (1961). *Development and use of weighted application banks.* Dubuque, IO: Brown Publishing Company.

Fine, S. A., & Cronshaw, S. (1994). The role of job analysis in establishing the validity of biodata. In G. S. Stokes, M. D. Mumford, & W. A. Owens (Eds.), *Biodata handbook* (pp. 39–64). Palo Alto, CA: Consulting Psychologists Press.

Gatewood, R., Feild, H. S., & Barrick, M. (2015). *Human resource selection.* Boston, MA: Cengage Learning.

Goldstein, I. L. (1971). The application blank: how honest are the responses? *Journal of Applied Psychology, 55*, 491–492.

Harold, C. M., McFarland, L. A., & Weekley, J. A. (2006). The validity of verifiable and non-verifiable biodata items: an examination across applicants and incumbents. *International Journal of Selection and Assessment, 14*(4), 336–346.

Hough, L. M., & Paullin, C. (1994). Construct-oriented scale construction: the rational approach. In G. S. Stokes, M. D. Mumford, & W. A. Owens (Eds.). *Biodata handbook: The use of biographical information in selection and performance prediction* (pp. 109–146). Palo Alto, CA: Consulting Psychologists Press.

Hough, L. M. (1984). Development and evaluation of the 'accomplishment record' method of selecting and promoting professionals. *Journal of Applied Psychology, 69*(1), 135–146.

Hunter, J. E., & Hunter, R. F. (1984). Validity and utility of alternative predictors of job performance. *Psychological Bulletin, 96*(1), 72–98.

Karas, M., & West, J. (1999). Construct-oriented biodata development for selection to a differentiated performance domain. *International Journal of*

Selection and Assessment, special issue: Background Data and Autobiographical Memory, 7(2), 86–96.

Keating, E., Paterson, D. G., & Stone, C. H. (1950). Validity of work histories obtained by interview. *Journal of Applied Psychology, 34*(1), 6–11.

Kőváry, Z. (2011). Psychobiography as a method. The revival of studying lives: new perspectives in personality and creativity research. *Europe's Journal of Psychology, 7*(4), 739–777.

Lautenschlager, G. J. (1994). Accuracy and faking of background data. In G. S. Stokes, M. D. Mumford, & W. A. Owens (Eds.), *Biodata handbook* (pp. 391–419). Palo Alto, CA: Consulting Psychologists Press.

Levashina, J., Morgeson, F. P., & Campion, M. A. (2012). Tell me some more: exploring how verbal ability and item verifiability influence responses to biodata questions in a high-stakes selection context. *Personnel Psychology, 65*(2), 359–383.

Mael, F. A., & Ashforth, B. E. (1995). Loyal from day one: biodata, organizational identification, and turnover among newcomers. *Personnel Psychology, 48*(2), 309–333.

McManus, M. A., & Kelly, M. L. (1999). Personality measures and biodata: evidence regarding their incremental predictive value in the life insurance industry. *Personnel Psychology, 52*(1), 137–148.

Mount, M. K., Witt, L. A., & Barrick, M. R. (2000). Incremental validity of empirically keyed biodata scales over GMA and the five factor personality constructs. *Personnel Psychology, 53*(2), 299–323.

Mumford, M. D., Costanza, D. P., Connelly, M. S., & Johnson, J. F. (1996). Item generation procedures and background data scales: implications for construct and criterion-related validity. *Personnel Psychology, 49*(2), 361–398.

Mumford, M. D., & Owens, W. A. (1987). Methodology review: principles, procedures, and findings in the application of background data measures. *Applied Psychological Measurement, 11*(1), 1–31.

Mumford, M. D., & Stokes, G. S. (1992). Developmental determinants of individual action: theory and practice in applying background measures. In M. D. Dunnette, & L. M. Hough (Eds.), *Handbook of industrial and organizational psychology* (2nd ed., pp. 61–138). Palo Alto, CA: Consulting Psychologists Press.

Mumford, M., Stokes, G. S., & Owens, W. A. (1990). *Patterns of life history: The ecology of human development.* Mahwah, NJ: Lawrence Erlbaum Associates.

Ones, D. S., Viswesvaran, C., & Reiss, A. D. (1996). Role of social desirability in personality testing for personnel selection: the red herring. *Journal of Applied Psychology, 81*(6), 660–679.

Oswald, F. L., Schmitt, N., Kim, B. H., Ramsay, L. J., & Gillespie, M. A. (2004). Developing a biodata measure and situational judgment inventory as predictors of college student performance. *Journal of Applied Psychology, 89*(2), 187–207.

Paunonen, S. V. (1984). Optimizing the validity of personality assessments: the importance of aggregation and item content. *Journal of Research in Personality*, *18*(4), 411–431.

Reilly, R. R., & Chao, G. R. (1982). Validity and fairness of some alternative employee selection procedures. *Personnel Psychology*, *35*(1), 1–62.

Robertson, I. T., & Smith, M. (2001). Personnel selection. *Journal of Occupational and Organizational Psychology*, *74*(4), 441–472.

Runyan, W. M. (1981). Why did Van Gogh cut off his ear? The problem of alternative explanations in psychobiography. *Journal of Personality and Social Psychology*, *40*(6), 1070–1077.

Schmidt, F. L., & Hunter, J. E. (1998). The validity and utility of selection methods in personnel psychology: practical and theoretical implications of 85 years of research findings. *Psychological Bulletin*, *124*, 262–274.

Schmitt, N., Gooding, R. Z., Noe, R. A., & Kirsch, M. (1984). Meta analyses of validity studies published between 1964 and 1982 and the investigation of study characteristics. *Personnel Psychology*, *37*, 407–422.

Schmitt, N., Jennings, D., & Toney, R. (1999). Can we develop measures of hypothetical constructs? *Human Resource Management Review*, *9*(2), 169–183.

Schmitt, N., & Kunce, C. (2002). The effects of required elaboration of answers to biodata questions. *Personnel Psychology*, *55*(3), 569–587.

Schmitt, N., Oswald, F. L., Kim, B. H., Gillespie, M. A., Ramsay, L. J., & Yoo, T.-Y. (2003). Impact of elaboration on socially desirable responding and the validity of biodata measures. *Journal of Applied Psychology*, *88*(6), 979–988.

Schrader, A. D., & Osburn, H. G. (1977). Biodata faking: effects of induced subtlety and position specificity. *Personnel Psychology*, *30*(3), 395–404.

Song, G., Wu, J., & Wang, S. (2019, September). Recent ten years of biodata research: hotspots, progress and prospects [Paper presentation]. In *Advances in Economics, Business and Management Research* (Vol. 94). 4th international conference on Economy, Judicature, Administration and Humanitarian Projects (JAHP 2019), Kaifeng, China (pp. 961–965). Amsterdam: Atlantis Press.

Speer, A. B., Siver, S. R., & Christiansen, N. D. (2020). Applying theory to the black box: a model for empirically scoring biodata. *International Journal of Selection and Assessment*, *28*(1), 68–84.

Stokes, G. S., & Searcy, C. A. (1999). Specification of scales in biodata form development: rational vs. empirical and global vs. specific. *International Journal of Selection and Assessment, special issue: Background Data and Autobiographical Memory*, *7*(2), 72–85.

Stokes, G. S., Mumford, M. D., & Owens, W. A. (Eds.). (1994). *Biodata handbook: Theory, research, and use of biographical information in selection and performance prediction.* Palo Alto, CA: Consulting Psychologists Press.

Sulastri, A., Handoko, M., & Janssens, J. M. A. M. (2015). Grade point average and biographical data in personal resumes: predictors of finding employment. *International Journal of Adolescence and Youth, 20*(3), 306–316.

Sulloway, F. (1996). *Born to rebel.* New York City, NY: Pantheon Books.

Taylor, J., Furnham, A., & Breeze, J. (2014). *Revealed: Using remote personality profiling to influence, negotiate and motivate.* Hampshire, UK: Palgrave Macmillan.

Therivel, R. (1993). Systems of strategic environmental assessment. *Environmental Impact Assessment Review, 13*(3), 145–168.

Wernimont, P. F. (1962). Re-evaluation of a weighted application blank for office personnel. *Journal of Applied Psychology, 46*(6), 417–419.

9   Big Data

What is it?
It consists in capturing, storing, analysing, sharing and linking huge amount of (electronic) data created through computer-based technologies and networks, such as smartphones, computers, cameras, sensors, etc. The idea is to explore an individual's electronically stored behavioural footprint to derive a rich and accurate profile of their beliefs and behaviours.

How does it work?
Assessors and selectors obtain access to many types of Big Data. They may apply an AI algorithm to this data to look for a particular personality or motivational profile or may simply inspect it for patterns to try to answer certain questions.

What of the evidence?
There is a lot of evidence, some equivocal, some oversold by consultants, as to what and how much you can know about an individual from his or her electronic footprint.

Practical problems: cost, ethics, politics
The major problems are cost and ethics: the cost of getting the data and doing the analysis (compared to getting the same information from other techniques) and the considerable ethical problems of using data without candidate permission.

Recommendations for use
'Watch this space': there are lots of dramatic and important technical advancement in data capture, storage and analysis. Big data will probably need to be supported by other data sources.

9.1.1 *Introduction*

One of the most interesting and 'advertised' developments in the world of assessment has been the exploration of Big Data. The definition of what precisely constitutes Big Data is not that clear, but it is now over 20 years old. Big Data is also known as *data mining, knowledge discovery* in databases, data or *predictive analytics* or *data science*. It has traditionally been associated with computer science, statistics and business, and now it is making inroads into psychological research and applied practice. There is a growing infrastructure for dealing with Big Data, some of it being open source and free to use (Harlow & Oswald, 2016).

It is important to examine the practicality–effectiveness trade-off, and distinguishing Big Data from machine learning (because you can have one and not the other). Furthermore, there is a difference between a lot of data and Big Data. Machine learning can be very usefully applied to any size data set. The main aim of Big Data is creating a holistic picture from as many differing sources of readily available information. This can then expand out to new technology: What does the step count/pedometer in a phone tell you about a person? How do they buy things? Do they do transactional purchases or subscriptions? When they type on a keyboard or phone, how quickly and accurately do they do this?

It presents, for the assessor, opportunities to accumulate information about an individual never before available. The question is whether the effort involved in attempting to obtain this (unique) data is worth it from a selection perspective.

For those in the business of assessment and evaluation it means there is often a surprising amount of information about an individual 'on the web'. Naturally, for well-known and public figures in a number of worlds from business to media, sports to politics, a great deal is known and has been written about them. Many have *Wikipedia* entries and it is easy to 'google' them. However, there are a range of very well-established websites like Facebook and LinkedIn where people post their profiles. These are often 'advertorials' about themselves, but also ways of communicating with others throughout the world.

Some people make strenuous efforts to not appear on any form of social media, which is telling its own way. Indeed, some organisations offer a service to those in assessment to 'scrape the web' and 'trawl public records' to write a report on any particularly nominated individual.

The most-researched tool is the use of *social media*, which is the term used for internet-based tools used on computer, tablets and smart phones. These are designed to help people interact and share information, ideas and opinions. Millions of people of all ages organise their lives online and communicate using social media. Therefore, they leave a substantial digital footprint, which can be used by many people for many reasons.

Big Data has been defined as 'massive amounts of electronic data that are indexable and searchable by means of computational systems . . . stored on servers and analysed by algorithms' (Lane, 2016, p. 75). There are sceptics and enthusiasts, but also cynics who reject the notion that 'bigger is better' or 'more will reveal the truth', such there are great enthusiasts of the digital era (Gonzalez, 2017). There are already scandals in the use of Big Data, such as the Cambridge Analytic affair.

One aspect of Big Data analysis is on large groups rather than single individuals. An example of such analysis is one conducted by MIT Media Lab (Thompson, 2016) of Twitter use during the 2016 US presidential elections. The analysis, based on over a billion tweets, showed that Clinton and Trump supporters, largely self-selected who to follow, and consequently lived in separate media bubbles, with little interaction between them.

Big Data is defined as anything that is too large for typical database tools to be able to capture, store, manage and analyse (George et al., 2014). However, some researchers prefer to define Big Data by its 'smartness' than by its size, for example, the extent to which a dataset is able to provide the material to conduct fine-grained analysis that can accurately explain and predict behaviour and outcomes (Mahmoodi et al.,2017).

Gosling and Mason (2015) have argued that:

> The Internet has transformed society and changed the way people think about and interact with the world and with each other. The Internet has created new forms of behavior (such as online gaming, virtual worlds, and crowdsourcing) and new ways for people to interact with each other (such as online forums, social networking sites, and photo sharing sites) – with both positive and negative effects. In fact, over the past 20 years many different effects of the Internet on people have been studied, including the potential for addiction, the inducement of isolation or loneliness, cyberbullying, the spread of rumors, political polarization and filter bubbles , and the Internet's influence on political movements.
>
> *(p. 880)*

Hariri et al. (2019) noted that Big Data analysis is difficult to perform using traditional data analytics as they can lose effectiveness due to the five Vs:

> *Volume* refers to the considerable amount of data generated continually. This is about the size and scale of a dataset. Huge volumes of data can introduce scalability and uncertainty problems (e.g. a database tool may not be able to accommodate infinitely large datasets).
> *Variety* refers to the different forms of data in a dataset, including structured data, semi-structured data and unstructured data. Structured data (e.g. stored in a relational database) is mostly well organised and easily analysed, but unstructured data (e.g. text and multimedia content) is random and difficult to analyse. Semi-structured data contains some ways to separate data elements. They note that uncertainty can become apparent when converting between different data types, in representing data of mixed data types, and in changes to the underlying structure of the dataset at run time. Traditional Big Data analytics algorithms face challenges for handling multi-modal, incomplete and noisy data.

> *Velocity* is about the speed of data processing. The speed with which the data is processed should meet the speed with which the data is produced.
> *Veracity* represents the quality of the data (e.g. uncertain or imprecise data). A lot of Big Data is inconsistent, noisy, ambiguous or incomplete. Data veracity is categorised as good, bad or undefined.
> *Value* represents the context and usefulness of data for decision-making: quite simply is it worth the effort compared to other methods.

Over the last decade there have been a number of reviews of the new 'Big Data era'. Many have seen this as a very exciting time to advance assessment particularly through the use of machine learning (Bleidorn & Hopwood, 2019). Researchers have noted a 'data divide' where both researchers and possible respondents are Big Data Rich or Big Data Poor. Most believe that Big Data will complement and extend traditional research. There are three ways in which this is done (Adjerid & Kelley, 2018):

Big 'n': Collecting data from very large populations.
Big 'v': Collecting data from highly varied variables to study human behaviour.
Big 't': Collecting data over long periods of time.

This allows for all sorts of research given the Big/Small and N/V/T options like Big N, Small V. Big T which is traditional research expanded. All three being Big (NVT) offers perhaps the most exciting new possibilities. But there are also many challenges, which include access to the data and technical challenges like cleaning the data. Mayer-Schönberger and Cukier (2013) certainly argued that big data will be very disruptive. Furthermore, whilst being great enthusiasts for the new technology, they do see problems and the downside of over-reliance on this data.

Data mining, it is argued, promotes objectivity in assessing, classifying and profiling because decisions are made by a *formal, objective and constant algorithmic* process, which is more disinterested and unbiased than human decision-making. This feature of objectivity should reduce human error and bias. According to some of the literature, automatic data mining could also be used to discover and assess discriminatory practices in classification.

However, there are also pitfalls in using Big Data and machine learning. First, although data may be in abundance, it is biased towards data that is available (often a by-product of endeavours other than to measure a variable for research purposes) and that is quantifiable. Factors that are not easily quantifiable may be overlooked and it becomes a case of using data that is available, rather than data best suited to answer a given question. Second, there may be systematic differences in the population and what Big Data about them is available, which is likely to bias outcomes unless correctly identified and controlled for. Third, when big data is coupled with deep-learning algorithms, the process becomes so complex it is impossible for humans to evaluate them.

Yet it should be noted that lots of sites and environments are not open for analysis, which may create various distortions (Labrinidis & Jagadish, 2012). Indeed, this is a problem which involves a number of concerns around such things as privacy, proprietary algorithms and security data, as well access to the community of scholars interested in the usual academic pursuits of data sharing, replication and hypothesis testing.

A fundamental principle in psychology is that past behaviour is often a good (perhaps the best) predictor of future behaviour. As a result, with the explosion of Big Data, data mining techniques (which find patterns in the data) are increasingly used to identify markers of talent. There are various areas that allow researchers to collect data: social media, smart phones, wearable devices (see Section 8.1).

However, there have been some attempts to use social media statistics to help selectors. Some years ago people had the idea that they could use social media to rate people. The 'Klout Score' of 'influence' was based on an individual's social media presence and people were scored on a 1–100 scale. Some employers were using

Klout scores when selecting and recruiting candidates (at the neglect of other important data) but became defunct probably because of questionable legality and gross misuse/misunderstanding by employers as to what the score indicated. Klout was very interesting to follow at the time, because so many people willingly made important decisions based on it, at the expense of common sense and established selection methodologies.

This illustrates some of the most fundamental issues with Big Data. The fact that it is now possible to obtain all sorts of information about an individual only helps the selector if he/she knows what the data show: i.e. how are they related to ability, personality or motivation.

9.1.2   Self-Presentation and Relationships

Around 20–30 years ago people in certain fields hired 'publicity agents'. Their job was to keep an individual in the public eye, ensuring they had a positive profile. At the same time, in certain countries, there was a *Who's Who* publication that listed 'the great and the good' with personal entries. Some were difficult to get into and rigidly policed by those trying to ensure only certain people got in, and more importantly, their profile was accurate. In other cases these were business ventures where people of very varied backgrounds paid for their entry.

The world has changed dramatically with social media, personal pages, websites and even personal TV channels. This could be described as digital self-representation. It is a way of 'sharing yourself' with others: a sort of 'public advertorial', an open CV. Consider the story of Facebook. It was started in 2004 and now has over 2 billion users.

Indeed, using Wikipedia it is possible to know the whole story of this amazingly successful organisation. It currently notes:

> Facebook can be accessed from devices with Internet connectivity, such as personal computers, tablets and smartphones. After registering, users can create a profile revealing information about themselves. They can post text,

photos and multimedia which is shared with any other users that have agreed to be their 'friend', or, with a different privacy setting, with any reader. Users can also use various embedded apps, join common-interest groups, buy and sell items or services on Marketplace, and receive notifications of their Facebook friends' activities and activities of Facebook pages they follow. Facebook claimed that it had more than 2.3 billion monthly active users as of December 2018.

(Wikipedia)

People create and curate their Facebook profiles. They post pictures and videos and list their friends. For the potential assessor this provides unrivalled information about an individual and more particularly their self-presentation strategies and their network. There are many options in different social media websites: private communication (i.e. one to one), public communication (one to many) and collaborative communication (many to many) data. Also, public and collaborative communication could also be private within the group of participants (private channel of the organisation).

One of the most interesting aspects of social media is the availability of digital relationship data, which describes the explicit connections and ties between users/members on the platform. This can reveal social relationship patterns and social network structures. This is often explicit data on digital friendships and followership. People build virtual communities based on both physical and online activities. People have followers or friends on various social platforms (Facebook, LinkedIn, Twitter, Instagram). They can also follow someone to maintain friendships, business relationships or track important content of another relevant user. The size and homo- and heterogeneity of those networks is often of considerable interest to the researcher and the assessor. The question is why add people to your list?

Of considerable interest is not only the 'static' webpages but the frequency and content of public and private communication. Tweets can be analysed to infer individual connections between people, from which it is possible to build network representations of communities. This usually requires network analysis.

9.1.3   Social Media Analytics

By collecting information from an individual's Facebook or Twitter profile, a selector can allow for more selective recruitment due to the growing ability to analyse an applicant's personality from what they post online. This also contributes to understanding the compatibility for a potential job applicant with the organisation, which is a growing concern for firms as person-to-organisation fit is crucial. A rapid rise in businesses employing this technique has been observed – for example, IBM created 'Watson' which works by translating open text into personality traits – such as Extraverts mentioning 'bars', 'drinks' and 'Miami' significantly more often than introverts do. So, a company simply has to paste an individual's Twitter posts into Watson, and their basic personality traits can be computed (IBM Watson Analytics).

However, it should be pointed out that algorithms that count target words can introduce inaccuracy, just as spell checkers often do for spelling. For example, if a person wrote 'On our day off, we went to **Miami** and had **drinks** in several **bars**' or 'On our day off, our last choice would be to go to **Miami** and have **drinks** in **bars**', both statements may be coded as indicators of Extraversion or sociability. All intelligent reviewing systems still struggle with structure and syntax. The risks of mechanical algorithms include undetectable but inevitable degradation of validity and virtually undetectable and untraceable adverse consequences for individual job candidates. This can have serious methodological and legal problems and implications.

As with a lot of new technologies, the business world appears to be getting ahead of academic research. However, there are a number of studies that have recently been conducted that attempt to assess the use of social media as a new personality assessment tool (Correa et al., 2010; Park et al., 2015). For instance, there have been studies that look at whether Twitter and Instagram usage predicts personality (Ferwerda et al., 2015; Skowron et al., 2016) as well as links between mobile apps usage and personality (Xu et al., 2015).

A good example of developments in this field is that by Stachl et al. (2019), who wondered whether smartphone usage revealed the personality traits of the user. They obtained data from 743 participants for 30 consecutive days of smartphone sensing and computed variables (15,692) about communication and social behaviour, music listening behavior, app usage behavior, mobility, and general day- and nighttime activity. Their analysis explored how these variables predicted self-assessments of the Big Five personality traits at the factor and facet level. They showed how a combination of rich behavioral data obtained with smartphone sensing and the use of machine learning techniques predicted particularly Extraversion, Openness and Conscientiousness above chance.

Over the past decade, research into social media platforms and personality has increased dramatically, with 1,180 articles published up to May 2020 on personality and at least one of the following platforms: Facebook, Twitter and LinkedIn. The range of topics examined is wide, but they divide into four general areas of interest: mental health and life satisfaction; self-presentation and communication online; social capital, selection and evaluation; and large-scale communication.

As part of their review, Ihsan and Furnham (2018) identified 30 studies in this area. Table 9.1 identifies over various studies that have been conducted in the last decade that has evaluated if the different features of social media (e.g. profile pictures, status, number of likes, number of friends) can help predict a user's personality.

The research has grown with social media; the earliest research in this area (before the emergence of social media) focused on the internet as an entirety or the ownership of websites. In 2006, Machilek, Schutz and Marcus compared a relatively large sample of personal website owners to a group of non-website owners on the Big Five dimensions of personality, narcissism, self-monitoring and

Table 9.1 *Studies using Facebook data*

Authors	Year	Type of technology	Findings
Kosinski et al.	2014	Contents of Personal Websites and Facebook Activity	Data collected from more than 350,000 US Facebook users (and their personality assessments) showed that there are psychologically meaningful links between users' personalities, their website preferences and Facebook profile features. • Website audience personality profiles were developed, such as of deviantART.com, which showed that this website attracts an audience that tends to be liberal and artistic rather than conservative and traditional (i.e. with high Openness), shy and reserved rather than outgoing and active, etc. • Found significant correlations between Facebook profile features and psychological traits: liberal and open-to-experience individuals tend to 'like' more items on Facebook, post more status updates and join more groups, or that Extroversion relates to the number of Facebook friends.
Celli et al.	2014	Facebook Profile Pictures	Bag-of-Visual-Words technique was used to automatically predict personality and interaction styles from profile pictures on Facebook. • Agreeableness and extraversion can be more easily predicted among personality traits, while dominance and affect achieve performances slightly above f1 = .6. Emotional stability is the most difficult trait to predict. • Extroverts and stable people tend to have pictures where they are smiling and they appear with other people. Introverts tend to appear alone, neurotics tend to have images without humans and close-up faces, etc.
Kosinski et al.	2013	Facebook Likes	Based on the myPersonality database and using relatively straightforward methods (singular value decomposition and linear regression) showed that Facebook likes are highly predictive of personality and number of other psychodemographic traits, such as age, gender, intelligence, political and religious views and sexual orientation. • There are examples of likes most strongly associated with given personality traits. For example, users who liked 'Hello Kitty' brand tended to have high openness, low conscientiousness and low agreeableness.

Schwartz et al.	2013	Facebook Statuses	Applied differential language analysis to uncover features distinguishing demographic and psychological attributes to 700 million words, phrases and topic instances collected by myPersonality from Facebook status updates of 75,000 participants. Findings showed a striking variation of language driven by personality, gender and age. This work confirmed existing observations (such as neurotic people's tendency to use the word 'depressed''.
Hall et al.	2014	Facebook Profile Pictures	Findings indicate that observers could accurately estimate extraversion, agreeableness and conscientiousness of unknown profile owners. Profile pictures were useful for estimating extraversion and agreeableness.
He et al.	2014	Facebook Wall Posts	Concluded that the textual posts on the Facebook Wall could partially predict users' self-monitoring skills and that the typical networking language, emoticons and internet slangs, are robust predictors to classify high and low self-monitors. Expressions related to family topics were found more likely used by low self-monitors.
Quercia et al.	2012	Facebook Popularity	Studied the relationship between Facebook popularity (number of contacts) and personality traits. • Found that Extroversion predicts the number of Facebook contacts. • No statistical evidence for the relationship between popularity and self-monitoring – a personality trait describing an ability to adapt to new forms of communication, present oneself in likeable ways and maintain superficial relationships.
Golbeck et al.	2011	Facebook Profile	Attempted to predict personality from Facebook profile information. They used a very rich set of features, including both Facebook profile features and also the words used in status updates. Results showed that using the profile data as a feature set, they were able to train two machine-learning algorithms – m5sup'Rules and Gaussian Processes – to predict each of the five personality traits to within 11% of its actual value.
Gosling et al.	2011	Facebook Activity	Revealed several connections between personality and self-reported Facebook features. For example, they showed the positive relationship between Extroversion and frequency of Facebook usage and engagement in the site. As in offline contexts, Extroverts seek out virtual social engagement, leaving behind a behavioural residue such as friendship connections or picture postings. However, their work was based on a relatively small sample of 157 participants, again limiting the reliability and generalisability of their results.

485

Table 9.1 (cont.)

Authors	Year	Type of technology	Findings
Amichai-Hamburger and Vinitzky	2010	Facebook Activity	Found several significant correlations; they found that Extroversion was positively correlated with the number of Facebook friends, but uncorrelated with the number of Facebook groups. Additionally, they found that high Neuroticism was positively correlated with users posting their own photo, but negatively correlated with uploading photos in general.
Back et al.	2010	Facebook Profiles	Data gathered from various Online Social Network sites showed that online profiles reflect the actual personality of their owners rather than an idealised projection of desirable traits. Accuracy was strongest for extraversion and openness and lowest for neuroticism.
Ross et al.	2009	Facebook Profiles	The study proposes a number of hypotheses but reports only one significant correlation – between Extroversion and group membership. A relatively small ($n = 97$) and homogeneous sample (mostly female students studying the same subject at a single university), and a potentially unreliable approach to collecting data (participants' self-reports of their Facebook profile features, rather than direct observation) may have prevented the authors from finding more significant connections and make it difficult to extrapolate findings to a general population.
Evans et al.	2008	Facebook Profiles	Examined what aspects of the Facebook profile individuals use to form personality judgements. Findings show that certain features are difficult to grasp for people. For example, while the number of Facebook friends is clearly displayed on the profile, people cannot easily determine features such as the network density (whether a user's friends know each other).

self-esteem based on visitors' self-reports (Marcus et al., 2006). They found that, compared with the general adult population, website owners scored lower on Extraversion, Agreeableness and Conscientiousness, and higher on Openness to Experience. Due to the self-report nature of this study, the internal validity of the findings was called into question. Vazire and Gosling (2004) reported that observers' identity claims from websites are used to convey valid information about personality and that website observers were generally accurate in their assessments of website authors' personalities.

An emerging conclusion from social media-based research is that individuals' profile pictures can also say a lot about their personality traits. For example, Hall et al. (2014) reported that observers could accurately estimate Extraversion, Agreeableness and Conscientiousness of unknown profile owners based on profile pictures. Celli et al. (2014) suggested that people who are more Extraverted and Stable tend to have pictures where they are smiling. Furthermore, they appear more with other people. On the other hand, Introverts tend to appear alone whilst Neurotics tend to have images without humans and close-up faces.

Various other social networking site features have been shown to predict personality traits. Some researchers have studied the relationship between Facebook popularity (number of contacts) and personality traits. They found that Extraversion predicts the number of Facebook contacts; however, these findings were not statistically significant (Quercia et al., 2012).

Similarly, Gosling et al. (2011) showcased a positive relationship between Extraversion and frequency of Facebook usage and engagement. Parallel to offline behaviour, Extraverts seek out virtual social engagement, leaving behind a digital trail of behaviour such as friendship connections or picture postings. However, their work was based on a relatively small sample of just over 150 participants, again limiting the reliability and generalisability of their results. Overall, it would appear that Extraversion is one of the more predictable traits by information gathered from social media. This was corroborated by Celli et al. (2014), who reported that Agreeableness and Extraversion can be more easily predicted among personality traits, while Emotional Stability (low Neuroticism) is the most difficult trait to predict.

Other features include an individual's Facebook likes, which was discovered by pioneering researchers at Cambridge who developed the *myPersonality* database (Kosinski et al., 2013). This database includes more than six million Facebook users who have been able to take a variety of personality and ability tests by installing myPersonality. Alongside this, the majority of users have also given consent for access to their Facebook information, including likes. Based on this wealth of information, Kosinski and colleagues showed that Facebook likes are highly predictive of personality and number of other psycho-demographic traits, such as age, gender, intelligence, political and religious views and sexual orientation. For example, they found significant correlations between Facebook profile features and psychological traits such as individuals who are more liberal and Open-to-Experiences tending to like more items on Facebook, posting more status updates and joining more groups.

However, there are some reports that point towards Big Data (particularly, Kosinski's model) as the 'culprit' behind Brexit and Trump's presidential win. Cambridge Analytica (CA) allegedly sold their information to an election-influencing company. By December 2015, CA claimed to have collected up to 5,000 data points on over 220 million Americans. In September, the Trump campaign spent $5 million with CA to target potential voters. The company has denied the claims but, regardless, it highlights the potential danger Big Data has (Doward & Gibbs, 2017). In the aftermath of the CA scandal, doubts have been raised as to the extent the analysis were used, or if they were mainly a marketing gimmick, as CA were unable to extract sufficiently precise results for use in their campaigns.

Another commonly used method in research to assess personality is a *linguistic analysis* technique used on information gathered from social media. This method is extremely useful when it comes to understanding and individual's personality based on the words they use. For example, Qiu et al. (2012b) concluded that tweets do contain valid linguistic cues to personality. In particular, Extraversion was found to be positively correlated with positive emotion words and social process words, Agreeableness was found to be negatively correlated with negation words and Openness was found to be negatively correlated with second-person pronouns, assent words and positive emotion words.

Furthermore, Schwartz et al. (2013) applied differential language analysis to uncover features distinguishing demographic and psychological attributes of 700 million words, phrases and topic instances collected by myPersonality from Facebook status updates of 75,000 participants. Their findings showed a striking variation of language related to personality, gender and age. This work confirmed existing observations such as Neurotic people's tendency to use the word 'depressed'.

Nevertheless, despite some organisations believing that information gathered from social media sites are more well rounded and uncover an individual's true personality, this does not always appear to be the case. The issues that occur with traditional methods remain true for newer methods. For example, individuals may intentionally or unintentionally misrepresent themselves online as they formulate a profile that showcases their ideal selves rather than what truly symbolises their actual personality (Green, 2013).

Research has emphasised that personal accomplishments and positive attributes are more likely to be advertised online rather than the negatives (Qiu et al., 2012a). This can have great implications on the selection process, and recruiters must use social media with caution. Indeed, the social media may paradoxically be much more prone to impression management than either interviews or standard personality questionnaires (Buffardi & Campbell, 2008).

It has become apparent that some people have more than one social network identity. Furthermore, as it becomes more widely known that social network identities are being used for selection, it is both possible and likely that *impression management and self-editing* will increase, which in turn lowers reliability and validity. Indeed, there are reputation-defending and reputation-restoring organisations that, for a fee, try to enhance a person's public face and profile, which would lead the data analysis to be incorrect. Thus, it might be possible to create personal websites designed specifically to make the person look like an ideal citizen and employee, namely, high on Conscientiousness and Agreeableness as well as being socially self-conscious and concerned.

Social media sites have been freely available online (World Wide Web) for the past 25 years. In the early 2000s, sharing your name on the open internet was considered unsafe, so people used pseudonyms for their online identities. Creating websites or other content online was restricted to the tech savvy and therefore considered odd. By the mid-2010s, it became commonplace to share, indeed advertise personal details, in real time on open platforms. In recent years, there is a backlash to this and many people are very wary of communicating this way. Thus some platforms, like Snapchat, which deletes messages after they have been seen once; WhatsApp, which offers an encrypted messaging service; and other closed groups, have become increasingly popular.

Other social networking tools are also being deployed in the work environment, such as Slack and Microsoft Teams (over 12 million and 44 million daily users respectively as of March 2020). The Covid-19 pandemic dramatically affected the use of online communication providing even more Big Data for analysts.

A recent study underscores issues related to impression management and how it results in context collapse, where users' enacted content sharing strategies, including aspects such as changes in linguistic style, expressed emotions and private nature of content, depend on their imagined audience. The results showed that posts were targeted to the lowest common denominator of the imagined audience, where users with a more heterogeneous audience share less personal information, though with more positive words (Gil-Lopez et al., 2018). These contextual factors, and other shifts in demographic uses, preference and practices should be taken into consideration when evaluating results from studies conducted at a given time period on a given sample.

9.1.4 Problems, Perils and Promises

Both consultants and researchers are required to abide by a number of ethical guidelines in the assessment of people. Every so often there are very high-profile, and thus well-known, litigation cases where people attempt to sue test publishers, test administrators, organisations and consultants because of decisions based on judgements and test scores. They are usually, but not exclusively, people from minority groups of many types who feel the tests are unfairly discriminated against them.

Is Big Data prone to any particular issues? For instance, there is also the question of what meaning should be given to low-frequency users of social media. Are they disadvantaged in some way? Do these tests discriminate against older and poorer people who may reside in rural settings? What about users of older, outmoded systems compared to those using the latest competing systems? These problems could lead to many unintended consequences and legal cases.

The new technologies and Big Data present a range of new problems. The first is obtaining data about an individual without their consent. How would candidates feel about organisations that were scraping as much data from the web and other open sources about them? There are important questions about the accuracy of these data and who indeed is supplying them. Next, there are many potential issues around surveillance (Furnham & Swami, 2015).

It seems sensible that two things are done concerning the ethics of the new technologies. First, ethics committees need experts and specialists on these new technologies to inform other committee members. Second, the committees could also benefit from the insight of users and researchers who themselves do not have any financial interest in the development or sale of those technologies.

The advent of new technologies has provided a whole new research area for ethicists, a potential field day for lawyers and considerable problems for consultants and others who use these technologies. To a large extent this is a new virgin territory.

As Favaretto et al. (2019) have noted:

> Practices of automatic profiling, sorting and decision making through data mining have been introduced with the prima facie concept that Big Data technologies are objective tools capable of overcoming human subjectivity and error resulting in increased fairness. However, data mining can never be fully human-free, not only because humans always risk undermining the presumed fairness and objectivity of the process with subconscious bias, personal values or inattentiveness, but also because they are crucial in order to avoid improper correlations and thus to ensure fairness in data mining. It thus seems that Big Data technologies are deeply tied to this dichotomous dimension where humans are both the cause of its flaws and the overseers of its proper functioning ...
>
> The difficulties encountered in adequately regulating discrimination in Big Data, especially from a legal point of view, could be partly related to a diffuse lack of dialogue among disciplines. The reviewed literature in fact pinpointed that while on the one hand, unfair discrimination is a complex philosophical and legal concept that stores difficulties for trained data scientists , Big Data, on the other, is quite a technological field so philosophers, social scientists and lawyers do not always fully understand the implications of algorithmic modelling for discrimination.
>
> *(pp. 22–23)*

9.1.5   Experts View

The following brief was sent to a number of people experts and those working in the assessment business. Most, but not all, were trained psychologists, others were entrepreneurs and those working in test development and sales. Some were chosen because they were young

(<30 years) and 'tech savvy' while others were often much older (>50 years) with years of experience in this business. The aim was to look at the range of replies, paying particular attention to their use of Big Data.

> **Think of somebody you know that you are interested in: it may be a boss, a neighbour, a teacher. Let us assume that they are not particularly well known or famous.**
>
> **Your task is to understand this individual: to draw up a rich psychological profile on him/her for a variety of reasons.**
>
> **You have enough time (as much as a week) and a reasonable budget to assist you. You are being paid by an assessment company to do this.**
>
> **How can you use the internet, Big Data, or legally sourced and available data to inform your profile?**
>
> **Where would you begin? Facebook? LinkedIn? Where else?**

Response 1

If we're looking at new things/tech:

TV/Film – What do they watch on Netflix? Do they prefer binge watching TV shows or do they watch films? Are they documentary or sit-com people?

Music – What do they listen to on Spotify? Do they listen to albums or playlists? Their own playlists (creative curators) or premade playlists?

Radio – Do they listen to podcasts? What kind – people-affairs, culture, art, comedy? What time of day do they listen to podcasts – commuting or at home?

Purchase history – What do they spend their money on? Can we use modern banking apps like Monzo to track how they categorise their spending? Is it on dinner, going out for drinks, hiring music spaces? Do they buy the same coffee at the same place at the same time every day (high routine)? Do they do sporadic purchasing?

Just focusing on social media, there are too many platforms now, so age has become a key moderator that needs to be considered (these are very loose rules of thumb, but could be interesting):

What is their age?:

40+: look to Facebook.

Extraversion/Narcissism –

How many photos do they post? How many friends do they have? What types of photos do they post – is it pictures of themselves, pictures of their family, pictures of landscapes, pictures of them playing sports? This also gives an indication of what is central to their identity.

Value signalling –

How many times do their profile pictures include banners about politics or a geopolitical event?

Are their banners more political (Vote Labour; Leave Means Leave; Pro-EU, etc.) or are they referencing geopolitical tragedies (e.g. changing their profile picture to have the colours of the Lebanese flag in reference to the protests there) – people who do this last one are called Tragedy Hipsters, they usually couldn't care less about Lebanon, but changing their profile pictures gives an opportunity to signal that they are more in touch with non-mainstream political issues than the average person, therefore better than everyone else.

30–40: look at Twitter.

Followers to following ratio – gives an idea of if they are projectors or reflectors? (stealing from your drains and radiators analogy).

What do they follow? News sites, sports, celebrities, influencers, friends? What do they post? Do they reply to other people's posts? Do they post their own content? Their own content – what is it about? High-level socio-political commentary or do they comment on the qualia of their stream of consciousness?

Younger than 30: look at Instagram and TikTok.

What is their followers to following ratio? How often have they posted in comparison to the number of people they are following?

This gives an indication of whether they use social media as a means of following and viewing others or whether they use it is as a platform to talk about themselves. Are they projectors or reflectors?

The more they follow, there is an argument that they crave external stimulation.

What do they follow? People, animals, culture, magazines, influencers, music, etc.?

Response 2

It is quite easy to use Instagram to get a seemingly good impression of what someone was like without even messaging them.

How often they posted and what type of photos they posted are huge. You genuinely want to stay clear of anyone that posts too frequently from my experience.

As far as content goes, you have: pictures of others; pictures of wildlife, environment/pictures of self, taken by others/pictures of self, taken by self in order of decreasing wholesomeness and increased narcissism (and/or insecurity) – multiply the last two with frequency as it's expected that you'll post photos of yourself on the platform unless you're a photographer. A lot of people use these sites to market their ideal self so by their posts you can see what they think is most valuable in people.

You can see a similar thing with LinkedIn as some people write about how their whole paradigm has changed because they went to a lecture/conference for a few hours and how they're a much better, smarter and more employable person.

Narcissism and (secondary) psychopathic behaviour is also pretty normal and easy to see in such platforms.

Getting their Reddit (massive forum site) username if they had one could also show a huge amount about their specific interests or values (fitness, cooking, trading cards, woodwork, philosophy, etc.)

Their job itself is likely a considerable marker of their testosterone (men)/agreeableness in general and shows what they're interested in (as long as it's a career). Alternately, a lack of career at a young age may also be telling (but less so if they're of low socio-economic status or in minority groups).

Response 3

I would first apply the obvious social media, but there are MANY of them: Facebook, Twitter, LinkedIn, Instagram, TikTok, etc. This information can be rich, meagre, or non-existent. In any case it will tell us something about the person. That is important because a social media profile can be used for later disambiguation. Social media usually contain pictures and activities that let us know age, ethnicity and affiliations to use as filters in later searches.

From there, I would move to various search engines. Google, Yahoo and DuckDuckGo will give different types of information. It is rare to find someone who today does not exist in *any* of these search engines. Our profile is now building. What we find, we find, but lack of presence can be telling here as well.

Now to the better sources. If we have possibilities of disambiguation, we can search newspapers and other media. There is a vast ocean of local newspapers, global outlets, professional periodicals and reports from clubs and associations. Working on the papers from my grandfather I discovered that even the Freemasons sometimes publish financial reports when they have to; these have signatories.

With this in hand, one may now approach official records within the legal domain – school alumni rosters, company presentations, business transactions, boards of companies, directories of properties, taxation records, donators to public causes. Such sources are diverse and difficult, but if you already have half a profile, you know what to look for.

Now to the grey zone. Once you have *some* information you may go to the national archives. For Britain, the one in Kew is perfectly searchable online. There are also library sources. While this information tends to be of the archival and ancient kind, one may find a lot about a living person's family, background, cultural history and other footprints that provide context to more erratic pieces of information collected at an earlier stage of the search.

The final possibility is to establish a fictional family (this is possibly illegal, but I am not quite sure) on websites like 'MyHeritage' and create a family with very close social ties to the key person. Chances are that such websites will spontaneously direct you to information about the key person's family network if listed on the website.

With all this information, the person will need to be really young or intentionally invisible to dodge profiling. If you have a week and a reasonable budget, all this is within reach. Moreover, if you are a professional sleuth you can have a lot of these searches in store as generic approaches and they will take you very little time to get going.

Response 4

I would start with google, making a list of the profiles they have to get an idea about which type of activities are they into. This is not just your Facebook, Instagram, LinkedIn – I'd want everything they ever assigned their name to, even if it's 10 years ago. In summary, a full history of their accounts using Google.

I'd want someone to content analyse all information that is public and if possible, I'd also send a friend request to get access to a deeper layer of info. Even if they reject the invite, it means something (so that's an extra data point). I'd really like to get my hands on things they are being tagged in so accepting the friendship on Facebook or Instagram would come handy for that.

Assuming they have social media, I would want to track who is interacting with them on each platform. Have a summary of the people they most interact with and see if we have any patterns.

I'd want to have a breakdown of how regular they are posting on each platform and what type of content (perhaps any patterns based on the time of the day they are posting). I'd also want to track how many posts have been adjusted during that week. This could mean deleting the post or just editing it.

What are the posts sounding like? Is it call for action (i.e. buy my product) or sharing their opinions? I'd track emotion words used to describe different things. I'd want to see if anything obvious comes out of it and if I can make any inferences which I could confirm on a different platform.

If possible, I'd use Big Data to have a look at the things they interact with (i.e. likes on Instagram, Facebook, LinkedIn, Twitter).

I'd also love to tap into seeing what type of adverts are they being targeted with. Not sure this bit is legal.

Overall, I'd like to have a mind map of all the different platforms and how the content follows patterns or not. It would be fantastic to compare this against a psychometric test to confirm or infirm some of the hypothesis created.

Response 5

This is a tricky one and worth a lot of money. If one cares about the law, GDPR prevents you from collecting information without the approval of the person. So, it also means that there is nowhere to start without asking the person first.

Then, based on what one searches to understand and how they analyse the information, there will be different sources one person should try to access. For example, Facebook is a great source, which is why Cambridge Analytica was able to target adverts based on individuals' LIKES on articles (the number was that with a certain number of likes, they were able to understand the person better than their partner.

X and Y have built contextual analysis and text analysis, so that if someone wrote a 100-word essay, they would be able to draw your profile on 10+ traits. In that case, LinkedIn would be a good source for people who wrote candid content.

If one can do the connections with forums and blogs, the quality of the analysis is increased.

Twitter is a bit of a mix of both LinkedIn and Facebook with its offering.

Alternatively, you may want to see interviews on YouTube and with speech recognition, see how people express themselves.

Response 6

Good question! I'd start with social media profiles (Facebook, LinkedIn and others). These are self-reported indicators and a goldmine for such profiling. You get all sorts of info – from date of birth to travel locations to significant life events to likes and dislikes as well as friends and connections. One could look at connections in common and analyse these too. I know that journalists when researching a target individual create fake profiles and add friends of friends of the individual in question so that when they would want to add the target, they are more likely to accept since you have 'friends in common'.

Depending on the budget and reason for profiling, you could also get data from official resources – for example credit rating agencies. In my work we use databases to verify identities, addresses and passports.

Response 7

Legally the only thing you can do is to search for their profile on Google, Facebook, LinkedIn and all the possible social media sites (but Google search will give you everything) and then you can see what's public info.

You won't be able to run any algorithms unless you have tech that is authorised to scrape that data, and when we are talking about one person your clinical judgement will of course outperform any algorithm.

So, there's not too much hope for most people unless they are relatively successful, famous or in the business of self-promotion (or very careless). There are obviously age and culture and personality effects at play too.

Response 8

If they are active on a rant Facebook group, GoodReads, Reddit or Quora then people tend to write quite extensively on these forums, so lots of scope for linguistic analysis

Is there a pattern in the groups they join, e.g. Pinterest/Instagram -> Visual
Are they active across many -> Openness?

Do they respond quickly -> Conscientiousness?

Do they mainly agree or challenge – is there a pattern -> Agreeableness?

On LinkedIn, can you see contacts in common – does that allow some triangulation?

What do their hobbies say about extraversion and thrill seeking, if visible?

What is being screened out as well as screened in – and how might this show up on social media?

Do they have followers – becoming increasingly important for some roles – does their role require a high or low profile?

Some apps, e.g. Snapchat, give various ratings that can be informative.

Do they use social media professionally to initiate and move the debate or are they more comfortable sitting in an echo chamber?

Are they engaged with political opinion, e.g. constant #FBPE hashtags?

How much self-monitoring appears in their profiles?

Does their identity appear integrated or fragmented across the various media?

If you find their CV how do they describe their achievements? Do they associate/connect with a wide or narrow range of people – perhaps instrumental of affective/instrumental mindsets?

Response 9

Videos – YouTube, Internet, websites

Of all the sources I like videos most, particularly when the principal is engaging with others. Ideally, we should see the full body language and others in the same shot. Face to camera interviews and recordings of speeches are less useful.

Absence of internet profile: In this day a serious businessperson has to have a profile on the internet. Those who do not should have an explanation.

Property – Where and what sort of home does the principal live in. It's relatively easy to find addresses on the internet (e.g. Companies House) and then from Google Earth what kind of property do they live in. One I investigated had three homes each of which was at the end of a cul-de-sac or hidden away.

> **Family** – The principal may be careful about what he or she puts on the internet, but the children, spouse and friends often reveal incriminating details through Facebook, Instagram, etc. A Deutsch bank CEO was targeted by criminals through his daughters' Facebook accounts.
>
> The **website** of the principal's company – what does it say about the principal – is a good source for narcissists and can reveal a lot about him or her. I once looked up a CEO of an SME to find the first pages all dedicated to pictures of him in a very flattering light. The researchers who did some early work on him thought nothing of this display of narcissism.
>
> **Written work** – Twitter, Facebook, Instagram, etc. – the trick here is to find work you know they have written themselves rather than a PR person. Trump's tweets say a lot about him and we can learn a lot about Boris from his prolific published work.

The responses of these individuals reflect many things: their assessment experience and their knowledge of Big Data. Some clearly have a good idea of what they want to assess; others of what they can assess. Some are more sensitive to legal and moral constraints than others. Some see Big Data as central, others as a potential supplement to other data. Some use it to inductively explore, others to deductively confirm hypotheses.

9.1.6 Conclusion

For the person assessor and selector, Big Data presents an interesting practicality–effectiveness trade-off. Big data takes a lot of effort and a lot of computing power. How much effort has to be put in to do it properly in order to be able to get a powerful/meaningful profile? What are the smallest behavioural signals that have the biggest impact? Some believe it is deeply impractical: academically it is clearly fascinating.

Obtaining information about people is becoming easier than ever before. However, the assessor and evaluator need to be differentiating and discriminating and not prurient in the sense it is important to know *what* information is relevant. The information supplied by Big Data can be difficult to obtain and deeply unreliable, but it can also give unprecedented information about an individual's impression management and networking.

As ever the 'science' is behind the enthusiastic adoption of Big Data analysis. The question is – *what* do you want to assess and which is the most effective and valid way of doing so? For some the idea of 'scanning the web' for data to determine the Big Five personality characteristics of an individual as opposed to giving him or her a short questionnaire seems obvious. On the other hand, there are times when people are required to do an assessment when it is impossible to interrogate the individual by any media: it is then that Big Data comes into its own.

However, the ethical and legal questions still linger over Big Data as the observers discussed have noted. Indeed, the law is often even further behind the scientists in the business of passing judgements on new assessment methods. Sceptics and cynics see Big Data as an expensive and unreliable way of getting information about an individual, which can be obtained by more traditional methods. Enthusiasts herald the dawn of a new age of assessment where we have unprecedented opportunities to collect valuable information on an individual which really helps the business of selection.

REFERENCES

Adjerid, I., & Kelley, K. (2018). Big data in psychology: a framework for research advancement. *American Psychologist*, 73(7), 899–917.

Amichai-Hamburger, Y., & Vinitzky, G. (2010). Social network use and personality. *Computers in Human Behavior*, 26(6), 1289–1295.

Back, M. D., Stopfer, J. M., Vazire, S., Gaddis, S., Schmukle, S. C., Egloff, B., & Gosling, S. D. (2010). Facebook profiles reflect actual personality, not self-idealization. *Psychological Science*, 21(3), 372–374.

Bleidorn, W., & Hopwood, C. J. (2019). Using machine learning to advance personality assessment and theory. *Personality and Social Psychology Review*, 23(2), 190–203.

Buffardi, L. E., & Campbell, W. K. (2008). Narcissism and social networking web sites. *Personality and Social Psychology Bulletin, 34*, 1303–1314.

Celli, F., Bruni, E., & Lepri, B. (2014). Automatic personality and interaction style recognition from Facebook profile pictures. In *Proceedings of the 22nd international conference on multimedia* (pp. 1101–1104). Glasgow, UK: ACM. http://dx.doi.org/10.1145/ 2647868.2654977.

Correa, T., Hinsley, A., & De Zuniga, H. (2010). Who interacts on the web? *Computers in Human Behavior, 26*, 247–253.

Doward, J., & Gibbs, A. (2017, March 4). Did Cambridge Analytica influence the Brexit vote and the US election? *The Guardian.* www.theguardian.com/polit ics/2017/mar/04/nigel-oakes-cambridge-analytica-what-role-brexit-trump

Evans, D. C., Gosling, S. D., & Carroll, A. (2008).What elements of an online social networking profile predict target-rater agreement in personality impressions? In *Proceedings of the international conference on weblogs and social media* (pp. 1–6). Seattle, WA.

Favaretto, M., De Clercq, E., & Elger, B. S. (2019). Big Data and discrimination: perils, promises and solutions. A systematic review. *Journal of Big Data, 6*(12), 1–27.

Ferwerda, B., Schedl, M., & Tkalcic, M. (2015, September). Predicting personality traits with instagram pictures. In *Proceedings of the 3rd workshop on emotions and personality in personalized systems 2015* (pp. 7–10). Vienna, Austria: ACM.

Furnham, A., & Swami, V. (2015). An investigation of attitudes toward surveillance at work and its correlates. *Psychology, 6*(13), 1668–1674.

George, G., Haas, M. R., & Pentland, A. (2014). From the editors: big data and management. *The Academy of Management Journal, 57*(2), 321–326.

Gil-Lopez, T., Shen, C., Benefield, G. A., Palomares, N. A., Kosinski, M., & Stillwell, D. (2018). One size fits all: context collapse, self-presentation strategies and language styles on Facebook. *Journal of Computer-Mediated Communication, 23*(3), 127–145.

Golbeck, J., Robles, C., & Turner, K. (2011, May 7–12). Predicting personality with social media. [Paper presented at the 2011 annual conference on human factors in computing systems], Vancouver, Canada.

Gonzalez, R. J. (2017). Hacking the citizenry? Personality profiling, 'big data' and the election of Donald Trump. *Anthropology Today, 33*(3), 9–12.

Gosling, S. D., Augustine, A. A., Vazire, S., Holtzman, N., & Gaddis, S. (2011). Manifestations of personality in online social networks: self-reported Facebook-related behaviors and observable profile information. *Cyberpsychology, Behavior, and Social Networking, 14*(9), 483–488.

Gosling, S. D., & Mason, W. (2015). Internet research in psychology. *Annual Review of Psychology, 66*, 877–902.

Green, K. (2013). The social media effect: are you really who you portray online? *HuffPost*. Retrieved from www.huffingtonpost.com/r-kay-green/the-social-media-effect-a_b_3721029.html

Hall, J. A., Pennington, N., & Lueders, A. (2014). Impression management and formation on Facebook: a lens model approach. *New Media & Society, 16*(6), 958–982.

Hariri, R. H., Fredericks, E. M., & Bowers, K. M. (2019). Uncertainty in big data analytics: survey, opportunities, and challenges. *Journal of Big Data, 6*(44), 1–16.

Harlow, L. L., & Oswald, F. L. (2016). Big data in psychology: introduction to the special issue. *Psychological Methods, 21*(4), 447–457.

He, Q., Glas, C. A., Kosinski, M., Stillwell, D. J., & Veldkamp, B. P. (2014). Predicting self-monitoring skills using textual posts on Facebook. *Computers in Human Behavior, 33*, 69–78.

Ihsan, Z., & Furnham, A. (2018). The new technologies in personality assessment: a review. *Consulting Psychology Journal: Practice and Research, 70*(2), 147–166.

Kosinski, M., Bachrach, Y., Kohli, P., Stillwell, D., & Graepel, T. (2014). Manifestations of user personality in website choice and behaviour on online social networks. *Machine Learning, 95*(3), 357–380.

Kosinski, M., Stillwell, D., & Graepel, T. (2013). Private traits and attributes are predictable from digital records of human behavior. *Proceedings of the National Academy of Sciences, 110*(15), 5802–5805.

Labrinidis, A., & Jagadish, H. V. (2012). Challenges and opportunities with big data. *Proceedings of the VLDB Endowment, 5*(12), 2032–2033.

Lane, J. (2016). Big data and anthropology: concerns for data collection in a new research context. *Journal of the Anthropological Society of Oxford, 3*(1), 74–88.

Mahmoodi, J., Leckelt, M., van Zalk, M. W., Geukes, K., & Back, M. D. (2017). Big Data approaches in social and behavioral science: four key trade-offs and a call for integration. *Current Opinion in Behavioral Sciences, 18*, 57–62.

Marcus, B., Machilek, F., & Schütz, A. (2006). Personality in cyberspace: personal Web sites as media for personality expressions and impressions. *Journal of Personality and Social Psychology, 90*(6), 1014–1031.

Mayer-Schönberger, V., & Cukier, K. (2013). *Big data: A revolution that will transform how we live, work, and think.* New York: Houghton Mifflin Harcourt Publishing Company.

Park, G., Schwartz, H. A., Eichstaedt, J. C., Kern, M. L., Kosinski, M., Stillwell, D. J., Ungar, D. J., Seligman, M. E., & Martin, E. P. (2015). Automatic personality assessment through social media language. *Journal of Personality and Social Psychology, 108*(6), 934–952.

Qiu, L., Lin, H., Leung, A. K., & Tov, W. (2012a). Putting their best foot forward: emotional disclosure on Facebook. *Cyberpsychology, Behavior, and Social Networking, 15*(10), 569–572.

Qiu, L., Lin, H., Ramay, J., & Yang (2012b). You are what you tweet: personality expression and perception on Twitter. *Journal of Research in Personality, 46*(6), 710–718.

Quercia, D., Lambiotte, R., Stillwell, D., Kosinski, M., & Crowcroft, J. (2012, February). The personality of popular facebook users. In *Proceedings of the ACM 2012 conference on computer supported cooperative work* (pp. 955–964). Seattle, DC.

Ross, C., Orr, E. S., Sisic, M., Arseneault, J. M., Simmering, M. G., & Orr, R. R. (2009). Personality and motivations associated with Facebook use. *Computers in Human Behavior, 25*(2), 578–586.

Schwartz, H. A., Eichstaedt, J. C., Kern, M. L., Dziurzynski, L., Ramones, S. M., Agrawal, M., Shah, A., Kosinski, M., Stillwell, D., Seligman, M. E., & Ungar, L. H. (2013). Personality, gender, and age in the language of social media: the open-vocabulary approach. *PLOS ONE, 8*(9), 1–16.

Skowron, M., Tkalčič, M., Ferwerda, B., & Schedl, M. (2016). Fusing social media cues: personality prediction from Twitter and Instagram. In *Proceedings of the 25th international conference companion on world wide web* (pp. 107–108). Geneva, Switzerland: International World Wide Web Conferences Steering Committee.

Stachl, C., Au, Q., Schoedel, R., Buschek, D., Völkel, S., Schuwerk, T., Oldemeier, M., Ullmann, T., Hussmann, H., Bischl, B., & Bühner, M. (2019, June 12). Behavioral patterns in smartphone uage predict Big Five personality traits. Retrieved from https://doi.org/10.31234/osf.io/ks4vd.

Thompson, A. (2016, December 8). Journalists and Trump voters live in eparate online bubbles, MIT analysis shows. *Vice News*. www.vice.com/en_us/article/d3xamx/journalists-and-trump-voters-live-in-separate-online-bubbles-mit-analysis-shows

Vazire, S., & Gosling, S. D. (2004). e-Perceptions: personality impressions based on personal websites. *Journal of Personality and Social Psychology, 87*(1), 123–132.

Xu, R., Frey, R. M., Vuckovac, D., & Ilic, A. (2015). Towards understanding the impact of personality traits on mobile app adoption – a scalable approach. In *Proceedings of the 23rd European conference on information systems* (pp. 1–12), Münster, Germany.

10 The Future of Assessment

How will technical, social, economic and legal forces influence the future of people assessment? How has the assessment and selection industry embraced changes in technology and the efforts of researchers to validate techniques?

We live in exciting times, particularly with respect to technological development and the internet being present in an ever-increasing amount in our daily lives. We are promised new methods which will both optimise and revolutionise assessment: it will be cheaper, more accurate and free from all sorts of bias.

New technologies include smartphone and mobile sensing, ambulatory assessment and ecological momentary sampling, text mining (e.g. from Twitter or Facebook), sensors and wearables and virtual and augmented reality.

The central question in assessment is the 'what' not the 'how' question: that is, *what* we are trying to predict/understand (i.e. how hardworking is the person, do they cope with stress well, have they got integrity) rather than *how* we measure this. Those interested in assessment often seem transfixed by the 'how' questions which do change, as opposed to the 'what' questions, which often do not.

Equally, it is important to ask whether a new technology adds *more, new, relevant* information that we *really need* rather than simply new ways of collecting and refining data. Many in the selection business have observed that technology is more innovative about collecting than interpreting data. Similarly, do those who collect good psychometrically valid data know how to use it wisely, or are they doing little more than automated headhunting?

Academics are getting more interested in how different traits *interact* (Conscientiousness and Neuroticism), which gives a more subtle and nuanced interpretation but one which is inevitably more complex. Just like the 'how' questions, the 'what' questions are becoming more sophisticated.

As the world becomes a smaller place and there are large movements of people from the developing to the developed world, there is the question of cross-cultural validity (i.e. how psychological constructs transpose from one culture to the next and how does that affect the validity of the instrument). This is especially true in countries where we have to test and select over many different cultures. The question is, 'are some assessment techniques more or less prone to cultural effects and what are we going to do about them?'

Since selection, whatever the technique, has more and more legal consequences than ever before, being able to demonstrate predictive validity becomes all the more salient. Those who use new technology (AI algorithms) should expect a number of lawsuits and would do well to start preparing their defence based on all the relevant criteria as well as predictive validity.

There is also the question of whether new technology improves the breadth or depth. Those who buy assessment are, of course, most interested in predictive validity but are also becoming aware of other issues like being a good team player, can they become good leaders, are they strategic enough?

How have things changed from 50, 25 or even 10 years ago? What methods do we still employ and why? How will the brave new world of Big Data, neuroscience and AI change completely how we assess people? What information can we retrieve from the internet and organisational data banks, like criminal and medical history? What will turn out to be 'flash in the pan' over-hyped and under-delivered promises ... and what will endure?

There are many developments in the psychological assessment of people (Bersin & Chamorro-Premuzic, 2019). The old trio of application form, interview and letters of recommendation seem to be outdated.

So do personality tests, even when done online. Techniques go in and out of fashion that does not always have to do with their validity.

There has always been the call for faster, cheaper, more accurate and more fake-resistant ways of assessing people. There has also been a call to measure different aspects of individuals from the *shape* of their head to what is *inside it* and how it *works*. Popular media are full of reports on the brave new world of testing based on new mobile technology and how it has replaced the tired old world of question-naires and interviews. Many commentators have discussed the use of mobile devices (Arthur et al., 2014; Illingworth et al., 2015; Morelli et al., 2014) and Big Data (Guszcza & Richardson, 2014) for more accurate and subtle assessment of individuals at work.

Are there many fundamental changes in

1. *What* we are trying to assess? The answer appears to be no: selectors are still interested in an individual's ability, personality and motivation, as well as their integrity and health. Whilst new concepts appear every so often, there has not been much change in the fundamental features of what people are trying to assess.
2. *How* can we assess individuals? This is about the development of new measurement techniques which may be superior to those used in the past. There has always been and remains great changes in this aspect of assessment.
3. The *cost* of those assessments? Inevitably selectors want the best possible cost-effective methods though many seem willing to trade off reliability and validity for cost. A related question is organisational budgets and it seems some, realising the cost of selection errors, are willing to spend greater amounts in the hope of better assessment and selection.
4. *What we are allowed to* assess? For many, the new world is one of increasing legislation where there are a number of questions and details it is unadvisable and illegal to ask as they may be related to anti-discrimination laws. This differs from country to country depending on a variety of political factors.
5. *Who* does the assessment? This is about whether companies should outsource assessment to experts or do it in-house. To a large extent this question depends on what is assessed and how it is done.

6. How is the assessment data *used*? Is the data fed into a complex and sophisticated algorithm or used more impressionistically by an individual or small team? Is it stored and used to help validate instruments and decisions? This needs to be decided upfront.

7. To what extent is the assessment data *fed back* to the individual and or used by HR to develop a training program to train them. This means the assessment can have multiple uses.

8. Where is data *stored* and who has access to it? Data privacy and storage laws have greatly increased in the last decade (GDPR) as have its abundance in 'cloud' storage and server farms.

Every generation of researchers has attempted to describe processes and exploit the assessment technology of their time. Two of the most famous personality theorists of the twentieth century, Hans Eysenck and Raymond Cattell, were particularly imaginative in trying to invent new ways of measuring personality. Eysenck explored many different methods based in biology (the lemon drop test), electricity (EEG techniques) and mechanical tasks (pursuit rotor task), while Cattell completed a long book on the 'objective' measurement of personality. Current technology, particularly brain scanning, appears to offer even more and better opportunities to assess people (Farr & Tippin, 2017; Finn et al., 2015).

For nearly two decades researchers have noted the possibility of using the internet to do personality research (Buchanan & Smith, 1999). Chapman and Webster (2003) pointed out 15 years ago that the new assessment technologies (predominantly online) have specific goals: improve efficiency, enable new screening tools, reduce costs, standardise the HR system, expand the applicant pool, promote the organisational image and increase applicant convenience. There are now companies who track huge numbers of people on the web and build various profiles, but do not follow any classical or modern personality theory.

However, there are also *unintended consequences* and effects of these developments. Thus, the use of the internet not only expands the applicant pool but also increases the number of under-qualified and out-of-country applicants. It is easy to be flooded with inappropriate applicants in the sense that many people lacking the required and specified qualifications, experience or place of domicile apply online because it is so convenient, quick and easy. There is also the loss of personal touch that both assessor and assessee value and respect. There are further concerns about cheating if timed ability tests are used. Also, there are still concerns about adverse impact, which means that certain groups simply do not have access to the technology to take the tests.

Current technology, particularly brain scanning (see Chapter 7), appears to offer even more and better opportunities to study individual differences. The past decade has seen a great expansion of many new technologies in the workplace, some of which have been directed at personality assessment and personnel selection. Ranging from social media analytics for selection to Big Data mining for employee improvement, there has been a great interest in the development of new, valid and efficient ways to assess both job applicants and holders.

In 2010, Stamper reported, based on a survey in the USA, that 45% of hiring managers were using information found from social networking sites to inform their hiring decisions. Furthermore, 35% of that group did not hire at least one applicant based on what they found. Moreover, more than 70% of Forbes Global 2000 companies (2013) surveyed said they intended to use technologies such as gamification for marketing and customer retention.

Chamorro-Premuzic et al. (2016) reported how talent identification in the HR world is shifting from the traditional methods of assessment, including job interviews, assessment centres, cognitive ability tests, personality inventories, biodata, situational judgement tests (SJTs), 360-degree feedback ratings, resumes, letters of recommendations and supervisors' ratings of performance. They identified the four primary new technologies of talent identification. These include: digital interviewing and voice profiling, social media analytics, web scraping and text analytics, internal Big Data and talent analytics and gamification.

They also predicted that 'profiling tools will become invisible to individuals and require no deliberate attention from job applicants or incumbents. Most people will be profiled already, and if they aren't, assessment will operate in the form of covert or subtle algorithms embedded in other activities, including fun and interactive, game-like experiences' (p. 39). Yet, it is important to note that they have further highlighted that there is little or no academic research for some of these methods, suggesting that the validity and reliability of these tools are still unestablished (Winsborough & Chamorro-Premuzic, 2016).

10.2 MARKETING IN THE BRAVE NEW WORLD

Those who favour and sell gamified and other products argue that many employers are overwhelmed with large application volumes. Quite naturally they want to reduce the time and costs associated with CV screening and interviewing. They believe they need a clear and fair method to differentiate candidates. More importantly they want methods that are focused on diversity and inclusion. Equally, importantly they want an excellent experience for their candidates.

Those who advocate the new technologies, like gamification, use the following catchphrases to sell their ideas and product:

'Next-generation technology'

'21st-century generation'

'Digs deeper'; 'Reveals more'

'Powered by Neuroscience' ; 'State-of-the-Art'

'More diverse choices'

'Authentic' and 'Real-World'

'Disruptive'

'Exciting, New and Different'

Those in game-based assessment (GBA) all claim that the candidate experience of GBA is better than traditional psychometrics. Research has tried to catch up, and a recent paper by Landers et al.

(2020) found that GBA versions of SJTs only improve the candidates' perception of the technological sophistication of the hiring company, but did not lead to more positive candidate experience, attitudes or perceptions of attractiveness of the organisation.

Some advocates of GBA also claim that the candidate experience is better as it reduces the number of candidates dropping out of the selection process (i.e. candidates do not have the inclination nor attention span to complete an ordinary psychometric assessment). This could mean prototypic 'millennials', who may be 'incapable' of taking traditional psychometric assessments. Yet, if a candidate does not have the motivation or the attention span to complete a traditional psychometric, do they deserve to be selected? At the very least, dropping out would save the company time in selecting them out.

Some boldly say that their techniques have *better psychometrics:* particularly predictive validity. That is, that they are more accurate than the 'old', well-used and tried methods. They suggest that their new methods in fact lead to a reduction/avoidance of 'older method' issues/artefacts (e.g. impression management). That is, the more traditional methods have well-known problems associated with them and these new methods largely overcome them.

They also suggest that many new methods provide a better candidate experience: that is that candidates are much more positive about the whole experience. This leads, of course, to better PR for the tester and company doing the assessment and selection. These methods, they argue are more up to date, fairer and more engaging, all of which reflect very well on the selectors.

Researchers in this area know how difficult it is to validate assessment techniques because of problems of getting hold of big-enough samples with comprehensive, salient and subtle work-outcome measures. It comes as a shock to young researchers that organisations appear to have so little and so poor appraisal data on their staff. Yet, those who advocate the new technology often make claims about improved and incremental validity, which seems rather dubious.

10.3 BEWARE THE JINGLE-JANGLE EFFECT

The *jingle-jangle fallacy* refers to the specious idea that two different things are the same because they bear the same/very similar names (*jingle fallacy*), or that two identical or very similar concepts are different because they have different labels (*jangle fallacy*). In both cases discrepancies occur due to the attention given to the name/brand rather than the product.

For the psychometrician, the jangle fallacy describes the inference that two tests of whatever sort with *different names/labels* measure essentially quite *different constructs/ideas*. On the other hand, a jingle fallacy is based on the assumption that two measures that have the same name measure the same construct.

The question is what jingles and why and what jangles and why? The world of psychological tests jangles more noisily than a gamelan orchestra. Lexical psychologists who have studied the words we use to describe personality in many different languages have found evidence of little more than five to seven concepts.

Fashions change; ideas and measures need revitalisation. So, it is not difficult to take an old test and idea and repackage it, which is, of course, what many do. It is manufacturers who prefer the jingle fallacy.

This can happen in the consultancy and testing world, where someone has had a monopoly for a famous, expensive and well-known product. The jinglers provide a very similar, much cheaper version, that tries to capture the market. The question for psychometricians and managers alike is the underlying test validity of both.

10.4 COMPARE AND CONTRAST

Academics, consulting psychologists and new start-up entrepreneurs attempt to exploit the opportunities that new technology offers to assess people more accurately, easily and cheaply. Many are early adopters, indeed even pioneers, in the field. Others find that it is client demand that causes them to investigate, and then use, new tools and techniques that show that they are at the cutting edge of

Table 10.1 *A comparison of old and new techniques*

Old methods	New tools	Dimension assessed
Interviews	Digital interviews Voice profiling	Expertise, social skills, motivation and intelligence
Biodata Supervisory ratings	Big Data (internal)	Past performance, current performance
IQ/SJTs Self-reports	Gamification	Intelligence, job-related knowledge, big five and minor personality traits
Self-reports	Social media analytics	Big five personality traits and values
Resumés References	Professional Social networks	Experience, past performance, technical skills and qualifications
360 ratings	Crowdsourced	Any personality trait, competencies, reputation

psychometrics (Furnham, 2018). Some will inevitably be in the late majority, while others might even be laggards. The question for many must be the investment of time and money in techniques that in the end fail to deliver what they promise and may indeed cause many additional problems.

There are changes in the law, and all the issues surrounding discrimination. There are changes in how tests are administered and scored. There are changes in how tests 'get to market'.

Chamorro-Premuzic et al. (2016) compared 10 old and new techniques (Table 10.1).

They conclude

In a hyperconnected world where everyday behaviors are recorded, unprecedented volumes of data are available to evaluate human potential. I-O psychologists need to recognize the impact our digital lives will have on research methods, findings, and practices. We believe that these vast data

> pools and improved analytic capabilities will fundamentally disrupt the talent identification process. There are several key points to be derived from our review. First, many more talent signals will become available. Second, even if these emerging signals are weak or noisy, they may still work additively and be useful. Third, new analytic tools and computing power will continue to emerge and allow us to improve and refine the prediction of behavior in a wide range of contexts, probably based on the additive nature of these signals. Alternatively, if they do not prove to be additive, we anticipate that subsets of these signals will allow more specific prediction of performance. That is to say, computing power and the vast number of data points will allow for much greater alignment between the criterion and the predictor, which is a fundamental tenet of validity.
>
> *(p. 633)*

Finally, they note that most of the innovations have yet to demonstrate compelling levels of validity. There is a substantial gap between what science prescribes and what HR practitioners do. Also the history of science is much more one of adventitious and serendipitous findings than many people realise. Raw empiricism has often produced marvellously useful outcomes. There are two fundamental questions underlying the assessment process: (a) what to assess and (b) how to assess it?

In another paper that covered the same ground but aimed at HR people, Chamorro-Premuzic et al. (2017) concluded:

> Although we advocate for the benefits accruing from the datafication of talent, it is also important to consider some limitations and negative consequences of these novel approaches to talent identification. As new tools are developed and begin to be deployed in the workplace, there are three issues pertaining to the employee-employer relationship that must be resolved: a) clear boundaries around data ownership and sharing must be established; b) data privacy and access must be consensual and transparent; and c) data should be used ethically and in a non-discriminatory manner. Although regulatory bodies have already established best practices

> regarding these issues for the use of traditional psychological assessments, much work remains to be done in order to update these guidelines beyond HR and organization psychology, considering the intersectional nature of data, machine learning & human behaviour.
>
> *(p. 15)*

There are plenty of speculators and futurologists in this area, both academic and non-academic, the latter often being science journalists, practitioners and consultants. An example is McHenry (2017), who is both an academic and a test publisher. He made five assertions about the future of psychometric tests:

> '1. Smartphones will replace computers for employee assessment.
> 2. High-quality psychometric testing services will be sold direct to consumers.
> 3. Advances in the neuroscience of personality will reveal which are the most valid individual differences to measure and how best to measure them.
> 4. The digital badging movement, coupled to the use of big data and new forms of digital CV, will render many of the current applications for high-stakes testing redundant.
> 5. The basis for employee development will in the near future be derived from the data yielded by wearable devices and not from psychometric tests.'
> (p. 268)

In a similar vein Iliescu and Greiff (2019), looking at the impact of technology in testing practice and policy, suggested that those interested address four observations:

(1) 'Without a closer integration of technology, testing as we know it may disappear – but it may do so equally *because* of the integration with technology

(2) Psychological testing will continue to generate data, but it will also begin to preferentially use existing data, that was routinely collected for other objectives

(3) We have no clear criteria on which to decide whether psychological testing is "better" than technology-driven profiling and prediction

(4) Active advocacy for psychological testing is critical in the future, if we want to become more visible for society.' (p. 151)

One of the most comprehensive and up-to-date reviews called 'Personnel selection in the digital age' Woods et al. (2020) reviewed all recent research 2010–2020. Their focus was on *digital selection procedures* (DSP) and the main applications and emergent evidence. They observed:

> Digital technology is flexible and easily updated and adapted and so information from users, clients and others can be used to continually and rapidly improve the way that, for example, software or online systems function ... The rapid configurable nature of digital assessments means a fundamental shift in the way we approach validation, from an 'endpoint' of instrument creation to an ongoing accumulation of insight into a technique or methodology.
>
> *(p.71)*

They were equally interested in the new technology and the adaptation to existing method. There are many applications of online methods:

> The use of online applications for the purpose of screening applicants increases efficiency by shortening hiring cycles, leading to a significant reduction in selection costs, while simultaneously expanding applicant pools ... Online applications have also shown to be more effective in assuring objectivity in the handling of job applications and reducing the potential for adverse impact for protected groups. However, peer reviewed literature reveals little on the validity of online applications.
>
> *(p. 45)*

Moreover, online testing can be combined with AI technology to use pre-established criteria in algorithms to choose the best candidate (as measured by education, job history). They detail many studies which compare old and new methods (electric vs paper-and-pencil; proctored vs unproctored) and different tests (personality vs intelligence). Most showed no differences. However, they do note the problem of impersonation and fraudulent completion of tests. Furthermore, they noted that candidates often preferred internet testing over the traditional methods.

New developments in SJTs include the use of videos with some evidence that they were more valid predictors of work performance than traditional written methods. There is a great interest in *digital interviews* where people record video or digital answers to predetermined questions. This data can be subject to all sorts of AI and other analysis. However, studies suggest that candidates do not like these techniques and consider them less fair and stilted and 'creepier and less personal' than the traditional methods though that may change over time.

In examining *gamified assessments*, they note arguments in favour of reduced faking and social desirability while promoting 'fun, transparency, challenge and interaction'. But they conclude:

> Surprisingly, despite much buzz about the use of gamified assessments in practice, there remains scarce published literature on the construct validity of gamified assessments and applicant reactions to them in the peer reviewed IWO [Industrial, work and organisational] psychology literature.
>
> *(p. 68)*

Next, with respect to using social media and network sites to gather digital footprints they note that it is possible to gather information that would seem to predict work success like breadth of professional and non-professional experience social capital, interest in updating their knowledge. But they suggest caution in the use of such profiles and have raised a number of concerns over veracity, validity, personal information usage, compliance procedures and other important issues. They also observe that people are more likely to use impression management tactics in their social media to enhance their chances in getting the job. Also adverse impact on the profile ratings present a serious potential bias issue among gender, age and minority groups.

In this excellent review they cover various crucially important issues:

Validity: This is clearly the most important issue and they conclude like so many others:

> Alongside issues of construct validity is arguably the most critical gap currently in the literature on the validity of DSPs; namely the absence of peer-reviewed published studies of criterion validity. In the papers we reviewed, only two reported criterion-related validity of digital forms of assessment in the context of selection.
>
> (p. 69)

Adverse impact: It is argued that new technology can be used to reduce human bias in selectors, but many maintain biases (through AI technology) that are found in society.

Privacy: Clearly some people are really put off by the idea that selectors themselves will screen all their online content. Furthermore, it can be challenged in the law.

Digital Familiarity: Access to, and familiarity with, technology may discriminate older, poorer people in developing countries as there is a digital divide.

As such they developed a useful 10-point research agenda:

1. 'What are appropriate and effective benchmarks for evaluating the construct validity of DSPs?
2. How can validity evidence be applied most effectively in the rapid design, improvement and deployment of DSPs?
3. What are the criterion validities of different forms of DSPs?
4. Do DSPs outperform non-digital selection procedures in terms of validity in any specific situations?
5. What are the incremental criterion validities attained through using a combination of DSPs and non-digital methods?

6. What are the effects of potential new forms of adverse impact and bias in the use of DSPs, and in what ways do they exacerbate or ameliorate unfairness concerns in selection?
7. How do DSPs shape applicant reactions towards the hiring organization?
8. How should the basis for digital selection decisions be presented to applicants to ensure transparency?
9. What are the ethical and privacy considerations that should be considered by the organizations to enhance applicant reactions to DSPs?
10. Are there generational or other relevant demographic differences in applicant reactions to DSPs?' (p. 70)

This is their conclusion:

Our view is that the application of DSPs have forged ahead of scientific research and that in some areas organizations are using these new technologies rather 'blind' to their validity, adverse impact, privacy, or impact on applicants. Given the speed of advancement of some of the pertinent technologies this is perhaps unsurprising; what is now called for is a period of realignment between research and practice in IWO psychology in our view where these concerns can be examined and addressed by applied research efforts into DSP in employee selection ... The pace of development of digital technology is increasingly incompatible with the slower processes of research dissemination in the field. The rise of DSPs is one of the most prominent early manifestations of this tension. Maintaining the centrality of our research evidence in the practice of selection will require changes to how we make available the findings of research to ensure they are relevant to state-of-the-art practice. But this issue is not peculiar to selection research, and rather is reflective of the impact of digital technology across business and management. Successfully meeting our call to action requires new learning by psychologists about the epistemologies, techniques and challenges of multi-disciplinary teams, and clarity about the benefits that psychologists can bring (i.e. the incentives for others to collaborate with us). However, by doing so and adapting to the digital age, selection researchers have an opportunity, as arguably in the past, to lead development of the tools, methods and processes of IWO research and practice, and ensure its continued impact in, and relevance to, organizations in the future.

(p. 74)

10.5 A SCEPTIC'S RESPONSE

Sherman (2019) notes in a blog in *Psychology Today*

Almost every week I learn about a new psychological assessment company entering the marketplace. Although each company is different, many tell the same story. First, they tell you that hiring is broken; personality tests don't work anymore; recruiting is out-of-date. Second, they tell you that their company has the answer. Finally, they hit you with the marketing smokescreen: a list of sophisticated-sounding technological advancements designed to confuse you, misguide you, and make you feel like you are missing out. You are not missing out, but you are falling for the common marketing trends used by these new companies. In this article, I expose these trends so that you won't fall for them.

Trend #1: Neuroscience

Some companies measure how fast you react to flashing objects on a computer screen and say that their assessments are based on neuroscience. Neuroscience is the study of the structure and function of the nervous system. Even though such a broad definition leaves room for debate, the reality is that neuroscience concerns the function of individual neurons and the brain (i.e., a large mass of neurons).

Trend #2: Big Data and Deep Learning

Some companies brag about their stacks of big data and their use of machine learning or artificial intelligence to produce talent insights. However, if you dig deep, you find that most of the data these companies collect are useless; they aren't even using it. For example, millions of mouse-movements, keystrokes, and response times can be measured in a 10-minute assessment. But are they consequential? Do they predict anything? How is moving your mouse five pixels to the left before you respond to a question even relevant to your job as a store clerk? Evidence indicates that these sorts of micro-movements don't predict anything and aren't job-relevant ... The second thing you find as you dig deep (and you should be digging deep) into these assessment companies is that the sophisticated statistical methods they tout don't provide the new insights they promise.

Trend #3: Gamification

... The idea is that if job applicants have more fun taking the assessment, they will be less likely to drop out of the application process. Although the data show that candidates do enjoy game-based assessments, the data also indicate that gamification doesn't improve performance predictions. Research indicates that applicants who drop out during the assessment process are unlikely to be your strongest candidates anyway ... In addition, assessments that claim to be game-based often aren't games at all. In fact, most are just boring psychology laboratory tasks, like the Go, No-Go. Dr. Richard Landers – a global expert on game-based assessments – points out that dressing up boring tasks and adding arbitrary point systems doesn't make something a game.

Trend #4: Profile Matching

First, they assess your high-performers. Next, they see what differentiates your high-performers from a larger population of people who have taken the assessments. The differences between the two create a high-performer profile. At face value, this approach sounds perfect, but it is deeply flawed ... Although this profile matching approach used by many companies seems intuitive, only a proper validation study that differentiates high and low performers will give you an accurate profile. Don't fall for assessments that are only validated on high-performers.

Trend #5: Emphasizing Irrelevant Information

... New and old assessment companies often emphasize the total number of applicants, time to hire, and the diversity of the hiring class as selling points. The odd thing about emphasizing these is that you don't need an assessment company to do any of them. A simple lottery will do. That is, if you hire people randomly, you are sure to increase the total number of applicants and the diversity of the hiring class, and likewise you will decrease time to hire. The problem is, when it comes to performance, hiring randomly doesn't work.

When it comes to performance, the only thing that matters is validity: how well does the assessment predict performance? The reality is that some assessments predict job performance better than others. Assessment companies that don't show or emphasize validity probably don't have any. With no validity, they have no choice but to emphasize irrelevant features. Only two things matter in psychological assessment: fairness and predicting performance. Companies that emphasize neuroscience, big data, and gamification may be trying to distract you from the fact that their assessments don't predict workplace performance.

10.6 CONCLUSION

Differential psychologists are traditionally interested in assessing ability, personality and motivation. Academia is not immune from fad, fashion and folderol. To the outsider, some of these debates and issues look petty, puerile and pointless. Yet the academic world and the applied consultancy world of assessment and selection are closely related. Many academics work with and for test publishers; some even start their own business. In doing so they have to deal with the fact these worlds have different timeframes, values and perhaps even ultimate aims.

Furthermore, ordinary people are becoming more 'psych savvy'; many do tests, on varying quality, online. They get the feedback, learn the jargon. Learned societies like the APA and BPS are taking more interest in the use and abuse of testing.

Perhaps it is possible to classify attitudes to the future of assessment on two dimensions: enthusiastic–pessimistic and naïve–sceptical, such that we have naïve enthusiasts who see and welcome the brave new world and sceptical pessimists who reject all it stands for. Clearly the academic position is the enthusiastic (for progress) but sceptical about overclaiming.

Nevertheless, it is a particularly interesting time to be alive for those interested in the whole business of assessment and selection. As noted in Chapters 1 and 2, many aspects of the world have affected the way in which we appraise, evaluate and, hence, assess people. Thus, all those in the business need to know the options available to them, and their respective advantages and disadvantages, which was the motivation for writing this book.

REFERENCES

Arthur Jr, W., Doverspike, D., Muñoz, G. J., Taylor, J. E., & Carr, A. E. (2014). The use of mobile devices in high-stakes remotely delivered assessments and testing. *International Journal of Selection and Assessment, 22*(2), 113–123.

Bersin, J., & Chamorro-Premuzic, T. (2019). New ways to gauge talent and potential. *MIT Sloan Management Review, 60*(2), 1–7.

Buchanan, T., & Smith, J. L. (1999). Research on the Internet: validation of a World-Wide Web mediated personality scale. *Behavior Research Methods, Instruments, & Computers, 31*(4), 565–571.

Chamorro-Premuzic, T., Akhtar, R., Winsborough, D., & Sherman, R. A. (2017). The datafication of talent: how technology is advancing the science of human potential at work. *Current Opinion in Behavioral Sciences, 18*, 13–16.

Chamorro-Premuzic, T., Winsborough, D., Sherman, R. A., & Hogan, R. (2016). New talent signals: shiny new objects or a brave new world? *Industrial and Organizational Psychology, 9*(3), 621–640.

Chapman, D. S., & Webster, J. (2003). The use of technologies in the recruiting, screening, and selection processes for job candidates. *International Journal of Selection and Assessment, 11*(2–3), 113–120.

Farr, J. L., & Tippin, N. T. (2017). *Handbook of employee selection.* New York City, NY: Routledge, Taylor & Francis Group.

Finn, E. S., Shen, X., Scheinost, D., Rosenberg, M. D., Huang, J., Chun, M. M., Papademetris, X., & Constable, R. T. (2015). Functional connectome finger-printing: identifying individuals using patterns of brain connectivity. *Nature Neuroscience, 18*(11), 1664–1671.

Furnham, A. (2018). The great divide: academic versus practitioner criteria for psychometric test choice. *Journal of Personality Assessment, 100*(5), 498–506.

Guszcza, J., & Richardson, B. (2014). Two dogmas of big data: understanding the power of analytics for predicting human behavior. *Deloitte Review, 15*, 161–175.

Iliescu, D., & Greiff, S. (2019). The impact of technology on psychological testing in practice and policy. *European Journal of Psychological Assessment, 35*(2), 151–155.

Illingworth, A. J., Morelli, N. A., Scott, J. C., & Boyd, S. L. (2015). Internet-based, unproctored assessments on mobile and non-mobile devices: usage, measurement equivalence, and outcomes. *Journal of Business and Psychology, 30*(2), 325–343.

Landers, R. N., Auer, E. M., & Abraham, J. D. (2020). Gamifying a situational judgment test with immersion and control game elements. *Journal of Managerial Psychology.* https://doi.org/10.1108/JMP-10-2018-0446

McHenry, R. (2017). The future of psychometric testing. In B. Cripps (Ed.), *Psychometric testing: Critical perspectives* (pp. 269–281). London, UK: Wiley.

Morelli, N. A., Mahan, R. P., & Illingworth, A. J. (2014). Establishing the measurement equivalence of online selection assessments delivered on mobile versus nonmobile devices. *International Journal of Selection and Assessment, 22*(2), 124–138.

Sherman, R. A. (2019, October 17). Beware these marketing trends in psychological assessment: and why you shouldn't fall for them. *Psychology Today.* www .psychologytoday.com/gb/blog/the-situation-lab/201910/beware-these-marketing-trends-in-psychological-assessment?amp

Stamper, C. (2010). Common mistakes companies make using social media tools in recruiting efforts. *CMA Management, 84*(2), 12–14.

Winsborough, D., & Chamorro-Premuzic, T. (2016). Talent identification in the digital world: new talent signals and the future of HR assessment. *People and Strategy, 39*(2), 28–31.

Woods, S. A., Ahmed, S., Nikolaou, I., Costa, A. C., & Anderson, N. R. (2020). Personnel selection in the digital age: a review of validity and applicant reactions, and future research challenges. *European Journal of Work and Organizational Psychology, 29*(1), 64–77.

Index